STUDIES IN IMPERIALISM

general editor John M. MacKenzie

When the 'Studies in Imperialism' series was founded more than twenty-five years ago, emphasis was laid upon the conviction that 'imperialism as a cultural phenomenon had as significant an effect on the dominant as on the subordinate societies'. With more than ninety books published, this remains the prime concern of the series. Cross-disciplinary work has indeed appeared covering the full spectrum of cultural phenomena, as well as examining aspects of gender and sex, frontiers and law, science and the environment, language and literature, migration and patriotic societies, and much else. Moreover, the series has always wished to present comparative work on European and American imperialism, and particularly welcomes the submission of books in these areas. The fascination with imperialism, in all its aspects, shows no sign of abating, and this series will continue to lead the way in encouraging the widest possible range of studies in the field. 'Studies in Imperialism' is fully organic in its development, always seeking to be at the cutting edge, responding to the latest interests of scholars and the needs of this ever-expanding area of scholarship.

Missionary families

MANCHESTER
1824

Manchester University Press

SELECTED TITLES AVAILABLE IN THE SERIES

MISSIONARIES AND THEIR MEDICINE
A Christian modernity for tribal India
David Hardiman

CONFLICT, POLITICS AND PROSELYTISM
Methodist missionaries in colonial and postcolonial Upper Burma
Michael D. Leigh

WELSH MISSIONARIES AND BRITISH IMPERIALISM
The Empire of Clouds in northeast India
Andrew J. May

GENTEEL WOMEN
Empire and domestic material culture, 1840–1910
Dianne Lawrence

EUROPEAN EMPIRES AND THE PEOPLE
Popular responses to imperialism in France, Britain, the Netherlands, Belgium, Germany and Italy
John M. MacKenzie (ed.)

Missionary families

RACE, GENDER AND GENERATION ON THE SPIRITUAL FRONTIER

Emily J. Manktelow

MANCHESTER UNIVERSITY PRESS

Published by Manchester University Press
Altrincham Street, Manchester M1 7JA, UK
www.manchesteruniversitypress.co.uk

British Library Cataloguing-in-Publication Data is available

Library of Congress Cataloging-in-Publication Data is available

ISBN 978 0 7190 9670 9 paperback

First published by Manchester University Press in hardback 2013

This paperback edition first published 2015

Printed by Lightning Source

CONTENTS

LIST OF FIGURES

Note: The family trees in this book are compiled using James Sibree, *A Register of Missionaries, Deputations etc., from 1796–1923* (London: London Missionary Society, 1923), the LMS's *Register* of missionary children, and for family information past the first generation of missionary children, online genealogical information compiled by private family historians and verified where possible. See also the Moffat family tree in Cecil Northcott, *Robert Moffat: pioneer in Africa 1817–1870* (London: Lutterworth Press, 1961).

GENERAL EDITOR'S INTRODUCTION

There is no better focus for inter-cultural contacts of all kinds than overseas Christian missions. Given the very nature of their proselytising ambitions, they were established in the midst of indigenous communities, often on or beyond the frontiers of colonial societies. In such locations, missionaries set about learning the local language both for the purposes of preaching and communication, but also in order to translate the Bible, that central ambition of each newly located mission. But their inter-culturalism went much further than this. Missionaries invariably regarded the transmission of their own cultural norms, what they regarded as elements of 'civilisation', as central to their purposes. These behavioural standards might include, in their eyes, such forms as domestic architecture, the structure of the family (including, of course, monogamy), clothing, aspects of western education and medicine, hygienic practices and 'modesty' in behaviour and demeanour (often represented in anxieties about indigenous music and dance, discussion of sexual and other basic practices, and respect for the Christian god, his representatives and converts). But it was generally impossible for missionaries to be entirely unaffected by the people among whom they had settled. Such people were not passive recipients of the message of the mission. Through their own agency, they also created reciprocal influences upon the white inhabitants of the mission, including various forms of resistance, even producing syncretic religious compromises. Moreover, the missionaries were inevitably sucked into local politics and, indeed, frontier warfare, sometimes conflicts between whites and 'natives' such that their position became a highly dangerous one.

If all this is well known, it is also the case the missions were sites of inter-generational and gendered contact as well as inter-racial. After some initial hesitancy, missionary societies began to realise that the western-style family might itself act as an instrument of conversion, by precept and example, and also through the activities of the various members of a missionary's family. Missionary wives became unofficial and unpaid missionaries themselves with carefully delineated gendered roles – and this was also true of children as they grew up. On the indigenous side, missionaries attempted to create routes into local societies both through the elders and through the children. Above all, women seemed to constitute, through their power over the upbringing of children, an important field for both forms of education (often domestic and practical) and conversion. All such activity provoked extensive debates within the councils of parent missionary societies, as well as among practical missionaries on the ground. But the debates that have been least recognised have been those connected with the family policy to be adopted towards the proselytisers themselves. Should missionaries be married before they entered the field? What should be the arrangements for the education and training of the resultant children? Could missions become, in a sense, almost self-sustaining through the eventual employment of those children once they had reached adulthood? Was it indeed possible that such children were themselves more valuable as a result of their rearing within the missionary environment? To what extent had they received a dual socialisation, Christian and western, local and indigenous?

But of course inter-cultural contacts presented threats as well as opportunities. Missionaries could well be led astray, not least by 'sexual opportunity' in a setting of complex and sometimes unequal power relations (in both directions). Their wives and daughters might be seen as highly vulnerable. Above all missionary children, inhabiting as they did a 'grey area' between the two cultures, constituted the very embodiment of just such threats and opportunities. As they grew up, their contacts with indigenous people were often more frequent and 'easier' than those of their parents. They learned the language and in some cases adapted to environmental and social conditions more readily, partly because they had often known no other home. And, of course, all of this was mediated by relations between husbands and wives, between children and parents, and among siblings of both sexes. All sorts of questions were raised. What should be the roles of husbands or of wives in such settings, far from their home societies? How should they behave as fathers and as mothers? How far should they set about building cultural bridges with those whom they were setting out to convert? To what extent should their children be the instruments in such bridge-building? How could they train those children up for the maintenance of the 'civilised' norms they professed, educate them in the learning of their own societies, as well as maintain their adherence to the Christian principles central to their existence as missionaries? Was all of this best achieved at home, in schools in the colonial setting, or by transmission of those children back to the home society, even if only temporarily? And what distinctions should be made between boys and girls?

These are the questions that have not been addressed before. Emily Manktelow does so in this volume by concentrating on the London Missionary Society and on the first half of the nineteenth century when many of these issues were in a state of flux, when policies were being initially formulated. Her book should act as a model for further studies in respect of other societies and further 'spiritual frontiers' (as she calls them). We need to know, for example, the extent to which there were different responses and different results across the continents, or whether policies changed and developed in the course of the nineteenth century. To what extent did the imposition of more formal aspects of imperial rule produce significant changes? Were there any differences among the various Christian denominations or the ethnic origins of the missionaries (in the British case, Scottish or Irish, English or Welsh)? Moreover, as we enter the twentieth century, at a time of very different technologies and transport arrangements, were these relationships and arrangements transformed again? To what extent did the establishment of missionary dynasties, as Manktelow identifies them, ensure that succeeding generations passed through these transformations in conditions? And most importantly of all, how did these gendered and generational familial relationships affect the actual conduct of the missions themselves? There is a rich vein of enquiry here and Manktelow has done missionary scholarship a considerable service by opening it up in such an illuminating fashion.

John M. MacKenzie

ACKNOWLEDGEMENTS

This book has accumulated many gratitudes along the way. My first, and most fundamental, acknowledgement is to the Arts and Humanities Research Council without whose funding this project may never have happened. The overseas portion of the research has been generously supported by the University of London Central Research Fund, the Royal Historical Society, and the David M. Stowe Fellowship (Yale Divinity School). The archivists at the School of Oriental and African Studies have been a constant and unstinting source of knowledge and assistance and I must thank Jo Ichimura, Gillian Butler and Lance Martin in particular, for their help and friendship. Many a happy day has been spent in their company. While overseas I benefited from the expertise of archivists at the National Library of South Africa, the Cory Library at Rhodes University, the National Library of New Zealand and the Library of Yale Divinity School. My thanks also to the Council of World Mission for permission to use numerous images from their archive, and to the Basel Mission archive and the University of Cambridge Library in the same vein.

Sources of inspiration there have been many (including the works of Rhonda Semple, Liz Buettner, Clare Midgley and Catherine Hall, all of whom I have been fortunate enough to meet and converse with about my research at various stages), but I can only thank one person for always keeping me grounded. Professor Andrew Porter has guided my work for many years, and can always be relied upon for sound commentary, constructive criticism and unstinting wit and wisdom, for which I remain ever grateful. I have also received a great deal of support from the staff at King's College London; special thanks to John Stuart and Ludmilla Jordanova, as well as many others in the department for their kindness and confidence. Thanks also to Clare Midgley and Deborah Gaitskell for their constructive criticisms and continued support. And what would we do without good and generous proofreaders? Dave Monger, Bronwen Everill, Liz Harvey, Annie Selway, Rachel Johnson, Claire McCallum and various members of my family have all read parts of the book. Thanks also to the staff and reviewers at Manchester University Press, and the blind reviewers at the *Journal of Imperial and Commonwealth History* and the *Journal of Women's History* for their helpful comments and guidance. Parts of this work have also benefited from the comments and questions of various conference and seminar participants over the years. The regulars of the Imperial History seminar and the Christian Missions in Global History seminar at the Institute of Historical Research have been particularly helpful, and I must especially thank my fellow conveners of the latter for their enthusiastic encouragement.

Contrary to expectation, I did not find this process an isolating one, and have been lucky enough to make many good and lifelong friends along the way. My special thanks must go to Ben Bankhurst, Rachel Bright, Esme Cleall, Bronwen Everill, Laura Ishiguro and Annie Selway in particular. In the last two years I have found much joy and friendship at the University of Exeter, and while I cannot thank everyone by name, special thanks to Antonella Liuzzo Scorpo, Laura Sangha, Sara Barker, Claire McCallum and Jenny Lea for making me feel so at home there. *My* family have always been, and remain, the ultimate inspiration for my work, and my parents and siblings have certainly earned recognition here for their generosity, encouragement and support. In the next generation too, my nieces Grace and Robyn have kept me in touch with reality, and have always been wonderful and entertaining distractions from my work! During the original research my baby nephew Joseph cuddled me back into good spirits on more than one occasion; and since then his younger siblings Megan and Sam have done sterling work in the same direction. Nothing I have ever done or will ever do could be achieved without the love and encouragement of my family, whose actions remind me every day that mere words will never be enough. Thank you.

LIST OF ABBREVIATIONS

AtPQ	Answers to Printed Queries
BM	Board Minutes
CLRU	Cory Library, Rhodes University
CP	Candidate Papers
CWM/LMS	Council for World Mission/London Missionary Society
EM	*Evangelical Magazine*
LMS	London Missionary Society
MDC	Madras District Committee
MIL	Madagascar Incoming Letters
NLNZ	National Library of New Zealand
NLSA(CT)	National Library of South Africa (Cape Town)
NSW	New South Wales
SAIL	South Africa Incoming Letters
SI(T)IL	South India (Tamil) Incoming Letters
SSA	South Seas Academy
SSIL	South Seas Incoming Letters
SSM	South Seas Mission
SSJ	South Sea Journals
WOL:SS	Western Outgoing Letters: South Seas

PREFACE

Being thematic in structure, this book does have a tendency to rove fairly freely around time and space, particularly in the chapters more interested in cultural, rather than chronological, trends. Chapter 2 aims to provide a chronological scaffold, but it might also be useful for the reader to orientate themselves within the contexts and characters of the book: London, Tahiti and South Africa; and the main missionary families involved.

Contexts

This book is placed within three main contexts: the Pacific 'South Seas Mission' of the London Missionary Society (LMS) (and more particularly, Tahiti); southern Africa, through the LMS's 'South Africa Mission'; and the LMS hierarchy and directorate in London. What you will not find within this book, however, is a sense of metropole and periphery, despite its use of the idea of the 'spiritual frontier'. Rather, the LMS in London was part of an uneven, but complex web of relationships that stretched across the missionary world. While London may be thought of as some sort of hub within that web, taking in and dispersing information about its mission stations and mission actors, the missionary enterprise was shaped by interactions between London and individual mission stations, as well as by the transglobal connections that existed between mission stations themselves – mediated often, indeed, by familial relationships, as well as associations based upon friendship, professional affiliation and regional networks.

London

Many of the most famous missionary societies that were founded at the turn of the nineteenth century sprang up in London, the home of a strong evangelical network then centred around Baker's Coffee House in Change Alley, the Castle and Falcon public house on Aldersgate Street, Spa Fields Chapel in Finsbury (connected with the famous Countess of Huntingdon's Connexion), and Freemason's Hall in Great Queen Street. Indeed, the Missionary Society (as the London Missionary Society was known until 1818) was founded in 1795 out of a series of small meetings held primarily at Baker's Coffee House ('which at that time was used for an hour or two every Tuesday morning as a place for chat and the interchange of news by the London ministers'),[1] the

Castle and Falcon (which was also the site of the inaugural meeting of the Church Missionary Society, in 1799), and finally a large meeting, of over 200 people, at Spa Fields Chapel. The Directors of this new society, meanwhile, were drawn from all over the country, including Cambridge, Warwickshire, Sudbury, Sheffield, Birmingham and Scotland, thereby creating a national religious network that would be consolidated by the later creation of numerous auxiliary societies (the grass-roots organisations of the missionary movement). Even in 1795, pledges of monetary aid and regional public promotion of the Society flowed in from such places as Axminster, Derby, Glasgow, Taunton, Essex, Nottinghamshire and Warwickshire.

The London Missionary Society became one of the hubs of the London evangelical network, connecting sites such as Salisbury Square (the eventual home of the LMS's headquarters, as well as the primary site of many of the other missionary societies); Exeter Hall (erected between 1829 and 1831, the Freemasons' Hall having been deemed too small for the purpose of popular missionary and anti-slavery society meetings);[2] Spa Fields Chapel (which remained a hub of evangelical activity); the Religious Tract Society (founded in 1799 in Paternoster Row); the *Evangelical Magazine* (a monthly periodical which served as a forum for the dissemination of revival news, information and ideas among Anglicans, Independents and dissenters, and had been founded in the same year as the LMS, sharing a number of founders and editors with the LMS's directorate, and serving as its unofficial mouthpiece until the founding of the LMS *Chronicle*), which also found a home in Paternoster Row; and existing evangelical networks at Baker's Coffee House, the Castle and Falcon, Tottenham Court Chapel, Surrey Chapel and other prominent places of non-conformist worship (e.g. Walworth, Shacklewell and Blackfriars Road).

Missionary students, meanwhile, were educated among the dissenting academies of London, including Homerton Academy, Cheshunt College, New College, the Home and Colonial School Society, Highbury College and Hoxton Academy. The LMS founded their own school at Gosport, in Hampshire in 1800 (under the auspices of David Bogue, one of the LMS's founding members and a prominent evangelical leader). The Mission Schools for the education of missionary children were both founded in Walthamstow, though the girls' school (Walthamstow Hall) ultimately moved to Sevenoaks in Kent. The boys' school, meanwhile, was moved south of the river to Mottingham.

The LMS thus became part of, and intersected with, numerous evangelical networks, at home and abroad. National networks of evangelical activity included the home towns of its directors, local hubs of interest and activity, and later the extensive network of mission auxiliaries that transected the country. In London itself, the LMS was at the heart of the city's evangelicalism, and would remain so for many years.[3] London, meanwhile, formed part of an increasingly global evangelical network, intersecting with both the British Empire, and beyond. At the same time, webs of contact, information and supply linked local hubs of evangelical knowledge and activity: from the connections formed between local auxiliaries, through the links forged between mission sites themselves, and finally to those links made between missionaries in the field, and particular auxiliary organisations – often those situated in the missionary's home town.

South Seas Mission

The inaugural mission of the LMS, the South Seas Mission (SSM) was founded in 1797 with the arrival of thirty missionaries from London. This first contingent was something of a motley crew – four were ordained, five were married, and its ranks were made up of skilled artisans and 'pious mechanics' including carpenters, tailors and weavers.[4] 'The reason why there was so undue a proportion of handicraftsmen and tradesmen was, undoubtedly, the belief that the natives would speedily see the value of European civilization, and be glad to learn trades', noted the LMS's official historian, Richard Lovett, in 1899.[5] The mission proceeded by placing eighteen missionaries at Tahiti (including all of those who were married), ten at Tonga and two at the Marquesas (though one returned immediately to Tahiti).

Tahiti itself was then under the control of the *ari'i rahi* (paramount chief) Pomare I (so-called by the missionaries). The Pomare family had been the most successful in capitalising on the increasing trade links with Europeans in the mid-late eighteenth century – their chiefdom (one of many on the island) encompassing the sheltered Matavai Bay which was used as a harbour by passing and visiting ships. Visiting Europeans, meanwhile, recognised their local authority and scaled it up to the island as a whole – believing them to be kings and queens.[6] Their rise to paramount power in the late eighteenth and early nineteenth centuries would have a profound impact on the LMS's fledgling mission there as the missionaries allied themselves with this well-known family, and ultimately converted to Christianity important elements within it. At the time of their arrival, however, the political situation in Tahiti was far from stable, and in Tonga too, power struggles between the local rulers marked the early years of mission activity in the South Seas. In 1798 four of the Tahitian missionaries were assaulted, stripped and maltreated by a group of 'unfriendly' natives. Frightened by their precarious situation, and unhappy that they were forbidden to marry the locals (see Chapter 2), eleven of the missionaries (including four of

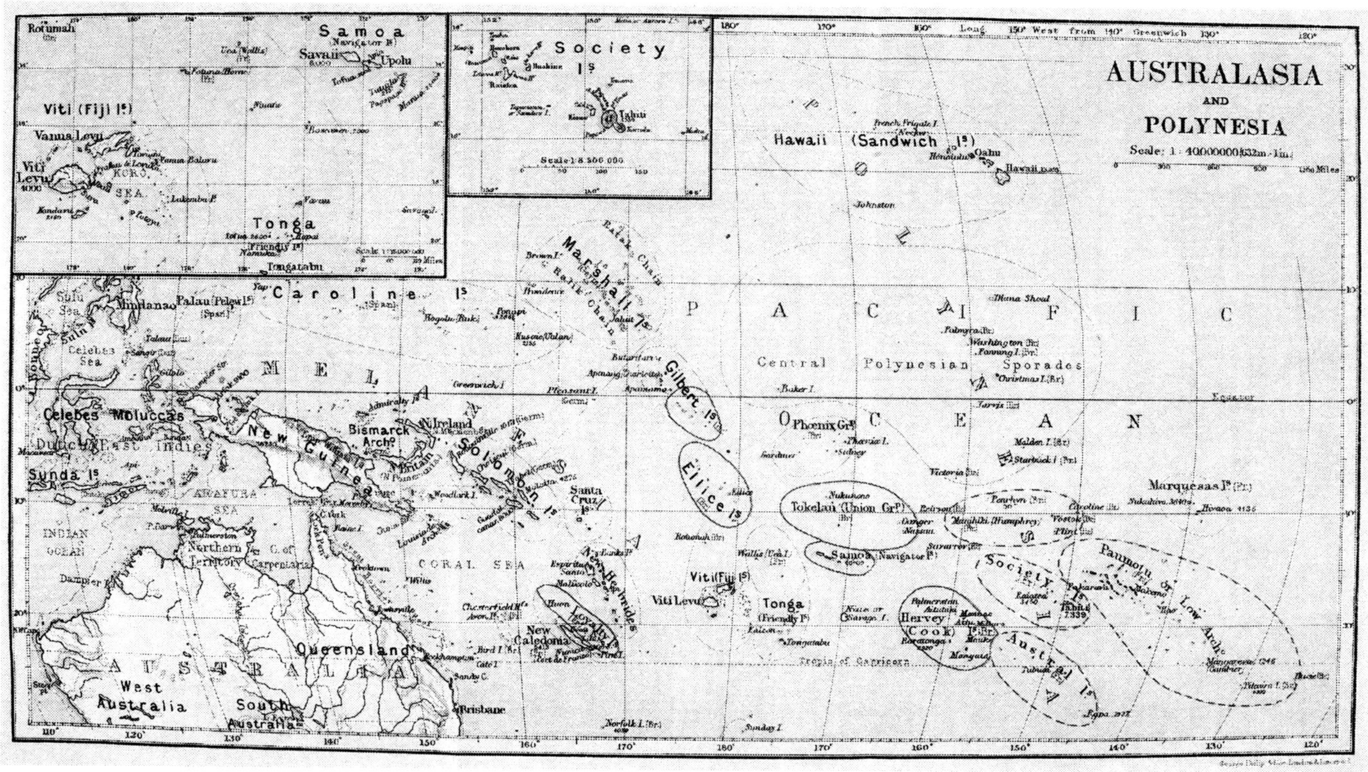

Figure 1 Australasia and Polynesia.

those who were married) resolved to leave the mission for the safety of Port Jackson, New Holland. In Tonga, meanwhile, three of the missionaries were killed in May 1798 having become embroiled in local conflict. By January 1799 the Tongan missionaries had also fled. The SSM then, did not get off to a good start. War broke out in Tahiti in 1807, leading the married missionaries then on the island to move to Huahine, and in 1808 Pomare II and the remaining missionaries fled to Eimeo (later Moorea). By 1809, all but Henry Nott and James Hayward had retired to Port Jackson, there to wait out the war. But better news was on the horizon. Pomare II eventually declared himself interested in Christianity, the 'idols' were abandoned, and by 1815 it seemed that the civil war was over, with Pomare as the victor. More and more of the missionaries scattered around the Pacific region returned to their work, and by 1816, with mass conversions apparent around the islands, Tahiti, Moorea, Tapuamanu and Tetaroa were confidently declared '*Christian Islands*'.[7] Pomare was officially baptised in 1819, and 'from this period until the time of the French intervention the work of the Tahiti Mission consists chiefly of a record of evangelistic and educational work at the different stations occupied by the missionaries'.[8] Consolidation and expansion followed, and the ties tightened between the missionaries and the Pomares. Mrs Hannah Crook attended the birth of Pomare's first son, and the prince was educated at the South Seas Academy, alongside the children of the missionaries. Pomare II died in December 1821, succeeded by his second son, then eighteen months old, who became Pomare III and was himself succeeded by his 14-year-old sister Queen Pomare IV in 1827.

Queen Pomare IV was the last of the family to exercise independent rule in Tahiti, which was declared a French protectorate in 1842. Years of rebellion followed, but by 1847 the French hold over the island was complete. Queen Pomare was retained as a figurehead, but European settlers ultimately carved up the island into fenced plantations, under the protection of martial law. As for the missionaries, their work continued, but from a rather more precarious position than before, and in active competition with both French Catholicism and the Paris Evangelical Society. Pomare IV died in 1877 and was succeeded by her son Pomare V until his forced abdication by the French in 1880, when Tahiti formally became a French colony.

Despite these ups and downs, the SSM was something of a flagship mission for the LMS. Parts of its history had been disastrous, but the mass conversions occasioned by Pomare II's personal conversion *c.*1812 led to the missionaries becoming an integral part of the island's history, involved in education, politics and the law. News from the Pacific was often first in the LMS's regular publications, and the

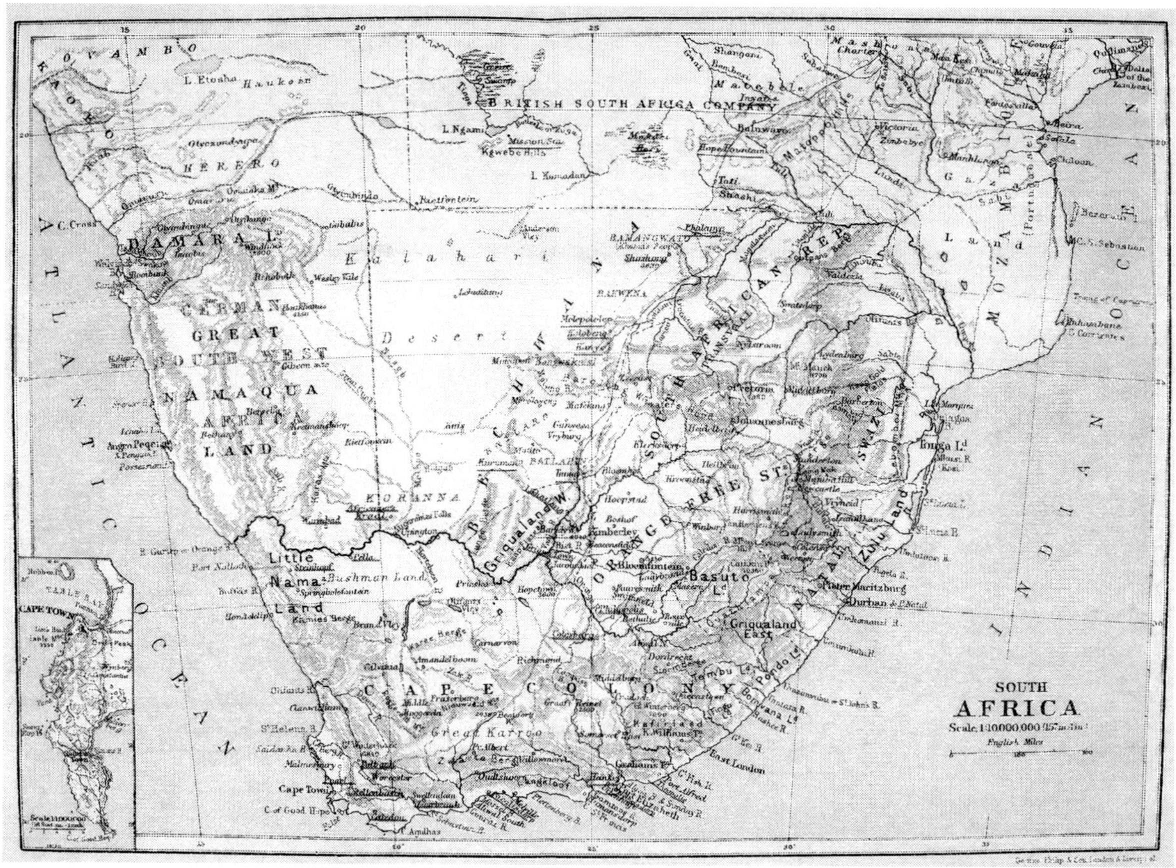

Figure 2 South Africa.

Note: Kuruman is between the 'E' and 'C' of BECHWANA; Molepolole under the 'A'; and Inyati above the word 'company' in the BRITISH SOUTH AFRICA COMPANY.

mission gave the LMS at least one true missionary hero, in the shape of John Williams, who was famously killed on the island of Erromango in 1839. The SSM also gave the LMS at least one prolific writer and mission-publicist, William Ellis, who later became the LMS's foreign secretary.[9] For our purposes what is important about the SSM is that it became a proving ground for LMS policy on the family – and many of the most tense debates about the role of the family were played out there. The reasons for this are addressed in the introduction, but the public and private history of the SSM is one of the most important for historians who wish to understand the LMS's early mission endeavour.

South Africa Mission

The story of the South Africa Mission of the LMS is well known, in no small part owing to its engagement with the early history of empire, and of white settlement in particular. It is a history filled with famous characters: Johannes Vanderkemp, John Philip, Robert Moffat, John Mackenzie and David Livingstone. This second mission of the LMS was founded in 1799 when Vanderkemp, John Kitcherer, John Edmonds and William Edwards dropped anchor in Table Bay. The Cape itself was oscillating between the control of the Dutch and the British, the latter having taken over in 1795 (they later ceded the territory back to the Dutch in 1803, but regained it in 1806). The history of European settlement in southern Africa meant that the South Africa Mission was always an expanding one – interested from the first designs of Vanderkemp in pushing inwards towards the local African populations: the so-called 'Kafirs' (a general term, Arabic in origin meaning 'non-believer', but used generally for black Africans in the sixteenth to nineteenth centuries), the 'Hottentots' (modern-day Khoikhoi or more broadly Khoisan), and the Xhosa. It was also a largely successful mission, capitalising on (or mitigating against) the dislocation and dispossession of the local people occasioned by European settler-colonialism.

The South Africa Mission is most famous for its political and humanitarian agenda (often much against the designs of the LMS hierarchy in London). Vanderkemp was a famous egalitarian, quick to baptise local converts, and uninterested in the precepts of 'civilisation' as embodied in dress or custom. His closest missionary ally was undoubtedly James Read, who joined the mission in 1800 (having first been captured by the French when bound for the SSM in 1798). He and Vanderkemp founded the famous mission station at Bethelsdorp (near Port Elizabeth) in 1803 which became the centre of African Christianity in the early nineteenth century. Vanderkemp and Read engaged in constant political tussles with the British government in the colony, fighting in particular for the rights of the local people. In 1812, after the death of Vanderkemp in 1811, Read was intimately involved in the so-called 'black circuit' – a series of court cases brought by the Khoikhoi against the white farmers and settlers.

Read was replaced as the mission's superintendent by John Philip, having been accused of serious immoralities (including adultery, and fathering an illegitimate child) in 1817. Although his remaining relationship with the LMS was rocky, his popularity among the local converts ensured his continuation as a missionary, and ultimately as an independent pastor to the 'free Khoi' Kat River Settlement from 1829. Philip, meanwhile, had begun his own campaign for racial equality in the Cape. His *Researches in South Africa*, and parliamentary campaigning, are often cited as crucial to the passing of Ordinance 50 in the colony, which ended indentured labour, abolished the offence of 'vagrancy', and established the ideal of equality under the law. Philip and Read both returned to Britain in 1835 to report to Thomas Buxton's Select Committee on Aboriginal Tribes (in reference to the recent 'frontier wars' against the Xhosa). In the end, however, the political activities of both Read and Philip earned the unease and later ire of their fellow missionaries and the LMS, who increasingly turned towards apoliticism as a mission policy. For the most part it was impossible for the South Africa Mission to remain entirely apolitical, however, and its history is marked by its context, often right on the frontier of British (and Dutch) expansion. Missionaries in South Africa were often embroiled in local and colonial issues, and lived sometimes precarious lives in the midst of war and violence. It remained famous, however, for its complex and ambivalent interactions with imperial advance; and its early years of evangelical humanitarianism became an important element in the missionary movement's self-justification and interaction with the moral side of empires and imperialism.

Characters

The most important family, or indeed missionary dynasty, in this book is that of the Moffats and their offshoots: the Livingstones and the Prices. The choice of this missionary dynasty is both pragmatic and methodological. As historians of mission in Africa will know, the extended Moffat family is exceptionally well documented, with contemporary publications (including Robert Moffat's *Missionary Labours and Scenes in South Africa* and David Livingstone's *Travels and Researches*), post-mortem reflections (most especially John Smith Moffat's biography of his parents, *The Lives of Robert and Mary Moffat*) and a wealth of both historical writing and primary sources (all beautifully archived by the School of Oriental and African Studies in London and Rhodes University Library in Grahamstown). At the same time, the Moffat family stretched across southern Africa's spiritual frontier throughout its generational history. Robert and Mary Moffat struck out and made their home at Kuruman, in the modern-day north of South Africa, a place then very much on the geographical, colonial and spiritual frontier, though later a busy hub of regional missionary activity. The Prices ventured further north into Shoshong and Molepolele some thirty years later, and made their life in the latter, situated in modern-day Botswana. Of course, the Livingstones famously travelled even further north, initially as a family, and later Livingstone alone. The Moffats' second living son John Smith Moffat was also a missionary, first to Inyati (in modern-day Zimbabwe) and later taking over the mission station at Kuruman. The Moffats' second daughter Ann also married a missionary, Jean Fredoux, though they do not appear in these pages, being of a different missionary society; while Jane, their youngest, remained with her parents in Africa, working as an unofficial missionary, until their retirement to England in 1870.

Robert and Mary Moffat

Robert Moffat was born in Scotland in 1795 into a strictly Calvinist family. In 1815 he travelled to Manchester to meet with William Roby (a Congregationalist minister and evangelist in Lancashire), in order that he might give himself to be a missionary. It was in the job as a gardener that Roby initially found him at Dukinfield, Manchester that Robert met and fell in love with his future wife, Mary Smith. Theirs was a love story that did not run smoothly, however. Moffat offered himself to the LMS and ultimately sailed for South Africa in 1817, but without his beloved Mary who, as is well documented, was reluctant to leave her ageing parents without their consent. Two years of heartache and heartbreak followed (which Robert spent in Great Nama Land, modern-day Namibia), until, at last, Mary's parents gave their permission for the marriage, and Mary journeyed to South Africa, where they were married in Cape Town in 1819.

From their marriage until 1823, the Moffats lived in Dithakong, a station pioneered by James Read, Robert and Ann Hamilton, and a number of Bethelsdorp converts in 1815. Troubled times and wars followed, but ultimately the station was re-established as New Dithakong, or Kuruman, in 1824, having been moved closer to the eye of Kuruman – a fresh water spring that was key to Kuruman's later productivity. Again, the Moffats found themselves in the middle of intense frontier conflicts – the price of living on that intersection between the geographical, colonial and spiritual frontier. At the same time,

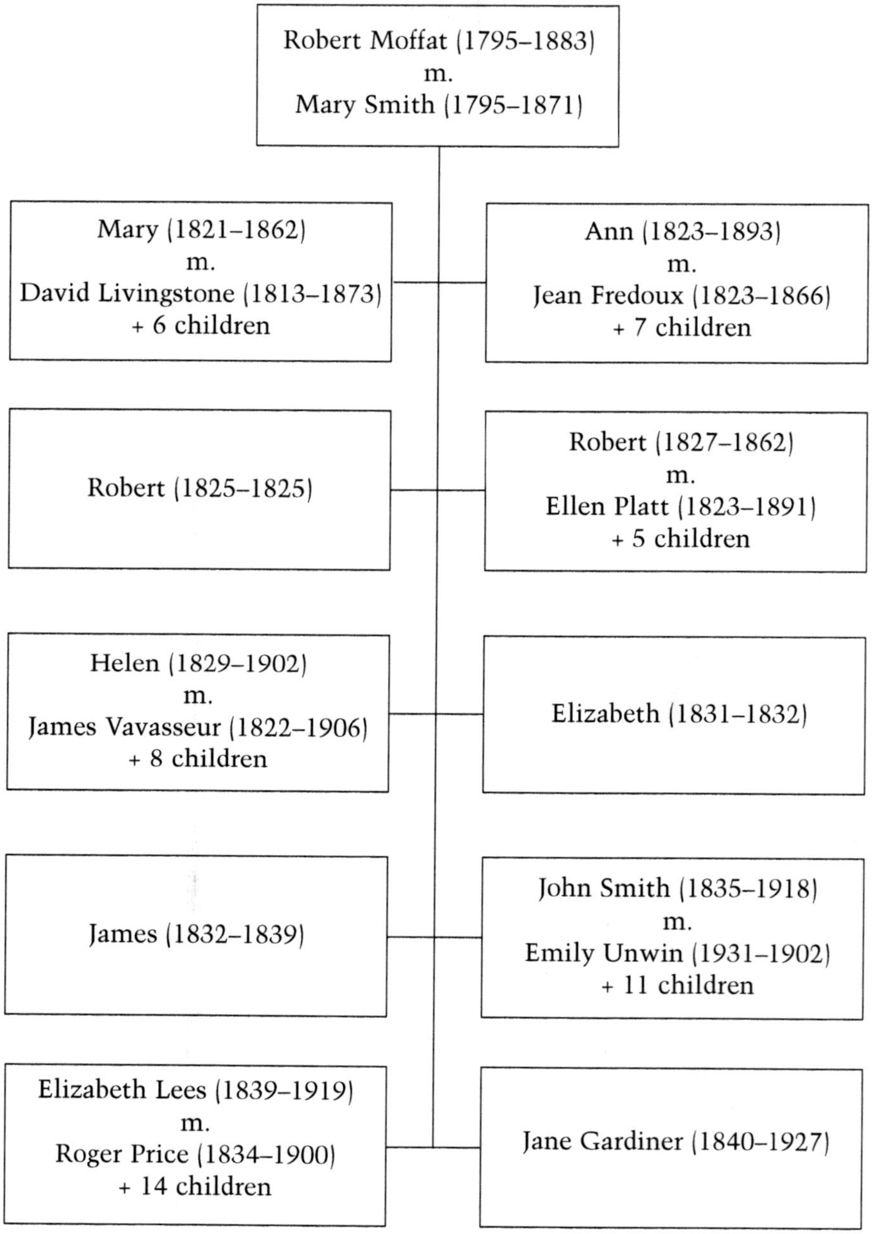

Figure 3 Moffat Family Tree.

Figure 4 Robert Moffat.

however, they built up a strong and thriving mission station (that still survives today), complete with church, school and homestead. Robert started to produce the first seTswana Bible (finished in 1857), and Mary produced eight children (later followed by two more). Both created what was to become a mission hub in South Africa, responsible for refuelling mission stations for miles around, and caring for missionaries bowed down by the pressures of itinerant and frontier mission work in the further north.

The Moffats returned to England in 1838, gaining a daughter on the voyage, and losing a son (to the measles). They stayed in England for three years, Robert touring the country promoting the mission, his translation work and his book, *Missionary Labours and Scenes in South Africa* (published in 1842), Mary fostering the female evangelical networks that were such an important part of their life in Kuruman, and upon whom they often relied for material and emotional support. They returned to South Africa in 1843. Robert finished his Bible translation in 1857, and engaged in the foundation of numerous new mission stations, including the mission to the Ndebele at Inyati, to be staffed by his son John and his new wife Emily (Unwin), and the Kololo mission whose disastrous end would bring young widower Roger Price into the Moffat fold through his marriage to their daughter Elizabeth (Bessie).

The Moffats reluctantly retired from the mission in 1870, leaving behind them a difficult legacy for their son John to negotiate on their behalf – something he did not do entirely successfully, giving up the mission and joining the British Bechuanaland colonial service in 1879. Robert and Mary Moffat, meanwhile, went to live with their daughter and her family, the Vavasseurs, in Brixton, where Mary died only six months after their arrival in 1871. Robert, accompanied still by his youngest daughter Jane, travelled the country for the next two years, promoting mission work and finally settling down in Brixton in 1873. In 1874 he identified the body of his son-in-law, David Livingstone – the seventh of his children and children-in-law that he had outlived. Robert himself died in 1883, and was buried in Norwood Cemetery with Mary, who had been 'indeed a missionary *second only to himself!*'[10]

Figure 5 Mary Moffat.

Mary and David Livingstone

The life of David Livingstone is of course well known, and hardly needs reiterating here. Nonetheless, the Livingstone marriage is less often the site of historical enquiry, despite some recent trends to victimise Mary, which are discussed later in the book. The salient facts will, I think, suffice. David was born in 1813 in Blantyre, to a poor family whose daily life was structured around the working rhythms of Monteith's cotton mill. An extremely determined autodidact, and supported by a family enthusiastic about such an education as could be gained within the confines of mill life, David ultimately offered himself to the London Missionary Society in 1838. Inspired by his father-in-law to be, Robert Moffat, and put off his course to mission work in China by the outbreak of the Opium Wars, David eventually sailed for South Africa, famously and unusually unmarried, in 1840.

Mary was one of the Moffat clan, born and bred in South Africa, and educated in Grahamstown (with her younger sister Ann, but unlike her youngest sisters who were educated in Britain) from the age of nine. She accompanied her parents to Britain in 1838, and returned with them to Kuruman in 1843, where she worked at the mission schools, helped her mother in her domestic and mission duties, and ultimately trained herself for what would be her eventual vocation: missionary wife (with all the public and private duties that entailed). David and Mary had first met when Livingstone came out to meet the Moffats on their return to Kuruman in 1843. Their acquaintance was consolidated in 1844 when Livingstone returned to Kuruman to convalesce after being mauled by a lion. At the end of that trip he proposed (under an almond tree that was later split by lightening), and the couple married at Kuruman in 1845. Two years later, and after the birth of their first two children, they headed north to Chonuane, and then west to Kolobeng (see figure 2; Kolobeng is beneath Molepolole).

In 1848 Mary and their three children returned to Kuruman, while Livingstone prepared for an expedition into the north with explorer William Oswell. In 1849 the expedition travelled to Lake Ngami (see figure 2; beneath the 'British' of BRITISH SOUTH AFRICA COMPANY), returning then to Kolobeng in order to collect the Livingstone family, and gearing up for a second expedition to the Botletle River (also known as the Zouga). This was the more ill-fated of their family expeditions – two of their children died, and they returned to Kolobeng only just in time for the birth of their fourth child (who lived for only six weeks). Mary also was very ill, that journey being the root of her lifelong facial paralysis. The family returned to Kuruman in 1850, but embarked for their second expedition in 1851, this time reaching the Chobe river

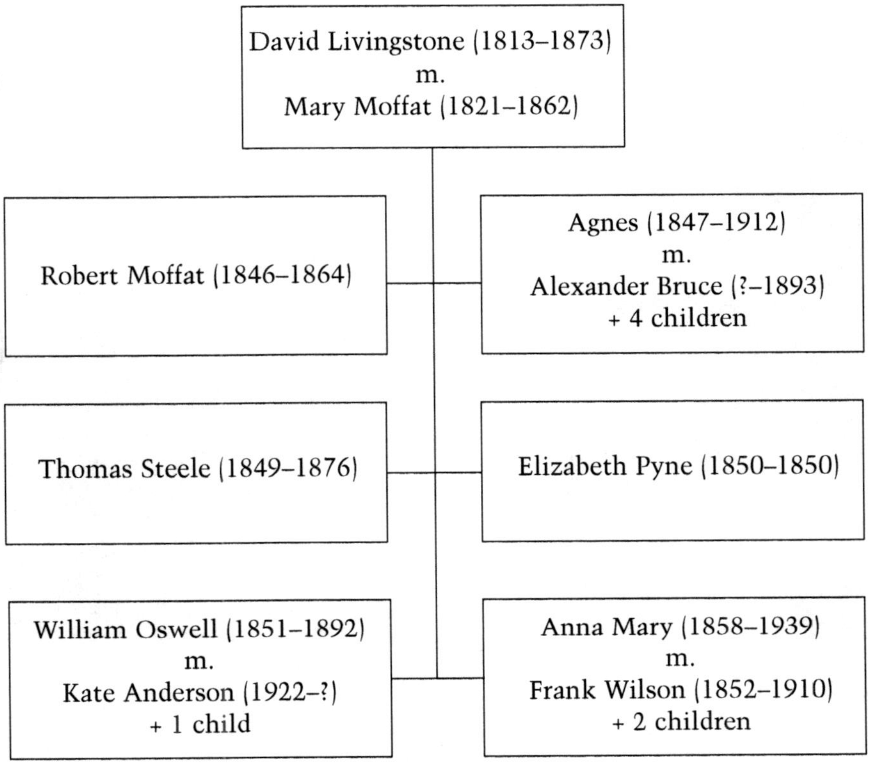

Figure 6 Livingstone Family Tree.

(despite nearly dying of thirst en route). Leaving the family at the river, David proceeded to the Zambesi river, and ultimately determined that it required further navigation. He rejoined his family, and the Livingstones headed south to the Cape, with the intention that Mary and the children should leave for Scotland, while David should return to the Zambesi for further explorations.

By 1852 then, the family had temporarily split. Mary embarked for Britain with the children; David was back into the north. During the years 1852–56 David travelled across Africa, while Mary and the children travelled across Britain. They met again in December 1856 at Southampton. During the next two years the Livingstones travelled around the country, David giving lectures and speeches about his experiences, and publishing his book, *Travels and Researches in South Africa* in 1857. In the same year he resigned from the LMS and in 1858 the Livingstones (minus their three older children, who were left with

Figure 7 David Livingstone.

Figure 8 Mary Livingstone.

relatives in Britain, to be educated) set off for the ill-fated Zambesi expedition.

Realising that she was pregnant again, Mary headed up to Kuruman, while David continued on the expedition (which was itself delayed until 1860). After the birth of Anna Mary in November 1858, Mary returned briefly to Scotland, meeting David again in 1862, having sailed with the young Scots missionary James Stewart (with whom some said she had had an improper friendship) and having travelled to the mouth of the Zambesi to meet him. As the expedition assembled the *Lady Nyasa*, a portable steamer more appropriate than previous vessels for exploring the waterways of central Africa, Mary died of fever in April 1862.

With Mary's death, the idea of the 'Livingstone family' also died. Although David returned to Britain (and his children – except Robert who had travelled to America to fight in the civil war, where he died in 1864), he did not stay long. Having published his second book *Narrative of an Expedition to the Zambesi and its Tributaries* in 1865 he left for his final expedition in 1866, famously dying (to cut a long story short) while out there in April 1873.

Roger and Elizabeth Price

Elizabeth Lees Moffat (known as Bessie) was born on board ship, while anchored in Table Bay, on 16 March 1839. Her family were en route to England for the Moffat's first furlough since their arrival in South Africa in 1817 and 1819, and would remain there for the first four years of Bessie's life. Indeed, her time at the Moffat mission station at Kuruman was short-lived compared with her childhood in England, which included not only those first four years, but later seven years at Walthamstow Hall, school for the daughters of missionaries (where she resided 1847–54). When she returned to Kuruman as a 15-year-old in 1854, however, she was returning to the place she considered home, and to the region to which she would devote her life.

She first met Roger Price in 1858 when he was en route to the new (and ultimately disastrous) mission to Inyati. Roger was a Welshman, born in South Wales in 1834, and was then accompanied by his first wife, Isabella Slater, whom he had married between ordination and embarkation for South Africa. The Prices and the Helmores (Henry Helmore, his wife and four of their children) proceeded into the north to found their new mission, but met with a great deal of disaster, including the death by fever (though Roger thought by poisoning) of Mr and Mrs Helmore, two of their children, and ultimately Isabella Price and their infant daughter Eliza.[11] Roger returned to Kuruman with the two remaining Helmore children in February 1861, and was

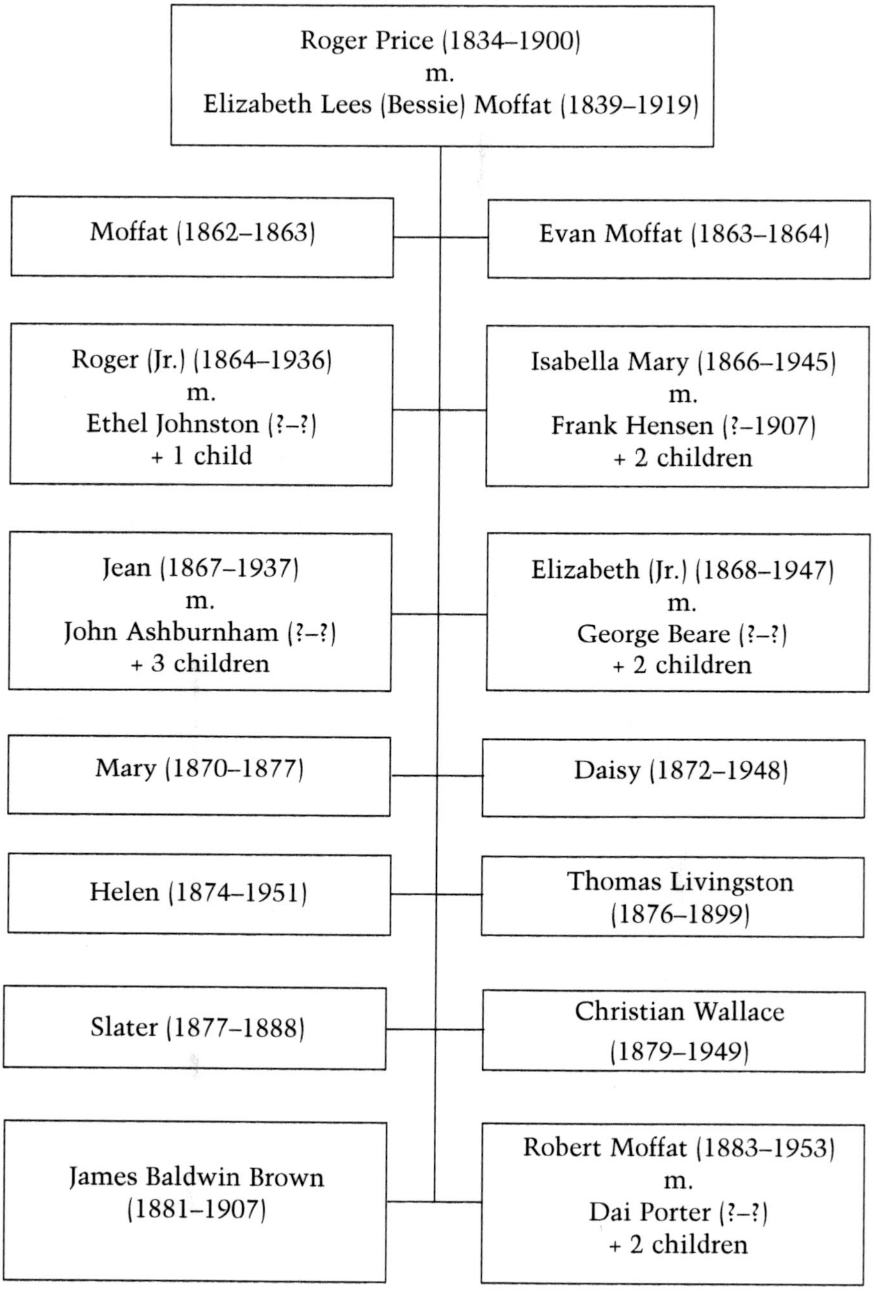

Figure 9 Price Family Tree.

Figure 10 Elizabeth and Roger Price.

there nursed back to health by the Moffats, including 22-year-old Bessie. Roger and Bessie married in the autumn of that year.

In May 1862 the Prices arrived at their first mission station, Shoshong, where they remained for four years until 1866 (Shoshong is next to the 'N' in Bechwana in figure 2). This was what Una Long has called Bessie's 'baptism of suffering' for it was there that her first two children were lost to fever.[12] They returned to Kuruman in February 1866, and in July of that year proceeded to their new station at Logagen (later Molepolole), where they would tend to the Bakwena people, who had recently settled there themselves, under the Chiefdom of Sechele (whom Livingstone had converted to Christianity – though it was not a stable conversion – in 1846).

The Prices had a long and prominent missionary career. Roger Price was appointed the leader of the Ujiji expedition during their first furlough in Britain 1875–79 (though he was later removed from the post owing to his objections about its viability); they remained at Molepolole for eighteen years; and were ultimately appointed to work at the Moffat Institute in Kuruman in 1885. They had fourteen children (ten of whom survived into adulthood), undertook educational, medical and spiritual work throughout their lives, and Roger accompanied the LMS's Foreign Secretary on his deputation to North Bechuanaland and Matabele Land (so-called) in 1883–84. Roger died at Kuruman in January 1900, and was buried next to the grave of his first son Moffat Price, whose grave also commemorated the deaths of Isabella and Eliza Price. Bessie Price moved to Cape Town (where four of her children then lived), and died there nineteen years later in 1919.

My discussions of the Tahiti context have been less driven by particular families than by crystallising events. The South Seas Mission was often a place where debates about the family were played out: a result of both its being the first mission of the LMS, and its island location. Nonetheless, one family in particular has made its imprint on my discussions there: the Crook family.

William and Hannah Crook

William Pascoe Crook (1775–1846), former gentleman's servant and later tin-worker, arrived in the South Seas in 1797 with the first fleet of missionaries dispatched by the LMS (a year earlier, in 1796). He was dropped off at the Marquesas in June of that year, and, after the departure of his colleague John Harris, toiled there alone until the *Butterworth* 'rescued' him and returned him to England in May 1799.

Crook had had a rather distressing time during his year in the Marquesas. There 'ever[y] temptation ha[d] been of such a strange sort' that he wished to 'blush and be confounded before the Lord'.[13] After

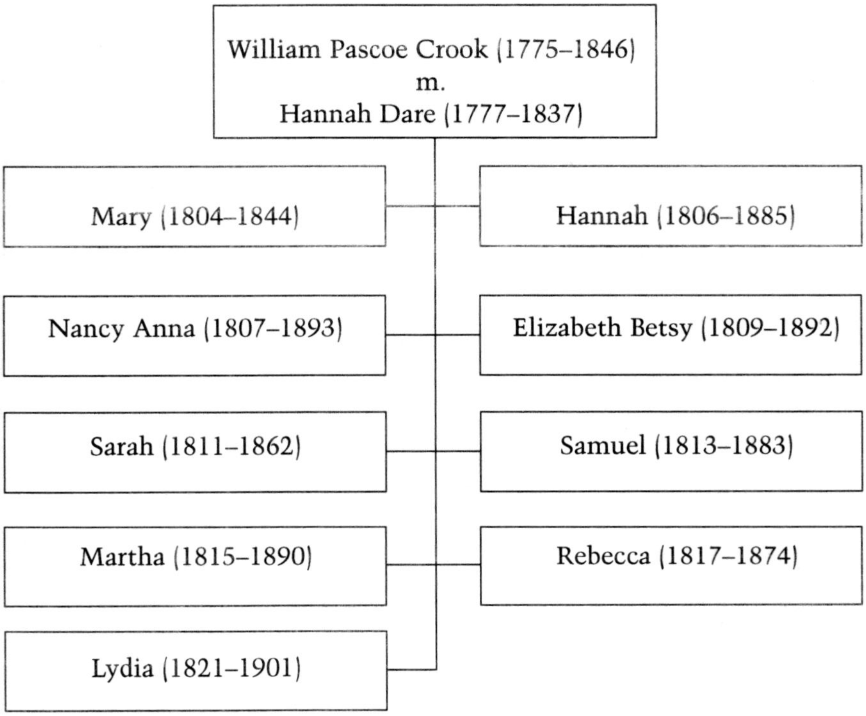

Figure 11 Crook Family Tree.

a year of temptations, argues Alex Calder, 'Crook long[ed] to reconstitute his identity in the confirming looks of someone who knows how to read him rightly' – in other words, his desire to 'blush and be confounded before the Lord' was, among other things, a need to be reconstituted as a white, western man, a pious missionary, and a martyr to temptation, rather than its slave. Upon his return to England he worked on a dictionary of the Polynesian language, wrote up an account of his experiences, and married a respectable young Englishwoman – Hannah Dare (1777–1837).

William and Hannah sailed together for Tahiti in 1803, stopping off at Port Philip, and three weeks later, Sydney. 'But painful intelligence awaited him there, for on his arrival in that city he found that the Society Islands were all at war, and that the missionaries had all left except two, Mr. Hayward and Mr. Nott.'[14] This was the 'separation', as it was known, and equated to the abandonment of the South Seas Mission in 1798 by eleven of its missionaries, supposedly spooked by a 'plan to seize our women and property', but probably as much to do

Figure 12 William Pascoe Crook.

with the difficulties, temptations and dangers of missionary work for a group of highly unprepared and idealistic young men (and a small handful of women).The Crooks settled in Sydney, William founding a school and for some time being the colony's official chaplain, Hannah setting up a millinery business. But though at this time their 'prospects in life were highly flattering ... [they] could not be happy, but sold all off, and returned to the mission, considering that only to be [their] proper place'.[15]

The Crooks had an illustrious career in Tahiti, and were strongly connected with the Pomare family; but with nine children – eight of whom were girls – they found themselves constantly perplexed by how to ensure their temporal and eternal well-being, which makes them of particular interest in this book. While the Crook children were often of great assistance to the mission – particularly the two elder daughters, Mary and Hannah Jr – by 1827 the Crooks were in a deep quandary about their futures. So concerned were they, and so unhelpful was the LMS in their response (as explored in later chapters), that the Crooks felt forced to abandon their mission – a rare and striking case in which missionaries put their family ahead of their vocation. They returned to Sydney in 1830, and continued their religious and philanthropic work until their respective deaths in 1837 and 1846.

Notes

1 Richard Lovett, *The History of the London Missionary Society, 1795–1895* ([S.I.]: Frowde, 1899), vol. 1, p. 13.

2 See, for example, *Random Recollections of Exeter Hall, 1834–37* (London, 1838), pp. 1–20.

3 It is interesting to note that the current Council for World Mission (which absorbed the LMS, and the Colonial Missionary Society, in 1966) is now in the process of moving out of its offices in Great Peter Street, London, for a new headquarters in Singapore – an attempt, among other things, to shed the idea of London as the metropole of its operations, with all of the colonial and imperial connotations that may go with it.

4 For a full list of missionaries and their trades see Lovett, *The History of the London Missionary Society*, vol. 1, p. 127.

5 Ibid., p. 127.

6 See Jennifer Newell, *Trading Nature: Tahitians, Europeans and ecological exchange* (Honolulu: University of Hawai'i Press, 2010), pp. 16–18 for a good introduction to this family.

7 Lovett, *The History of the London Missionary Society*, vol. 1, p. 211.

8 Ibid., p. 223.

9 Norman Etherington, 'William Ellis', *Oxford Dictionary of National Biography*.

10 John Smith Moffat, *The Lives of Robert and Mary Moffat* (T. Fisher Unwin, London, 1885), p. 457. For more details on the lives of Robert and Mary Moffat see Elizabeth Elbourne, 'Robert Moffat', *Oxford Dictionary of National Biography* (which has been used extensively for this passage) and John Smith Moffat, *The Lives of Robert and Mary Moffat*, which has been used extensively throughout this book.

11 It seems to me particularly interesting that Roger and Bessie named their first daughter Isabella, and one of their later sons Slater, speaking perhaps not only to the rhetorical purchase of missionary martyrdom to Protestant evangelicals, but also to the long-term emotional consequences of this first tragedy in Roger's life.

12 Una Long (ed.), *The Journals of Elizabeth Lees Price: written in Bechuanland, Southern Africa 1854–1883 with an Epilogue: 1889 and 1900* (London: Edward Arnold, 1956), p. 17.

13 Alex Calder, 'The Temptations of William Pascoe Crook: an experience of cultural difference in the Marquesas, 1796–98', *Journal of Pacific History* 31 (1996), 144–61.

14 'Biographical Sketch of the Life and Labours of the Late Rev. William Pascoe Crook', *The Melbourne Argus*, 14 August 1846.

15 Ibid.

CHAPTER ONE

Introduction

'Originally,' wrote Richard Lovett in his centenary history of the London Missionary Society (LMS) in 1899, 'the idea was that the Christian family would be an educative and helpful influence to the natives, and as the European children grew up they also would take part in missionary labour, and be all the better qualified for the work from their intimate knowledge of native life.' So far, so good. Unfortunately 'this was a fond imagination, but, like so many others, it fared badly under the rough trial of experience'.[1] Throughout its history the LMS was constantly disappointed with the behaviour and function of missionary families. Forced at every institutional level to deal with

Figure 13 'The missionary at home'.

them (much against its will), the LMS seemed to find nothing but difficulty in these families, even as individual missionaries wove the family into mission theory and objectives. Wives put domesticity before their work; children turned to the worst kinds of juvenile deviancy; and fathers complained bitterly and constantly about their parental autonomy. This was not what the LMS had envisioned when it counselled that at each station they would have 'a little model of a Christian community, an economy of well regulated families'.[2]

Missionary families were the building blocks of an enterprise that spanned the globe in the nineteenth (and twentieth) century. Around 10,000 missionaries were dispatched from Britain in those first hundred years; over 1,300 by the LMS alone – all this, 'not including the wives', yes, but also not including the children, the grandchildren, the sisters and aunts. For thousands of people around the world, missionaries were the point of contact between the local and the global. These exchanges were managed by missionaries, but were mediated by families – and while Lovett's quote eloquently demonstrates both the LMS's ambivalence about the role of the family, and the mission historian's tendency to ignore their influence, the mission family should not be ignored in the history of this cultural, material and spiritual encounter.

This book explores both the institutional and the intimate history of the missionary family. This is not a project many historians of Christian mission have pursued, and although there are some notable exceptions, mission historians tend to operate within a system of assumed knowledge: that is, we all think we know about the missionary family (after all, it is a constant background presence in the writings and ruminations of the missionaries themselves), but without a real working knowledge of how it fitted into the missionary enterprise, the lived experience of individual missionaries, and the mission's global and spiritual objectives. In fact, the LMS at least found itself constantly embroiled in the intimate history of the family, much against its will, and individual missionaries struggled to balance the personal and the professional in such a way that ultimately the personal *became* the professional; the private became the public, most famously through the precepts of the civilising mission, but more generally in the everyday experience of mission lives. This book provides the context for this re-imagination of the mission experience.

At the end of eighteenth century the Pacific voyages of Captain Cook, the so-called 'swing to the east' occasioned by British victory in the Seven Years War, and the consumer revolution in imperial goods all came together to spark a wide-ranging British interest in the non-Christian world.[3] That, combined with a dramatic reassessment of Britain's religious trajectory through the evangelical revival (which stressed vital and personal religion over nominal and ceremonial religious performance), culminated in the 1790s with the foundation of numerous evangelical missionary societies whose existence shaped, and were shaped by, the parameters of Britain's global encounter.[4] Cook's voyages in particular were 'as the spark to tinder' in the minds of early missionaries and mission supporters,[5] and in the imperial world there was developing a 'many-sided reassessment of Britain's overseas responsibilities', spurred on by abolitionist rumblings for the ending of the slave trade,[6] and evangelicalism's active engagement with community, nation and world.

The LMS, with whom this book is primarily concern, was founded within this context in 1795 by a group of evangelically minded individuals inspired by the Apostolic injunction to 'Go ye into all the world, and preach the Gospel to every creature.'[7] It had been preceded some three years earlier by the Baptist Missionary Society (founded in 1792) and was followed by the Edinburgh (Scottish) and Glasgow Missionary Societies in 1796 and the Church Missionary Society in 1799. These organisations would ultimately dispatch thousands of missionaries across the globe, initially unschooled, pious and apostolic; increasingly educated, professional and socially oriented. Mission activity crept into the four corners of the globe, impacting profoundly on indigenous peoples, the domestic social and cultural history of Britain itself, and on the broader history of Britain's global century.

Despite this, the figure of the missionary him/herself, the nature of missionary stations, and the configurations of the missionary family remain obscure in much mission writing. Thomas Beidelman evocatively remarked, in the 1970s, that while anthropology has been increasingly interested in the study of modern societies, such work 'dims with the colour line', concerned with 'exotic societies, but not with ... the study of colonial groups such as administrators, missionaries, or traders'.[8] Excepting important work undertaken on female missionaries,[9] this remains a problem.[10] Why mission scholars are reticent about writing anthropologically or historically about missionaries themselves Beidelman unintentionally acknowledged when remarking that while there have been 'some highly sophisticated studies of mission by missionaries themselves ... none of these writers appears to have had any interest in relating his findings to theories or problems outside the mission community'.[11] In the words of Lovett,

> missionary history is hardly worth the telling, unless it leads the reader to bring the experience of the past to bear upon the missionary problems of to-day, and enables him to solve the problems of to-day by the insight

> and the instinct, as it were, that reward the patient investigator into the deeds and the purposes of those who have gone before. A knowledge of the history of all the societies is of little service unless the conscience of the reader is enlightened, his love for those for whom Christ died deepened, and his zeal for the furtherance of the great missionary cause strengthened.[12]

From its inception, then, mission history, hagiography and missiology have been intimately linked: an uncomfortable beginning for historians now more interested in the social, cultural and economic dynamics of what was never a purely spiritual encounter. Breaking away from earlier traditions of hagiography and missiology has been the more recent objective of mission historians, and one strikingly achieved. Mission history has grown into a complex and sophisticated discipline, from the books of A. F. Ajayi and Emmanuel Ayandele in the 1960s, to the more recent works of Brian Stanley and Andrew Porter, the Comaroffs and Catherine Hall (among many others).[13]

The price of this historical legitimacy, however, has been a focus on the public history of the missionary endeavour, brought about by a close (and fruitful) association between mission history and the history of imperialism.[14] This has meant that while imperial history itself has embraced the importance of studying the personal and the intimate (particularly in the field of sexual relationships and their role in constituting racial categories and the colonial encounter),[15] mission history has been most effectively mined in its public intersection with imperial history, and has lagged behind in explorations of the affective and the personal. Taking the missionaries themselves as a legitimate site for historical analysis divorced from their effect on public processes of 'modernisation', 'civilisation' and colonial engagement, remains scholastically taboo.[16]

The trouble is, this way of approaching mission history (in the words of mission historian Natasha Erlank),

> perpetuate[s] the dominance of [a] kind of history which give[s] precedence to attitudes and relationships that have to do with public 'political' issues, mediated in public spaces. This kind of history privileges political and public events and in doing so dismisses the importance of events and relationships that occur in more private arenas, including the home.[17]

'The public sphere is assumed to be capable of being understood on its own', notes political scientist Carole Pateman, 'as if it existed *sui generis*, independently of private sexual relations and domestic life.'[18] The ever-present proximity of mission history's problematic predecessors has in some ways obstructed a fruitful avenue for analysis:

missionaries themselves as personal, emotional and three-dimensional individuals in the historical landscape. It was with this in mind that this project was embarked upon; not with an idea of the necessarily public importance of private life, but with an understanding of history as rooted in the intimate and the personal, historical sites that have value in themselves, and not necessarily as ciphers for deeper understandings of public history. After all, 'historians of colonialism cannot write "against the grain" of imperial history and state-endorsed archives without attending to the competing logics of those who ruled and the fissures and frictions within their ranks'.[19]

As such, this project has been much inspired by the words of anthropologist Greg Dening, who has argued that 'to write the history of men and women one has to compose them in place and in their present-participled experience'.[20] With regard to missionaries, thinking about their role in a family, evolving through the life-cycle, is to 'present-participle' them: to acknowledge their humanity, their emotions, their reality as living beings. To analyse their impact, historians must analyse (emotionally *and* critically; spiritually *and* historically) their existence, and the day-to-day fabric of their lives. Mission history, the missionary, and the missionary family are legitimate sites of historical enquiry on their own terms. Catherine Hall has certainly recognised this in her powerfully complex reading of the interrelated histories of Britain and Jamaica:

> Public metropolitan time was cross-cut with public colonial time; both were cross-cut again by familial time, private time, the time of birth, emigration, marriages, new homes and death. It was these cross-cutting patterns which constituted 'imperial men', and out of which they made, and told, their stories.[21]

Mission and colonial historian Sujit Sivasundaram, meanwhile, has recently urged that 'more attention should be paid to the lived experience of evangelicalism'.[22] In the period covered in this book in particular (the nineteenth century), family life and the lived experience of family structures were integral parts of the lived experience of evangelicalism, increasingly instrumental in an emerging middle-class evangelical domesticity.[23] 'Now the wheel has come full circle', notes mission historian Neil Gunson, 'as missiologists and academic historians look again at mission origins and mission values.'[24]

For me the present-participling of missionary history means creating and exploring a familial context in which to place missionaries, their thoughts and actions. I approached this project in the belief that present-participling historical actors is a worthy objective in itself. Broader arguments relating to the family's integral role in the public history of Christian mission have found me nonetheless, and against expectation it has become increasingly evident that an understanding of mission family life transforms understandings of mission history itself. In the words of Erlank again, there is a 'need for gendered analyses of history ... in order to examine both people's personal lives in their own right and the ubiquitous, though overlooked, importance of those lives to those canons of "proper" history'.[25] This has certainly been the case here. Missionary families were integral to the evangelical missionary endeavour in the nineteenth century. They profoundly influenced missionary activity across a spectrum of involvement that encompassed sheer presence (indicating 'peaceful' intentions and normative exemplarity) to active engagement in mission objectives (through both female and juvenile participation). This book thus rests upon three interconnected arguments: that the history of the family cannot be ignored in mission history; that the intimate, emotional and personal cannot be written out of broader historical processes; and that historians must create research models sensitive to emotion, intimacy and personality. The family can no longer be legitimately ignored in mission history, and a clear understanding of its role and presence utterly transfigures our understanding of the missionary enterprise itself.

The family in mission history

The appearance of the missionary family in mission history then, has been patchy, if not entirely absent. Laudable mentions appear in Jeffrey Cox's works on mission,[26] Catherine Hall's *Civilising Subjects*,[27] and Rhonda Semple's *Missionary Women*, which displays a real interest in taking the history of the family further in mission studies.[28] Recent work by Esme Cleall has also sought to challenge the historiographical absence of missionary families, using 'families and households as a way in which to explore the intersections between gender, sexuality and race as they developed as discourses of difference'.[29] Hers, in particular, is a skilled utilisation of family discourses to think about the ways in which difference was constructed, embedded and understood on colonial frontiers and at home. Aside from these exceptions, however, the family has appeared in three main areas of mission research: a small, but fascinating body of work on missionary sexuality, the vibrant and important historiography of the missionary wife, and the recently emerging field of scholarly biography.

Missionary sexuality

In the early years of the missionary enterprise (discussed in Chapter 2), most LMS missionaries were dispatched from Britain unmarried, with a view to integrating with the communities in which they were placed. The specificity of that particular historical moment has led to some interesting work on missions and sexuality, primarily focused on an early history of interracial sexual relationships, particularly in South Africa. Before families could emerge, the boundaries and limits of legitimate missionary sexuality had to be established, promoted and enforced. Sexuality has been seen not only as the means by which appropriate missionary relations became racially demarcated, but as part of a 'hidden agenda of how to define the very nature of the missionary enterprise in its relationship to British colonialism'.[30] Earlier forms of Christian universalism came increasingly into confrontation with a settler racism emerging and solidifying in the face of cultural encounter, and a set of colonial relationships increasingly structured along hierarchies of race.[31] The sexual deviancy (marked by adultery and non-marital sex rather than interracial marital relationships themselves) of early South African missionaries undermined an early evangelical 'syncretistic approach to the evangelisation of Africans' and moved the LMS in particular towards a new generation's call for 'greater conformity to European settler standards of living and values'.[32] This shift in relations between missionaries, settlers and Africans (in this context) was constituted on the site of legitimate sexuality. Doug Stuart, Julia Wells and Elizabeth Elbourne have all seen this episode as crucial in the resituating of sexuality on to racial hierarchy, and the increased (though not uncomplicated) commonality of opinion between missionaries influenced by the fusion of 'Christianity, commerce and civilisation' and settlers influenced by biological racism.[33] Chapter 2 of this book, meanwhile, situates this regional drama into its broader global (mission) context, and maps the consolidation of racial sexual boundaries in South Africa on to the issue of the missionary family more broadly. In so doing, it places South Africa's history of syncretism into the wider historical context of evolving mission theory and notions of what constituted a missionary.

The existing research on missionary sexuality, meanwhile, has drawn upon a clear inheritance from studies of imperial sexuality, a particularly vibrant and sophisticated area in recent imperial history. Earlier accounts of white women disrupting, through their presence and overt racism, previous forms of racial and cultural intermixing,[34] have been roundly dismissed by feminist historians, who point out both that private sexual relationships were as fractured by the dictates of power and oppression as much as public colonial relationships,[35] and that white women were no more or less racist than their masculine counterparts.[36] Yet the notion that sexuality, or what Ann Laura Stoler more broadly calls *affect*, is crucial to colonial history has survived unscathed. Stoler in particular has turned the earlier idea of the destructive female on its head, thinking about the ways in which 'gender inequalities [were] essential to the construction of colonial racism and imperial authority'.[37] Inspired by, but also critical of, the works of Foucault, Stoler desired not only to establish that 'the discursive management of the sexual practices of coloniser and colonised was fundamental to the colonial order of things', but further to 'look at how his [Foucault's] insights play out in a colonial setting ... [and] suggest that a wider imperial context resituates the work of racial thinking in the making of European bourgeois identity'.[38] Stoler's later work *Carnal Knowledge* delved further into the imperial experience itself, powerfully arguing that the politics of sexuality was crucial to the racial organisation of the colonial state. 'The task is ... to identify the regimes of truth that underwrote such a political discourse and a politics that made a racially coded notion of who could be intimate with whom – and in what way – a primary concern in colonial policy.'[39]

Racial intimacy and the ways in which sexuality has been crucial to the constitution of racial boundaries and colonial hierarchies has become a site of sustained and sophisticated historical enquiry, with writers such as Pamela Scully, Adele Perry, Sylvia Van Kirk and Ann Stoler leading the way.[40] This book owes a profound debt to imperial history's engagement with the family, and the research methodologies utilised in that body of work. Elizabeth Buettner's *Empire Families* has also been an inspiration, sparking an interest in global families, which provided a pathway out of the methodological dilemma occasioned by careful thought on the notion of 'women's history' early on in the project. Like Jane Haggis and Barbara Caine, I have become increasingly uncomfortable with the notion of 'women's history' as the site of discrete historical enquiry.[41] Just as 'the idea of discussing the Strachey women without encompassing the Strachey men became impossible' for Caine in her excellent family biography *Bombay to Bloomsbury*, so an exploration of missionary women (where this project began, many years ago) without placing them within their family context became methodologically unworkable.[42] Yet simply locating missionary women in their familial context is also a limited project. The mission family could not make sense without a clear conceptualisation of familial masculinity. While historical masculinity (both evangelical and imperial) is a field of burgeoning analytical study,[43] its place in mission history has developed more slowly, despite increasing historical recognition that 'men constantly travelled back and forth across the frontier of domesticity'.[44] Recent works are beginning to tackle this issue, reflecting on both the difficulties of exploring missionary masculinity,[45] and finding ways to overcome them.[46] This book places both male and female missionaries into the more intimate, and yet also broader historical context of their family lives.

The missionary wife

Women's history itself has profoundly influenced my research and writing and, along with imperial history, is probably the most direct of this book's intellectual inheritances. In mission history it is also the second site in which missionary families have appeared. Feminist scholarship has revitalised, renovated and resuscitated mission history to an extraordinary degree. Historians cannot now ignore the crucial role women played in that enterprise, and it has become commonplace to acknowledge that the missionary movement was an increasingly feminised one, numerically and ideologically.[47] The historiography of missionary women has been singularly vibrant, particularly in the North American context,[48] but with a strong presence in British historiography as well, particularly when intersecting with imperial history.[49]

Since the publication of Patricia Grimshaw's *Paths of Duty* the role of the family in this body of research has focused on missionary wives' spiritual agency and vocational professionalism: how far were women able to exercise their vocation while still fulfilling their familial and domestic obligations; how far were missionary wives actually missionaries themselves, in both perception and reality? While Grimshaw has argued that missionary wives were continually frustrated in their public activity by the ways in which family life and female domestic obligation evolved (in the Pacific), others such as Dana Robert have looked at the ways in which these frustrations were incorporated into new mission ideologies that had space for female private action *as* female public action.[50] More recent interventions by Clare Midgley and Alison Twells have considered the role of the missionary public's expectations, perceptions and reflections on the issue of female professionalism, as well as the ways in which domestic mission ideologies reflected and fed into expansive notions of 'missionary domesticity' at home and abroad.[51]

Chapter 3 of this book deals directly with this body of literature, examining the ways in which female professional and spiritual agency was incorporated into a domestic ideology, in order to resolve some of the tensions and contradictions inherent in the lives of missionary women and their enforced focus on domesticity. It argues that situating missionary wives firmly within their familial, as well as their individual, regional and chronological context, allows for greater complexity and nuance in approaching the question of female vocation. The companionate missionary marriage in particular, was able to catch and patch some of the fractures between expectation and reality in the mission field, for both husbands and wives. Yet while missionary families are clearly fundamentally present in discussions of female professionalism in the mission context, they are often no more than a passive backdrop in these writings, taking the form of undifferentiated infants, children and adolescents whose main engagement with mission was one of obstruction. It is into this apparent backdrop that this book delves, bringing complexity and nuance to the backroom cast of missionary lives.

Historical biography

In so doing it takes a cue from recent trends in mission biography, which perhaps more than any other body of mission-family literature has sought to interweave the family with the public history of mission. Mission history (and history more generally) has had a troubled relationship with biography, 'reflect[ing], in part, the lack of engagement by practitioners of biography with social historiography and critical theory', argue David Lambert and Alan Lester in their book *Colonial Lives*.[52] Missionary biography in particular has been utilised by generations of mission supporters (and institutions) to further the particular agenda of their chronological, ideological or missiological project.[53] While families have often been part of the triumphalist narratives of mission hagiography – as a site of muscular Christianity, a sufferer of exemplary martyrdom (female and juvenile in particular), and the means through which male missionaries proved their masculinity – this has made mission biography an unstable and potentially unreliable source for mission historians (unless one is studying the very chronological, ideological and missiological shifts such biographies reflect).

Despite this chequered history, however, biographies are making a comeback. In *Colonial Lives* Lambert and Lester have argued that a properly nuanced form of biographical life-writing 'remains a powerful way of narrating the past'.[54] That two chapters within that book deal directly with missionaries (Lancelot Threlkeld, missionary to the South Seas and Australia, and William Shrewsbury, missionary in the Caribbean and Africa) demonstrates the way in which historical and analytical mission biography is finding a place at the centre of this historicising of the biographical form.[55] Clare Midgley has also made the case for utilising mission biographies more effectively. As 'multi-layered' texts, female biographies (for example) are able to illustrate 'how male missionaries wished to present their wives to the British public as [much as] about the views, motivations, activities, and self-presentation of missionary women themselves'.[56] By revisiting more hagiographical texts through a revitalised conceptual framework, reading with and through them, these literary sources can be further mined for both content and form.

In the 1980s mission historian Andrew Ross was undoubtedly at the forefront of this biographical resurgence, with his historical, critical and complex biography of John Philip.[57] While this earlier foray into historical biography focused predominantly on the public nature of Philip's life and work, owing largely to limited source material, it was also a highly nuanced reading of his life in both its public and private context, with note made of the role of his wife and children throughout.[58] Ross's later biography of David Livingstone was another example of both critical mission biography, and how the mission family can be woven into historical analysis. Livingstone's family make frequent appearances throughout that biography, and their importance to his life and work are duly and regularly acknowledged.[59] So too the biographical accounts in *Colonial Lives* thread the missionary family into the public world of the missionary enterprise, with Lester and Lambert's chapter on William Shrewsbury achieving this integration most effectively by seeking to 'situate Shrewsbury within an increasingly difficult and even traumatic set of familial relations, which came to problematise his missionary zeal'.[60] There they argue that Shrewsbury's political views were not just transformed (from universalistic optimism, to a more close-minded racial pessimism) through his transnational trajectory, but through the experience of his family life, and the disruptions his Christian mission caused to it.[61] In short, questions of whether a mission continually obstructed by the seeming obstinacy of 'barbaric' people was really worth the pain and suffering of his family led to the fractures in his humanitarian universalism. His public life course is thus rendered both insensible and deeply distorted without reference to his family life. To imagine that missionaries (female or male) operated within a professional existence unconcerned with the impact their vocational choices had on their children and families would be extremely blinkered. Some of the most basic conceptual underpinnings of the missionary enterprise were troubled and shaken by parental anxieties and domestic concerns, to the extent that some missionaries abandoned the very universal humanitarianism that underpinned the entire enterprise.

The missionary family

Aside from these historiographical areas, however, the missionary family has often been an unacknowledged absence in mission history. This is surprising for several reasons. The language of the missionary endeavour was a familiar one. The hidden hierarchies embedded in missionary activity were obscured through a long lexicon of familial rhetoric.[62] Christians were brothers and sisters, missionaries were fathers and mothers, converts were eager children. At the same time, missionary families were ubiquitous. The vast majority of missionaries were married, and the missionary family was engaged in a constant cycle of reproduction, with missionary women having children well into their forties. Mission life *was* family life in the most profound sense. As Hall has noted,

> Family was indeed a many-layered concept in this context: there was the family of origin, the family of marriage, the family of the chapel, the mission family, the family of Baptists at home and the family-to-be in the sky – this last providing the key to the overarching spiritual nature of the Christian family.[63]

The missionary enterprise was structured linguistically, metaphorically and actually by the rhythms, cycles and realities of family life.

The absence of the family in mission history is also surprising given the class dynamics of mission. Early missionaries were notoriously low on the social scale, recruited predominantly from the artisan class and inhabiting what John Comaroff has called 'the ideological core yet the social margins of bourgeois Britain'.[64] Often with little or no formal education, and given no training before being dispatched, they established their 'respectability' through their piety, and perhaps more importantly through 'cultivat[ing] middle-class attitudes'.[65] Respectable domesticity became a social marker for both missionaries and indigenous converts. The self-help evangelicalism of missionaries also became a common trope in the mission hagiography.[66] At the same time 'the missionary imperial project was central to the construction of Victorian middle-class identity, or at least to one influential version of it', argues Susan Thorne.[67] Non-conformist piety and evangelical association became the means by which 'Victorian evangelicals constructed their case for respectability'.[68] Domesticity and the family were crucial to this process of acquiring that valuable commodity: respectability. Manifesting correct domestic relationships was an essential part of middle-class social status.[69] It thus becomes increasingly surprising that the mission family itself (manifesting practical evangelicalism, performative domesticity and family respectability) has received so little historical attention.

Missionary families were also central to missionary engagement, both practically and ideologically. Family members consistently interacted with mission objectives, passively demonstrating domestic normativity and actively engaging in missionary activity. Ideologically, family (and domesticity) was crucial to the idea of Christian modernity. If middle-class domesticity was integral to the respectability of the missionary family, western familial relationships were even more crucial to the material manifestation of internal religious conversion. Missionaries constantly meddled in indigenous family structures,[70] were 'firm believers in what they saw as a proper gender order, in which men worked for money and women stayed at home', and were instrumental in non-western contexts in the emergence of a 'new marital economy ... modelled on that of the English middle classes'.[71] 'Missionaries had few qualms about asserting to non-Western peoples the virtues of their own ideal gender arrangements, with the Christian family as their crucible', argues Grimshaw.[72] At the same time, adds Cleall, 'the family was a key site in which missionaries agonised over the boundaries between "heathen" and "Christian", and, in so doing, deliberated over questions that had no easy answers'.[73] Indigenous families were not only a site of change, but a site for complex questions over the boundaries of spiritual and material conversion. The prioritisation of the family was a mutually constitutive encounter for missionaries, seeking to legitimise their own social mobility through the performance of indigenous cultural and material conversion.

Methodologically, however, this thesis has not sought to read family life back from preaching into practice. Such a stratagem would be unsound, due in no small part to the rupture between what missionaries preached about family, and what they practised.[74] The line between 'say' and 'do' was riven by fractures, gaps and inconsistencies. These need not demonstrate a deep-seated hypocrisy within the missionary endeavour. Rather, for missionaries the fundamental and eternal importance of their vocational calling justified the gaps between their rhetoric and their experience. Public female activity (in the face of a preached domestic economy based on separate spheres) could be justified through the importance of the mission itself (and in particular the need to 'uplift' indigenous women).[75] The splintering of the nuclear family through juvenile repatriation[76] (while preaching normative familial relationships) was a price to be paid by missionary families for the sake of the cause. Though missionaries promoted an upper working-class dynamic of hard work, self-help and emergent respectability for indigenous converts,[77] they themselves aspired to, and increasingly came from, middle-class attitudes, practices and communities.[78]

Indeed, many of the gaps between missionary prescription and their own family practices can be explained by different class expectations. Missionaries aimed to replicate respectable working-class values in their converts, while they themselves sought to inhabit a middle-class consciousness. Thus when missionary institutions trained indigenous women to be domestic servants, with a view to ultimately securing respectable upper-working-class marriages, they were certainly not advocating that this was the appropriate trajectory for their own daughters.[79] The perceived and prescribed class differences between missionaries and their converts make any attempt to understand the missionary family through the domestic relationships they advocated for convert families a highly problematic strategy. At the same time, the fractures between the universalist ideal of spiritual and material conversion and the realities of missionary judgement of the convert domestic space, further problematises such a project.[80] For that reason indigenous peoples do not appear as frequently in this book as they might have within a different methodological frame. The focus of this work is the missionary family. The mission impact on indigenous families has been dealt with extensively elsewhere.[81]

Methodology

Perhaps the most distinctive thing about this book is its situating of the missionary family within the institutional context of official mission strategies, policies and objectives. As an institution the LMS was continually forced, by both its missionaries and the missionary public, to interfere in and be preoccupied by family issues, even if these were not translated in meaningful ways into their public-facing literature or identity. By the mid-nineteenth century it had become a professional institution which had to provide a level of social welfare for the families of its missionaries, including financial security in the face of death, investment in the future careers of missionary children, and ultimately expensive 'homeland' education in order to further facilitate the 'gentrification' or 'bourgoisement' of missionary families. As such, the LMS became intimately involved in mission family life: an outcome completely unsolicited, unforeseen and discomforting.

This book thus makes extensive use of the LMS's institutional records. Board Minutes, Annual Reports, official transactions and publications, registers, statistics and outgoing correspondence have been extensively mined for information. But the missionary endeavour was by no means a one-way encounter, and these records have been met in equal measure with the correspondence, writings and journals of missionaries themselves, seeking to explore not only the ideal conditions expected and projected by London, but the way in which the missionary endeavour was forged out of a transnational encounter between, and within, complex missionary networks.

The aim is thus to think about the missionary family in its global context, but the book is nonetheless anchored in the regional specificities of the Pacific (South Seas Mission) and southern Africa (South African Mission), in order to promote both focus and depth. These were the first two missions of the LMS, out on the absolute border of the spiritual frontier, and both were sites of complex interchange between missionaries in the field and the London hierarchy. At the same time, while much of the material has the potential to speak about the evangelical missionary enterprise more broadly, practical issues of source material (particularly important when dealing with intimacy, sexuality and emotion, areas already obscure in the most verbose of archives) have limited its scope to the LMS. Chronologically, its focus on the nineteenth century maps on to what I have considered the ascendancy of the missionary family, as explored in Chapter 2. It was during those years, and particularly before the systematic employment of female missionaries from 1875 (in the LMS), that the missionary family was the primary agent of mission activity, and during which debates about its role, rights and responsibilities were thrashed out and defined.

Many of these formal debates on the role and existence of the missionary family were played out between London and the Pacific context. This was not only because the South Seas Mission (SSM) was the first mission of the LMS, but because many of the most pressing 'dangers' facing missionary families (sexual temptation, missionary deviance and juvenile transgression) seemed to be more ubiquitous there. At the same time, it has been suggested by island historians that the ubiquity of islands in the Pacific region made it the frequent site of historical experimentation. Islands were 'consumable', and thus their histories often display the microcosms of broader historical processes and the evolution of ideas, experiments and practices (colonial, western, modernising).[82] South Africa was also a place for early debates and experimentations, with sexual syncretism being particularly well known in that geographical context. The hardships of that mission (on the 'frontiers' of 'civilisation') also made it an area where family issues were negotiated and defined. Meanwhile, the fame of many South African missionaries, and the Moffat-Livingstone family in particular, has resulted in a wealth of surviving source material for the mission historian, much of it more private, personal and intimate than that connected with the SSM, and thus of particular use in this project.

Indeed, it is in thinking about these two regions in particular that I have found the notion of the 'spiritual frontier' to be especially useful. What I am really trying to evoke when using this idea is the perception of isolation and distance that missionaries entertained when their work took them to (or beyond) the corners and borderlands of 'western civilisation'. At the same time, it should suggest the idea of contact and exchange – material and cultural, but particularly in this context, spiritual. The missionaries in these pages were often those charged with being the first to bring the Christian message to non-western peoples. This produced a particular kind of missionary world-view, very different from the understanding missionaries had of themselves and their work in urban or colonial centres, such as Cape Town, Sydney or Madras. Working on the edge of the Christian and 'civilised' world gave these missionaries a unique perspective, but also exerted certain pressures upon them that their brethren in more developed areas of mission activity would not have felt so keenly. This was especially true when it came to families on the colonial frontier, and missionaries fretted continually about the material and spiritual legacy of their vocational choice upon their children, whose birthplace on the apparent edge of the world made them peculiarly vulnerable to life's temporal difficulties and temptations. This was the sense missionaries had of their world and work on the spiritual frontier, and to really understand their family life, we need to appreciate their sense of being both pioneering, and vulnerable.

Despite its unacknowledged absence from mission history then, the family was completely formative in the practice and evolution of mission. The profundity of its role will provide the main content of this book; the dynamics of its existence an ever-intriguing, fascinating and imaginatively inspiring aspect of the cultural history of mission within it.

Notes

1 Richard Lovett, *The History of the London Missionary Society, 1795–1895* ([S.I.]: Frowde, 1899), vol. 1, pp. 295–6.

2 'Letter of Instructions from the Directors of the Missionary Society to Captain Robson of the Missionary Ship, Duff', *Evangelical Magazine* (hereafter *EM*) (January 1799), p. 9.

3 James Cook, *The Voyages of Captain James Cook: illustrated with maps and numerous engravings on wood: with an appendix giving an account of the present condition of the South Seas Islands, etc.* (London, 1842); Vincent Harlow, *The Founding of the Second British Empire, 1763–1793*, 2 vols (London: Longmans, 1952–64); C. A. Bayly, *Imperial Meridian: the British Empire and the world, 1780–1830* (London: Longman, 1989); Peter Marshall, *Oxford History of the British Empire, vol. 2, The Eighteenth Century* (Oxford: Oxford University Press, 1998); T. H. Breen, '"Baubles

of Britain": The American and Consumer Revolutions of the Eighteenth Century', *Past and Present*, 119 (1988), 73–104; Joanna de Groot, 'Metropolitan Desires and Colonial Connections: reflections on consumption and empire', in Catherine Hall and Sonya Rose (eds), *At Home with the Empire: metropolitan culture and the imperial world* (Cambridge: Cambridge University Press, 2006), pp. 166–90. See also Andrew Porter, 'Trusteeship, Anti-Slavery, and Humanitarianism', in Andrew Porter (ed.), *Oxford History of the British Empire, vol. III* (Oxford: Oxford University Press, 1999), pp. 198–222, and Porter, 'Religion, Missionary Enthusiasm, and Empire', in Porter (ed.), *Oxford History of the British Empire vol III*, pp. 222–46.

4 Boyd Hilton, *Age of Atonement: the influence of evangelicalism in social and economic thought, 1795–1865* (Oxford: Clarendon, 1988); David Bebbington, *Evangelicalism in modern Britain: a history from the 1730s to the 1980s* (London: Unwin Hyman, 1989); Roger Martin, *Evangelicals United: ecumenical stirrings in pre-Victorian Britain,1795–1830* (Metuchen, NJ and London: Scarecrow, 1983); Mark Noll, *The Rise of Evangelicalism: the age of Edwards, Whitefield and the Wesleys* (Nottingham: IVP, 2004).

5 Ralph Wardlaw Thompson and Arthur Johnson, *British Foreign Missions, 1837–1897* ([S.I.]: Blackie and Son Ltd, 1899), pp. 8–9 cited in Anna Johnston, *Missionary Writing and Empire, 1800–1860* (Cambridge: Cambridge University Press, 2003), p. 117. See also Rod Edmond, *Representing the South Pacific: Colonial discourse from Cook to Gauguin* (Cambridge: Cambridge University Press, 1997), p. 98.

6 Andrew Porter, *Religion versus Empire? British Protestant missionaries and overseas expansion, 1700–1914* (Manchester: Manchester University Press, 2004), p. 39. On anti-slavery see Roger Anstey, *The Atlantic Slave Trade and British Abolition, 1760–1810* (London: Macmillan, 1975); David Brion Davis, *Slavery and Human Progress* (New York and Oxford: Oxford University Press, 1984); and Robin Blackburn, *The Overthrow of Colonial Slavery, 1776–1848* (London: Verso, 1988).

7 [Original emphasis] 'To the Evangelical Dissenters who practise Infant Baptism', *EM* (September 1794), p. 379.

8 Thomas O. Beidelman, 'Social Theory and the Study of Christian Missions in Africa', *Africa*, 44 (1974), 235–49. Quote on p. 235.

9 See particularly Fiona Bowie, Deborah Kirkwood and Shirley Ardener (eds), *Women and Missions: past and present: anthropological and historical perspectives* (Providence, RI and Oxford: Berg, 1993) for a joint anthropological and historical approach. See also notes 48 and 49 below.

10 Exceptions include Sarah Caroline Potter, 'The social origins and recruitment of English Protestant missionaries in the nineteenth century', PhD thesis (London: University of London, 1974); Thomas O. Beidelman, *Colonial Evangelism: a socio-historical study of an East African mission at the grassroots* (Bloomington: Indiana University Press, 1982); Stuart Piggin, *Making Evangelical Missionaries, 1789–1958: the social background, motives and training of British protestant missionaries to India* ([S.I.]: Sutton Courtney Press, 1984); Catherine Hall, *Civilising Subjects: metropole and colony in the English imagination, 1830–1867* (Oxford: Polity, 2002); and Elizabeth Elbourne, *Blood Ground: Colonialism, missions, and the contest for Christianity in the Cape Colony and Britain, 1799–1853* (Montreal; London: McGill-Queen's University Press, 2002) which have all looked at missionaries (male and female) in their own right as well as part of broader historical processes.

11 Beidelman, 'Social Theory', p. 235.

12 Lovett, *History of the LMS*, vol. 1, vii–viii.

13 A. F. Ade Ajayi, *Christian Missions in Nigeria, 1841–1891. The making of a new elite* (London: Longmans, 1965); Emmanuel Avankanmi Ayandele, *The Missionary Impact on Modern Nigeria, 1842–1914: a political and social analysis* (London: Longmans, 1966); Brian Stanley, *The Bible and the Flag: Protestant missions and British imperialism in the nineteenth and twentieth centuries* (Leicester: Apollos, 1990); Jean and John Comaroff, *Of Revelation and Revolution, vol. 1 Christianity, colonialism, and consciousness in South Africa* (Chicago: University of Chicago

Press, 1991) and vol. 2, *The Dialectics of Modernity on a South African Frontier* (Chicago, London: Chicago University Press, 1997); Hall, *Civilising Subjects*; Porter, *Religion versus Empire?* For a recent review of the shape of mission literature, see Andrew Porter, 'Evangelical Visions and Colonial Realities', *Journal of Imperial and Commonwealth History*, 38:1 (2010), 145–55. See also the many references to each author in the bibliography.

14 Porter, 'Evangelical Visions'.

15 Kenneth Ballhatchet, *Race, Sex and Class under the Raj: Imperial attitudes and policies and their critics, 1793–1905* (London: Weidenfeld & Nicolson, 1980); Sylvia Van Kirk, *Many Tender Ties: women in fur-trade society in Western Canada, 1670–1870* (Winnipeg: Watson and Dwyer Publications, 1980); Ann Laura Stoler, *Race and the Education of Desire: Foucault's History of sexuality and the colonial order of things* (Durham, NC and London: Duke University Press, 1995); Ann Laura Stoler, *Carnal Knowledge and Imperial Power: race and the intimate in colonial rule* (Berkeley and London: University of California Press, 2002); Adele Perry, *On the Edge of Empire: gender, race, and the making of British Columbia, 1849–1871* (Toronto and London: University of Toronto Press, 2001); Durba Ghosh, *Sex and the Family in Colonial India: the making of empire* (Cambridge: Cambridge University Press, 2006); Pamela Scully, *Liberating the Family? Gender, professionalism, and the Victorian idea of Christian mission* (Woodbridge: Boydell Press, 2003).

16 Beidelman, 'Social Theory'.

17 Natasha Erlank, 'Jane and John Philip: partnership, usefulness and sexuality in the service of God', in John de Gruchy (ed.), *The London Missionary Society in Southern Africa: historical essays in celebration of the bi-centenary of the LMS in Southern Africa, 1799–1999* (Cape Town: David Philip, 1999), pp. 86–93, quote on p. 83.

18 Carole Pateman, *The Disorder of Women: democracy, feminism and political theory* (Cambridge: Polity, 1989), p. 3, cited in Erlank, 'Jane and John Philip', p. 83. See also Jean Bethke Elshtain, *Public Man, Private Woman: women in social and political thought* (Princeton, NJ: Princeton University Press, 1981); Elizabeth Fox-Genovese, 'Placing Women's History in History', *New Left Review*, 133 (1982), 5–29; Joan Wallach Scott, *Gender and the Politics of History* (New York: Columbia University Press, 1988); Carole Pateman, *The Sexual Contract* (Cambridge: Polity, 1988). In imperial history Ann Stoler has long argued for the importance of the intimate: see Stoler references in the bibliography, and in particular, 'Tense and Tender Ties: The Politics of Comparison in North American and (Post) Colonial Studies', *Journal of American History*, 88:3 (2001), 829–65; and 'Matters of Intimacy as Matters of State: a response', *Journal of American History*, 88:3 (2001), 893–97.

19 Stoler, 'Matters of Intimacy', p. 895; Ann Laura Stoler, *Along the Archival Grain: epistemic anxieties and colonial common sense* (Princeton, NJ: Princeton University Press, 2009).

20 Greg Dening, *Performances* (Chicago: Chicago University Press, 1996), p. 17. See also Hans Medick and David Warren Sabean (eds), *Interest and Emotion: essays on the study of family and kinship* (Cambridge: Cambridge University Press, 1977).

21 Hall, *Civilising Subjects*, p. 65.

22 Sujit Sivasundaram, *Nature and the Godly Empire: science and evangelical mission in the Pacific, 1795–1850* (Cambridge: Cambridge University Press, 2005), p. 57.

23 Ian Sellers, *Nineteenth-century Nonconformity* (London: Edward Arnold, 1977), ch. 1; Leonore Davidoff and Catherine Hall, *Family Fortunes: men and women of the English middle class, 1780–1850* (London: Hutchinson, 1987); Susan Thorne, *Congregational Missions and the Making of an Imperial Culture in Nineteenth-century England* (Stanford, CA: Stanford University Press and Cambridge: Cambridge University Press, 1999), pp. 53–88. For gender's importance to class formation see Catherine Hall, *White, Male and Middle Class: exploration in feminism and history* (Cambridge: Polity, 1992), pp. 205–55.

24 Neil Gunson, 'Christian Encounters with the Other', *Journal of Pacific History*, 39:2 (2004), 259–66. Quote on p. 259.

25 Erlank, 'Jane and John Philip', p. 83. See also Joan Wallach Scott, *Gender and the Politics of History* (New York: Columbia University Press, 1988).

26 Jeffrey Cox, *Imperial Fault Lines: Christianity and colonial power in India, 1818–1940* (Stanford, CA: Stanford University Press, 2002), pp. 76–84; and *The British Missionary Enterprise since 1700* (London: Routledge, 2008), pp. 107–13.

27 Hall, *Civilising Subjects*, pp. 86–98.

28 Rhonda A. Semple, *Missionary Women: gender, professionalism and the late Victorian idea of Christian mission* (Woodbridge: Boydell, 2003), pp. 38–43, 103–5 and throughout.

29 Esme Cleall, 'Thinking with Missionaries: discourses of difference in India and southern Africa, *c.*1840–1895', PhD thesis (University College London, 2009), p. 83.

30 Julia C. Wells, 'The Scandal of Rev. James Read and the Taming of the London Missionary Society by 1820', *South African Historical Journal* 42 (2000), 136–60. Quote on p. 136.

31 Elbourne, *Blood Ground*, pp. 197–232.

32 Wells, 'Scandal of Rev. James Read', p. 136.

33 Doug Stuart, '"Of Savages and Heroes": Discourses of Race, Nation and Gender in the Evangelical Missions to Southern Africa in the Nineteenth Century', PhD Thesis, Institute of Commonwealth Studies (University of London, 1997), pp. 262–73; Julia C. Wells, 'The Scandal of Rev. James Read'; 'Curing the "Public Evils": The contested terrain of male missionary sexuality in early nineteenth-century LMS missions at the Cape of Good Hope', *Le Fait Missionnaire*, special issue 'Sex and Mission', 11 (2001), 45–72; and 'The Suppression of Mixed Marriages among LMS Missionaries in South Africa before 1820', *South African Historical Journal* 44 (2001), 1–20; Elbourne, *Blood Ground*, pp. 197–232.

34 Ballhatchet, *Race, Sex and Class*, p. 5; Ronald Hyam, 'Empire and Sexual Opportunity', *Journal of Imperial and Commonwealth History* 14:2 (1986), 34–90. See also Claudia Knapman, *White Women in Fiji 1835–1930: the ruin of empire* (London: Allen & Unwin, 1986), pp. 1–18.

35 Mark Berger, 'Imperialism and Sexual Exploitation: a response to Ronald Hyam's "empire and sexual opportunity"', *Journal of Imperial and Commonwealth History* 17:1 (1988), 83–9.

36 Margaret Strobel, *European Women and the Second British Empire* (Bloomington: Indiana University Press, 1991); Nupur Chaudhuri and Margaret Strobel (eds), *Western Women and Imperialism: complicity and resistance* (Bloomington: Indiana University Press, 1992); Claudia Knapman, *White Women in Fiji 1835–1930: the ruin of Empire* (London: Allen & Unwin, 1986).

37 Ann Laura Stoler, 'Carnal Knowledge and Imperial Power: gender, race and morality in colonial Asia', in Micaela di Leonardo, *Gender at the Crossroads of Knowledge: feminist anthropology in the postmodern era* (Berkeley: University of California Press, 1991), pp. 51–101. Quote on p. 52.

38 Stoler, *Race and the Education of Desire*, pp. 4 and 5.

39 Stoler, *Carnal Knowledge*, p. 2.

40 Scully, *Liberating the Family*; Perry, *On the Edge of Empire*; Van Kirk, *Many Tender Ties*; Sylvia Van Kirk, 'From "Marrying In" to "Marrying Out": changing patterns of aboriginal/non-aboriginal marriage in colonial Canada', *Frontiers: A Journal of Women's History* 23:3 (2002), 1–11. See also Kathleen M. Brown, *Good Wives, Nasty Wenches, and Anxious Patriarchs: gender, race, and power in colonial Virginia* (Chapel Hill and London: published for the Institute of Early American History and Culture, Williamsburg, Virginia by the University of North Carolina Press, 1996); Philippa Levine, *Prostitution, Race, and Politics: policing venereal disease in the British Empire* (New York; London: Routledge, 2003); Ghosh, *Sex and the Family*.

41 Jane Haggis, 'White Women and Colonialism: towards a non-recuperative history', in Clare Midgley (ed.), *Gender and Imperialism* (Manchester: Manchester University Press, 1998), 45–75; Barbara Caine, *Bombay to Bloomsbury: a biography of the Strachey family* (Oxford and New York: Oxford University Press, 2005), pp. 1–3.

42 Caine, *Bombay to Bloomsbury*, p. 2.

43 Norman Vance, *Sinews of the Spirit: the ideal of Christian manliness in Victorian literature and religious thought* (Cambridge: Cambridge University Press, 1985); J. A. Mangan and James Walvin (eds), *Manliness and Morality: middle-class masculinity in Britain and America, 1800–1940* (Manchester: Manchester University Press, 1987); Michael Roper and John Tosh (eds), *Manful Assertions: Masculinities in Britain since 1800* (London and New York: Routledge, 1991); Hall, *White, Male and Middle Class*; Mrinalini Sinha, *Colonial Masculinity: the 'manly Englishman' and the 'effeminate Bengali' in the late nineteenth century* (Manchester: Manchester University Press, 1995); John Tosh, *A Man's Place: masculinity and the middle-class home in Victorian England* (New Haven, CT and London: Yale University Press, 1999) and *Manliness and Masculinities in Nineteenth-century Britain: essays on gender, family and empire* (Harlow: Pearson Longman, 2005), p. 2 in particular.

44 Martin Francis, 'The Domestication of the Male? Recent research on nineteenth- and twentieth-century British masculinity', *The Historical Journal* 45:3 (2002), 637–52. Quote on p. 643.

45 Rhonda Semple, 'Missionary Manhood: Professionalism, belief, and masculinity in the nineteenth-century British imperial field', *Journal of Imperial and Commonwealth History* 36:3 (2008), 397–415.

46 Esme Cleall, 'Missionaries, Masculinities and War: The London Missionary Society in Southern Africa, *c.*1860–1899', *South African Historical Journal* 61:2 (2009), 232–53. See pp. 232–42 in particular for an overview of the field.

47 Stephen Maughan, 'Regions Beyond and the National Church: Domestic Support for the Foreign Missions of the Church of England in the High Imperial Age, 1870–1914', PhD thesis (University of London, 1995), pp. 258–372; Thorne, *Congregational Missions*, pp. 17 and 89–123; Semple, *Missionary Women*; Cleall, 'Missionaries, Masculinities and War', pp. 235–6; Cox, *British Missionary Enterprise*, pp. 196–8.

48 R. Pierce Beaver, *American Protestant Women in World Mission: history of the first feminist movement in north America* (Grand Rapids: William B. Eerdmans, 1980); Diane Langmore, *Missionary Lives: Papua, 1874–1914* (Honolulu: University of Hawaii Press, 1989); Jane Hunter, *The Gospel of Gentility: American women missionaries in turn of the century China* (New Haven and London: Yale University Press, 1984); Patricia Grimshaw, *Paths of Duty: American missionary wives in nineteenth-century Hawaii* (Honolulu: University of Hawaii Press, 1989); Patricia Ruth Hill, *The World their Household: the American woman's foreign mission movement and cultural transformation, 1870–1920* (Ann Arbor: University of Michigan Press, 1985); Dana L. Robert, *American Women in Mission: a social history of their thought and practice* (Macon, GA: Mercer University Press, 1996); Dana L. Robert (ed.), *Gospel Bearers, Gender Barriers: missionary women in the twentieth century* (New York: Orbis, 2002); Myra Rutherdale, *Women and the White Man's God: gender and race in the Canadian mission field* (Vancouver: University of British Columbia Press, 2002).

49 Bowie, Kirkwood and Ardener, *Women and Missions*; Mary Taylor Huber and Nancy C. Lutkehaus (eds), *Gendered Missions: women and men in missionary discourse and practice* (Ann Arbor: University of Michigan Press, 1999); Hall, *Civilising Subjects*; Semple, *Missionary Women*. See also various chapters in Robert Bickers and Rosemary Seton (eds), *Missionary Encounters: sources and issues* (Richmond, Surrey: Curzon Press, 1996); Clare Midgley (ed.), *Gender and Imperialism* (Manchester: Manchester University Press, 1998); Andrew Porter (ed.), *The Imperial Horizons of British Protestant Missions, 1880–1914* (Grand Rapids, MI: W. B. Eerdmans Pub., 2003); Philippa Levine (ed.), *Gender and Empire* (Oxford: Oxford University Press, 2004); and Hilary M. Carey (ed.), *Empires of Religion* (Basingstoke: Palgrave Macmillan, 2008) which deal with gender and mission. See also works by Hilary Carey, Jane Haggis, Deborah Gaitskell, Patricia Grimshaw, Jane Healey, Margaret Jolly, Clare Midgley, Dana Robert, Kathryn Rountree, and Karel Schoeman in the bibliography.

50 Patricia Grimshaw, '"Christian Woman, Pious Wife, Faithful Mother, Devoted Missionary": Conflicts and Roles of American Missionary Women in Nineteenth-Century Hawaii', *Feminist Studies* 9:3 (1983), 489–521; Dana L. Robert, 'Evangelist or Homemaker? Mission strategies of early nineteenth-century missionary wives in Burma and Hawaii', *International Bulletin of Missionary Research* 17:1 (1993), 4–12.

51 Clare Midgley, 'Can Women be Missionaries? Envisioning female agency in the early nineteenth-century British empire', *Journal of British Studies* 45 (2006), 335–58; Alison Twells, *The Civilising Mission and the English Middle Classes, 1792–1850: the 'heathen' at home and overseas* (Basingstoke: Palgrave Macmillan, 2009).

52 David Lambert and Alan Lester (eds), *Colonial Lives across the British Empire: imperial careering in the long nineteenth century* (Cambridge: Cambridge University Press, 2006), pp. 18–19.

53 See, for example, John MacKenzie, 'David Livingstone: the construction of the myth', in Graham Walker and Tom Gallagher (eds), *Sermons and Battle Hymns* (Edinburgh University Press, 1990), pp. 32–3.

54 Lambert and Lester, *Colonial Lives*, p. 20. See also pp. 16–21.

55 Anna Johnston, 'A blister on the Imperial Antipodes: Lancelot Edward Threkheld in Polynesia and Australia', in Lambert and Lester, *Colonial Lives*, 58–87; Alan Lester and David Lambert, 'Missionary Politics and the Captive Audience: William Shrewsbury in the Caribbean and the Cape colony', in Lambert and Lester, *Colonial Lives*, 88–112.

56 Midgley, 'Can Women be Missionaries?', p. 341.

57 Andrew C. Ross, *John Philip (1775–1851): missions, race and politics in South Africa* (Aberdeen: Aberdeen University Press, 1986).

58 Ibid., particularly pp. 1–10.

59 Andrew C. Ross, *David Livingstone: mission and empire* (London and New York: Hambledon & London, 2002), e.g. pp. 48–51, 58–62, 64–5, 82–4, 107, 112–15, 132–4, 177–9, 188–93, 197–8, 215–17, 231–2, 237.

60 Lester and Lambert, 'Missionary Politics', p. 91.

61 Ibid., p. 110.

62 See Alison Twells, 'Missionary "Fathers" and Wayward "Sons" in the South Pacific, 1797–1825', in Trev Lynn Broughton and Helen Rogers (eds) *Gender and Fatherhood in the Nineteenth Century* (Basingstoke: Palgrave Macmillan, 2007); and Anne McClintock, *Imperial Leather: race, gender and sexuality in the colonial conquest* (New York and London: Routledge, 1995), p. 45.

63 Hall, *Civilising Subjects*, p. 94. See also Cleall, 'Thinking with Missionaries', pp. 88–91.

64 John Comaroff, 'Images of Empire, Contests of Conscience: models of colonial domination in South Africa', in Frederick Cooper and Ann Laura Stoler (eds), *Tensions of Empire: colonial cultures in a bourgeois world* (Berkeley, CA and London: University of California Press, 1997), pp. 163–97. Quote on p. 168. See Potter, *Social Origins*; Neil Gunson, *Messengers of Grace: evangelical missionaries in the South Seas, 1799–1860* (Melbourne and Oxford: Oxford University Press, 1978), p. 31; Piggin, *Making Evangelical Missionaries*; Andrew F. Walls, *The Missionary Movement in Christian History: studies in the transmission of faith* (Edinburgh: T. & T. Clark, 1996), ch. 12; and Cox, *British Missionary Enterprise*, p. 79.

65 Gunson, *Messengers of Grace*, p. 31. See also Catherine Hall, 'Missionary Stories: Gender and Ethnicity in the 1830s and 1840s', in *White, Male and Middle Class*, pp. 205–55. See pp. 239–41 in particular.

66 See Mackenzie, 'David Livingstone', p. 32.

67 Thorne, *Congregational Missions*, p. 56.

68 Ibid., pp. 56–7. See also Alison Twells, '"Happy English Children": class, ethnicity, and the making of missionary women in the early nineteenth century', *Women's Studies International Forum* 21:3 (1998), 235–45.

69 Davidoff and Hall, *Family Fortunes*; Tosh, *A Man's Place*. See also Adele Perry, 'From "The hot-bed of Vice" to the "Good and well-ordered Christian home": first nations housing and reform in nineteenth-century British Columbia', *Ethnohistory* 50:4 (2003), 587–610.

70 Jean and John L. Comaroff, 'Home-Made Hegemony: modernity, domesticity, and colonialism in South Africa', in Karen Tranberg Hansen (ed.), *African Encounters with Domesticity* (New Brunswick: Rutgers University Press, 1992), pp. 37–74 and *Of Revelation and Revolution*, vol. 2; Margaret Jolly and Martha Macintyre (eds), *Family and Gender in the Pacific: domestic contradictions and the colonial impact* (Cambridge: Cambridge University Press, 1999); Catherine Hall, 'White Visions, Black Lives: the free villages of Jamaica', *History Workshop Journal* 36:1 (1993), 100–32; Scully, *Liberating the Family*; Perry, 'Hot-bed of Vice'.

71 Hall, *Civilising Subjects*, pp. 122 and 125.

72 Patricia Grimshaw, 'Faith, Missionary Life, and the Family', in Philippa Levine (ed.), *Gender and Empire* (Oxford: Oxford University Press, 2004), pp. 26–280. Quote on p. 270.

73 Cleall, 'Thinking with Missionaries', p. 125.

74 Ibid., pp. 83–151. See also Deborah Gaitskell, 'Devout Domesticity? A century of African women's Christianity in South Africa', in Cherryl Walker (ed.), *Women and Gender in Southern Africa to 1945* (Cape Town: David Philip, 1990), pp. 251–72. Quote on p. 254.

75 Antoinette Burton, *Burdens of History: British feminists, Indian women and imperial culture, 1865–1915* (Chapel Hill and London: University of North Carolina, 1994); Midgley, 'Can Women be Missionaries', p. 348; Clare Midgley, *Feminism and Empire: women activists in imperial Britain, 1790–1865* (London: Routledge, 2007), pp. 65–91 and Susan Thorne, 'Missionary-Imperial Feminism', in Huber and Lutkehaus, *Gendered Missions*, pp. 39–66.

76 Sending children 'home' for their education.

77 See Comaroffs, *Of Revelation and Revolution*, vol. 2, pp. 119–217.

78 For contradictions more generally between preaching and practice see Huber and Lutkehaus, *Gendered Missions*, pp. 14 and 18–21; Thorne, 'Missionary-Imperial Feminism'; and Thomas O. Beidelman, 'Altruism and Domesticity: images of missionary women among the Church Missionary Society in nineteenth-century East Africa', in Huber and Lutkehaus, *Gendered Missions*, pp. 113–43.

79 Deborah Gaitskell, 'Housewives, Maids or Mothers: some contradictions of domesticity for Christian Women in Johannesburg, 1903–39', *The Journal of African History* 24:2 (1983), 241–56.

80 Cleall, 'Thinking with Missionaries', p. 129 (and 117–30).

81 Comaroffs, 'Home-Made Hegemony'; Comaroffs, *Of Revelation and Revolution*, vol. 2; Jolly and Macintyre, *Family and Gender in the Pacific*; Hall, 'White Visions, Black Lives'; Scully, *Liberating the Family*; Perry, 'Hot-bed of Vice'.

82 Rod Edmond and Vanessa Smith (eds), *Islands in History and Representation* (London: Routledge, 2003).

CHAPTER TWO

The rise and fall of the missionary wife

> If single men went, which probably will be most desirable to begin, they would do well to form matrimonial connections with the first converts of the natives, especially with those connected with the superior families; who would thus, receiving them into their bosom, be more engaged to protect them.
> (LMS Director Thomas Haweis on the ideal marital condition of early missionaries, 1795)

On 29 June 1803, James Read, evangelical Protestant missionary in southern Africa, married 'a young Hottentot woman' by the name of Elizabeth Valentyn. He was followed in his choice of an African wife by the superintendent of the mission Johannes Vanderkemp (who had presided over the ceremony) when *he* married a 14-year-old Malagasy girl named Sara Janse three years later in 1806. These cases are well known among mission historians, and represent a small, but infamous number of missionaries who chose to marry indigenous women in the early nineteenth century. Later generations of missionaries and mission writers found such marriages deeply scandalous, and railed against missionaries who adopted indigenous dress and customs. It is thus often assumed that marriages of this type, so contrary to later racial and sexual mores (in evangelical and colonial cultures), swam against the tide of missionary thinking, and were deemed to be as scandalous at the time as they would be later. After all, evangelical missionary culture was based on upper-working- and lower-middle-class respectability, a respectability defined by its difference from the 'other'.

This chapter shows such an assumption to be completely incorrect and traces the institutional history of the missionary couple's (and thus the missionary wife's) place within LMS mission objectives in the nineteenth century from initial institutional ambivalence about the missionary wife (and preference for racial intermarriage and cultural integration), through her ascendency in mid-century, to her partial marginalisation upon the arrival of single 'lady' missionaries from 1875 onwards. As such, this chapter provides the chronological, conceptual and discursive framework for what follows in the ensuing chapters, which delve more deeply into the intimate history of the missionary family. The white missionary family in the nineteenth century was not an assumed presence in the missionary endeavour, but rather developed out of early mission experiences: the realities of indigenous conversion, an interplay between the mission society and the sending culture, the impact of the culture in which each mission station evolved, and the personalities of prominent individuals at home and in the field.

It was on the issues of race, legitimate marriage, missionary sexuality, and female vocation (in other words whether, and how, white women could be missionaries), that complex debates about the nature of the missionary enterprise were negotiated and defined. The rise and demise of missionary wives, and more broadly the changing dynamics and interplay between the white missionary couple and evangelical mission theory, dramatically shaped the history of the evangelical missionary movement in the nineteenth century. These changes chart the course from what I call integration (whereby missionaries were encouraged to integrate with local cultures through interracial marriage and cultural mixing), to civilisation (i.e. 'the civilising mission' whereby missionaries sought a wholesale physical, material *and* spiritual transformation from their converts, who would thus adhere to western cultural norms), and ultimately to what Jeffrey Cox calls institutionalisation (that is, the shift in missionary practice away from the home and family, towards the mission institution – e.g. schools, hospitals and orphanages).[1] None of the most important, course-shifting changes in the missionary enterprise can be understood or appreciated without attention to marriage, female agency and missionary domesticity. The rise and demise of missionary wives signpost, and constitute, some of the most profound changes in nineteenth-century mission history itself.

Integration and improvisation

For the LMS the nature of the missionary, the nature and existence of the missionary's wife, and consequently the form of the missionary enterprise itself, were all very much open concepts in the late eighteenth century. Fired by millenarian expectations, and improvisational in its scope, the LMS, and indeed its Baptist counterpart the BMS, were in a rush to establish as many missions as quickly and cheaply as possible in their early history.[2] Their particular sense of

Christian mission thus evolved through innovation, and through interactions between the Congregationalist, Independent, or Baptist sending culture, their agents in the field, and the indigenous cultures that received them. Missionaries' wives, and the preponderance of the missionary couple as the primary agent of mission, were certainly not the building blocks of these voluntarist missions. For the LMS in particular, the missionary couple's later ascendancy was the result of debate, dispute and compromise.

In its early years the society was profoundly convinced that dispatching single male missionaries was the most appropriate beginning for their evangelical mission. After all, fiscal and physical pragmatism supported marital ambivalence. Pre-embarkation marriage was extremely costly; including women in a potentially dangerous enterprise threatened the propriety of a respectable institution; and women and families were burdensome, requiring expensive and inconvenient material and physical concessions that the LMS were unwilling to provide, while at the same time potentially distracting male missionaries from their spiritual work. This attitude rested upon a conceptualisation of missionary masculinity that had little room for the personal, and mission femininity that had little room for the professional, but would ultimately lead, in its ambivalence, to the reshaping of the latter into the industrious missionary wife with which we are familiar.

The LMS had both ideological and practical reasons for wishing to leave white women out of its early enterprise. Ideologically, gendered and racialised understandings of safety, sexuality and propriety militated strongly against their inclusion. Women were perceived as threatening to the mission in a number of ways. Fears over their safety loomed large. After all, even male missionaries 'must be well apprised of the Difficulties and Dangers of the Undertaking, and be willing thro divine help to encounter them'.[3] 'The personal security of the female is an article of such importance, that we cannot forcibly [enough] inculcate upon you a constant attention to it', the LMS Directors wrote to Captain Robson of the mission ship *Duff* during its second missionary voyage in 1799.[4] White women in particular would excite 'the passions of the islanders', exposing them to the unacceptable risk of personal molestation and assault; or to the kind of black male and white female sexuality that exercised the anxieties of colonial officials and agents throughout the imperial experience, be it 'black peril' or consensual intercourse. As a philanthropic organisation based upon aspirational middle-class values, the LMS was highly sensitive to accusations of impropriety, and running underneath all of these anxieties was the general concern about appropriate gender roles. As Patricia Grimshaw has highlighted, 'would they appear, with their wives' active participation, to be contravening the Protestant churches' dichotomy of gender'?[5]

Practical considerations also weighed heavily on the minds of the early LMS Directors. Pre-embarkation marriage was expensive, both in terms of actual costs incurred, and in being unable to defer later domestic costs on to local communities. More supplies would be required by the mission stations, which were supplied directly from Britain, and later through the nearest European colony. There was concern about incurring costs should the missionary die, leaving an impoverished wife and family on the hands of the mission institution.[6] In 1799 it was noted in the Annual Report that '*eighty-nine* persons [had already been] sent out; including women and children. Some of these must be maintained in their stations at a large expense.'[7] In the same year, expensive alterations had to be made to the missionary ship *Duff* 'for the greater accommodation of ten married Missionaries, besides children; and for about twenty single men'.[8] Once salaries were paid to missionaries in the 1810s, the problem of financing families increased even further. 'My private expenses are now nearly or quite double what they were when single, so that this year it has cost me nearly or quite 50*l.* when I used to be able to live for 30*l.*', wrote James Read (South African missionary 1800–52) in 1807.[9] His appeal for a larger salary led the Directors to ask Johannes Vanderkemp, Superintendent of the South African Mission (1799–1811), to suggest what monies a married missionary *could* live upon. His suggestion that an extra £10 per annum should be received for a wife, and £5 per annum for each child,[10] was enacted by the LMS throughout their missionary stations. Missionary families were both expensive and inconvenient.

More worrying still was the notion that families would be detrimental to the mission itself. Evangelical culture was inextricably connected with the family, and the concomitant duties of men and women within the domestic sphere.[11] The LMS was concerned that missionary families could be a distraction from the objectives of the missionary, and that male missionaries would be unable to fulfil their dual, and equally important, responsibilities under the conditions of the mission.[12] The notion that a man's familial responsibilities were an essential duty, and that God 'has not placed an essential duty in a state of variance with another [i.e. duty to the mission]', caused the Directors a profound ideological headache.[13] As early as 1795 LMS Director Thomas Haweis had anxiously expressed the wish that 'a missionary, as far as possible, should neither be engrossed in labour, nor his attention distracted, and his anxiety exercised about his own or his family's provision'.[14] In particular the problem centred on children and whether a missionary could be both an effective proselytiser and father. Not only would the presence of families at the mission, 'abridge the usefulness [of the missionary] and limit his sphere of activity', but would also lead to the 'neglect [of the] formation of the morals of his own children'.[15] 'Wives and children are tender names, and, in the general course of things, the pledges of public virtue, as well the comforts of private life; but we persuade ourselves they will be often found the greatest impediments to missionary engagements', noted the LMS's unofficial mouthpiece, the *Evangelical Magazine*, in 1797.[16]

Perhaps it was for the best then, that married men had in several cases 'professed themselves discouraged, solely by the difficulty of securing support to themselves, and those whom God has committed to their care, in a heathen country'.[17] A fast-paced pragmatism and improvisational mission culture recognised the difficulty of attracting well-educated and ordained ministers to the cause, and the LMS (like the BMS) was subsequently built on the enterprising piety of single male artisans imbued with Protestant evangelicalism's drive for self-improvement. In seeking pious, intrepid missionaries with low material expectations, the LMS turned to the lower classes for its recruitment. Thus of the first thirty missionaries who arrived at the Pacific in 1797 only four were ordained and only five were married. Their ranks included carpenters, smiths, tailors, shoemakers and weavers, leaving more ideological room for racial and cultural integration between two sets of people (the 'heathen' and the lower classes) often described within the same rhetorical tropes, and both embodying the uplifting potential of Christian conversion.[18]

Thus, in 1795 Thomas Haweis sowed the seeds for marital and cultural integration. Haweis, the first of the LMS Directors to take up the question of marriage, was one of the most important founding members of the Missionary Society, whose interest in missions was long-standing, and who had attempted to launch a mission to the South Seas while part of the Lady Huntingdon Connexion.[19] This scheme had been a failure, but in 1794, having been involved in the foundation of the LMS, he assured Melville Horne, in a review of the latter's *Letters on Missions* in the *Evangelical Magazine*, that 'there are not now wanting men ready to hazard their lives ... for the work'.[20] For Haweis, the answer to the question of whether missionaries should be married, while admittedly requiring 'mature deliberation', was a simple one. Once again promoting the South Seas as a prime site for the mission in 1795, he noted that there 'a gracious women [*sic*] would be of most excellent use among the females, if such could be trusted in the country without particular danger of exciting the passions of the islanders'. If, however

> single men went, which probably will be most desirable to begin, they would do well to form matrimonial connexions with the first converts of their natives, especially with those connected with the superior families; who would thus, receiving them into their bosom, be more engaged to protect them.

Not only would intermarriage entrench early missionaries into indigenous communities, but further, 'if the labours of the Missionaries were not crowned with immediate success in the conversion of many, a very few families established would offer a seed to be brought up in the nurture and admonition of the Lord, and probably equally taught both language of father and mother'.[21] Children of mixed racial and cultural ancestry could thus be an asset to the mission, and could extend the scope of Christianity from within the indigenous community itself.

As an early mission ideal, then, integration was the result of pragmatic negotiations between practical and ideological concerns. It reflected prevailing understandings of race and class, and highly racialised and gendered concerns about the fragility of white women, their safety in missionary contexts, the sexual proclivities of indigenous men, and the internal polarity within the concept of femininity between moral agent and sexualised object which made them both a sexual and physical liability. At the same time it rested on an implicit undercurrent of superiority, and the belief that while adherence to western 'civilisation' was unnecessary, it would naturally flow from association and conversion. Thus:

> Should any Brother marry a Native, they should build a little house near their Brethren, and come under the same regulations as our own married brethren, their wives associating with our believing women, and on no account separate, but live a daily communion and worship under the same roof.[22]

While a small number of white women and ordained men were to form the foundation of this new church of men, its bedrock would be pious mechanics and indigenous wives, and its cornerstone mixed-race missionary children who 'equally taught both language of father and mother' and 'brought up in the nurture and admonition of the Lord' would form a strata of semi-native catechists able to extend the scope of Christianity from within the indigenous community itself.[23]

While integration thus demonstrated a possessive acceptance that conversion would be swift, and that 'our natives' would consequently be drawn to missionary marriage, it was also a theory of mission that spoke to a particular set of early LMS mission objectives and relied on a distinct lack of biologically determined prejudice. This was a moment truly built on the humanitarian universalism that characterised this late-eighteenth and early-nineteenth form of non-conformist evangelicalism, a mission identity that fitted well with other evangelical projects of the time, including the founding of Sierra Leone (the 'Province of Freedom'), and the movement for the abolition of the slave trade. Like both such projects, however, it was a universalist vision that, in reality, met with mixed success, and out of its ashes would rise the figure of the (white) missionary wife.

The rise of the missionary wife

The rise of the missionary wife as we know her was slow and gradual within the early history of the LMS. While there was never a missionary enterprise that did not include a female presence, her ascendance within mission thought and practice evolved over the early decades of mission endeavour, and did not really pick up pace until the 1820s, nor predominance until mid-century. The LMS itself spent its early years vacillating on the issue, due in no small measure to the pressure of a missionary public steeped in a culture of evangelical domesticity. Even Haweis worried in 1795 that 'we seem hitherto to have preferred batchelors [*sic*], but we wish also to join married men, and their wives, if on further enquiries, white women will be found not to endanger the mission. I think they will greatly advance it'.[24] The missionary public made its case for missionary marriage through the continuing difficulty of finding recruits, and fitted its argument into broader discussions on the socio-economic and educational status of evangelical missionaries. If married men were to be discouraged, too few ordained men would be able to take up the mission; and while the LMS was happy to construct mission masculinity in terms of unschooled, but skilled, piety, the missionary public were less enamoured of those 'godly mechanics' who made up the first fleet. By November 1795, and in the continued context of a shortage of volunteers, it had been resolved that 'married Men, with their Wives, are eligible for the Mission; if approved of by the Committee of Examination'.[25]

After all, certain benefits could accrue from the inclusion of missionary women. In 1799, with the second voyage of the *Duff* for the South Seas Mission (SSM), it was noted that the presence of women and children at the mission could be beneficial, and some form of policy relating to missionary families, as well as a protean mission theory based on the power of the normative Christian household, began to develop. Predominantly, the ideal remained single men, as befitted an organisation reaching out and growing into unknown corners of the world: 'with respect to the settlement of new Missions our recommendation is, that they consist of single Brethren *only*; as it would be evidently improper ... to place women and children in situations where their security and accommodation have not been previously... ascertained'.[26] Nonetheless, stable families had the potential to complement the mobility of single brethren: 'We shall have at each a little model of a Christian community, an economy of well regulated families', who would be able 'to take under their immediate care, a considerable number of children or young persons, and instruct them, both by precept and example, in every branch of domestic, social, and sacred duty'. Missionaries' wives would have their own value in this formulation for 'by this means the female natives will also be accessible to instruction, without which every plan of Missions will be inadequate and inefficient'.[27] At the same time theirs was a pre-emptive presence against the possibility of single male missionaries falling into (non-marital) sexual relationships with the women under their tutelage. 'Avoid as much as possible, all occasions of temptation', the Directors instructed the single men. 'Should any native woman seek instruction in private, let one of our women – sisters be their teacher.'[28] While missionary families would thus be fixed and able to teach the islanders, the single brethren 'will occasionally take their circuits through the contiguous islands, and prepare the way for the entrance of the kingdom of God among them'.[29]

Thus was beginning to gradually evolve a gender-divided theory of mission for the LMS. The seeds of exemplary domesticity were sown in familial example, as was a form of female vocation through teaching. Predominantly, apostolic proselytisation would be undertaken by single men, whose itineration flowed from a steady, family base; one they would join upon their own intermarriage with indigenous converts. But throughout this there remained one important caveat for integration and intermarriage: 'only in the Lord is the dear Apostolic order'.[30] Marriage had to occur within the confines of Christian conversion and baptism. It was this rule, and the creeping colonialisation of missionary culture, that would spell the end of evangelical integration, and would lead to the more assured rise of the missionary wife.

Between 1800 and 1818, generational change among the missionaries, developments in political and racial discourse, and realities in the field turned against the existence of racial intermarriage. In the Pacific, the first, flagship mission of the LMS, integration ultimately collapsed in the face of a distinct lack of conversions, leaving young male missionaries unprotected against the seemingly peculiarly acute temptations of the local women. Without the marital home as a bastion of respectability, they were more likely to acclimatise too completely to local customs and mores that were uniquely antithetical to evangelical respectability.[31] Missionary culture had space for racially mixed marriages, but not for religiously mixed ones. In sending young single men to the SSM the LMS had simply not foreseen a circumstance in which 'heathen' peoples would reject the Good News of the Gospel. This inevitably led them into difficulties when the peoples of the Pacific refused to embrace Christianity, and with no sanctioned outlet for their sexual curiosity and desire, it was almost inevitable that the issue of marriage to unconverted women was soon raised. 'If any brother should find himself disposed to marry one of the native women, would it be thought by the society an improper act?' asked Francis Oakes (South Seas missionary, 1797–98) in 1797.[32] 'Reference was had to the word of God, by which it was proved to be an unlawful action for any brother to marry a native woman in her present state, an idolatress ... [and] each brother acknowledged, That to marry an heathen woman was directly contrary to the word of God, and resolved, in the Lord's strength, to abide as they were.'[33]

Despite this optimistic reliance on the constancy of faith, the issue of marriage to non-Christian women was raised again in January 1798 when John Cock requested that he be allowed to marry an indigenous woman. He was also 'immediately answered in the negative, and informed, that the church had already determined such conduct, in any of her members, to be a departure from the faith'.[34] The issue of mixed marriages crystallised in the Tahitian mission with the prolonged dispute between John Jefferson, the superintendent of that mission, and one of the few ordained men, Rev. Thomas Lewis. Lewis requested his own permission to marry some months later. While 'the conversation then turned upon the inconsistency and unlawfulness of the action ... [and the] ... impropriety of a Christian man's marrying an heathen harlot', Lewis would not let the issue go, and shortly afterwards declared his 'fixed determination to take to wife one of these natives, and abide faithfully towards her until death'.[35] He was excommunicated in August 1798, having been reminded that '*if any missionary be connected with an heathen woman, he should no longer be considered as a missionary, or a member of the church* [original emphasis]'.[36] Lewis died in November 1799, apparently as a result of foul play on the part of his wife's lover, but equally likely having 'dash[ed] himself against the stones' outside their shared home, perhaps in response to his continued alienation from the religious and social community that had rejected him.[37]

Here, as would later happen in South Africa, it was the power dynamics of the mission that were played out on the issue of legitimate missionary sexuality (just as the politics of colonial societies were performed on issues of racial intimacy). Thomas Lewis, an ordained minister, came up against the superintendent of the mission, who was both unordained and had previously been scolded for Arminian religious principles. Their broader power struggle was resolved on the issue of sexuality. It did not have to be so. The Tongan situation made clear that some missionaries were willing to negotiate the rules laid down by the society, in order to stave off the greater sin of fornication. There, 'It had been reported by the natives … that [missionary George Veeson] had entered into a state of cohabitation with some of the native women and some parts of his conduct but too well corresponded with such a practice.'[38] Despite showing 'very little appearance of either shame or regret', he was not condemned by the community, but rather they agreed to marry him to the woman with whom he had been living.[39] Seth Kelso, mission superintendent, presided over the ceremony, but 'after having gone some length in the business, the poor woman burst into tears, and refused to come under the obligations she was made to understand were necessary to become his wife, alledging [*sic*] as her reason, that no due affection subsisted between them'.[40] Despite this, Veeson was not cut off from the Society. 'At the instance [*sic*] of brother Kelso it was resolved to try what another month's earnest prayer in his behalf would produce, and if no change of his temper and conduct appeared by our next meeting, we should then proceed to cut him off.'[41] Ultimately, Veeson refused to change his ways and was excommunicated on 6 January 1798 (though he was eventually reinstated after confessing his sins, and did not leave the mission until 1802).[42]

The realities of the SSM had failed to live up to the optimistic expectations of either the LMS hierarchy in London, or the missionaries in the field. The indigenous peoples had refused to flock to the new religion, and a lack of female converts had fatally undermined the integrationist principle. These early experiences on the ground reshaped the parameters of the mission experience in the South Seas. In short, an over-optimistic sending culture, the sexual desires of the young men dispatched, and the apparently peculiarly sexualised society of the Pacific had come together to dictate the need for white women in a respectable evangelical enterprise. Intermarriage, however optimistically defined, could no longer stand as a valid option for the South Seas missionaries. The mission's experience in the field compelled the directors to adjust their expectations, and make provision for alternative marital trajectories within their endeavour. In September 1804 they thus resolved,

> That if any of the Brethren be strongly persuaded that his stability and usefulness as a Missionary at Otaheite [Tahiti] would be promoted by his entering into the marriage state, he be advised to state his wishes to his Brethren there, and with their permission return to England for that purpose.[43]

While this resolution did not reflect a new embracing of pre-embarkation marriage within the LMS, it did demonstrate a reluctant accommodation of forces beyond their control. As a capitulation to reality it was by no means ideal, forcing unnecessary expense and inconvenience upon the mission, but the change in policy it embodied was inescapable. The blow was cushioned by a resolution that it was 'desirable, that by undertaking some employ on board the ship, he [the returning missionary] may relieve the Society from the expense of his passage'.[44] Further, the Society 'require[d] that this liberty be restricted to two or three Brethren, till their return back to Otaheite allow this indulgence to be extended to others'.[45] While marriage to white women in Britain remained an 'indulgence' in the eyes of London, single men were not sent to the South Seas again, and in 1809 the LMS sent out 'four pious women' who were to live in Port Jackson under the protection of Church Missionary Society agent Rev. Samuel Marsden. 'The single Brethren at Taheite [*sic*], who wish to change their condition, will, probably, visit them at that place; and should they marry, the Mission will probably derive much stability and encouragement from that measure.'[46] Not only had intermarriage as an ideal failed to materialise in the context of the SSM, but disintegration took with it the ideal of single missionaries, and the conception of the missionary enterprise embodied in their existence. It was on the issue of legitimate sexuality and marriage that the very nature of the missionary endeavour there had been decided and defined.

While the policy of intermarriage had quite conclusively failed in the Pacific, this optimistic fulfilment of the universalist ideal was enacted with somewhat more success in South Africa. It was there that James Read married Elizabeth Valentyn in 1803, and Johannes Vanderkemp wed Sara Janse in 1806. In the South African Mission the idea that through their own example the missionaries could influence the indigenous Africans to live according to a Western ideal of nuclear, Christian family, and that some level of 'civilisation' would flow from conversion, was high on the mission's agenda.

> The inconstancy of the Hottentots in their matrimonial connections, subjects us to great irregularities: we exhort, as much as possible, those who are still heathen, to abide with their wives, and not to leave or change them, as their custom is; and those who believe in Christ, we oblige, with consent of the unbelieving moiety, publicly to bind themselves to each other in inviolable ties of matrimony. In this manner, Brother Read was married, on the 29th June, to a young Hottentot woman, by Brother Van der Kemp.[47]

The 'first fruit of his marriage' was born on 15 May 1804,[48] and fulfilled in her birth the Missionary Societies' ideal of a 'seed to be brought up in the nurture and admonition of the Lord'.[49]

Vanderkemp himself was a strong believer in the essential and spiritual equality of all peoples.[50] Yet his career, and his personal actions, pushed the ideology of the LMS to its limits, if not to breaking point. His career was one of political action in defence of the local Khoikhoi, who faced oppression and violence in South Africa during both Dutch and British rule.[51] He was notorious for adopting African dress and customs, and practised in his personal life the same political ideals he preached in his public life. As James Read noted of him, some years later,

> The whole system of civilisation does not consist in dress, if Mr V was indifferent about one thing more than other, it might be thus: not that he disliked to see people decent, but he hesitated about using compulsion – he wished it to proceed from principle, and to put as much as possible the means into their hands, in doing of which however much opposition has been met with.[52]

The South African Mission, meanwhile, was the ideal situation for these integrationist ideals to be put into practice. The region had been exposed to Christianity by both western colonisation and earlier Moravian missions in 1737. While in the Pacific the missionaries could interact with no form of indigenous Christian community, the South African Mission could preach to peoples who had already been exposed to Christian teaching. Indeed when the Moravian missionaries returned in 1792, there existed a number of Africans who remembered their former missionary, and who continued to preach from the old Dutch Bible they had been given.[53] Mixed marriages in southern Africa were not incompatible with the apostolic injunction of conversion and the guidelines of the Missionary Society. Not only was there a tradition of indigenised Christianity, but displacement and slavery, as well as the social benefits that accrued from membership of the mission, contributed to a high level of conversion.[54] While in the Pacific the missionaries made little headway until the conversion of King Pomare in 1812,[55] by which time mixed marriages had already been abandoned, Vanderkemp was almost immediately head of a large body of people moving through 'Caffraria' to Graaff-Reinet.[56] The South African context was both practically and spiritually more conducive to the ideal of integration and intermarriage. A number of South African missionaries thus married African women, contributing to the universalist culture that marked South African evangelicalism in this period.

Despite this initial success however, in South Africa integration ultimately collapsed in the face of a colonial culture increasingly inimical to universalist racial politics, and a new generation of missionaries whose arrival signalled the rising importance of commerce and civilisation to Christian conversion. The abandonment of mixed marriages in southern Africa, as in the Pacific, was dictated from below, rather than from London, and was the result of complex interactions between the sending culture, the receiving community, and (more particularly in South Africa), prominent individuals.[57] A new missionary generation, increasingly uncomfortable with what was beginning to be viewed as the over-familiarity between missionaries and the local population, increasingly turned towards white women as the antidote.[58] 'The missionary character is not to be brought down to Hottentots; but His [*sic*] character raised to the missionary', argued the most vociferous critic of integration in South Africa, missionary George Thom (1812–18).[59] His critique demonstrated the growing missionary internalisation of an emerging colonial culture constituted through the prism of demarcated racial boundaries.

> *Three* missionaries have Hottentot wives which has lowered their character in the eyes of the farmers and indeed of the whole colony. It cannot be expected that the manners and sloth of a Hottentot will improve a Missionary, and he can never take her into any family ... Two extremes should be avoided particularly with Hottentots, too much familiarity and too much distance.[60]

In league with a number of his missionary colleagues, Thom was eventually able to engineer the so-called 'South African Synod', a convention of LMS missionaries opposed to intermarriage, which met in 1817 and ultimately exposed numerous missionary immoralities (including adultery and extramarital fornication) among the mission community, and particularly among those who had married African women.[61] These mission immoralities fundamentally undermined intermarriage as an institution in itself, brought down by the propensity of its proponents to stray outside acceptable evangelical behaviour and an emerging discomfort (in the mission and imperial world) with interracial integration.

The South African Synod, meanwhile, fitted into a larger debate on missionary marriage and legitimate missionary sexuality. These issues had driven a wedge through the SSM, and had, prior to that, occupied the thoughts of the London directors and the missionary public throughout the LMS's early history. Here, these debates would come to a head in a most dramatic way. The findings of the South African Synod were deeply scandalous. The missionaries' severe immoralities profoundly undermined the mission's moral legitimacy. But the very evolution of George Thom's thinking on issues of sexuality, marriage and intermarriage, and his wide-ranging comments on all three, reflected the continuing sense in which the LMS and its missionaries were grappling with issues that were constantly shifting and changing in perspective as marital policies, and the nature of mission itself, continued to evolve. Thom frequently concerned himself with the practical mechanics of missionary marriage: intermarriage, provision for widows and orphans, and the legal status of non-conformist marriage in southern Africa. These issues were part of a much broader debate: the nature of missionary marriage itself, and how far the LMS was responsible for it. More than being personally influential, Thom's thoughts and actions represented the culmination of disputes and debates that had criss-crossed the missionary world throughout its formative years. While the South African Synod marked the end of mixed marriages in the missionary enterprise (for the nineteenth-century LMS at least), it was in some ways no more than a marker in a process that had been evolving since 1795. In general, Thom's was a call for regulation and order in missionary marriages: both in their implementation, and in the LMS's policy toward them. In that he conformed not only to evolving marital practice, but to the increasing centralisation of LMS control more generally. From this point on in the mission world, legitimate marriage and mission sexuality began to be racially, as well as religiously, defined, and a space for white missionary women within that enterprise began seriously to emerge.

Integration had foundered on the rocks of conversion and colonialism, thus creating a place for white women in an enterprise that had been profoundly ambivalent about their utility and presence. At the same time, it could be argued that mission's rejection of racial and cultural syncretism, and its gradual inhabitation of a colonial mindset increasingly defined by mission's explicit promotion of western cultural and religious superiority, marked its integration into a settler-colonial and imperial enterprise. Yet, if the South African Synod did in fact mark mission's 'commitment to ... bring its activities more closely into line with the fundamentally racist view of British colonial society', as argued by Julia Wells, it was a reluctant accommodation on the part of the LMS. It reflected more the *personal* triumph of a renegade faction, jealous of the influence and affection of James Read and his Bethelsdorp cohort, and a new generation (influenced by changing evangelical and imperial mores), rather than the institutionalisation of colonial thought and practice.[62] The tensions between evangelical humanitarianism and a more colonial (and/or racialist) perspective would continue to be played out between prominent individuals within the missionary enterprise. In the Pacific, moreover, the decline of integration had everything to do with the failure of mission objectives (i.e. conversion), as well as personal (and theological) disputes being played out on the issue of sexuality, and seemingly little to do with the enclosure of evangelical missionaries into a colonial mindset and theoretical framework.

What the collapse of integration did usher in were two profound and interlinked changes in LMS mission objectives: the rise of the civilising mission, and the systematic inclusion of white missionary women. Similar processes in the imperial world[63] have led some historians to argue that the 'memsahib' and white women more generally became the guardians of racism, having, in the Indian context, 'hastened the disappearance of the Indian mistress ... [and] fostered the development of exclusive social groups'.[64] This theory has been concretely dismissed by feminist historians, who point out that sexual relationships were as fractured by the dictates of power and oppression as directly colonial relationships,[65] and who further undermine the link drawn between white women and racism.[66] Indeed, the relationship between women and colonialism is rather more complex than this early school of thought recognised. As even Ronald Hyam (an early proponent of the former view) himself has noted, 'if the mems[ahibs] contributed to racial exclusiveness it was because they were by their very presence meant to do so'.[67] Adele Perry has also noted that 'white women, colonial promoters argued, were crucial in the effort to discourage sex and marriage between white men and First Nations women'.[68] Western women, in colonial rhetoric, embodied a discomfort with the homosocial culture, and racial intermarriage, of the frontier. 'This meant that white women had a special responsibility as exemplars of civilised standards.'[69] The systematic introduction of women into the colonial space was here a symptom rather than a cause of changing colonial mores.

So too in the mission field women rhetorically embodied the rise of 'civilisation' and increasing evangelical, imperial and colonial discomfort with cultural and racial integration. As individuals they were not more racist or chauvinist than men, but the institutional (or state) encouragement of their systematic inclusion reflected the consolidation of these characteristics at societal (and institutional) level. In the missionary endeavour both the rise of civilisation as a precursor to conversion, and the systemisation of pre-embarkation marriage resulted from the failure of integration, with profound ramifications for the nature of the missionary enterprise. Marriage, patterns of marriage and legitimate sexuality were the sites at which these broader processes were negotiated and defined. Integration had foundered on two prominent sandbars: the lack of instant conversion leading to a number of racial intermarriages occurring outside conversion, and the worrying propensity of missionaries within interracial marriages to stray outside that relationship, undermining mixed marriage through their sexual misbehaviour. Both of these clashed with a mission rhetoric that marked itself off from amoral colonial interracial relationships. In the mission world, legitimate sexuality had to exist within marriage and within Christianity. The failure of early missionaries to conform to these two codes of practice spelt the end for an integrationist policy based on a utopian vision of racial intermarriage and cultural intermixing.

Of the six missionaries whose marital status is known who were sent to South Africa between 1817–24, only two were single, compared with previously when certainly over a half, and probably over two-thirds, had been unmarried.[70] In more general terms pre-embarkation marriage became more common, and numbers of single missionaries fell across the board. In 1818 the *Evangelical Magazine*'s lead article for the month of May was a long and detailed list of all the mission stations and Protestant missionaries currently serving with any missionary society overseas. Of the LMS missionaries recorded, 72 per cent were (or had been) married. Prior to 1818, only 28 per cent of the 107 LMS missionaries dispatched, had been married.

The South African Synod and its consequences thus marked a clear watershed in LMS marital politics. From that point pre-embarkation marriage became the norm, and with it the very nature of mission was transfigured. Mission theory became familial, indigenised Christianity became problematic, and racial politics became codified into more colonial discourses of difference. Yet as these figures also indicate, this process had been occurring throughout the early history of the LMS. By 1818 the pendulum had swung completely to the systematic inclusion of white women in the missionary enterprise. In so doing it was also veering towards civilisation and away from integration. Events in the field had spiralled out of London's control, and had forced a grudging acceptance of pre-embarkation marriage on to the LMS that would denote not only a change in marital policy, but a shift in the nature of mission itself. By 1818 the most appropriate agent of mission was the missionary couple. The white western missionary's wife had to be integrated into the enterprise. Her existence had been by no means implicit, necessary or assumed. Rather, the nature of her existence had been very much open to negotiation. Her ultimate characteristics were the result of early mission failures rather than evangelical ideologies and the LMS would remain ambivalent about her presence throughout the years of her ascendancy. From 1818 her position was consolidated within mission infrastructures, but by the 1840s LMS ambivalence began to resurface, and the cracks would once again appear between LMS ideals, and the reality of the field.

Widows and orphans

By 1818 the London Missionary Society had not exactly reversed its policy on marriage then, but had finally and gradually come to the realisation that pre-embarkation marriage would become foundational to the enterprise, and that the missionary couple, the embodiment of a unique and particular notion of mission (based on permanency, stability and 'civilisation'), would be its most appropriate agent. Missionary women were fundamental to this change, not only in the fact that their systematic inclusion in the enterprise marked its most obvious manifestation, but more to the point in the ways in which they exercised their spiritual agency, and transformed the nature of mission in the process. Female missionary agency is discussed further in Chapter 3, particularly the ways in which these women balanced the divergent demands on their time by creating a female mission theory complementary to their domestic obligations and mission objectives. This chapter is about the institutional framework within which missionary men and women functioned, and how it adapted to the changing shape of mission on the ground. For the LMS the realisation that missionary women were becoming an integral part of their endeavour came with a whole new set of difficulties and problems, issues to be resolved, and policy matters to be created and negotiated. For the two next decades the LMS hierarchy in London created an institutional framework for missionary families, forging a path that was as much a negotiation with their mission objectives, missionaries in the field and the missionary public at home as it was an imposition of mission ideology. This would manifest in the creation of a charitable fund for widows and orphans (in 1824), a series of resolutions designed to legislate for missionary children (the 1828 Resolutions), and the foundation of two schools for missionary children in London (in 1838 and 1842). The latter two of these initiatives is discussed further in Chapter 4. For now attention is on the former: the creation of the Widows and Orphans Fund.

The LMS was at heart an ideological institution. Its ultimate objective was a religious one: the spiritual transformation of non-western peoples. At different times throughout its existence, this would mean different things: from integration to civilisation to indigenisation. Its essential message remained the same, however: that God's 'light' be shone into 'heathen darkness'. Despite this ideological basis, the institutional side of mission was directed by its fiscal responsibilities, and the constant need to juggle millennial haste and optimism with the realities of a crowded philanthropic marketplace, and a public 'sometimes ... tempted to grow weary in well-doing'.[71] The first two decades of the nineteenth century had witnessed various attempts on the part of the Directors to cushion the financial impact of its own endeavour (in order, ultimately, to allow for more missions throughout the world). This was the primary reason for its ambivalence about missionary families, for its desire to recruit working-class men (who were more likely to accept a role in this initially unpaid enterprise), and its prioritisation of integration. Intermarriage meant the incorporation of missionaries into indigenous domestic economies, thus relieving the LMS of their expense and material provision.[72] An integrationist mission would be materially and spiritually self-sufficient and self-replicating. The LMS's greatest fear about including white women in its enterprise was of incurring financial responsibilities that would limit its global scope in the great ticking countdown to the millennium, and the second coming of Christ.

It has already been noted that missionaries returning from the South Seas for the purpose of marriage were to find some employment on board ship in order to pay their own way. This was only one attempt on the part of the Directors to limit the fiscal impact of missionary women and families. In May 1807 they had resolved that 'it is reasonable in the marriage of a Missionary, that the friends of the Female provide for the expenses attending her equipment and passage to the place of Destination, or a part thereof', in order to 'economise the funds of the Society and preserve them from unnecessary charges'.[73] In 1818 the *Annual Report* further lamented 'not only that the Missionaries derive little or no support from the places in which they reside, but that their claims on the Society augment in proportion as their families enlarge'.[74] The LMS was realising that exponential growth of the missionary enterprise might not be feasible while the mission remained financially dependent on London, and that growing missionary families would only perpetuate this broader financial problem.

Nonetheless, by 1818 it had become apparent that missionary wives (and consequently missionary families) were to be an integral part of the undertaking and that their presence and provision had to be fully integrated into the institutional framework of the LMS. In May of that year, the Directors passed a series of Resolutions, consolidating and defining the status of missionaries' wives and further integrating them, and missionary children, into their institutional mechanisms of control. The ideology of 'mission first; family second', articulated and formulated in these Resolutions, would fundamentally shape the history of the mission family. At the same time as exerting control, however, the 1818 Resolutions also found a place for wives in the missionary enterprise, and thereby shaped the terms of engagement between family and mission.

The primary concern of the 1818 Resolutions was to determine what was expected of, and what would happen to, their families in the event of a male missionary's death.

> The Directors do not consider the engagement into which a Female Missionary has entered with the Society, as necessarily dissolved by the decease of her husband, but on the contrary, she will be expected to remain at her station, or exert herself according to her ability in the maintenance of her self and family, and generally to promote the objects of the mission.[75]

Widows had to apply to the newly centralised 'Mission Committee' to leave the mission station, were granted one year's 'frugal maintenance' upon their return to Europe and must 'with the assistance of friends, have taken the necessary measures for procuring a subsistence'. Missionary orphans meanwhile, became 'an obligation' to their station. They were 'on no account to be sent to Europe without the authority of the Directors, unless it should be by the express desire of friends who shall have previously engaged to defray the expenses of their passage and to provide for their future subsistence'.[76]

The LMS's continued ambivalence was clear, and mission families were not to be a drain on fiscal or material resources. In making this clear, however, the Directors were also drawing missionary women into an official and individual relationship with the missionary institution. Even the death of their husbands did not absolve these women from their implicit obligation to the mission itself. At the same time as their labour on behalf of the mission was both implicitly and explicitly co-opted, the LMS recognised, created and confirmed a space for female activism in the missionary enterprise. Missionary marriage created a triangle of multilateral relationships: between the LMS and the missionaries (male and female), the missionaries and the LMS, and between the spouses themselves. Upon the death of the male missionary, the female missionary's connection with the Society as expressed in these Resolutions did not cease, but was transformed into a bilateral engagement that continued to demand female missionary service. This was a state of affairs, however, that did not last.

The explicit functions of the Resolutions were less than revolutionary, and fell far short of what both the missionary public and missionaries themselves had hoped for. The issue of the widows and orphans of missionaries had been brewing for some time. The

Evangelical Magazine had, from its foundation in 1792, dedicated its profits to the Widows and Orphans of Ministers Fund, and its pages had been alive with debate on issues of stipends and salaries for ministers and ministers' dependants from an early date.[77] The South African Synod had also been concerned with the status of missionary widows and orphans: 'Does the Society provide for the widows and orphans of deceased Missionaries? No explicit sum is promised by the Directors, and what we see printed on the subject and what we have heard from them when presented is exceedingly unsatisfactory.'[78] It is worth remembering here that the South African Synod was a grass-roots phenomenon, reflecting that generation's personal, rather than official, views: 'It is the universal voice of all the Missionaries within the Colony and so far as we know of those without the Colony that widows and orphans should be immediately provided for ... it has been and is a source of great uneasiness in the breasts of married Missionaries, that no specific provision is made for widows and orphans.'[79]

The Widows and Orphans Fund, like the foundation of the London mission schools for missionary children twenty years later, reflected the strong influence of an engaged missionary public when united with missionaries on the ground – connected by strong trans-local missionary networks that linked missionaries to local auxiliaries and evangelical luminaries. The timing of its foundation, meanwhile, was dictated (as usual) by events. It was the case of Jane Smith, wife of Demerara missionary John Smith, which finally forced the LMS to make genuine provision for missionary widows and orphans. John Smith (a former tradesman from the Midlands) had been accepted as a missionary by the LMS in 1816 and after a short spell at Gosport Seminary College had sailed for the West Indies, with his new wife Jane, in January 1817. Arriving in Demerara in February he soon became acquainted with the island's social and racial tensions and aligned himself with a missionary contingent politically active in evangelical humanitarianism.[80] Rebellion broke out in 1823 and John Smith was 'taken into custody on the evening of the 21 August, and all his papers seized' as white islanders railed against meddling missionaries accused of inciting rebellion, but more generally seen as the enemy of white planters, owing to their education and conversion of the slaves (acts which blurred the corrosively necessary line between human and chattel).[81] He was bought before a court martial on 13 October and charged with four charges of inciting rebellion and conspiracy. In a trial used as an 'opportunity to condemn indirectly all those who threatened slavery as an institution',[82] Smith was found guilty and sentenced to death, pending the King's decision. The death penalty was ultimately commuted, but not before John Smith had 'died quietly' in prison on 6 February 1824.[83]

Most of the letters and petitions that flooded into the *Evangelical Magazine* and the LMS headquarters thereafter related to the need to clear John Smith's name of all charges. Many also referred to the situation of his widow. 'The Committee unite with all Christians in expressing their tenderest sympathy for the forlorn widow of their departed brother, and will most cordially concur with the Directors in promoting any plan that may be adopted for her comfort', wrote the Glasgow Missionary Auxiliary in May 1824.[84] Subscriptions were raised on her behalf, and by June of that year over £96 had been raised in reference to the case, £3 14*s* 6*d* for the direct benefit of Jane Smith.[85]

> With the bereaved widow the thousands of our British Israel sincerely sympathise; for her, their fervent prayers ascend to heaven; and for her future support a liberal subscription is commenced, not only by the Missionary Society, but also by persons of various denominations, not connected with it, whose hatred of oppression and persecution, and whose love of liberty and of religion, have inclined to engage in this labour of love, and which we doubt not will be crowned with distinguished success.[86]

The philanthropic and religious public took on the case of Jane Smith in an unprecedented fashion, the appeal tapping into a pool of support connected with the abolition movement. The LMS also had an appeal on her behalf, but sought to ensure that most of the Fund would be garnered from outside support, so as not to deplete the General Fund for missionary work. By September they were

> desirous to obviate a mistaken impression ... that a large sum has been raised for the benefit of the Widow of the late Rev John Smith, Missionary at Demerara: they beg to assure the Public, that the amount already received is very small, and to urge upon them the desirableness of making for her a moderate provision for life.[87]

By May 1825 nearly £1,900 had been raised for Jane Smith's support,[88] and by 1826 the total had reached £2,874.[89]

The 'Fund for the Widows and Families of deceased Missionaries, who had been employed by the London Missionary Society', was founded on 4 May 1824, just in time for a triumphal declaration of intention at the Annual May Missionary Meetings. While the Annual Report stated that the Fund had been under advisement 'during the past year',[90] it had in fact only been discussed since 22 March when the Committee of Examination had recommended that 'a paper be prepared ... on the subject of providing for the widows and children of missionaries'.[91] In response to a missionary public aroused by what seemed a direct attack on the missionary enterprise by the colonial government, and the continual (if less vociferous) calls from its missionaries that more provisions needed to be made for widows and orphans, the

LMS reluctantly committed its resources to their financial security. Its reticence in doing so was clear, however. By its triumphal foundation in May, none of the details of the Fund had been worked out, and the announcement was uncharacteristically short on detail. It was not until June that a committee was even appointed to 'prepare the detailed plan of the W&O Fund', nor until December that the Society matched the £1,000 donation from the *Evangelical Magazine* which had been resolved in a meeting of *their* Trustees on 15 May.[92]

The Society remained reluctant to see the Fund acquire monies that would otherwise be put to the general use of the missionary enterprise. It was hoped that the new fund could 'receive, from a humane and generous Public, extensive support ... Without detriment to the General Income of the Society.'[93] The point was reiterated in the auxiliary Circular.

> It is the desire of the Directors that the Members and Friends of the Society should be earnestly invited to contribute ... and they cherish the hope, that whatever may be contributed toward the WIDOW'S AND ORPHAN'S FUND, will in no degree lessen the amount of the GENERAL INCOME of the SOCIETY.[94]

It seemed at first that their concerns were well justified. Despite an initial flurry of giving which resulted in a first annual income of nearly £1,200, in the second year this had dropped to only £287. The Directors lamented that 'this interesting object does not appear to have attracted that share of benevolent attention which they anticipated'.[95] In 1827 the Fund did not even raise this much, with a derisory total of £273.[96] Nonetheless, by mid-century its fortunes had increased. The fund became self-sustaining in 1851, and garnered an average annual income of £2,700 between 1836 and 1895, dramatically evidencing the missionary public's collusion in the missionary family's ascendancy.

Missionary wife marginalisation

The union between an interested missionary public and missionaries in the field was one that would mark the institutionalisation of the missionary family, but its lack of complete compliance with LMS institutional mores meant that the hierarchies of mission would never be completely convinced about the utility of missionary wives and missionary children, relative to their financial cost. This underlying ambivalence would reach a flashpoint in the 1840s, as the LMS baulked at the growing sense that it was being forced to take on an increasingly involved role in the intimacies of the missionary family. This would become most obvious in the case of South Seas missionaries William and Lillias Mills, but reflected far wider trends to do with the institutionalisation of the missionary enterprise, the codification of mission centralisation, and the marginalisation of the missionary family as the primary mission institution.

By the mid-nineteenth century the mission world was swirling around the fixed point of the missionary family. The decline of 'commerce, Christianity and civilisation' as a missionary slogan,[97] the maternalisation of metropolitan and colonial cultures,[98] and the increased institutionalisation of the missionary enterprise were all changing the configurations of mission masculinity and femininity.[99] While missionary families stayed the same, the world around them was shifting in such a way that precluded their adaptation to new missionary norms. While this did not entail the complete marginalisation of the missionary couple, it did ultimately lead to a bifurcation in missionary practice: between that based around the mission home, and that based around the formal mission institution. By the 1870s the ideological ascendancy of the missionary family was slipping away, unable to keep up with the institutionalisation of the enterprise. The missionary family would no longer be the primary agent of conversion after this period, but would rather be one of a number of divergent options, including both single women, and (once again) single men.

In terms of gender, this was a divergence with the most profound ramifications for women, largely because of the sudden influx of single female missionaries in the later years of the nineteenth century (for the LMS from 1875). While missionary masculinity gradually transmuted away from itineration and preaching towards the more institutional medical and educational services, missionary discourse no longer had room for an ideal of female action which travelled between domestic obligation and spiritual activism (as described in Chapter 3). It was now *men* who had privileged access to that public–private journeying, as the middle-class home became increasingly reified, and as masculinity increasingly encompassed both work removed from the home, and the home itself.[100] The emergence of single female missionaries, meanwhile, meant that one end of the female missionary spectrum could be inhabited by missionary wives (the domestic end), while the other (the spiritually active, or 'public' end) could be embodied by these new 'lady' missionaries. As Jane Haggis has argued for the Indian context, mission femininity became 'bifurcated: the missionary wife increasingly viewed as an amateur appendage to her husband, firmly secured in the domestic sphere, while the single woman attains a new status as a professional worker'.[101]

The main obstacle to missionaries' wives full interaction with their vocational leanings was the existence of children. In those early years of negotiation in the history of the LMS (1794–*c.*1800), it had been questioned whether a male missionary could fulfil both the role of missionary and father.[102] By the end of missionaries' wives' ascendancy the same questions were being asked of her. The wives of missionaries throughout the missionary enterprise negotiated the terms of their engagement with missionary activity. This negotiation was dependent on their physical location, their personal circumstances, and their position in the female life-cycle. While newly-weds and older missionary women could often accommodate mission activity with their domestic responsibilities, particularly when they had older children to assist them, many of those missionary wives who had young children, or lived in isolated geographical contexts with little domestic or social support, found that their maternal and wifely obligations overrode their personal sense of vocation and adherence to the precepts of mission.

The foundation of the mission schools for missionary children in London in the 1830s and 1840s would make these negotiations easier in practical terms (though emotionally more difficult), and would relieve a later generation of missionary women from some of the burdens associated with raising children in the missionary context. The LMS hierarchy was however, as so often, undecided about the ways in which its own policies were evolving, and concerned about the dual obligations exerted on its male and female missionaries. Increasingly, in the mid-nineteenth century its concerns crystallised into a barely suppressed anger at the responsibilities that were being forced upon it, as well as reticence about prioritising female mission over maternal commitment.

For the South Seas Mission of the LMS, the beginnings of this bifurcation in mission femininity can be seen as early as the 1840s. In 1846 William and Lillias Mills left their station in Samoa and sailed for England with a shipment of missionary children bound for the new mission schools in London. Owing to the 'affectionate addresses' of the farewell meeting before they left for Samoa in November 1835, the couple anticipated a friendly and warm reception from the Directors.[103] When they arrived, however, they were met with a 'chill', blowing across a growing concern within the LMS that their missionaries (and mothers in particular) were abdicating their parental responsibilities.

> after some notice being taken of the ship's return, a gentleman who sat on the chairman's right, got up, and with no little warmth, and somewhat of anger in his voice said – Mr Chairman now are 20 children thrown upon us, who knows but that next week 20 more may be sent home to us. Are we to be Grandfatherly to all these Missionary children?[104]

'The unexpectedness of the whole affair preventing me from replying as I would otherwise have done', William Mills remarked. 'A wound was inflicted by that meeting, which was not healed', added his wife.[105] Indeed, the wound never did heal and they left Samoa for New South Wales, giving up missionary work in 1856.

On their return to Samoa in 1847, their experiences fed into a much larger debate about parental prerogative and the missionaries' fears that fiscal pragmatism on the part of the LMS was eroding their rights as parents (see Chapter 4). On a more personal level Lillias Mills's reaction to this 'chill', and what seemed to her as a direct attack on her prioritisation of mission over maternity, sheds important light on both female negotiation of home and mission and LMS reticence about the female missionary role. She wrote to the Directors upon her return to Samoa, that

> it has been my privilege to spend twelve years of hard labour among the Samoan females. While my children were younger, I was able, though with difficulty, to superintend their education also, but for a considerable time past, the demands for native education have been overwhelming, and the claims of my children upon my time have also increased. Both could not be answered, consequently either must be relinquished. For some years longer I could very well have educated my children and kept them from injurious intercourse with the natives, by giving up my entire time to them, but this, though not unscriptural, would have been a painful alteration, in the interesting state of the Mission. After prayerful consideration, we resolved on parting with our children, that they might enjoy the advantages of education in a civilised land, and that I might be able to give my undiminished time to the native females.[106]

Although 'for some years longer' she 'could very well have educated [her] children', Mills deemed her missionary responsibilities the more pressing obligation. While in the early nineteenth century the Directors of the LMS has been unequivocal in their demand for female vocational activity, even in the face of widowhood, by mid-late century shifting and crystallising ideals of femininity, increasingly constituted as a domestic identity in the face of emerging proto-feminisms in Britain which were destabilising gendered assumptions of place and subordination, were leading to serious doubts about how far they could support missionary women, about whose presence they had always been ambivalent, in their desire to prioritise mission over family obligation. Reflective of broader trends, including the rise of faith missions and the collapse of 'commerce, Christianity and civilisation' as a missionary slogan, the Mills dispute marked the beginning of the missionary wife's marginalisation in the last quarter of the nineteenth century. Although wives remained an important part of the missionary enterprise (indeed, up to the present day), they were increasingly professionally sidelined through a late Victorian rise in maternalism, and the parallel emergence of *social* maternalism, that is, single female evangelical and philanthropic action.[107]

While the dispute between Lillias Mills and the Directors was both personal and regional, it fed into a larger global debate about the role of missionaries' wives in the missionary enterprise, and reflected a continued caution on the part of the LMS in London in its tacit approval of female mission. In 1849, not long after the Mills controversy, David Livingstone wrote to his parents, on the topic of his brother Charles joining the African mission,

> his being engaged frightens them, for they have resolved to send out none who are married. They have been so often plagued by young men going out at great expense with their wives with them, and then returning, that they have adopted the rule in all cases to send out the young man alone, and see whether he is capable of standing the climate and fit for missionary operations first. He may then return and marry if he will.[108]

In February 1864, William Ellis (SSM, 1817–22; foreign secretary, 1833–41; Madagascan missionary, 1862–65) drew a direct line between frustrated missionary-wife professionalism and the need for single female missionaries. The Madagascar mission was in need of 'a thoroughly good strong efficient school Master and *Mistress* ... The wives of the Missionaries though willing are not able to do more than give a partial attention to the female pupils in the schools.'[109] With the proximity of Catholic nuns in the vicinity, Ellis further remarked on their ability to be single-mindedly vocational.

> We sorely feel the necessity for some counterpart to these indomitable Catholic Sisters who seem never tired in their service to as bad a cause as could be benefited by their good deeds. In our small community we have got no '*sisters*' – the care of children and home puts help in this direction out of the question.[110]

At the same time the notion of professionalism in mission as something *schooled* (for men and women) was taking hold, hand in hand with an increased secularisation or socialisation of missionary practice ever more concerned with medicine and education as institutional activities.[111] As mission became institutionalised, with the increased foundation of schools and hospitals, so it became increasingly clear that wives would find it difficult to keep up with mission theory and infrastructure. Mrs Mills's decision to prioritise education over motherhood, and the LMS's institutional reaction to that decision, began to demonstrate the fractures opening up between formalised missionary practice and informal female vocational activity. It was no coincidence that William Ellis's desire for lady missionaries in Madagascar was connected with the needs of an educative institutional establishment. It was, by mid-century, becoming increasingly clear that wives could not keep up with institutionalised mission infrastructures.

Institutionalism squeezed missionaries' wives out of mission professionalism, if only patchily out of mission practice. Many (if not the majority) of wives continued to have extensive involvement with active mission, continuing in their roles as teachers, nurses and spiritual leaders (the latter, after all, having always been an unofficial, and deeply unacknowledged role).[112] Both missionary institutions, and single missionary women were built and deployed unevenly, anyway. Missionary wives continued to have an important role in the missionary enterprise after the introduction of single female missionaries, both within the roles they had always inhabited, and in new, institutionalised or 'professionalised' roles – particularly at the cross-over points where missionary women became missionary wives (through post-embarkation marriage).

Nonetheless, having proved the importance of their work in the mid-nineteenth century (as explored in Chapter 3), particularly to indigenous women, wives were gradually pushed aside by those single female missionaries who could devote their entire time and energies to it. Female ('lady') missionaries were explicitly recruited to replace many of the functions of missionaries' wives, a convenient compromise for an institution whose very foundations had been based on the principles of single missionaries. It is little wonder then that 'the changeover from wives and daughters to single professional ladies was not without its difficulties ... the different categories of women saw the world and their work in different ways'.[113] From 1875 (in the LMS) the role of missionaries' wives was increasingly undercut by the formal vocationalism of female missionaries. Instead of two gendered spheres of activity, there were now three, but it was the missionary wife's sphere that came off the most diminished and undervalued, a deeply unfitting response to the ways wives had themselves transformed mission practice.

Conclusion

It was on the issue of female mission engagement that complex debates about the nature of mission were negotiated and defined, and it was the ways in which white women moved within the patriarchal and professional structures of mission that shaped mission theory. The LMS had built racial intermarriage into its early mission objectives. Young and single male missionaries were to marry 'the first converts of their natives', thereby integrating themselves into suitably Christianised local domestic and moral economies.[114] This idealised racial and cultural integration, however, had been thrown into chaos by the lack of indigenous conversions. The LMS's firm belief in the efficacy of young, single and pious artisans was undermined by the dynamics of societies whose sexual and cultural practices differed so dramatically from the evangelical respectability of the sending culture. At the same time 'heathen' and colonial environments alike undercut the evangelical universalism on which integration was based, and generational change was embodied in vociferous individuals who turned towards the inclusion of white missionary women as a way of turning against a racial integration that was increasingly inimical to emerging settler-colonial cultures and evangelical mores.

Spurred on by their own vocational desires, meanwhile, white women from the 'missionary middle-class'[115] in Britain took the opportunity to enter the mission field in their droves, often marrying men they barely knew in order to fulfil their vocational calling, and actively reshaping the dynamics of voluntarist mission in the process. The LMS was forced to make institutional provision for these women, which manifested in the creation of the Widows and Orphans Fund in 1824. This was a reluctant accommodation on the part of the LMS, however, which remained ambivalent about the financial cost of missionary wives and families, relative to their utility to the cause. Thus, when faced with the increasing demands of missionary families, they turned their ire on missionary women, and found in single female missionaries the perfect antidote to complicated female action. The role of single women was simple: to replace the role of missionary wives who could not balance their vocational and domestic concerns. In this, the LMS partially ignored the ways in which missionary women had woven domesticity into vocation (see Chapter 3), but also conformed to the institutionalisation of their enterprise, and its increased focus on professionalisation. In so doing they undoubtedly marginalised the missionary wife, but by no means stamped her out. Missionary wives were, and had always been, highly resilient to the contradictions inherent within their vocation; and it is to the ways in which they balanced these contradictions that we now turn.

Notes

1 Jeffrey Cox, *The British Missionary Enterprise since 1700* (London: Routledge, 2008), pp. 171–96.
2 Ibid., pp. 81 and 82–3.
3 LMS Board Minutes (hereafter BM), 28 September 1795, p. 99 Fiche Box Number (hereafter FBN) 1/Slide 2.

4 'Letter of Instructions from the Directors of the Missionary Society to Captain Robson of the Missionary Ship, Duff', *EM* (January 1799), p. 9.

5 Patricia Grimshaw, 'Faith, Missionary Life, and the Family', in Philippa Levine (ed.), *Gender and Empire* (Oxford: Oxford University Press, 2004), 260–280. Quote on p. 266.

6 BM, 12 February 1798, p. 236 1/6.

7 *Annual Report* (1799), p.xviii. When salaries were paid to the missionaries, from the first decade of the nineteenth century, this came even more to the fore, particularly in South Africa.

8 *EM* (November, 1798), p. 470.

9 *Transactions of the Missionary Society* (hereafter *Transactions*) (London, 1813) vol. 3, p. 153.

10 Ibid., p. 249.

11 Anthony Wohl (ed.), *The Victorian Family: structure and stresses* (Croom Helm, London, 1978); Catherine Hall, 'The Early Formation of Victorian Domestic Ideology', in Sandra Burman (ed.), *Fit Work for Women* (London: Croom Helm, 1979); Rayna Rapp, Ellen Ross and Renate Bridenthal, 'Examining Family History', in Judith L. Newton, Mary P. Ryan and Judith R. Walkowitz (eds), *Sex and Class in Women's History* (London, Boston, Melbourne and Henley: Routledge & Kegan Paul, 1983); Leonore Davidoff and Catherine Hall, 'The Architecture of Public and Private Life: English middle class society, in a provincial town 1780–1850', in Derek Fraser and Anthony Sutcliffe (eds), *The Pursuit of Urban History* (1983). Catherine Hall, 'Private Persons versus Public Someones: class, gender and politics in England, 1780–1850', in Carolyn Steedman, Cathy Urwin and Valerie Walkerdine (eds), *Language, Gender and Childhood* (1985), pp. 10–33; Leonore Davidoff and Catherine Hall, *Family Fortunes: men and women of the English middle class, 1780–1850* (London: Hutchinson, 1987); Leonore Davidoff, Megan Doolittle, Janet Fink and Katherine Holden, *The Family Story: Blood, Contract and Intimacy, 1830–1960* (London and New York: Longman, 1999). For evangelicalism and fatherhood see David Roberts, 'The Paterfamilias of the Victorian Governing Classes', in Anthony Wohl (ed.), *The Victorian Family: Structure and Stresses* (London: Croom Helm, 1978), pp. 59–81; Anthony E. Rotundo, 'Patriarchs and Participants: A Historical Perspective on Fatherhood', in Michael Kaufman (ed.), *Beyond Patriarchy: Essays on Pleasure, Power, and Change* (Toronto and New York: Oxford University Press, 1987); Michael Roper and John Tosh (eds), *Manful assertions: masculinities in Britain since 1800* (London: Routledge, 1991); and John Tosh, *A Man's Place: masculinity and the middle-class home in Victorian England* (New Haven, CT and London: Yale University Press, 1999).

12 See Chapter 5, p. 158.

13 *Annual Report* (1797), p. xii.

14 *Sermons Preached in London* vol. 2 (London, 1795), p. 164.

15 *Annual Report* (1797), p. xi.

16 'An Address from the Ministers of Christ in the Direction of the Missionary Society, to their Brethren in the Gospel Ministry', *EM* (September 1797), p. 367.

17 *EM* (August 1797), p. 330.

18 See John Galt, *All the voyages round the world: from the first by Megellan in 1520 to Krusenstern in 1807/ now first collected by Capt. Samuel Prior* [i.e. John Galt] (London, 1820), p. 354 and Richard Lovett, *The History of the London Missionary Society, 1795–1895* vol. 1 ([S.I.]: Frowde, 1899), p. 127.

19 Lovett, *History of the LMS*, vol. 2, p. 11; Edwin Welch, 'Thomas Haweis' entry in the *Oxford Dictionary of National Biography*.

20 Thomas Haweis, 'Review of Horne's Letters on Missions', *EM* (November 1794), p. 478.

21 Thomas Haweis, 'The Very Probable Success of a Proper Mission to the South Sea Islands', *EM* (July, 1795), p. 267.

22 'Counsels and Instructions of the LMS', South Seas Incoming Letters (hereafter SSIL), FBN 10/ Slide 415.

23 Haweis, 'The Very Probable Success of a Proper Mission to the South Sea Islands', p. 267.
24 *Sermons Preached in London*, vol. 2, pp. 172–3.
25 BM, 9 November 1795, p. 51.
26 'Letter of Instructions from the Directors of the Missionary Society to Captain Robson of the Missionary Ship, Duff', *EM* (January 1799), p. 9.
27 Ibid., pp. 13–14.
28 'Counsels and Instructions for the Regulation of the Missionaries' [undated], SSIL 10/ 415.
29 'Letter of Instructions from the Directors of the Missionary Society to Captain Robson of the Missionary Ship, Duff', *EM* (January 1799), p. 14.
30 'Counsels and Instructions', SSIL 10/415.
31 See George Veeson, *An Authentic Narrative of Four Year's Residence at Tongataboo* (London, 1810). For the unsanctioned marriage of Rev. Thomas Lewis, see *Transactions* vol. 1 (1804), pp. 58–147.
32 *Transactions*, vol. 1, p. 15.
33 Ibid., p. 16.
34 Ibid., p. 24.
35 Ibid., p. 57.
36 Ibid., p. 58.
37 Ibid., p. 147.
38 Diary of John Buchanan, Seth Kelso and James Wilkinson, Tongataboo, 1797–1800. South Seas Journals (hereafter SSJ), Box 1.
39 Ibid., 1 October 1797.
40 Ibid., 21 October 1797.
41 Ibid., 2 December 1797.
42 Ibid., 6 January 1798. See also Veeson, *An Authentic Narrative.*
43 *Transactions* vol. 3, p. ii.
44 Ibid.
45 Ibid.
46 Ibid., p. 288.
47 Ibid., p. 166.
48 Ibid., p. 239.
49 Indeed, their later son James Read Jr became a missionary for the LMS in South Africa.
50 Ido H. Enklaar, *Life and Work of Dr. J. Th. van der Kemp, 1747–1811: missionary pioneer and protagonist of racial equality in South Africa* (Southern African Biographical and Historical Studies, 28: Blakema, 1988); Elizabeth Elbourne, 'Review Article: Concerning Missionaries: the case of Van der Kemp', *Journal of Southern African Studies* 17:1 (1991), 153–64.
51 Adrian Hastings, *The Church in Africa: 1450–1950* (Oxford: Clarendon Press, 1994); Elizabeth Allo Isichei, *A History of Christianity in Africa: from antiquity to the present* (London: SPCK, 1995); John de Gruchy (ed.), *The London Missionary Society in Southern Africa: historical essays in celebration of the bi-centenary of the LMS in Southern Africa, 1799–1999* (Cape Town: David Philip, 1999); Elizabeth Elbourne, *Blood Ground: Colonialism, missions, and the contest for Christianity in the Cape Colony and Britain, 1799–1853* (Montreal; London: McGill-Queen's University Press, 2002).
52 Answers to the Questions of George Thom, January 1814, South Africa Incoming Letters (hereafter SAIL) 5/3/A.
53 Hastings, *The Church in Africa*, pp. 197–8; John Philip, *Memoir of Mrs Matilda Smith late of Cape Town, Cape of Good Hope* (London, 1824), p. 53.
54 Elbourne, 'Concerning Missionaries'. See also Norman Etherington, 'Missions and Empire', in Robin W. Winks (ed.), *Oxford History of the British Empire*, vol. 5 *Historiography* (Oxford: Oxford University Press, 1999), pp. 303–14.
55 See Preface, p. xix.
56 *Transactions*, vol. 1, p. 430.

57 See Elbourne, *Blood ground*, pp. 227–32 for more details on the South African context.
58 See Ronald Hyam, *Empire and Sexuality: the British experience* (Manchester: Manchester University Press, 1990), p. 119; Adele Perry, '"Fair Ones of a Purer Caste": White Women and Colonialism in Nineteenth-Century British Columbia', Feminist Studies 23:3 (1997), 501–24; and below, pp. 37–8.
59 George Thom to London, 27 October 1813, SAIL 5/2/E.
60 Ibid., 16 February 1814, SAIL 5/3/C.
61 Elbourne, *Blood ground*, pp. 227–32.
62 Julia C. Wells, 'The Scandal of Rev James Read and the Taming of the London Missionary Society by 1820', *South African Historical Journal* 42 (2000), 136–60. Quote on p. 137.
63 Sylvia Van Kirk, 'From "Marrying In" to "Marrying Out": Changing Patterns of Aboriginal/Non-Aboriginal Marriage in Colonial Canada', *Frontiers: A Journal of Women's History* 23:3 (2002), 1–11; Adele Perry, *On the Edge of Empire: gender, race, and the making of British Columbia, 1849–1871* (Toronto and London: University of Toronto Press, 2001); Barbara Bush, *Slave Women in Caribbean Society 1650–1838* (Currey, 1990); Ann Laura Stoler, *Race and the Education of Desire: Foucault's History of sexuality and the colonial order of things* (Durham, NC and London: Duke University Press, 1995); Ann Laura Stoler, *Carnal Knowledge and Imperial Power: race and the intimate in colonial rule* (Berkeley and London: University of California Press, 2002); Ann Laura Stoler, 'Making Empire Respectable: The Politics of Race and Sexual Morality in Twentieth-Century Colonial Cultures', *American Ethnologist* 16:4 (1989), 634–60; Durba Ghosh, *Sex and the Family in Colonial India: the making of empire* (Cambridge: Cambridge University Press, 2006).
64 Kenneth Ballhatchet, *Race, Sex and Class Under the Raj: Imperial attitudes and policies and their critics, 1793–1905* (London: Weidenfeld & Nicolson, 1980), p. 5. See also Ronald Hyam, 'Empire and Sexual Opportunity', *Journal of Imperial and Commonwealth History* 14:2 (1986), 34–90; and *Empire and Sexuality*.
65 Mark Berger, 'Imperialism and Sexual Exploitation: a response to Ronald Hyam's "Empire and Sexual Opportunity"', *Journal of Imperial and Commonwealth History* 17:1 (1988), 83–9.
66 Margaret Strobel, *European Women and the Second British Empire* (Bloomington: Indiana University Press, 1991); Nupur Chaudhuri, and Margaret Strobel (eds), *Western Women and Imperialism: complicity and resistance* (Bloomington: Indiana University Press, 1992); Claudia Knapman, *White Women in Fiji 1835–1930: the ruin of Empire* (London: Allen and Unwin, 1986).
67 Hyam, *Empire and Sexuality*, p. 119.
68 Perry, '"Fair Ones of a Purer Caste", p. 505.
69 Marilyn Lake, 'Australian Frontier Feminism and the Marauding White Man', in Clare Midgley (ed.), *Gender and Imperialism* (Manchester: Manchester University Press, 1998), pp. 123–36. Quote on p. 126.
70 James Sibree, *A Register of Missionaries, Deputations etc., from 1796–1923* (London Missionary Society 1923).
71 'An Appeal to the Pastors of our Churches in Behalf of the Institution for the Education of the Daughters of Missionaries', *EM* (February, 1848), p. 93.
72 Early missions were provisioned directly from London, and later in the Pacific from New South Wales.
73 BM, 25 May 1807, p. 48.
74 *Annual Report* (1818), p. 46.
75 BM, 18 May 1818, p. 189.
76 Ibid., pp. 188–93.
77 *EM*, October 1797, February, May and November 1798, April 1803, November 1807, and January 1811.
78 South African Synod, SAIL 7/2/C, p. 36.
79 Thom to London, 12–22 August 1817, SAIL 7/2/C, p. 37.

80 For more on the missionary interaction with the West Indies see Mary Turner, *Slaves and Missionaries: the disintegration of Jamaican slave society, 1787–1834* (Urbana: University of Illinois Press, 1982); David Brion Davis, *Slavery and Human Progress* (New York and Oxford: Oxford University Press, 1984); Andrew Porter, 'Trusteeship, Anti-Slavery, and Humanitarianism', in Andrew Porter (ed.), *Oxford History of the British Empire*, vol. III (Oxford: Oxford University Press, 1999), pp. 198–222 and 'Religion, Missionary Enthusiasm, and Empire', in Porter (ed.), *Oxford History of the British Empire* vol. III, pp. 222–46; Gad Heuman, 'The British West Indies', in Porter (ed.), *Oxford History of the British Empire* vol. III, pp. 470–94; Catherine Hall, *Civilising Subjects: metropole and colony in the English imagination, 1830–1867* (Oxford: Polity, 2002); Porter, *Religion Versus Empire?*, pp. 84–90; and Alan Lester, 'Humanitarians and White Settlers in the Nineteenth Century', in Norman Etherington (ed.), *Missions and Empire* (Oxford: Oxford University Press, 2005), pp. 64–85.

81 *EM* (January, 1824), p. 30. See also Michael Craton, *Testing the Chains: resistance to slavery in the British West Indies* (Ithaca, NY and London: Cornell University Press, 1982); Emilia Viotti da Costa, *Crowns of Glory, Tears of Blood: the Demerara Slave Rebellion of 1823* (Oxford: Oxford University Press, 1994).

82 Da Costa, *Crowns of Glory*, p. 252.

83 Ibid., p. 274.

84 *EM* (May 1824), p. 232.

85 *EM* (June 1824), p. 284.

86 *EM* (August 1824), p. 341.

87 *EM* (September 1824), p. 409.

88 *Annual Report* (1825), p. 152.

89 *Annual Report* (1826), p. lxiv.

90 *Annual Report* (1824) p. 135.

91 BM, 22 March 1824, p. 71.

92 BM, 14 June 1824, p. 131; 20 December 1824, pp. 261–3; 17 May 1824, p. 121.

93 *Annual Report* (1824), p. 135.

94 *Annual Report* (1825), p. 151.

95 *Annual Report* (1826), p. 97.

96 *Annual Report* (1827), p. 112.

97 Brian Stanley, 'Commerce and Christianity: Providence Theory, the Missionary Movement, and the Imperialism of Free Trade', *The Historical Journal* 26:1 (1989), 71–94; Andrew Porter, 'Commerce and Christianity: the Rise and Fall of a Nineteenth-Century Missionary Slogan', *The Historical Journal* 28:3 (1985), 597–621.

98 Anna Davin, 'Imperialism and Motherhood', *History Workshop Journal* 5:1 (1978), 9–66.

99 Cox, *British Missionary Enterprise*, pp. 171–95.

100 Tosh, *A Man's Place*.

101 Jane Haggis, 'Ironies of Emancipation: Changing Configurations of "Women's Work" in the "Mission of Sisterhood" to Indian Women', *Feminist Review* 65:1 (2000), 108–26. Quote on p. 108.

102 See above, p 26.

103 Lillias Mills to London, 6 November 1849, SSIL 22/4/C.

104 William Mills to London, 16 July 1850, SSIL 23/5/C.

105 Lillias Mills to London, 6 November 1849, SSIL 22/4/C.

106 Lillias Mills to London, 29 December 1847, SSIL 20/6/D.

107 See Clare Midgley, *Feminism and Empire: women activists in imperial Britain, 1790–1865* (London: Routledge, 2007), pp. 123–46.

108 Livingstone to his parents, 25 September 1849 in David Livingstone, *Family Letters, 1841–1856* vol. 1 *Edited with an introduction by I. Schapera* (London: Chatto & Windus, 1959), p. 67. For a slightly later chronology of 'sexual asceticism', in the East African Mission of the Church Missionary Society see Thomas O. Beidelman, 'Contradictions between the Sacred and the Secular Life: The Church Missionary

Society in Ukaguru, Tanzania, East Africa, 1876–1914', *Comparative Studies in Society and History* 23 (1981), 73–95, pp. 90–3. There is evidence, outlined above, that the LMS also revisited its marriage policy from the 1860s. It has not left a strong footprint in the records, however, suggesting either a particular regional specificity, or an unofficial implementation, unevenly applied.

109 William Ellis to London, 3 February 1864, Madagascar Incoming Letters (hereafter MIL) 7/1/A. See also Ellis to London, June 26 1864, MIL 7/2/A.

110 Robert Toy to London, 30 June 1864, MIL 7/2/A. See also Cox, *British Missionary Enterprise*, pp. 189–90.

111 Ibid., pp. 171–95.

112 Judith Rowbotham, '"Soldiers of Christ?": Images of Female Missionaries in Late Nineteenth-century Britain', *Gender and History*, 12 (2000), 82–106.

113 Rhonda A. Semple, *Missionary Women: gender, professionalism and the late Victorian idea of Christian mission* (Woodbridge: Boydell, 2003), p. 91. See also Haggis, 'Ironies of Emancipation', p. 111.

114 Haweis, 'The Very Probable Success of a Proper Mission to the South Sea Islands', p. 267.

115 Twells, *The Civilising Mission*, p. 7.

CHAPTER THREE

Missionary marriage

> One great trouble was the kindling of a smoky wood fire upon the flat hearth. Bending one day over this, her sickly babe wailing ... [and] after trying in vain with blurred and smarting eyes to get it alight, she burst into tears and said 'Is *this* the sort of work I have left home and friends to spend my life doing, in this uncongenial heathen land?' But she heard a voice within – 'Ah! If I may be the hewer of wood, and a drawer of water for the temple of God, am I not still blessed and privileged beyond words?' This – *this* my mother told me, was a landmark in her life ... She renewed her vows and went forward with fresh hope and courage. (Bessie Price talking of her mother, Mary Moffat)

Sometime around the early 1820s, Ann Hamilton, seasoned and, indeed, determined, wife of LMS missionary Robert Hamilton in southern Africa, stood before her young missionary colleague, superintendent of the station Robert Moffat, in order to answer his enquiries relating to her 'character' and 'conduct'. She had, in transpired, 'finally determined that Mr H[amilton] should never father another child by her' and had thus 'presumptuously and unscripturally' removed herself from their marital bed. In doing so she had not only acted 'contrary to Mr H's will[,] [her] own vow when married[,] and the command's [*sic*] of Jesus Christ', but had also done 'much injury to the cause of Christ' in the process.[1] Moffat proceeded to remind her of her duties as a Christian wife, quoting 'the 10 and 11 verses of the VII chapter of 1st Corinthians', and demanding that she repent and reconcile with her husband, in the process and at the same time bringing her 'public conduct' more into line with 'the character of a Missionary's wife'. Ann Hamilton refused, however, calling her husband 'a brute and declaring that his brutality was such as rendered it impossible for her to love him'. Her proposition the next day that 'a mutual forgiveness might be exercised on both sides and that nothing more be said on what was past' was rejected because 'reconciliation was connected with forgiveness ... [and] so long as her sins continued unrepented off [*sic*] forgiveness would avail her nothing'. Ultimately, having withdrawn her sexual and reproductive services from the mission, Ann Hamilton called upon herself a storm of ire that she could not withstand, and was in the end forced to leave the church, her mission and South Africa, returning to England as a fierce critic of the mission she had once been so desirous to serve.

The case of Ann Hamilton has been put to good use by historians of Christian mission, seen often as an exemplary instance of female vocation falling asunder to the sexual and reproductive demands of missionary men and a patriarchally structured mission society. Doug Stuart in his 1994 thesis 'Of savages and heroes' has noted that 'the real issue for Ann Hamilton was her passion for missionary work' and that while 'Ann Hamilton clearly viewed her marriage as a means to missionary activity' it was 'the demands of the marriage itself she was unwilling to accept'.[2] More recently Jeffrey Cox has argued that the case demonstrates that while missionary wives were duty bound to be useful, 'this utility had to be subordinated to the primary breeding function of the wife'.[3]

The case of Ann Hamilton certainly highlights the complex links drawn between mission, marriage, sexuality, reproduction and vocation: or in the words of Elizabeth Elbourne that 'the ability of missionary women to bear and nurture children was, among other things, a sign of male power'.[4] Sex, reproduction and domesticity are thus seen as the foundation stones of the female mission experience. In the words of Patricia Grimshaw, 'the story of the female missionaries to the Sandwich Islands offers a simple yet revealing tale of the foundering of female ambition for an independent public role on the rocks of sacred maternal obligation'.[5] Ann Hamilton, in rejecting this narrow definition of female vocation, went against a patriarchal mission structure that was too powerful to be overthrown.

Indeed, the question of female professionalism within mission circles has exercised historians of Christian mission since at least the 1980s, from Patricia Grimshaw's understanding of female vocational frustration outlined above, through Valentine Cunningham's assertion that 'missionary' was a 'male noun', to Clare Midgley's more recent assertion that women *could* be missionaries.[6] The body of literature that has grown out of these debates is a vibrant one, and has evolved through two distinct phases. Within early understandings of frustrated female vocation, pioneered by Grimshaw and more recently revived by Catherine Hall, wives were seen as inhabiting an entirely patriarchal mission system, one in which their identities and activities were subsumed within the professional and personal identity of the male missionary.[7] Missionary women thus 'received none of the public praise which was heaped upon their successful husbands',[8] while missionary men embodied the patriarchal systems of nineteenth-century society. In the words of Grimshaw, 'neither deep emotional bonds nor transplantation to an exotic setting ... had been sufficient to alter the traditional demarcation of labour within their own marriages'.[9] Within this patriarchal paradigm, the lives of missionary women were marked by vocational frustration and overwhelming domestic obligations which precluded the kind of spiritual agency embedded in the notion of female vocation. 'Except in crises such as childbirth and illness, husbands dissociated themselves from routine domestic chores and minor social obligations, despite their apparent sympathy for the wives' desire to teach.'[10]

While this school of thought excels at recognising the difficulties and frustrations faced by missionary wives in navigating structures of patriarchy, it has more recently been questioned by historians of missionary women who argue that wives were nonetheless able to reinscribe a notion of vocation into their domestic endeavours, and to 'carve out both psychological and institutional spaces for female missionary agency' within the missionary endeavour.[11] Clare Midgley has thus argued that missionary women were trumpeted and acknowledged within and *through* the still male-dominated organs of the missionary public: the periodical press and mission publications.[12] In the (British) private sphere meanwhile, social historian Alison Twells's notion of 'global domesticity' proves exceptionally useful in conceptualising the mission home, and mission domesticity, as a multi-dimensional mission institution. Twells has called for an understanding of domesticity that integrates and recognises its multi-layered and *global* obligations and aspect, in contrast to a sense of its confining parochialism.[13] While talking about the 'missionary class' in Britain, hers is a powerfully useful concept in thinking about missionaries' wives as mission agents in and through their domestic obligations.[14]

While the case of Ann Hamilton may highlight the depth of male power in mission stations, as Elbourne reminds us it also demonstrates 'that missionary women sometimes resisted the roles laid out for them'.[15] In this case, the kind of flat resistance that Ann Hamilton put up against her domesticity was too brittle to withstand the onslaught of male power embodied in her mission superior, Robert Moffat, and later from the superintendent of the South African mission John Philip. But we need not look far around the case of Hamilton to find a missionary woman more able to reinscribe vocation into her domestic and maternal commitments: Mary Moffat. At first exasperated by her domestic obligations, she ultimately found a path for vocation within evangelical domesticity. When kindling her smoky fire one day, with 'her sickly babe wailing ... [and] after trying in vain with blurred and smarting eyes to get it alight, she burst into tears and said "Is *this* the sort of work I have left home and friends to spend my life doing, in this uncongenial heathen land?"'[16] But if Ann Hamilton's 'evangelical faith ultimately trapped her in an unwanted and unendurable domesticity',[17] it was evangelical faith in the spiritual aspect of practical evangelicalism that lifted Mary Moffat out of hers, for she ultimately 'heard a voice within – "Ah! If I may be the hewer of wood, and a drawer of water for the temple of God, am I not still blessed and privileged beyond words?"'[18]

Both Ann Hamilton and Mary Moffat inhabited a transitional moment in LMS history. As integration ebbed away, and civilisation as a missionary precept flowed in, missionary women found themselves navigating the rapids of a redefining sense of female vocation. Not all missionary women were able to navigate those torrents successfully, but those that were (like Mary Moffat) established a pathway that was to be followed by successive generations of missionary wives. This pathway essentially revolved around the idea of combining religiosity and domesticity in order to reformulate female mission objectives. Female vocation became tied to mission domesticity, and the ability of women to find spiritual fulfilment in and through their domestic obligations. Female mission became exemplary, civilisational and companionate: three aspects of mission domesticity that gradually emerged in the early nineteenth century through female missionary agency.

But the difference between the Ann Hamiltons and the Mary Moffats of this transitional period was not simply force of will. Rather, the crucial difference often lay in marital context. It was the companionate missionary marriage that eased the transition, and created and sustained a conceptual space in which missionary women could define and redefine their sense of vocation within the missionary enterprise. It was the companionate nature of successful missionary marriages that made this possible, and that marked an important difference between total secular frustration on the one hand, and female vocation on the other. While Mary Moffat's arrival in South Africa was to Robert 'nothing less than life from the dead',[19] the Hamilton marriage was clearly and famously unhappy. While Mr Hamilton was apparently *'brutish'* and inattentive, 'her conduct from nearly the first he knew her was enough to drive every grain of love out of him'.[20] It was the level of companionship, and cooperation, within missionary marriages that made all the difference for female vocation, and it was the companionate missionary marriage that allowed missionary women, in various ways, to carve out a vocational place for themselves within the rising tide of the civilising mission.

Female professionalism on the spiritual frontier

Before we get to that, however, we need first to tie up how the LMS as an institution thought of the missionary wife in these years of transition; and what husbands and wives themselves expected out of female vocation. As outlined in Chapter 2, the missionary couple had become the primary mission agent by the 1820s. The idea of the single, peripatetic preacher had been superseded by the missionary family – settled, civilised and exemplary. Embarkation for the field was preceded by ordination and marriage, often on the eve of departure, in a conveyor belt of practical evangelicalism.[21] This was the norm until the systematic introduction of single female missionaries in 1875, and for over fifty years missionaries inhabited complex kin networks mediated by marriage, and exercised their vocation and profession within the context of missionary partnership.

This transition in missionary marriage theory, and the move from integration to civilisation, raised quite particular issues for those white missionary women who had already become part of the LMS's missionary endeavour. As the home became demonstrative

Figure 14 Illustration of mission premises at the Kuruman Station printed in oil colours by George Baxter [1842].

(and constitutive) of correct familial relationships, and Christianity increasingly conflated with western 'civilisation', so domesticity and the performance of domesticity, took on added importance. It was the fact that the more systematic inclusion of white women into the enterprise in these years was a direct ramification of integration's collapse and civilisation's increasing ascendency that made life so difficult for these already active missionary women. In the words of Patricia Grimshaw, evangelical women were caught between the extension of the female public role in industrialised societies on the one hand, and the simultaneous 'articulation of ideologies stressing the supreme moral and spiritual worth of home and family' on the other.[22] Mary Moffat, frustrated by her inability to devote as much time as she would have liked to directly vocational activities, 'made it a matter of serious consideration what we can but dispense with that takes up my time', but as a product of these new mission trends could not reconcile herself to the 'opinion of some that it is our duty to assimilate ourselves more to the manner of the people'.[23]

It is clear, after all, that as far as the LMS, the missionary public and individual missionaries (male and female) were concerned, the missionary wife was a missionary. This ideal was prevalent from the very beginning of the missionary enterprise in Britain and was expressed in public mission sources, as they grappled to delineate the roles and functions of the (gender-neutral) missionary, and private sources (including Board Minutes, official Societal transactions and missionaries' letters and journals). As outlined in Chapter 2, the response of the LMS to the white female presence in mission shaped the parameters of her professionalism and spiritual agency. Within a ubiquitous LMS context of fiscal and material pragmatism, it was clear that missionary wives would have to pull their own weight. The 1818 Resolutions had codified this into official policy, delineating the responsibilities of the 'Female Missionary', and confirming a bilateral relationship between missionary women and the missionary society. For the LMS it was clear that wives should be missionaries.

At the same time, missionary husbands and their wives also projected female spiritual agency on to their expectations of mission life. 'A missionary in this country without a wife is like a boat with one oar', wrote Robert Moffat in 1819. 'A good missionary's wife can be as useful as her husband in the Lord's vineyard.'[24] After all, notes Catherine Hall, missionaries were simply 'used to a world which was physically organised around the family enterprise ... it would have been unthinkable for women not to have contributed.'[25] When South African missionary Bastion Tromp informed the Directors of his intention to marry in 1806, he 'hope[d], when she becomes my wife, that the

Society may look upon her as a Missionary also'.[26] Reflecting on the life of Robert Moffat some years after Mary's death, the Home Secretary of the LMS noted that 'truly it was evident that in Mrs Moffat he had been singularly blessed with a noble and devoted wife, who was indeed a missionary *second only to himself!*'[27]

Yet it cannot be denied that the prevalence of this female-missionary ideal set many wives up for disaster. They frequently experienced deep and painful internal tensions when the realities of their lives in the field could not meet the ideal level of participation expected of them. In writing to Jane Philip in September 1821, Mary Moffat wished to assure her that

> it is much against my intentions that my time should be wholly taken up with domestic affairs and often causes depression of spirits[,] having come out with sanguine expectations of doing good, and almost every letter which arrives for me from England seems to reproach me, all like yours intimating that they expect me to be very active.[28]

Mary Moffat's missionary intentions initially fell flat in the face of pregnancy, childbirth and domesticity. She noted that Jane Philip 'who have never been without the limits of the Colony, will wonder to hear me say that at present I have no time to devote exclusively to what may be termed labour in the vineyard', but 'having a young child and there being such a difficulty of getting servants, and withal such a variety of work especially as we are newly come, have a house a[-]building and many people to provide for' prevented her from pursuing such activities.[29] This pointed comparison of material circumstances keenly demonstrates the sense Mary had of both her own inadequacy, but also of the impossibility of comparing herself, as a missionary's wife, with a contemporary so differently placed on the material and physical scale.[30] 'Mary has at all times her hands full of work', remarked Robert in 1822; 'there are fifty things to be attended to [here] unknown in England'.[31]

While public and private expectations of missionary women were that they would unequivocally be missionaries, the Moffats's need to continually justify Mary's preoccupation with domestic affairs suggests a certain level of discomfort with her early mission life, rooted in their own marital expectations, and the presumptions of the missionary public, both of which were founded on ideals of missionary partnership and mutual usefulness. 'The rough drudgery of those early days – few can imagine', wrote Elizabeth (Bessie) Price of her own early career on the expanding spiritual frontier, some forty years later.[32]

> *druggery* [drudgery] – *instead of teaching*. We wives have precious little of the latter. Our chief work is to keep the Husbands *up* – up from sinking down down gradually into native style of living – and from losing

> *heart and spirits* in that great work in which we but act as organ *blowers* to the musicians.[33]

Indeed, so disgusted was she with the domestic anchor on her vocational hopes that she wished to ensure no future missionary's wife would fall into that chasm between expectation and reality: 'should any of my dear correspondents be some day *thinking* of Missionary life in Africa – these details would prove valuable and prevent them being startled, disgusted and disappointed with the life they have to lead'.[34]

It is the contention of this chapter, however, that recognising the difficulties missionary women faced in navigating structures of patriarchy and domesticity need not lead us inexorably away from an understanding of their lives as vocational, spiritual and indeed professional. If Chapter 2 sought to answer the question of who the missionary wife could be, this chapter addresses the follow-up question, what could she do? What were the parameters of her professional, public or vocational existence? What did it mean for a white missionary woman to be a missionary wife? The answers to these questions are clearly complex, and variegated along lines of place, personality and perspicacity. But in thinking about missionary wives in the early to mid-nineteenth century, and within stable marriages, certain answers can be reached. Missionary women wove together their personal and professional lives, actively creating the theory of mission domesticity that allowed them a vocational existence within the precepts of evangelical domesticity, and increasingly filling out the role of what has, perhaps dismissively, been called helpmeet, to conform to their own marital and professional expectations.

The companionate missionary marriage and mission domesticity

The point here is that being highly driven women, missionaries' wives did not passively accept the subsumation of their spiritual agency. More than simply travelling between 'public' vocation and 'private' domesticity, missionary women developed over the course of the mid-nineteenth century an understanding of mission complementary to, and inextricable from, that domesticity. The way they did this was twofold, but both relied on the companionate missionary marriage. On the one hand, housekeeping became the pragmatic facilitation of male vocation, removing at least this one non-spiritual activity from his pantheon of secular missionary projects. On the other hand, missionary women came to an understanding of their role as wife that balanced these two primary and divergent demands on her time, enacting spiritual agency through domesticity. 'A unique woman's mission theory based on exemplifying the Christian home emerged naturally and gradually in the life of the mission', argues Dana Robert, moving beyond Grimshaw's elucidation of frustrated agency to explore how women coped with and integrated the realities of life into their sense of vocation.[35] Example and civilisation, plus domestic cheer and comfort, became the twin pillars of female mission, balancing domesticity with vocation, and all within the framework of the companionate missionary marriage.

The mission home and domestic example

Like many of her contemporaries, Mary Moffat came to understand her role as a female missionary as an exemplary one.[36] It became central to her sense of herself as a missionary's wife that she 'set before the heathen an example of cleanliness and decency[,] and I account it an honour that it is my lot to fill up such a station'.[37] Missionaries' wives internalised their own conceptual position as inextricably linked to the rise of the civilising mission. Good housekeeping would progress the cause of Christ through the union of the secular and the spiritual embodied in the real figure of the missionary's wife (and ultimately, the Christian convert). Developing a mission theory based on the realities of domesticity in the mission context was the primary way in which the wives of missionaries balanced their increasingly important domestic duties with their original vocational desires, and thus healed the rupture between expectation and reality. As Leonore Davidoff and Catherine Hall have demonstrated, the domestic space was not the same as the domestic sphere.[38] More recently, Alison Twells's notion of 'missionary domesticity' has reminded us that domesticity as an idealisation of women's roles was not necessarily a confining concept, but one 'shot through with social and global concerns'.[39] This was as true for missionaries' wives as it was for evangelical middle-class women at home. They too understood their domestic lives as promoting the mission in both direct and indirect ways, while at the same time seeming to conform to burgeoning domestic expectations. As Natasha Erlank describes for Jane Philip: 'At various times she managed to disguise her work as domestic labour, she managed to disguise it under the duties of marriage, and she managed to justify it because of its ultimate aim.'[40] Contemporary South African missionary George Barker certainly deemed his wife's domestic contribution as important to the mission. Her religion was 'carried into the most minute affairs of common life'.[41] In the mission context, domesticity denoted more than mere housekeeping, and was embedded with spirituality, example and vocation.

Meanwhile, determined missionary women also interlaced domesticity with direct mission action, often by mediating the mission home's oscillation between public and private space. The mission home was frequently a fraught place, where the fractures between expectation and reality crystallised in a variety of ways. Domesticity involved commitments and frustrations for both spouses who felt their time slipping away into secular pursuits. Missionary women dealt with this not only by making domesticity in itself mission work, but by utilising the domestic space as a place for direct missionary action. Bessie Price, constantly frustrated by her inability to successfully juggle the domestic and the vocational, nevertheless taught her servants in her own home to read, to speak English and to understand the Bible. This was something she could balance with her housekeeping and parental duties, because in her own eyes it was less demanding than teaching someone from outside the domestic circle. When asked by Bantsan (one of the local Chieftain Sechele's daughters) why she would not teach her English, Bessie exclaimed 'Because it is impossible! … to do so without neglecting my husband – or children – or housework – or my servants – for these more than fill up my time.'[42] Her refusal was based not only on the domestic pressures on her time, but on Bantsan's own position outside the domestic sphere. Teaching her would require 'careful application – far greater than I give in teaching the Alphabet and spelling to my servants class – and that is hard enough with my baby in arms'.[43] Yet Bessie clearly derived some satisfaction from this 'servants class', and not only because of the connections she inferred between their learning, and better behaviour as servants.

> My servants' class goes on briskly every afternoon – Lamucha [the nurse-maid] is struggling hard at her spelling and writes too with Liagoman [maid]. Mabo [maid] and she are exactly together in spelling – but alas! poor Mabo's faltering tongue will prevent her keeping pace with L[amucha]. That lassie behaves most beautifully! I wish *I* were as faultless in my behaviour to her as she in hers to me. Indeed, I seldom have to rebuke her, and am getting to *love* her – which I used not to do … I am just back again in that old happy berth that I was in at Shoshong as regards servants.[44]

The unsuitability of the new nurse-maid, Topsy, as carer for her children was probably not unconnected to her unwillingness to take these lessons seriously.[45]

Mission domesticity, meanwhile, was also not necessarily confining. Leading the local people in the reformulation of domestic space through the power of example also involved women leaving the domestic sphere, and imposing their perceived moral and temporal authority upon indigenous spaces and dwellings. 'Today I took a walk with the children', wrote Hannah Crook in 1821, 'my intention was to see if I could stir up the people to be more cleanly in their houses to partition them into rooms and make door[s] etc ... The first house I went into was unfinished ... It was in a sad dirty state and exposed to all weathers as it was quite open. I spoke to them of the evil consequences of living in such a state.'[46] For Hannah Crook, as for most missionaries, the state of the house, its layout, the number of occupants, and its level of cleanliness, were moral issues.[47] 'I want to see your good houses, those that have bedrooms and that are clean ... [the people] exclaimed Alas Alas we are shamed.' More importantly still, the baptised within the community were as bad as the unbaptised in their domestic situations.

> I observed you are our baptised people, and have heard that little paper read telling you what we wish you to do respecting your houses, your dress etc. some of you have been baptised a long time, and therefore you must have some good houses among you, let me see them. They replied again Alas Alas we are shamed. I went on looking into several houses as I replied. I said these houses are dirty. We cannot go into them for the fleas will torment us ... Show me I said but one clean house that I may go in and sit down.

Thankfully, 'some of them were considerably affected at this visit and are inclined to set about the necessary alterations', though how sincere these intentions turned out to be is not further remarked upon.[48] 'The colonial encounter was played out over the small details of daily living', notes Adele Perry: 'the adoption of Western-style houses thus came to stand in minutiae for wholesale acculturation of First Nations people to European norms, if not standards, of living'.[49]

The important point here, is that Hannah Crook used ideals of domesticity to tie together spirituality and morality, was not shy about using her own house as an example ('*You like to talk to me at our house*, do you not like us to come and talk to you at your houses[?]'),[50] and took her children with her, reinforcing the connections between family, domesticity and morality.

Of course, there is nothing new in this recognition that missionary women sought to refashion indigenous spaces and bodies.[51] For missionaries the home was both indicative and constitutive of correct familial relations, and correct familial relations were the surface representations of a deeper conversion to western spirituality. 'Would-be converts were told repeatedly that minimal Christian living standards had to be signalled in their dwellings and dress; the internal transformations assumed to be taking place inside them and their families had to be played out on socially legible surfaces, for all to read.'[52] Conversion was most legible in the (Christian) home, making that home a site for public consumption. This was not always easy for missionary women, however. As Mary Moffat reminisced to her daughter Bessie in 1854,

> Groups of idle curious women would come crowding about the door peeping in and filling the room with offensive odours from their greasy and unwashed bodies while she toiled within. Sometimes she would invite them in ... so that they might sit and become friendly – thus preparing the way she thought for those happy days when she having learnt their language should teach them to read their Bibles. They would chat and laugh together, examining and observing with their eyes every thing about the room, my mother trying to interest or amuse them – but their manners were offensive and repulsive and soon she was longing for the ordeal for be over. And when they were gone, the first thing she then did was to get a bucket of water, and with soap and scrubbing brush cleanse away all the grease and filth they had left.[53]

As this quote so amply demonstrates, the relationship between the missionary, the home, and the local people was fraught with internal tension. While Mary Moffat clearly wished to encourage these women's entrance of the mission house in order to become friendly, ultimately with a view to interesting them in both western practices and religion, at the same time these incursions were undercut by differing codes of sociability, and different habits of cleanliness. There is a clear sense that while Mary *wished* often to invite these women into her home, there was also a frustrated compulsion to do so, given that with or without invitation, they would 'come crowding about the door peeping in and filling the room with offensive odours'. Further, their presence was clearly a double-edged sword. While at first they could 'chat and laugh together', 'soon she was longing for the ordeal to be over', and as soon as they had departed, 'the first thing she then did was to get a bucket of water, and with soap and scrubbing brush cleanse away all the grease and filth they had left'.

Refashioning the female helpmeet

On the whole, however, a home-based mission theory for missionaries' wives allowed them to psychologically unite their divergent responsibilities, and coterminously freed their husbands to devote themselves more to *their* professional vocation. For it was not just female missionaries who felt frustrated by secular demands obstructing their spiritual agency. Male missionaries too were torn between their numerous temporal duties and their spiritual expectations. They constantly found their energies diverted into artisanal projects, such as construction, gardening, agriculture (including the extremely time-consuming work of irrigation), and smithing. 'There was something ludicrous in the contrast between the theory and the practice of missionary life', noted the Moffats's son John on becoming a missionary in the 1850s; 'The missionary in these barbarous regions must often turn up his sleeves and plunge into something very unlike a pulpit – content to be a hewer of wood and a drawer of water for the temple.'[54] When, in rare circumstances, housewifery was added to this list of temporal demands missionary men (and let us not judge them too harshly), felt it became too much. 'My house is always pretty clean, but oh what a confusion there is always among my linen. I have no patience', wrote Robert Moffat when it seemed that Mary would not be permitted to join him in South Africa.[55] 'No one can do anything for me in my household affairs. I must attend to everything, which often confuses me, and, indeed, hinders me in my work.'[56]

It was the middle-class ideal of the companionate marriage that provided a conceptual space in which missionary women could express and fulfil their vocation through the facilitation of their husbands' careers. Being providers of comfort and cheer (fundamental to notions of the companionate, as opposed to the pragmatic, marriage) became a way of fulfilling spiritual agency complementary both to normative domesticity, and the active engagement with mission that time and domestic pressure allowed. Mission domesticity thus not only provided a means to exemplary vocation, but became intertwined with ideas of comfort and tenderness in the mission home, and the subsequent emotional and physical furtherance of mission objectives.

This should by no means be seen as missionary women having 'fallen back on the role of the good helpmeet as compensation',[57] but as the way in which the wives of missionaries came to fuse their domesticity and periodic domestic confinement to their spiritual vocation. It thus became a prime, and indeed largely self-imposed, duty of missionaries' wives to provide comfort, both material and emotional, for their husbands. What was unique about this middle-class unification of domesticity and comfort in the mission context was the connection made between domestic comfort and effective mission. By providing comfort for her husband, the missionary wife could increase his efficiency in the spiritual work, thereby promoting the cause of Christ from the home. Mary Moffat implicitly linked example and civilisation with domestic cheer and comfort, the twin pillars of mission domesticity, when she wrote in 1821 that,

> I am convinced there is a necessity for Missionaries to have wives to cheer them under the multiple sorrows and toils of their lives to provide comfortable food for the support of their bodies under hard labour, and to enable them to set before the heathen an example of cleanliness and decency ... O that I may not be wanting in the duties thereof.[58]

Her daughter Bessie Price also understood her role as keeping her husband 'from losing *heart and spirits* in that great work'.[59] The wives of missionaries imbibed these domestic demands, taking pride in their fulfilment. For Mary, the years that Robert had toiled in Africa without her care were painful to recall, so much so that she frequently refused to let him itinerate or travel alone, for 'he does not take care of himself, and will not be at the trouble to make himself comfortable; and I think he had enough of that sort of life in Namaqualand [prior to their marriage]'.[60]

The spiritual importance of providing comfort, meanwhile, is amply demonstrated in wives' feelings of guilt when they failed to provide it. When the Moffats' son-in-law Roger Price returned to the wagon from a hard day of oxen-driving to find nothing prepared (as Bessie, his wife and new mother to their first son Moffat, had been sleeping), Bessie tormented herself with guilt and remonstrance. 'Ah it was agony to me! No candle lit – no coffee cooked, no wee supper table spread! And he poor fellow had such need of refreshment.'[61] So guilty did she feel about her domestic inadequacy, that she 'took some of the nice cool water, which he had brought on purpose for me to taste, and washed his poor muddy hands and face – sponging him an age as if to atone for my sleep'.[62] The sense of atonement in this passage speaks eloquently to her state of mind and the complex links drawn between domesticity, comfort and mission.

Female cultural and religious encounters flowed directly from their understanding of, and interaction with, mission domesticity. By mid-century this form of female mission had reached its ascendency, allowing missionary wives to be trumpeted in both their domestic and religious activities. White missionary women had successfully navigated the transition from integration to civilisation, and more than that had shaped the direction of that transition. Through the energies of the mission wife, and the agency of the missionary couple, the mission home had become the ascendant mission institution by mid-century. The missionary or spiritual frontier was here constitutive of complex notions of both mission and domesticity which, in their reformulation through missionary realities, allowed missionary women to fulfil both their domestic and spiritual responsibilities. Mission became something beyond proselytisation and education, and conceptually expanded to include domestication, and the power of example. Meanwhile, domesticity itself incorporated notions of temporal and emotional comfort, and thereby, mission efficacy. The companionate missionary marriage was crucial to this reformulation of mission objectives (male and female), and thus requires some further attention.

The companionate missionary marriage and marital expectations

Historians of Christian mission tend not to think about marriage as a category of analysis for missionaries themselves. While it is recognised that missionaries attempted to impose an ideal of western, Christian marriage on to their converts (most obviously in their battles against polygamy and bridewealth in Africa), the missionary's own marriage is less often interrogated and investigated. It can be easy for the historian to overlook those ephemeral facets of life that are either so implicit in the cultural baggage of the time or so personal, and at the same time every day or usual, that they are sometimes swallowed up in the historical sources.[63] Faith, fun and love often fall prey to this historical blinkering, and it is worth pointing out that love was deemed by many missionaries to be absolutely crucial to marriage, and that successful missionary marriages were founded on deep foundations of affection and romance, as well as common vocations, communal interest and feelings of absolute inter-reliance. Their understanding of marital felicity built upon the emerging notion of the companionate marriage and expanded it into the realm of vocational and spiritual complementarity.[64] It seems clear that both the Philip and the Moffat marriages were genuinely founded on deep mutual affection, and emotional, physical, intellectual and spiritual intimacy. The longevity and success of those marriages resulted from these strong personal ties of love, affection and tenderness, as well as mutual interest in the spiritual vocation.

On the spiritual frontier the importance of complementarity and companionship was amplified by the feelings of loneliness and isolation that many missionaries, and missionary families, experienced. Here was the main difference between a missionary family on the temporal, geographical and ideological frontier, and those missionary families who lived in large mission towns, or colonial hubs (such as Cape Town). When Robert and Mary Moffat's son John wrote a biography of their lives and marriage in 1885, he noted that from 1818 to 1819 his father 'did not see the face of a fellow countryman, or hear a word in his mother tongue'.[65] The contrast between his pious rendering of that time as a happy one (for his father was 'in entire sympathy with the chief [Afrikaner] and his brothers') and Robert's own writings at the time is stark. On rebuking his, then, lover Mary's lack of letters in November of 1818, Robert remarked that since her last in August 1817,

> I have anxiously waited from day to day and I am still left in the midst of perplexity and fears. Which fears have frequently exerted me to make

> the following questions. Has *Mary* carried her resolutions into execution in renouncing me laying the guilt on the guiltless? Or has my most beloved earthly friend left these regions of sorrow and ascended to the heavenly Canaan to her Father and her God and left me alone without a single friend who I can call my own or to whom I can open my heart.[66]

Heartbroken at her then rejection of his marriage proposal, he lamented the fact that, 'When I shall be called to weep it will be unknown and of course unfelt for, by that which before felt my sighs and answered each other[']s tears.'[67] These poignant letters speak not only to the Moffats' love and affection, but to the sense of complete isolation and loneliness Robert felt in those early years of his mission in Namaqualand. Writing to his parents in December of that year he noted that his colleague 'Ebner is gone, and has left me a solitary missionary with little prospect of having help.'[68]

It seems to have been well understood that loneliness was a corrosive condition for these early missionaries. When George Barker sank into a deep depression following the death of his wife in 1836 he was visited by Dr and Mrs Philip who 'deemed [it] advisable that I should visit Cape Town if not England for a change of scene and a little society'.[69] If even Barker's situation in 1830s Theopolis (nestled safely within the Cape Colony, and 35 miles, and a five-hour horseback ride, at speed, from Grahamstown) was deemed isolated enough to require a change of scene, imagine the isolation of Robert Moffat in 1810s Namaqualand.

The point here is that this level of isolation forged intense interpersonal relationships: be they of love or hatred. Marriage was a great tonic to isolation, but could not be successful without a strong mix of love and affection also. Historian of the Norwegian Missionary Society Line Nyhagen Predelli has noted that when Niels Wiig felt the urgent need to be married to save himself from illegitimate sexual contact, he 'did not want to marry a woman without feeling any love for her'.[70] Robert Moffat referred to Mary Smith (before their marriage) as his 'most beloved earthly friend', and the 'object of my affection'. When she wrote to him that she could no longer hold to her vow to marry him, his reply was filled with evidence of his intense love. 'When you acknowledged the injury you had done in "wronging" me asking pardon, I was melted into tears for I had pardoned and would have pardoned a thousand times more … I am now completely stripped or rather robbed of the object of my fondest hopes.'[71] Her letters too had been filled with 'tender addresses', and had 'proved heavenly mandates to my soul'.[72] The Philips too 'had a close relationship'. According to Natasha Erlank, 'their love and regard for one another did not diminish throughout their married life'.[73] And in corrosive marriages it was a lack of affection that often lay at the heart of burgeoning hatreds. When confronted with her husband during one of Robert Moffat's frequent mediations Ann Hamilton 'turned upon him and said very warmly you never loved me'.[74]

Mutual spirituality, kindness and love were fundamental to a happy missionary marriage, and a happy missionary marriage was fundamental to a successful mission. And this is the important point here: the companionate missionary marriage facilitated the success of missions on the spiritual frontier; and at the same time, facilitated female vocational agency. On the one hand, domestic normativity meant that correct domestic arrangements were an important part of mission work in itself. On the other, the companionate missionary marriage provided a conceptual space in which missionary women could weave domesticity into vocation, and could fulfil their spiritual agency through domestic action. Indeed, with the mission home and family constantly on display, as a site for emulation, it was important that missionaries not only had good relations within their marriages, but did not allow disagreements to disrupt their marital and domestic performance. 'Beware of little differences among yourselves, husband and wife. Should anything of that kind occur let kind talk always settle it and never let the Heathen see such an evil', counselled South Seas missionary John Williams in 1823.[75] Hannah Crook instructed her women against marital quarrelling. 'A man and his wife who attend our meetings with a desire to be baptised have given us much trouble by their frequent quarrels with each other', she wrote in 1820. 'I addressed them all on the evil of quarrelling especially with their own husbands.'[76]

As we have seen, within this very particular style of missionary marriage, wives were able to juggle the various domestic and vocational demands on their time by creating and promoting two female mission theories complementary to their public mission activities: the power of domestic example on the one hand, and the promotion of mission efficacy through domestic comfort and cheer on the other. The latter, in particular, relied on the complementarity of the companionate missionary marriage, and while not all missionary marriages were companionate in this way, those that were fostered a particular type of female vocation that reached ascendency in the mid-nineteenth century. These two theories, coupled with the active mission work wives were able to perform themselves, formed the basis of mission femininity in the mid-nineteenth century, and moved in union and parallel with each other through the female life-cycle, with active work and domestic comfort in particular tied to how much a missionary wife could achieve, given the particulars of her family life at any given time. Life-cycle and life-stage were crucial to female spiritual agency, and dictated both its public and private manifestations.

Domesticating the male (missionary)

What of the men, then? What made the missionary husband tick in the mid-nineteenth century? The figure of the missionary husband and father can be a particularly difficult one to glimpse in the historical record. As Rhonda Semple has noted:

> If manliness is about a professional production that limits a man's participation in the very home that denotes his status as professional, and if manliness requires that men not talk about their private domestic lives, then historians face a paucity of information that could answer the very questions we might like to ask of men in the past.[77]

What were male expectations of himself, and his wife? How did he understand a hierarchy of priorities ranging from proselytisation, through practical (and temporal) mission support, to familial obligations? How did he relate to his children? How did his existence and experience interact with the changing codes of evangelical fatherhood in the nineteenth century? Semple has flagged up the difficulties associated with these questions, as well as the lack of historical analysis that has yet been directed at the male missionary, as a gendered subject.[78] In many ways the missionary husband (and father) remains the most elusive figure in the mission record. Not only do male missionaries rarely leave personal sources (despite an abundance of official letters and journals), but to glimpse the level of personal (as opposed to spiritual or professional) introspection in male missionary writing is particularly difficult.

Despite these difficulties, however, it is possible to catch the personal male voice in the mission archive, even if it might be more episodic than continuous. Moments of difficulty and distress in particular can help us glimpse the missionary father and husband. This section seeks to answer some of these questions for missionary husbands, while Chapter 4 looks at missionary fathers. What did husbands expect of their wives; what did wives expect of their husbands; and what did husbands expect of themselves?

The missionary wife

The importance of having a wife for male missionaries is clear across the generations. Robert Moffat's frequent laments about his unmarried life were an eloquent testimony to the importance of matrimony, not only for practical purposes, but to provide comfort and company in situations of complete racial and cultural isolation. For over a year he was 'quite alone, [and] seldom [saw] a white face'.[79] When his new bride finally arrived in South Africa in 1819, 'it was to me nothing less than life from the dead'.[80] For many second-generation missionaries marriage was a vital prerequisite to missionary service. 'I should be unwilling to go out unmarried', wrote William Philip (son of Jane and John Philip) in his 1836 application, 'unless such circumstances occurred as would appear to intimate it to be the will of God that I should'.[81] With such an example of a missionary wife as Jane Philip before them, it is unsurprising that all of the Philip sons insisted on leaving for the field married.[82] Nor were second-generation missionaries the only candidates to make a stand on marriage. David Jones and Thomas Bevan, the first missionaries to Madagascar, refused to embark unmarried, with disastrous consequences when both wives, two newborn babies and Bevan himself died of Malagasy fever.[83] Male missionaries, cognisant of the difficulties of life in the field without wives, demanded marital agency from a society that was frequently unwilling to give it, in order to secure a partner in their work and troubles.

An influential component of this demand for marital agency was the need for a spiritually sanctioned outlet for male missionaries' sexual frustrations.[84] As Predelli has argued, 'marriage was a remedy for sexual and psychological frustration, and a controlling mechanism for male sexuality'.[85] While Catherine Hall's comments on the missionary family as 'a bulwark, a defence against the immorality of "the world", [and] a haven in which Christian morality was practised' are certainly not confined to missionary sexuality, providing legitimate sexual relations was a key function of the missionary marriage.[86] In contexts where sexual boundaries were seen as relatively loose it was doubly important that men had access to legitimate sexual contact. Robert Moffat was, before the arrival of his new wife, 'grateful for the sympathy you all manifest as it regards my critical situation among a kind of naked people of licentious habits. From the numerous examples of fallen missionaries, nor is our Society alone, you have abundant reason to infer that the path is slippery.'[87] When Mary Smith broke off their engagement in 1818, Robert was not shy about explicitly using the mission context for emotional blackmail.

> You seem to wish earnestly that I should marry. I ask to whom? you seem to think that there are suitable females in the Cape. It is possible tho I am yet unacquainted with any. You also entertain a fear lest I should marry a native with solitary warnings. I can only remark that I have seen and learned much during my stay in Africa[;] I have seen native wives and Cape ones too and my thoughts at present is that I could not easily brook the idea of taking a native but rather that than fall into sin.[88]

The sexual importance of missionaries' wives was also made clear at the South African Synod in 1817.

> Is there not a practice which has led to temptation and we fear may have led to sin – that of single Brethren travelling long journies, or of married Brethren without their wives so travelling that one or more Hottentot females without their husbands, or single went in the same wagon? Yes ... We therefore recommend that no single Missionary or married Missionary without his wife should travel journies with one or more Hottentot females who are unaccompanied with their husbands and we earnestly recommend this to be a standing Rule.[89]

The importance of sexuality to the marriage of John and Jane Philip has been explored in some detail by Natasha Erlank who concludes that it was a vital component to their marital relationship.[90] More generally, Rhonda Semple has noted that 'while acting out heterosexual desire was something to be controlled, it was also at the heart of Victorian masculine identity ... Certainly missionary men had physical desire and mission societies acknowledged that as a reality requiring their attention.'[91]

Like their contemporaries in Britain, missionary husbands demanded that their conjugal rights be fulfilled within their marriages. The marriage of Ann and Robert Hamilton is extremely informative here, for it seems to have been on the issue of sexual relations (and indeed the consequent frustration of female vocation through pregnancy) that their marriage foundered. As we have seen, Ann Hamilton was chastised for abandoning her marital bed 'contrary to Mr H's will[,] your own vow when married and the command's [*sic*] of Jesus Christ'.[92] She had 'resolved ... never to be united to Mr H as his wife' and was unwilling to 'sacrifice her body' to her husband. She refused a reconciliation for thereby 'he would satisfy his lust but who was the sufferer[?]'. Through this determination, Ann had submitted neither 'to reason [n]or scripture ... let your character or the cause of Christ suffer as they will'.[93] Her refusal to enter the marital bed was unscriptural, unreasonable, and apparently contrary to her duty as a wife.

But despite the importance of marital intimacy, missionary marriages cannot, of course, be simply reduced to sexual relations, or to the practical advantages of housekeeping and domesticity. When Sarah Barker died in 1836, her husband George was disconsolate. 'Oh! when the stroke came I found my strength perfect weakness.'[94] Barker's long period of stricken mourning (six years of trauma-induced depression) gives a powerful insight into what missionaries desired and expected of their wives, what qualities were most valued, and how being part of a missionary partnership and companionate marriage was deemed crucial to male understandings of mission. The qualities he chose to ascribe to his wife speak to what expectations he had held of her.

> My Dear partner was unknown to you, and how shall I describe her? Will my pen be faithful? ... as a wife how shall I describe her? Solomon has done it for me, Proverb 30 – 10 to 29.[95] As a mother? "Let her own works prove her in the gates". Yet my dear children are a living testimony of what a mother they have lost. As a Christian? Ah! she was one. But her religion was not a noisy boast, nor a vain shew. It was carried into the most minute affairs of common life. It was seen in her attachment to the house of God, but it was also displayed in her family concerns, her obedience to God's commands was evinced by her attention to her children, her affection to me, and in her solicitude for the welfare of all around her. Mrs Barker entered into the affairs of the Mission with all her heart, and was beloved by the natives, by whom she will be greatly missed. I may add she was respected by all who knew her, but especially by those who knew her best. She possessed a mind, which though devoid of external embellishments, was of no ordinary cast, and I have never regretted taking her advice. Such is my loss.[96]

In this moving tribute to his wife Barker expressed those qualities most important to him as a missionary husband: piety and affection, usefulness and advice, care and comfort. In so doing he succinctly articulated the feelings of missionary husbands across the globe, which extended well beyond the pragmatic expectations of missionaries' wives explored above. When South Seas missionary David Darling's wife died in 1858 he also mixed her assistance in the work with her more familial, and domestic duties: 'She has been a good wife to me, and a great assistant in all Missionary work; and brought up our family in the fear of the Lord; and always set a good example to the people, worthy of their imitation, for forty two years.'[97]

For missionaries matrimony not only provided legitimate sexual contact, but social support in a context of racial and cultural isolation. 'I have no society beyond my family, no friends to speak to', wrote Barker. 'I feel rather lonely, left alone in the house.'[98] Barker's eldest unmarried daughter Elizabeth came to 'take charge of my house' (leaving her own career as a teacher, and a 'circle of pious young people' to do so), but even so he felt 'half ill in consequence' of his wife's death: and that a year later.[99] While certainly much of his illness referred to a growing depression of spirits (which ultimately led to his removing to a more populated station), there is some inference that without the temporal care of his wife, his health had become neglected.[100] But ultimately he had lost much more than 'an help meet for me'.[101] He had 'lost my right hand and I feel it ... It is now 16 months that I have been a widower, and have not yet recovered my spirits.'[102] It was, after all, a wife's duty to keep her husband *'up'*. Without his wife Barker certainly fell 'down' and lost *'heart and spirits* in that great work'.

By 1841, four and a half years after his wife's death, Barker's thoughts began to turn to remarriage. He ultimately focused on two main facets of his wife's presence that he missed: her sympathy (emotional sustenance) and her assistance (practical support). 'When fagged almost to death, I do wish I had the sympathy of her I once had, and so often wish I had her assistance.'[103] In 1842 he remarked that his 'own heart still bleeds. Five years and an half has not healed the wound ... I thought, were I to be taken ill to night, what would be my earthly consolation, I have no heart bound to my fate, no sister to lend a helping hand.'[104] By March 1844 George had resolved to solve the problem, and had married Hilletje Smuts, a Dutch woman 45 years of age.[105] When choosing his new wife he had had two main requirements.

> The first consideration with me is the fear of God, and this I am happy to say she possesses, and without this all other things would have been vain. Piety is the first consideration for a missionary in matrimonial affairs ... Another consideration of almost equal importance is a sympathy with the Blacks.[106]

George Barker remained a missionary until his death in 1861, and the second Mrs Barker continued to receive a widow's allowance from the LMS, and live at the mission station in Paarl, until her own death in 1864.

What is clear about this episode in the life of George Barker is that for missionary husbands too domesticity was a concept entwined with notions of comfort and tenderness, and that sympathy, domesticity, practical evangelicalism and missionary activity were all interwoven in the figure of the missionary wife. Missionary husbands did not expect their wives to be anchored to the domestic sphere. Rather, they expected them, like the mission public, the LMS hierarchy, and the wives themselves, to be partners in their spiritual vocation. Being an extra oar on the mission boat meant taking on spiritual and, particularly, educative roles in the mission. As Natasha Erlank has argued, mutual 'usefulness' was a foundational concept in the Philip family, extending not only to their companionate marriage, but to their offspring.[107]

What is equally evident in Barker's writing, however, is that being a 'helpmeet' meant more than undertaking the vocational duties of education, conversation, and socialisation. As it became increasingly clear that much of missionaries' wives' time would be taken up with the domestic sphere, assistance came to mean for missionary husbands also, something beyond direct mission work. They began also to entwine missionary domesticity with comfort and emotional support, as a concept imbued with spiritual, and not just matrimonial, significance. Bessie Price worried that her own mental state (which continually swung between neurosis and depression in the early years of her career) would detrimentally affect her husband's, for 'if I chatter all my weak-minded thoughts to him, a pretty help-meet I'd make'.[108]

Missionaries' wives certainly expected to be interested in the workings of the mission, even when their time was too overtaken with domestic duties to undertake direct mission work. 'I try to do everything thoroughly and *heartily* – and am really interested in all my plans and works and in my dear Roger's equally', wrote Bessie in 1866.[109] She continually tormented herself with comparisons with her colleague Mrs Mackenzie, who was 'so *truly* a help-meet',[110] and found herself wanting, her mind 'running into certain ruts – over and over and over the same subjects'.[111] Male missionaries also wished their wives to be connected with their work. Here, 'the most reliable basis of companionate marriage ... shared cultural interests', took on a religious, vocational and professional cast.[112] When Robert Moffat was away itinerating, he 'became a little dejected. Tried in vain to sleep ... I no more enjoy the company and counsel of my beloved partner, with whom I was wont to commune.'[113] George Barker meanwhile, had 'never regretted taking her [his wife's] advice'.[114]

Missionary husbands

A question we rarely (if ever) ask about the history of Christian mission is what missionary wives expected of their husbands. While thinking about female professionalism may inevitably lead us to wonder what husbands expected of their wives, marital expectations held of husbands remain elusive in the historical record: not just for want of evidence, but for want of asking. As historians we are perhaps put off from asking the question because it does not fit easily into the codes of masculinity we are used to dealing with for male missionaries. What Janet Parsons has called 'the missionary family ethic' (whereby the first priority for the male missionary had to be the mission) has obscured our historical vision.[115] It is clear that the mission *was* always expected to come first by both parties in the companionate missionary marriage (as distinct, perhaps, from less companionate marriages in the mission field). When the long lamented Sarah Barker went into the premature labour that ultimately led to her death in 1836, her eldest daughter prepared to send a messenger to recall her husband. 'Mrs B replied, No your father is gone on a good work and I shall not call him back, God will take care of me. We ought to remember the hundreds at the Kat River who are destitute of a minister.'[116] George himself had determined to go despite the fact that he 'feared a premature birth'. He *had* agreed to delay his trip, however; though he had wished to go at 'the beginning of last month ... all was not right with dear Mrs Barker and she requested me to wait till the end of the month and see how she was then'.[117]

Both husbands and wives accepted the predominance of mission priorities. The primacy of mission over and above familial responsibilities was most evident in itineration. Male missionaries spent a large proportion of their time itinerating, particularly in areas where stations were far removed from one another, as in southern Africa. They had little hesitation in leaving their wives in oftentimes dangerous situations, certainly lonely and isolated ones, frequently when they were heavily pregnant or had young children to look after.[118] It was part of a wife's duty, in return, to support her husband's decisions on this point, and put no obstacle in the way of his mission work. 'Mrs M. was anxious to go too', wrote Robert Moffat of one of his journeys in 1823, 'but it being the cold season she considered that my attention to her and the children would unavoidably impede my progress in the language, and therefore resolved to stay behind'.[119] This was not an easy decision for either spouse in many cases. Mary Moffat's instincts were always to accompany her husband, yet she was also willing to be separated from him if it was deemed best for the mission: 'I feel a satisfaction in sacrificing my dear husband's company when I reflect that it is for the cause of Christ, and I feel persuaded that these journeys into the interior are of enormous importance to the kingdom of our Lord, as they prepare the way for the spread of the gospel.'[120]

Nonetheless, while often steeped in internalised piety, the sources do suggest that missionaries' wives at times (at least) wished their husbands would sometimes prioritise family over mission. 'I had my lonely supper like the rest of my lonely meals today', lamented Bessie Price, with some bitterness in 1866;[121] '[I] get so "pent up" somehow when Roger comes in of an evening.'[122] Missionaries' wives were frequently torn between wanting their husband's company, and the needs of the mission. Ann Hamilton, whose dedication to the mission was clear, was nonetheless deeply bitter about her husband's lack of attentiveness when she was ill, both on board ship bound for South Africa, and after the birth of their first child.[123] This inattention was her definition of the '*brutish*[*ness*]' she attributed to him.[124] Even Jane Philip, that most energetic of missionary ladies, felt some bitterness about her husband's separation from her in 1836 and 'wrote to John in Britain that she was "really angry and hurt" at his writing so seldom, and that she feared the kindness and caresses of so many other good ladies'.[125] Physical and emotional separation was one of the facets of the missionary life that missionary couples found perplexingly difficult.

The (racial and cultural) isolation of the missionary context, meanwhile, meant that missionary spouses were often completely dependent on one another. Aside from their normal domestic activities, husbands also found themselves implicated in domestic duties when their wives were ill or absent. 'Roger was my faithful nurse, doctor, friend and cook. He tended me and my wee thing in the most tender way and I was as comfortable and happy as a Queen', wrote Bessie Price after the birth of her second child in 1863.[126] Bessie's sister-in-law, Emily Moffat, had a similar experience when she was incapacitated by an abscess on her arm.

> *Poor John*, he has to be maid of all work; I with my poor arm am almost useless and have to be a passive onlooker (the hardest thing to me). When we outspan John has always to be making baby's food, and poultices for me; then making the bed.[127]

While she expressed some sympathy for her husband, it is also clear that she expected him to take on these duties, for who else would do it? Frontier mission life was complementary in the most profound of senses. While male missionaries were away, meanwhile, their wives often took over the running of the mission. Robert Moffat remembered later in life, that his wife had often 'in my absence … managed the station as well or better than I could have done myself!'[128] This mutuality of responsibility worked both ways and when missionary wives were incapacitated or absent, their husbands had an equal responsibility to take on their spouses' role: 'When husbands were ill, wives did as much of the work as they could for them, even to the point of occasionally reading a sermon. When wives were ill, husbands found their labours greatly increased', notes Catherine Hall.[129] Robert Moffat, in a letter to Mary while she was away with their daughters, usefully elided his many practical and substitute familial responsibilities when caring for their two sons (Jim and Jack) in her absence. 'I was alone for the evening, but not in solitude, for who could be in the company of Jim and Jack? Jim let me see that he could put his foot into either end of his shoes. I took the hint and repaired them.'[130]

We need to move away, however, from the idea that missionary husbands were only 'domesticated' in times of crisis. Domestic and fatherly responsibilities permeated the everyday realities of their existence (as explored further in Chapter 5). Amanda Vickery has argued that masculinity was earned, in part, through the economic ability to create a marital home, something which took on a literal, as well as a metaphorical, meaning in the mission context.[131] When Mary Moffat arrived in southern Africa in 1821, she set her mind to Anglicising her new home, a process in which her new husband was intimately involved. This domestic replication ranged from large-scale reorganisation to small-scale comforts and necessities.

> in this part of the country it is the custom to have the kitchen separate from the house, a thing few English women can reconcile their minds to; for when that is the case the kitchen of the missionary is the place of common resort, and if one turns one's back, perhaps half of the food is gone, and spoons, knife, fork, or whatever lies about, is away.[132]

'My good man dislikes it as much as I do', she noted with relief, 'and has promised to order things differently when he builds.'[133] More immediately: 'When we get settled, I wish very much to wash in the English way. We cannot at present for want of tubs, but Moffat has promised to make me some, as I know he will.'[134] The organisation of the missionary house to conform to western standards was a male *and* female occupation. While domesticity is often seen as a female-centric concept, in this context at least, it was integral to what it meant to be both husband and wife. Everyday missionary masculinity was as caught up in the civilising mission as was their wives' femininity. This was perfectly in line with the publicising of the private that exercised missionary women. As Perry has noted, 'men, like women, secure their gender identity through the family and its rightful container, the home'.[135] In the very building and ordering of the house, the Moffats exemplified what it meant to be a 'proper' husband and wife. Robert was conforming to his wife's expectations of him as a husband, making her housekeeping possible through his workmanship, while Mary was conforming to her role as his wife, creating the domestic space of the home within the geographical place of the house. This was family life as it should be: house, home, and family on display.[136] When Robert Moffat began his missionary career at Afrikaner's Kraal in southern Africa, he lamented the attention he had to pay to his domestic affairs, despite a 'wish to have almost nothing to do but to instruct the heathen', 'I am carpenter, smith, cooper, tailor, shoemaker, miller, baker, and housekeeper.'[137] Some years later his daughter Bessie would put it even more succinctly: 'The husband is jack of all trades and the wife maid of all work.'[138]

The double-blind: missionaries as husbands

But what, then, did missionary husbands expect of themselves? Teasing out what male missionaries expected from themselves as husbands is exceptionally difficult. There is the double-blind, with little personal evidence speaking to what mission husbands' self-expectations were, and an almost complete lack of public reflection on the missionary-as-husband. Nonetheless, in the mission context, masculinity was strongly connected with notions of family. Not only did their 'ability to rescue wives and children, and attention to a wife's welfare' exaggerate the missionary's 'chivalric "heroism"' (as argued by Esme Cleall), but the family was also a 'source of male authority'.[139] As Hall has noted, the 'missionary's role in the family enterprise was closely linked to his fatherhood – head of household, father of the family, father of the congregation, father of the children in "his" schools'.[140] In short, male missionaries' familial identities constituted and consolidated their sense of professional identity.

The specificities of the mission context magnified certain aspects of husbandliness, while at the same time contributing a new set of mission-specific duties and responsibilities. The role of the husband in childbirth, and his taking on the roles of midwife, doctor and nurse at that time, are discussed in more detail in Chapter 5. It was during confinement and childbirth that male missionaries stood on the cusp of their dual role as husband and father, fulfilling both a responsibility to their wives as husbands, and to their children, as fathers. At that point more than any other, they accepted those limited demands made of them as family men; and guiltily regretted those times that they were unable to fulfil those duties.

Absolute interdependence, meanwhile, meant that missionary couples had to be everything to one another. In describing Mary's arrival in southern Africa to her parents, Robert Moffat wrote to assure them that 'she is under the care of our ever-present God, and united to one who speaks as he feels when he promises to be father, mother, and husband to Mary, and will never forget the sacrifice you have made in committing to his future care your only daughter'.[141] Robert understood that in taking Mary away from her familial and social support system in Manchester he would have to be more than a husband to her. When writing this to Mary's parents, he was calling upon a cultural geography of relationships that defined husbands, mothers and fathers differently, each fulfilling separate, but equally important roles in the life of a woman. Because Robert had caused a rupture in these relationships, through his removal of Mary from her social and familial networks, it was his duty to expand his notion of husband to include and embrace the duties and functions of parent, spouse and friend. The missionary husband came to understand that his role was quite distinct from that of husband in Britain and therefore felt an acute responsibility for his wife's emotional and physical well-being.

Nonetheless, the mission was always the first priority of missionary couples and essentially, missionaries in companionate missionary marriages derived marital satisfaction from the success of the mission, in line with the mutual spirituality and usefulness which underpinned this idealistic manifestation of missionary marriage. Bessie Price certainly approved her husband's juggling of home and mission when she was confined after the birth of their son Evan in 1863: 'he never missed a day of school for me, or service'.[142] Both male and female missionaries fulfilled their spousal roles through their spiritual activities, and both husbands and wives derived marital *and* vocational satisfaction from each other's missionary efforts. This chapter concludes by taking one famous missionary marriage and putting it under the microscope. What conclusions can we draw by living (briefly) with the Livingstones?

Living with the Livingstones

In mission historiography the marriage of the Livingstones is often seen as unique, and uniquely bad. While there is little evidence that they were unhappy in their marriage, works cite David's willingness to both abandon his wife and family for the sake of exploration, and paradoxically to endanger his family by taking them with him into dangerous regions on foolhardy expeditions. Meanwhile, biographers of both David and Mary cite her drinking, and the unhappiness of her time in Scotland as evidence of their ill-matched matrimony and uniquely unsuccessful marriage.[143] By looking at their marriage in detail some general conclusions about missionary husbands in particular can be hinted at, while the broader institution of missionary marriage can be further interrogated. David Livingstone was in many ways unique, but here it is argued that in his family affairs, he was far from abnormal, treading instead a well-worn path between family and mission.[144]

Mary (Moffat) Livingstone has, in particular, been the subject of frequent jibes and judgements, from one biographer in particular. In a strange preoccupation with her physical characteristics it is noted that Mary was: 'by no stretch of the imagination beautiful [...] she was fat and plain and probably felt fortunate to be getting married at all [...] In later life Mary grew extremely fat but it is interesting that this should already have been such a feature in her early twenties'; and by 1857 she was 'a stout, heavy-jowled woman, slightly coarse-featured and with a large nose'. Livingstone was never romantic, but 'considering her appearance, he cannot be given much credit for this achievement'. Mary is at the same time mocked ('sophistication was certainly never one of Mary's qualities'), derided ('the disparity in the respective intellectual gifts of husband and wife sometimes worried Livingstone') and victimised ('poor Mary Livingstone was not to have a happy married life'); none of which seem to do justice to her character, her marriage, or her individual agency.[145] Perhaps this is due to a lack of sources. Mary's own voice is practically silent in the historical record. In addition, David Livingstone was not a man to mince words. Many of his comments, taken out of the context of his broader writings, and his gruff, though sardonic tone, can seem unnecessarily hurtful. On the birth of his first child he wrote to his father Neil, 'I would call him Neil, if it were not such an ugly name'.[146] He got himself into some trouble when quizzing his brother Charles about his fiancé. 'I asked him if she had *red* hair, and thought as he was tall he must have chosen a short dumpy body, which may have offended his reverence.'[147] This comment certainly puts his descriptions of Mary into perspective: 'a plain common sense woman, not a romantic. Mine is a matter of fact lady, a little thick black haired girl, sturdy and all I want.'[148]

There is no reason to suppose that Livingstone's prioritisation of more practical attributes was unusual in missionary (or indeed, nineteenth-century) marriages. As Jeal himself notes,

> what she lacked in refinement, she made up for in other ways. She was literate and had been taught by her mother all the household tasks a missionary's wife ought to be able to manage; ranging from making clothes to making candles and soap. She would never be homesick for England, since Africa had always been her home ... [and] Livingstone was also convinced that having a wife would help his missionary work; she could run an infants' school and would diminish the suspicions which Africans unfortunately felt about a bachelor missionary.[149]

These qualities made missionary daughters particularly attractive wives for missionaries. More generally, it speaks to many of the reasons that male missionaries decided to marry at all: the desire to have a partner in the field, the expectation that having a wife to care for the domestic arrangements of missionary life would free their time for more spiritual endeavours, and the need for legitimate sexual contact. Livingstone's priorities seem little different from other LMS missionaries, nor is his focus on the practical in any way unique. George Thom noted in 1814 that, 'Plain suitable women from Britain or Germany will do ten times more than women of this colony (the white)', and when the Directors dispatched 'four pious women' to the South Seas, it was clearly not with ideas of romantic love in mind.[150] 'Livingstone knew that a man in his position could not afford to be fussy', says Jeal.[151] Hopefully this chapter has gone some way in showing that David Livingstone made in Mary Moffat (Jr) a very suitable choice.

Undoubtedly, Livingstone had many reasons for marrying. One of these was a desire for independence – a strong aspect of his character and one profoundly facilitated by matrimony. He had resented his dependence on the Edwards, with whom he lived in the years prior to his marriage, and recalled with bitterness their 'neglect' after he had been attacked by a lion. 'Mrs E scarcely ever looked near me ... and to get my arm dressed even when crawling with maggots I had to send for Mr E ... It was evidently a grudge to him, and how could it be otherwise? ... Obligation on my part there is none.'[152] For him marriage meant freedom and comfort. 'O it is a blessing to be allowed to eat as one likes [cf. the Edwards' nutritional habits]. I can never cease admiring the freedom.'[153]

Marriage also meant Livingstone could devote his time to missionary labours more intensely. 'At present we have everything comfortable and clean, and I may without distraction devote myself to the great work for which I came into this country.'[154] This sentiment should look familiar to readers of this chapter; in his focus on the practical benefits of marriage, David was in no way unique. His marriage to Mary in particular came with many practical benefits. Her 'missionary-wife qualities' have already been mentioned, and through their marriage, he became intimately connected with an important and established missionary family. His marriage not only opened up parts of the interior that would only be accessible to the relations of Ramary (Robert Moffat's Setswana name), but also meant a steady supply of practical accoutrements, from ploughs and tools to corn, from the Moffat mission station at Kuruman. It does not diminish the Livingstone marriage to note that it came with practical benefits for both parties.

Indeed, Mary Moffat (Jr) was no dupe in this marriage, and her agency should not be so easily brushed aside in victimisation. 'Like Livingstone she had also had a meagre choice of partners; added to which she was fat and plain and probably felt fortunate to be getting married at all. Moffat's other two daughters eventually married missionaries too.'[155] While it is probably true that Mary did not have a vast pool of eligible men from which to choose, it is excessively reductionist to assume that she merely accepted David's proposal because of a lack of options. Many missionary children (both male and female) became missionaries themselves. Like their mother before them, Mary, Ann and Elizabeth Moffat all married missionaries for vocational fulfilment. Jeanie, who did not marry, exercised her vocation by assisting her elderly parents. It would be ridiculous to assume that the Moffat daughters married missionaries simply because they had no other options available to them. Nor should Livingstone's own dashing personality and handsome charm be entirely brushed aside.

Indeed, the success of the Livingstone marriage can in large part be attributed to their shared sense of missionary vocation, and their mutual spirituality. Mary is often seen as the unwilling participant in David's unfolding career. 'Dragging that poor girl, Mary Moffat, along until she was forced to a long rest in her grave' was Aloysius Horn's conclusion on the Livingstone marriage.[156] The characterisation of Mary Livingstone as victim rests on the belief that she was the unwilling participant in David's plans and activities; dragged along or abandoned at various points in his career with little or no say. 'There was no way for her to know that the way of life he would choose for both of them would place unsupportable demands on a wife and children.'[157] This characterisation not only robs Mary Livingstone of her agency, but rests on two rather faulty foundations: the first is a lack of sources expressing *her* views and opinions; the second is the ire with which Mary Moffat (Sr) viewed her son-in-law's career – a perspective often equated with her daughter's.[158] In fact Mary Livingstone seems to have been no unwilling appendage to her husband in his missionary aims.

In the first instance, it should not be forgotten that like most wives, Mary probably considered herself as much a missionary as her husband. Like her mother before her and her sister Bessie after her, Mary 'carried on both infant and sewing school herself in addition to her numerous domestic duties'.[159] Second, it is difficult to maintain an idea that Mary Livingstone was simply 'dragged' along by her domineering husband. Having finally left Chonuane (their first missionary station) for good, and arrived in Kolobeng (near Molepolole) in 1847 (with two young children aged 20 months and 3 months, respectively), David decided that he was feeling 'very languid and think a trip will do me good'. Mary was having none of it. 'I should like Mary to come too, but she is sick of waggon life.'[160] In 1850, while on an expeditionary trip to the north, 'Mary offered to remain with Lecultathebe [a chieftain] while I went North.'[161] Heavily pregnant, and with two young children, she had little intention of trekking northwards with her husband. Even in that infamous trip to the Zambesi River in 1851 (after an earlier trip north which had dangerously endangered the lives of Mary and the children),[162] her mother conceded that Mary *wished* to accompany her husband. 'Mary had told me all along that should she be pregnant you would not take her, but let her come out here after you were fairly off. Though I suspected at the end that she began to falter in this resolution.'[163] In explaining his reasons for travelling north, David was sure to note that, 'Mary reciprocates these sentiments', speaking to her agreement and an interesting need on his part to prove the mutuality of their decision-making.[164]

While Mary's own motives for these decisions are obscure in the record, it would not be too bold to imagine that she wished in some respects to emulate her parents, striking out into the 'dark interior' with a mission to save souls and establish a new Kuruman in the far north. In the words of Andrew Ross: 'Mary could now ... with Livingstone strike out in partnership into the Africa she loved.'[165] Whether the designs were hers, her husband's, or a combination of both, it would seem impossible to argue plausibly that Mary Livingstone was merely 'dragged' along in her husband's wake.

Even on that most famous point, Livingstone's sending his wife and children to Scotland, often seen as the ultimate moment at which David's domineering spirit got in the way of marital felicity, Mary was not totally submissive and there are several hints that the terms of their separation, and its being limited to two years, had been negotiated between the spouses. 'Don't know what apology to make you for a delay I could not shorten', wrote David in 1855. 'I am sorry you have been disappointed, but you know no mortal can controul [*sic*] disease.' With a note of some anxiety he jokes, 'But as you are a merciful kind-hearted dame, I expect you will write out an apology in proper form, and I shall read it before you with as long a face as I can exhibit.'[166]

Another part of the Mary-as-victim complex has been the notion that the Livingstone marriage was an unhappy one. 'Poor Mary Livingstone was not to have a happy married life. Had she known Livingstone's views on marriage before their wedding, she might have had second thoughts.'[167] But was their marriage an unhappy one? In the context of missionary marriage more generally, as explored in this chapter, it is difficult to argue that theirs was anything other than eminently typical. Built on practical concerns, mutual spirituality and undoubted affection, it was punctuated by frequent separation, between spouses and children, and ranged well below mission objectives in their mutual hierarchy of priority. Such a description could be used for many missionary marriages, including that of the Moffats, something Mary Moffat seems at times to have rather disingenuously forgotten in the scolding of her son-in-law.

The Livingstone marriage was built upon mutual affection and love, as well as good temperamental match. 'She was just the sort of partner required by the stubborn and unfathomable personality of David Livingstone', notes Janet Parsons.[168] It seems churlish to argue that there was no affection or romantic love in their courtship and marriage. 'That convenience was probably a part of it does not mean there was no affection between them,' argues Ross, 'nor does it mean that this affection did not grow and deepen into something very powerful.'[169] Both George Seaver and Ross have noted that there were romantic elements to their meeting and courtship: David was the 'romantic invalid', Mary the tender nurse, 'gentle, [and] steadfast [in] character'.[170] The first time Mary had met Livingstone 'he appeared galloping on horseback across the veld'; during the trip back to Kuruman 'the young tanned Scot could not have avoided being also in close and constant contact with Mary'. 'Her next meeting with him was when he came, the wounded hero, to convalesce at Kuruman.'[171] All in all, notes Ross, 'it was a better basis for marriage than that of many marriages in Victorian Britain'.[172]

Livingstone consistently referred to his wife as 'his rib', denoting both the sense of her as a part of him, and her presence as a fundamental part of his being. 'My dearest Mary, How I miss you now, and the dear children!' he wrote in 1852 when they had left for England.

> My heart yearns incessantly over you. How many thoughts of the past crowd into my mind! I feel as if I would treat you all much more tenderly and lovingly than ever. You have been a great blessing to me. You attended to my comfort in many many ways. May God bless you for all your kindnesses! I see no face now to be compared with that sunburnt one which has so often greeted me with its kind looks.[173]

Nor was his emotion here seemingly exacerbated by the knowledge they would be separated for their longest time yet. Though they do not survive, he alludes to the love letters he wrote to her during earlier, short-term itineration.

> You may read the letters over again which I wrote at Mabotsa, the sweet time you know. As I told you before, I tell you again, they are true, true; there is not a bit of hypocrisy in them. I never show all my feelings; but I can say truly, my dearest, that I loved you when I married you, and the longer I lived with you, I loved you the better.[174]

David was well aware that his letters, words and actions were not always as romantic as perhaps they could have been. During their engagement he wrote to Mary often, with news of the mission and his progress in building their house, drawing her into his professional and personal identity. 'And although the above does not contain evidence of it, you are as dear to me as ever, and will be so long as our lives are spared.'[175] David Livingstone 'never show[ed] all my feelings', and his tongue (and pen) could be as the lash, even to those he loved, but for a man who pioneered the notion of 'muscular Christianity' and religious masculinity, his letters stand up well against the likes of Robert Moffat and John Philip, men of an earlier and more romantically inclined generation.

Conclusion

An analysis of the marriage of the Livingstones illuminates the main trends and themes of missionary marriage, while at the same time making clear that theirs was pre-eminently typical for their professional, vocational and social context. In all things the mission came first. From the most obvious example of itineration, to the positively intimate, such as the guideline that marital squabbles be removed from indigenous scrutiny, missionary families in all their forms were subordinate to the requirements of the mission itself. The failures of the early missions, and in particular the sexual scandals that had accompanied the spiritual failures, placed the LMS in a difficult position. Having advocated single male missionaries as the most appropriate means of spreading the gospel, it became increasingly clear that missionaries needed wives. Yet, cultural notions of husbandliness and fatherhood seemed embedded with responsibilities that would harm the mission, by diverting the missionary's time and energy from his spiritual objectives.

Nonetheless, such marriages could often be companionate ones, based on mutual spirituality and a shared understanding that mission (and the eternal) must have priority over the family (and the temporal). Love and affection were deemed crucial to successful missionary marriages, as was a sense of partnership and vocational complementarity. These pre-embarkation ideals were gradually shaped and mediated by the realities of missionary marriage in the field. Expectations were tempered by mission life, and new requirements, demands and desires took shape in the mission context. Often based around the practical side of the missionary marriage, expectations of domesticity (male and female), tenderness and care came to shape these marriages, while mutual spirituality and interest in the mission gave them a particularly missionary aspect. In the words of imperial historian Mary Procida, 'the professional partnership between husband and wife often blurred visible distinctions between the imperial official and his spouse, effectively erasing the line between a private femininity and a public masculinity'.[176] Whatever the LMS's and the missionary public's expectations about the place of marriage within the priorities of missionaries, marriage came to be of primary importance in the mission field, and profoundly shaped the lived experience of mission. At the same time, it gradually incorporated into itself a whole new mission theology, based on domesticity and example that would become foundational to the missionary experience. For mission historians to let the importance of marriage be eclipsed by the more 'public' aspects of mission is to miss the profound influence that family life had, not only on missionaries themselves, but on the very missiological practice of the enterprise.

Ironically it was the nature of the missionary marriage as companionate that sowed the seeds of wifely decline. The male internalisation of the importance of normative domesticity led them to increasingly lobby the LMS for single women to assist in the more secular aspects of mission (e.g. teaching). Missionary women could not let domesticity slide for the sake of formal social activities (teaching, nursing etc.). That the ladies who these husbands were demanding turned out to be far more than assistants, and the ultimate underminers, in their formal professionalism, of their wives' vocational activities, is one of the many ironies of mission history.[177] Missionaries' wives had carved out a vocational space they could not fill within the changing shape of mission, and were ultimately superseded by the lady missionaries who came to 'assist' them. For the LMS meanwhile, these intervening years of mission family ascendancy caused profound and unique difficulties. How they dealt with the ascendancy of the mission family is the subject to which we will now turn.

Notes

1 Robert Moffat Journal, 31 July [undated], National Library of South Africa (Cape Town) (hereafter NLSA(CT)) MSB 858 LMS Miscellaneous 1(2). See also Karel Schoeman, *A thorn bush that grows in the path: the missionary career of Ann Hamilton, 1815–1823* (Cape Town: South African Library, 1995).

2 Doug Stuart, 'Of savages and heroes: race, nation and gender in the evangelical missions to Southern Africa in the early nineteenth century', PhD thesis (University of London, 1994), pp. 185 and 187.

3 Jeffrey Cox, *The British Missionary Enterprise since 1700* (London: Routledge, 2008), p. 111.

4 Elizabeth Elbourne, 'Mothers Milk: gender power and anxiety on a South African mission station, 1839–40', in Andrew May and Patricia Grimshaw (eds), *Missionaries, Indigenous Peoples and Cultural Exchange* (Eastbourne: Sussex Academic Press, 2010), p. 20.

5 Patricia Grimshaw, '"Christian Woman, Pious Wife, Faithful Mother, Devoted Missionary": Conflicts and Roles of American Missionary Women in Nineteenth-Century Hawaii', *Feminist Studies* 9:3 (1983), 489–521. Quote on p. 492.

6 Patricia Grimshaw, *Paths of Duty: American missionary wives in nineteenth-century Hawaii* (Honolulu: University of Hawaii Press, 1989); Valentine Cunningham, '"God and Nature Intended You for a Missionary's Wife": Mary Hill, Jane Eyre and Other Missionary Women in the 1840s', in Fiona Bowie, Deborah Kirkwood and Shirley Ardener (eds), *Women and Missions: past and present: anthropological and historical perceptions* (Providence RI and Oxford: Berg, 1993), pp. 85–105; Clare Midgley, 'Can Women be Missionaries? Envisioning Female Agency in the Early Nineteenth-Century British Empire', *Journal of British Studies*, 45 (2006), 335–58.

7 Hilary Callan and Shirley Ardener (eds), *The Incorporated Wife* (London: Croom Helm, 1984).

8 Catherine Hall, *Civilising Subjects: metropole and colony in the English imagination, 1830–1867* (Oxford: Polity, 2002), p. 95.

9 Grimshaw, 'Christian Woman, Pious Wife', p. 500.

10 Ibid. See also Line Nyhagen Predelli and Jon Miller, 'Piety and Patriarchy: Contested Gender Regimes in Nineteenth-century Evangelical Missions', in Mary Taylor Huber and Nancy C. Lutkehaus (eds), *Gendered Missions: women and men in missionary discourse and practice* (Ann Arbor: University of Michigan Press, 1999), pp. 67–112.

11 Clare Midgley, *Feminism and Empire: women activist in imperial Britain, 1790–1865* (London, 2007), p. 121. See also Dana L. Robert, 'Evangelist or Homemaker? Mission Strategies of Early Nineteenth-Century Missionary Wives in Burma and

Hawaii', *International Bulletin of Missionary Research* 17:1 (1993), 4–12; and Jane Haggis, 'Ironies of Emancipation: Changing Configurations of 'Women's Work', in the 'Mission Sisterhood' to Indian Women', *Feminist Review* 65:1 (2000), 108–26.

12 Midgley, 'Can Women be Missionaries?'.

13 Alison Twells, *The Civilising Mission and the English Middle Classes, 1792–1850: the 'heathen' at home and overseas* (Basingstoke: Palgrave Macmillan, 2009), p. 8.

14 See also Robert, 'Evangelist or Homemaker?' and Diane Langmore, *Missionary Lives: Papua, 1874–1914* (Honolulu: University of Hawaii Press, 1989).

15 Elbourne, 'Mothers Milk', p. 20.

16 Elizabeth Price, 'Reminiscences', in Una Long (ed.), *The Journals of Elizabeth Lees Price: written in Bechuanland, Southern Africa 1854–1883 with an Epilogue: 1889 and 1900* (London: Edward Arnold, 1956), p. 48.

17 Stuart, 'Of Savages and Heroes', p. 190.

18 Price, 'Reminiscences', in Long, *Journals*, p. 48.

19 Robert Moffat to Mr and Mrs Smith, 8 December 1819, in John Smith Moffat, *The Lives of Robert and Mary Moffat* (London: T. Fisher Unwin, 1885), p. 68.

20 Robert Moffat Journal, 31 July [undated], NLSA(CT) MSB 858 LMS Miscellaneous 1(2).

21 See Hall, *Civilising Subjects*, p. 91.

22 Grimhsaw, 'Christian Woman, Pious Wife', p. 492.

23 Mary Moffat to Jane Philip, 12 September 1821, South Africa Incoming Letters (hereafter SAIL) 8B/3.

24 Robert Moffat to his father, 16 April 1819 in Moffat, *Lives*, p. 45.

25 Catherine Hall, 'Missionary Stories: Gender and Ethnicity in the 1830s and 1840s', in Catherine Hall, *White, Male and Middle Class: explorations in feminism and history* (Cambridge: Polity, 1992), 205–255. Quote on p. 226.

26 Bastion Tromp to London, 3 March, 1806, SAIL 3A/2/B.

27 Original emphasis. Moffat, *Lives*, p. 457.

28 Mary Moffat to Jane Philip, 12 September 1821, SAIL 8B/3.

29 Ibid.

30 Andrew C. Ross, *John Philip (1775–1851): missions, race and politics in South Africa* (Aberdeen: Aberdeen University Press, 1986).

31 Robert to Alexander Moffat, 25 February 1822 in Robert Moffat, *Apprenticeship at Kuruman. Being the journals and letters of Robert and Mary Moffat 1820–1828. Edited by I. Schapera* (London: Chatto & Windus, 1951), p. 60.

32 Price, 'Reminiscences', in Long, *Journals*, p. 47.

33 Price to 'Dear English friends', 24 December 1862 in Long, *Journals*, p. 105.

34 Ibid.

35 Robert, 'Evangelist or Homemaker?', p. 9. See also Hall, 'Missionary Stories'; Midgley, 'Can Women be Missionaries', pp. 348–52; and Amanda Vickery, 'From Golden Age to Separate Spheres? A Review of the Categories and Chronology of English Women's History', *Historical Journal* 36:2 (1993), 383–414.

36 See Diane Langmore, 'The Object Lesson of a Civilised, Christian Home', in Margaret Jolly and Martha Macintyre (eds), *Family and Gender in the Pacific: domestic contradictions and the colonial impact* (Cambridge: Cambridge University Press, 1999); and Adele Perry, 'From "The Hot-bed of Vice" to the "Good and Well-ordered Christian Home": first nations housing and reform in nineteenth-century British Columbia', *Ethnohistory* 50:4 (2003), 587–610.

37 Mary Moffat to Jane Philip, 12 September 1821, SAIL 8B/3.

38 Leonore Davidoff and Catherine Hall, *Family Fortunes: men and women of the English middle class, 1780–1850* (London: Hutchinson, 1987).

39 Twells, *The Civilising Mission*, p. 8.

40 Natasha Erlank, 'Jane and John Philip: partnership, usefulness and sexuality in the service of God', in John de Gruchy (ed.), *The London Missionary Society in Southern Africa: historical essays in celebration of the bi-centenary of the LMS in Southern Africa, 1799–1999* (Cape Town: David Philip, 1999), pp. 86–93. Quote on p. 89.

41 George to Thomas Barker, 7 January 1837, NLSA(CT) MSB 57 1 (14).

42 Elizabeth Price to Jane Moffat (hereafter Price to Moffat), 22 August 1866, in Long, *Journals*, p. 215.
43 Ibid.
44 Price to Moffat, 3 September 1866, in Long, *Journals*, p. 222.
45 Ibid., 24 July 1866, in Long, *Journals*, p. 209.
46 Hannah Crook Journal, 12 December 1819, National Library of New Zealand (hereafter NLNZ), Micro-MS-0726, pp. 53–4.
47 Perry, 'Hot-bed of Vice'; Catherine Hall, 'White Visions, Black Lives: the free villages of Jamaica', *History Workshop Journal* 36:1 (1993), 100–32. For the British context see Jean and John L. Comaroff, 'Home-Made Hegemony: Modernity, Domesticity, and Colonialism in South Africa', in Karen Tranberg Hansen (ed.), *African Encounters with Domesticity* (New Brunswick: Rutgers University Press, 1992), pp. 37–74; and Jane Lewis (ed), *Labour and Love: women's experience of home and family, 1850–1940* (Oxford: Blackwell, 1986).
48 Ibid., p. 54. See Margaret Jolly, '"To Save the Girls for Brighter and Better Lives": Presbyterian Missions and Women in the South of Vanuatu, 1848–1870', *Journal of Pacific History* 26:1 (1991), 27–48.
49 Perry, 'Hot-bed of Vice', pp. 604 and 599.
50 *My emphasis.* Hannah Crook Journal, 12 December 1821, NLNZ, Micro-MS-0726, p. 54.
51 See, for example, Jolly, 'To Save the Girls'; Kathryn Rountree, 'Re-making the Maori Female Body: Marianne Williams's Mission in the Bay of Islands', *Journal of Pacific History* 35:1 (2000), 49–66; Deborah Gaitskell, 'Housewives, Maids or Mothers: some contradictions of domesticity for christian women in Johannesburg, 1903–39', *The Journal of African History* 24:2 (1983), 241–56.
52 Comaroffs, 'Home-Made Hegemony', pp. 54–5.
53 Price, 'Reminiscences', in Long, *Journals*, p. 47.
54 Robert Unwin Moffat, *John Smith Moffat CMG Missionary: a memoir* (London: John Murray, 1921), p. 97.
55 Robert Moffat to his parents, 15 December 1818 in Moffat, *Lives*, p. 41.
56 Ibid.
57 Grimshaw, 'Christian Woman, Pious Wife', p. 501.
58 Mary Moffat to Jane Philip, 12 September 1821, SAIL 8B/3.
59 Price to 'Dear English friends', 24 December 1862 in Long, *Journals*, p. 105.
60 Moffat, *Lives*, p. 103.
61 Price to her sister Helen, 21 November 1862 in Long, *Journals*, p. 85.
62 Ibid.
63 Adam Philips and Barbara Taylor, *On Kindness* (London: Hamish Hamilton, 2009). For 'affective' economies in imperial history see Ann Laura Stoler, 'Tense and Tender Ties: the politics of comparison in North American and (post)colonial studies', *Journal of American History* 88:3 (2001), 829–65. See also Matt Matsuda, *Empires of Love: histories of France and the Pacific* (Oxford: Oxford University Press, 2005); and Tony Ballantyne and Antoinette Burton (eds), *Moving Subjects: gender, mobility, and intimacy in an age of global empire* (Urbana, IL: University of Illinois Press, 2009).
64 Lawrence Stone, *The Family, Sex and Marriage in England, 1500–1800* (London: Weidenfeld & Nicolson, 1977), p. 217; Davidoff and Hall, *Family Fortunes*, pp. 321–56; John Tosh, *A Man's Place: masculinity and the middle-class home in Victorian England* (New Haven, CT and London: Yale University Press, 1999), pp. 53–78.
65 Moffat, *Lives*, p. 38.
66 Robert Moffat to Mary Smith, 25 November 1818, NLSA(CT) MSB 349 1 (1).
67 Ibid.
68 Robert Moffat to his parents, 15 December 1818, in Moffat, *Lives*, p. 41.
69 George Barker to his Sister, 11 May 1834, NLSA(CT) MSB 57 1 (14).
70 Line Nyhagen Predelli, 'Marriage in Norwegian Missionary Practice and Discourse in Norway and Madagascar, 1880–1910', *Journal of Religion in Africa* 31:1 (2001),

4–48. Quote on p. 29.
71 Robert Moffat to Mary Smith, 25 November 1818, NLSA(CT) MSB 349 1 (1).
72 Ibid.
73 Erlank, 'Jane and John Philip', p. 84.
74 Robert Moffat Journal, 31 July [undated], NLSA(CT) MSB 858 1(2).
75 John Williams to the new missionaries at Aitutake, 6 July 1823, South Seas Incoming Letters (hereafter SSIL) 4/1/A.
76 Hannah Crook Journal, 2 February 1820, NLNZ, Micro-MS-0726, p. 62.
77 Rhonda Semple, 'Missionary Manhood: professionalism, belief, and masculinity in the nineteenth-century British imperial field', *Journal of Imperial and Commonwealth History* 36:3 (2008), 397–415. Quote on p. 400.
78 Ibid. See also Esme Cleall, 'Missionaries, Masculinities and War: the London Missionary Society in Southern Africa, *c.*1860–1899', *South African Historical Journal* 61:2 (2009), 232–53.
79 Mary Moffat to her parents, 18 December 1818 in Moffat, *Lives*, pp. 51–2.
80 Robert Moffat to the Smiths, 8 December 1819 in Moffat, *Lives*, p. 68.
81 William Philip, Answers to Printed Queries (hereafter AtPQ), 20 July 1836, Candidate Papers (hereafter CP) 26/2/26.
82 Thomas Philip to London, 13 May 1843, CP 13/21.
83 Richard Lovett, *The History of the London Missionary Society, 1795–1895* ([S.I.]: Frowde, 1899), vol. 1, pp. 674–5. See also LMS Board Minutes (hereafter BM), 27 January 1817, pp. 11–2; 10 February 1817, p. 14; 28 April 1817, pp. 69–70; 10 November 1817, p. 29.
84 See Esme Cleall, 'Thinking with Missionaries: discourses of difference in India and southern Africa, *c.*1840–1895', PhD thesis (University College London, 2009), pp. 143–50. For marriage more generally see Davidoff and Hall, *Family Fortunes*, pp. 323–4 and Tosh, *A Man's Place*, pp. 57–9.
85 Predelli, 'Marriage in Norwegian Missionary Practice and Discourse', p. 10.
86 Hall, *Civilising Subjects*, p. 94.
87 Robert to Alexander Moffat, January 1823, in Moffat, *Apprenticeship*, p. 70.
88 Robert Moffat to Mary Smith, 25 November 1818, NLSA(CT) MSB 349, 1 (1).
89 George Thom to London, 12–22 August 1817, SAIL 7/2/C.
90 Erlank, 'Jane and John Philip'.
91 Semple, 'Missionary Manhood', p. 409. See also Predelli, 'Marriage in Norwegian Missionary Practice and Discourse'.
92 Robert Moffat Journal, 31 July [undated], NLSA(CT) MSB 858 LMS Miscellaneous 1(2).
93 Ibid.
94 George to Thomas Barker, 7 January 1837, NLSA(CT) MSB 57 1 (14).
95 That is, the Proverbs of Solomon.
96 George to Thomas Barker, 7 January 1837, NLSA(CT) MSB 57 1 (14).
97 David Darling to London, 25 February 1858, SSIL 27/2/C.
98 George Barker to his brother [unnamed], 4 April 1838, and to his sister Elizabeth, 14 June 1841, NLSA(CT) MSB 57 1 (14).
99 George Barker to his sister [unnamed], 20 December 1837, NLSA(CT) MSB 57 1 (14).
100 George to Elizabeth Barker, 20 December 1837, NLSA(CT) MSB 57 1 (14).
101 George to Thomas Barker, 7 January 1837, NLSA(CT) MSB 57 1 (14).
102 George Barker to his brother [unnamed], 4 April 1838, NLSA(CT) MSB 57 1 (14).
103 George to Elizabeth Barker, 21 October 1841, NLSA(CT) MSB 57 1 (14).
104 Ibid., 28 June 1842, NLSA(CT) MSB 57 1 (14).
105 Ibid., 6 November 1844, NLSA(CT) MSB 57 1 (14).
106 Ibid., 19 June 1844, NLSA(CT) MSB 57 1 (14).
107 Erlank, 'Jane and John Philip, p. 91.
108 Price to Moffat, 3 September 1866 in Long, *Journals*, p. 223.
109 Ibid.
110 Ibid., 11 July 1866 in Long, *Journals*, p. 184.

111 Ibid., 3 September 1866 in Long, *Journals*, p. 223.
112 Tosh, *A Man's Place*, p. 66.
113 Robert Moffat Journal, 25 May 1823 in Moffat, *Apprenticeship*, p. 83.
114 George to Thomas Barker, 7 January 1837, NLSA(CT) MSB 57 1 (14).
115 Janet Wagner Parsons, *The Livingstones at Kolobeng 1847–1852* (Gaborone, Botswana: Botswana Society, 1997), p. 68.
116 George to Thomas Barker, 7 January 1837, NLSA(CT) MSB 57 1 (14).
117 Ibid.
118 Cleall, 'Missionaries, Masculinities and War', pp. 243–5.
119 Moffat, *Apprenticeship*, p. 76.
120 Moffat, *Lives*, p. 125.
121 Price to Moffat, 3 September 1866 in Long, *Journals*, p. 225.
122 Ibid, p. 223.
123 Karel Schoeman, *A Thorn Bush that Grows in the Path: the missionary career of Ann Hamilton, 1815–1823* (Cape Town: South African Library, 1995), pp. 1–4.
124 Robert Moffat Journal, 31 July [undated], NLSA(CT) MSB 858 1(2).
125 Erlank, 'Jane and John Philip', p. 95.
126 Price to Moffat, 23 November 1863 in Long, *Journals*, p. 139.
127 Moffat, *John Smith Moffat*, p. 70.
128 Moffat, *Lives*, p. 458.
129 Hall, *Civilising Subjects*, p. 96.
130 Robert to Mary Moffat, April 1838 in Moffat, *Lives*, p. 220.
131 Amanda Vickery, 'The Din of Visiting Day: Publicising the Private Sphere', unpublished Keynote Paper at the University of Northampton Visiting Rites: accessing the English home, *c.*1650–1850 symposium, 10 September 2009. See also Carol Summers, 'Mission Boys, Civilised Men, and Marriage: educated African men in the missions of Southern Rhodesia, 1920–1945', *The Journal of Religious History* 23:1 (1999), 75–91.
132 Moffat, *Lives*, p. 85.
133 Ibid., p. 90.
134 Ibid.
135 Perry, 'Hot-bed of Vice', p. 596.
136 Lee Wallace, Lee, 'A House is not a Home: gender, space and Marquesan encounter, 1833–34', *The Journal of Pacific History* 40:3 (2005), 265–88. See particularly pp. 275–80. See also Jolly, 'To Save the Girls'; and Greg Dening, 'Towards an Anthropology of Performance in Encounters in Place', in Donald H. Rubenstein (ed.), *Pacific History: papers from the 8th Pacific History Association Conference* (Mangilao, Guam, 1992).
137 Robert Moffat to his parents, 15 December 1818, in Moffat, *Lives*, p. 41.
138 Price to 'English friends', 24 December 1862, in Long, *Journals*, p. 104.
139 Cleall, 'Missionaries, masculinity and war', pp. 241 and 239.
140 Hall, *Civilising Subjects*, p. 95.
141 Robert Moffat to the Smiths, 8 December 1819 in Moffat, *Lives*, p. 69.
142 Elizabeth Price Journal, 23 November 1863 in Long, *Journals*, p. 140.
143 For example, Tim Jeal, *Livingstone* (New Haven and London: Yale Nota Bene, 2001); Parsons, *Livingstones at Kolobeng*; Edna Healey, *Wives of Fame: Mary Livingstone, Jenny Marx, Emma Darwin* (London: Sidgwick & Jackson, 1986).
144 Cf. Parsons, *Livingstones at Kolobeng*, p. 33.
145 Quotes can he found in Jeal, *Livingstone*, pp. 58–62.
146 David to Neil Livingston, 17 January 1846, in David Livingstone, *Family Letters, 1841–1856*, 2 vols. *Edited with an introduction by I. Schapera* (London: Chatto & Windus, 1959), vol. 1, p. 160.
147 David to Janet Livingston, 20 April 1849 in Livingstone, *Family Letters*, vol. 2, p. 37.
148 Jeal, *Livingstone*, p. 60.
149 Ibid., pp. 59–60.
150 Thom to London, 16 Feb, 1814, SAIL 5/3/C.
151 Jeal, *Livingstone*, p. 58.

152 David Livingstone to Robert Moffat (hereafter Livingstone to Moffat), 1 July 1846, in Livingstone, *Family Letters*, vol. 1, p. 176.
153 Ibid.
154 David to Agnes Livingston (Sr), 14 May 1845 in Livingstone, *Family Letters*, vol. 1, p. 121.
155 Jeal, *Livingstone*, p. 60.
156 Cited in Jeal, *Livingstone*, p. 61.
157 Parsons, *Livingstones at Kolobeng*, p. 33.
158 David Livingstone, *Livingstone's Private Journals, 1851–1853. Edited with an introduction by I. Schapera* (London: Chatto & Windus, 1960), pp. 70–1.
159 Livingstone to Moffat, 11 August 1848 in Livingstone, *Family Letters*, vol. 1, p. 250.
160 Ibid., 29 September 1847 in Livingstone, *Family Letters*, vol. 1, p. 223.
161 Ibid., 8 July 1850 in Livingstone, *Family Letters*, vol. 1, p. 90.
162 Jeal, *Livingstone*, pp. 95–107.
163 Livingstone, *Private Journals*, pp. 70–1.
164 Livingstone to Robert Moffat Jr, 28 April 1851, in Livingstone, *Family Letters*, vol. 2, p. 131.
165 Andrew C. Ross, *David Livingstone: mission and empire* (London and New York: Hambledon and London, 2002), p. 50.
166 David to Mary Livingstone, 14 September 1855, in Livingstone, *Family Letters*, vol. 2, pp. 268–9.
167 Jeal, *Livingstone*, p. 61.
168 Parsons, *Livingstones at Kolobeng*, p. 32.
169 Ross, *David Livingstone*, p. 48.
170 George Seaver, *David Livingstone: his life and letters* (London: Lutterworth Press, 1957), p. 85.
171 Ross, *David Livingstone*, pp. 49–50.
172 Ibid., p. 50.
173 David to Mary Livingstone, 5 May 1852, in Livingstone, *Family Letters*, vol. 2, p. 182
174 Ibid.
175 Livingstone to Mary Moffat, 12 September 1844, in Livingstone, *Family Letters*, vol. 1, p. 106.
176 Mary Procida, *Married to Empire: gender, politics and imperialism in India, 1883–1947* (Manchester: Manchester University Press, 2002), p. 50.
177 Patricia Grimshaw and Peter Sherlock, 'Women and Cultural Exchanges', in Norman Etherington (ed.), *Missions and Empire* (Oxford: Oxford University Press, 2005), 173–193. Quote on p. 181.

CHAPTER FOUR

The missionary family

> The boys [of the South Seas Mission] ... are too young for labour. It will however be of the highest importance that they should have regular employment before habits of indolence are formed and matured. At present there is no *regular* and suitable employ for the females ... if this plan be continued the children of the Missionaries will neither be properly instructed or employed, but will contract habits of immaturity and sloth which will at once be destructive of their morals and destroy all hopes respecting their future temporal condition in the world. Proper education and regular occupation are indispensably necessary for them and without these the mission will be threatened with ruin.
> (James Hayward's 'Answers to Queries' from the Directors, 1819)

By the 1820s William Pascoe Crook was a lucky man. He had survived his first isolated encounter with the Marquesas islands and people (1797 and 1799) relatively unscathed, despite 'the dangers to which [he] was constantly exposed while labouring among these savage people'.[1] Having been 'rescued' by the *Butterworth* in 1799, he had also survived his return to England, despite the outbreak of hostilities with the French (which elsewhere resulted in the second missionary fleet to the Pacific being taken captive). In England he had been fortunate enough to marry one Hannah Dare, who would acquit herself faithfully and fruitfully as his wife on their return to the South Seas Mission (SSM) in 1816 (as well as during their thirteen years stranded in Australia from 1803, owing to the Tahitian civil war). She was a 'true missionary's wife, assisting her husband in "every good work"', holding frequent prayer and 'experience' meetings, teaching reading, writing and sewing, and organising philanthropic societies and events among the local mission community.[2]

By 1821 Crook was the father of nine children – eight daughters and one son – had a close relationship with the ruling Pomare family (he and his wife having been present at the birth of their son in 1819), and was an integral part of a thriving mission community on the island of Tahiti. Whatever pleasure he may have derived from his material and spiritual circumstances, however, it was not to last. By 1827 he and his wife were plunged into anxious doubt, not about their mission, but about their family, and more particularly 'the temporal and spiritual welfare of our offspring'.[3]

> What to do for our family we know not. It is a discouraging thing to think of. One or both of us the parents will soon be removed and our poor girls will be cast among semi-savages except they take refuge in some of the missionaries houses, and they have enough to do to take care of their own and in a short time will be in the same state as ourselves. We can form no virtuous connexions for our girls, nor can we put them into any situation where they may be useful to others. What to do for them we know not.[4]

The Crooks situation was particularly acute, having 'eight daughters[;] six of them ... arrived at womanhood and the other two are not far behind'. 'We have for many years thought to live and die in this land, but the duty of providing for our family has lately deeply impressed our minds.'[5] The only solution he could think of was to 'retir[e] to New South Wales till we can dispose of our family', there to 'make ourselves useful in any station we might be called to occupy'. 'We therefore as a family beg your advice and assistance', William wrote to the LMS hierarchy in London in January 1828.[6]

Unfortunately, the answer they received was less than helpful. Although they began by sympathising with his predicament, the Directors ultimately expressed the hope that 'you will be enabled to cast this, as all other burdens, upon Him who has enjoined upon his peoples, not to be anxious about to-morrow, but to rest assured, if they are engaged in doing his will, he will take care of them and theirs'. Further, he was reminded that the duty of a parent 'cannot be devolved on others', nor could his own duty to the mission be ignored. They rejected his plan to settle temporarily in New South Wales (at the Society's expense) for he could not 'be spared from your post so long as this would require, while the great expense which it would involve, the funds of the Society cannot bear, nor should we feel justified in giving them this direction'. Finally he was advised,

> Does it not appear to you possible, that the families of the Missionaries should, if possible, become settlers in the Islands? Were they forming, from time to time, connexions among themselves, and obtaining from the chiefs in different places, some piece of lands, or in some one place a large portion, either as temporary leases or as entire property, we do not see why, in this manner, they might not be able to provide for their families, and ultimately be a great blessing to the people.[7]

'We beg also to be informed if you and your Brethren bring up your children in the practice of any useful arts ... your best endeavours should be exerted on this facet, both with respect to males and females.'[8]

The mission's response to these ideas, which were ultimately suggested for the mission community as a whole, is dealt with in the ensuing pages. For now it suffices to say that the Crooks were not impressed: 'To us, your idea of civilising the country is very pretty in theory, but utterly impracticable.'[9] By the time they had received the Directors' advice a recent incident involving their son would undoubtedly have made their minds up for them. Young Samuel Crook was 'taken home' from the South Seas Academy (school for missionary children) in December 1828 (about a year after William Crook's first letter to the Directors), having 'received from the hand of a Hutae auri [i.e. a member of the religious Arioi society] the sign of native circumcision', a shocking cultural and spiritual transgression for his parents.[10] Faced with the apparent moral decline of their son, and the very real problem of disposing of their daughters, the Crooks in the end felt forced to abandon their mission – a rare and striking case in which missionaries put their family ahead of their vocation.[11] They returned to Sydney in October 1830, and continued their religious and philanthropic work as religious teachers and leaders. Hannah Crook died in Sydney in 1837, at the age of 60. Having at last been 'permitted to see his prayers answered for all his children', meanwhile, William died in Melbourne in 1846. Undoubtedly, they would have considered their move worthwhile when their eldest daughter Mary married CMS missionary Johann Handt in 1832. For missionaries, the best blessing on their parenting style was the continuation of the missionary endeavour into the next generation. Before that could happen, however, the institutional ambivalence of the directors had to be negotiated, and more often than not, circumnavigated.

The LMS, as we know, had always been ambivalent about the family, and their reaction here probably seems less than surprising. The Crooks had had reason to be hopeful however. Not only had they worked for the mission for more than ten years, but during that time the LMS had been forced to make a series of concessions to familial provision. Not only were allowances made for missionary children within the missionary's salary (which had been the case since the 1810s), but money was actually invested into the futures of the children themselves, including the establishment of regional schools and provision for apprenticeships into useful trades. At first glance the 1820s might look like a time of fiscal munificence on the part of the Directors, a stance seemingly at odds with their continued reluctance to make adequate provision for missionaries' wives in the same period.

On closer inspection, however, the LMS had not experienced a radical change in fiscal policy. Rather the mechanisms of support introduced for missionary children were all designed to promote one thing: their permanent residence at the mission. Fiscal pragmatism on the one hand, and the rise of the civilising mission on the other came together to support the promotion of this one end: 'the permanent establishment of the families of missionaries in the region of their birth'.[12] In this determination the Directors were conforming to a changing notion of mission, as shown in Chapter 2, and implementing a new conception of the primacy of the 'commerce, Christianity, and civilisation'.

> the Directors regard the permanent establishment of the families of missionaries in the Island [Tahiti], for which Divine Providence has signally rendered them instrumental in introducing the Gospel, as one of the leading means of perpetuating that blessing, and, at the same time, of advancing the progress of moral improvement, and social cultivation amongst the inhabitants.[13]

The above was an absolute articulation of the civilising mission, and reflected the acceptance of the missionary family as the primary means of mission activity within that mission enterprise. Both wife and child became instrumental to mission, and were thereby incorporated into the enterprise, with or without their individual consent. Yet, the policies promoted by the LMS over the course of the 1820s were not rooted in ideological largesse. At the same time as the permanent establishment of missionary families cohered with ideological change, it also conformed to the ever-present fiscal pragmatism of the Directors in London. In promoting the permanent establishment of families, the Board of Directors was side-stepping an emerging trend within missionary circles: a desire to send children home (i.e. to Britain), or in the case of the Crooks, to 'any other civilised country' for their education and temporal futures.[14] The consolidation of missionary families within LMS policy can be seen as a consistent attempt by the Directors to cushion against this costly and inconvenient possibility, and thus did not reflect a dramatic shift within the upper echelons of the Society, but rather continuity with the earlier financial mores of a humanitarian institution based on private charity. This shift manifested in two main ways: the establishment of regional schools for missionary children and the desire to create a new settler class based on missionary families. Neither scheme, however, could ultimately halt the call for systematic juvenile repatriation.

Regional schools

By the 1820s, and much against its will, then, the LMS found itself embroiled in debates about missionary children's material and spiritual welfare, as well as their effect on, and role within, the mission itself. While fiscal pragmatism dictated that a laissez-faire attitude towards the temporal affairs of missionaries would be the most financially practical, in the case of missionary children there were more fundamental forces at work, for they had the potential to both greatly enhance the missionary enterprise, and to fatally corrupt it. As early as the 1810s, the LMS found itself having to address quickly the problem of ill-educated and badly behaved missionary children. In 1819 South Seas missionary James Hayward warned that: 'Proper education and regular occupation are indispensably necessary for them' (that is, the '15 boys and 17 Girls belonging to the mission') and that without these 'the children of the Missionaries will neither be properly instructed or employed, but will contract habits of immaturity and sloth which will at once be destructive of their morals and destroy all hopes respecting their future temporal condition in the world'. This would be bad enough, but it was 'the mission [that would] be threatened with ruin'.[15]

In November 1820 the Directors thus held a meeting specifically summoned for the purpose of discussing missionary children's education. There it was resolved that 'suitable Seminaries should be established abroad for the education of the children of the missionaries ... one in India and another in South Africa'. Generational replication and fiscal pragmatism were integral to their conception: 'the mode of education given to the children of the missionaries shall be such as to qualify them for the offices of Schoolmaster and Schoolmistress, or for becoming missionaries, in case they should afterwards be called to the work' and the 'missionaries sending their children to the Institution shall contribute a moderate sum towards the expense of each child boarded and educated there'.[16]

A Committee of Education was established to flesh out the plan and in January 1821 provided a detailed report on how the Madras school for missionary children was to be run. Its location was to be somewhere within the Madras presidency, where the climate was 'favourable for the health of the Pupils'; other European children were to be admitted, in order to raise funds for the school, and the curriculum was to consist of 'English Grammar, Latin, Greek, Arithmetic, Book keeping, Mathematics, Geography etc – and if practicable, in some of the principal native languages, such as the Tamil, Teloogoo and Canara'.[17] These resolutions were 'sent out to the missionaries at the several stations in India, with a request that they will communicate to the Directors any remarks they may have'. Missionaries were also asked to 'communicate their ideas as to the expediency of educating promising young men born in the country, as teachers, in the same seminary'.[18] In both South Africa and India, the idea of uniting the school for missionaries' children with a 'native seminary' spoke to the overriding concern that the education of missionaries' children be directed towards the ultimate success of the mission itself, as well as an interesting conceptual slippage between missionary children and indigenous converts, who both, after all, inhabited something of an interstitial space between two cultures: connected to both, but unreservedly accepted by neither.[19]

These plans, however, met with a surprising lack of enthusiasm on the part of the missionaries involved. 'I am afraid it will prove a more delicate and difficult subject than may at first sight be thought – all the tenderest feelings are involved', wrote William Loveless (missionary in India, 1805–1823).[20]

> I fear your plan will not answer unless it be on a most liberal scale both as it respects the Talents of the Tutor and the respectability of the Institution ... I fear your ideas of its ultimately contributing either wholly or in part to support itself will prove groundless ... Keeping a school now is not what it was 10 or 12 years ago – Schools are found now in many of the principal settlements and unless superior advantages either from intellectual improvement or cheapness are to be obtained little is to be expected. Those who seek the former mostly send their children to Europe and the latter will afford no assistance to your plan.[21]

His pessimism was shared by John Philip in South Africa when he too was consulted by the Board. Having discussed the issue with two missionaries from India who were in South Africa at the time he informed the Directors that:

> Both agree in their opinion, and I am sorry to say that they do not seem to think that good is to be expected from a School on the plan proposed at Madras ... both agree that the attempt will require a great deal of money and that after that money is expended there are nine chances, it will fail, for one, that it will succeed.[22]

By then, however, the LMS had dispatched what became known as 'the Deputation', one of the primary objects of which was the foundation of regional schools for missionary children. Two pious gentleman, George Bennett and Daniel Tyerman, thus left London in May 1821, charged with inspecting the missions of the LMS throughout the globe, driving forward the centralising plans of the Directors, and bringing the missions into line with the new primacy of the civilising mission: 'The great objects of the Deputation will be, to make themselves thoroughly acquainted with the state of the Missions, and of the islands; and to suggest, and, if possible, carry into effect, such plans as shall appear to be requisite for the furtherance of the gospel, and for introducing among the natives the occupations and habits of civilised life.' To do this, they would 'form such arrangements as shall tend to the introduction of Christian Churches; the establishment and improvement of schools for the children of the Missionaries and of the natives, and eventually, of trades; and a proper and constant attention to the cultivation of the ground'.[23] Disposing properly of missionary children, then, and integrating them fully into the mission's objectives, was a crucial part of new mission strategy.

The Deputation arrived in the SSM (its first stop), in September 1821, and having 'become acquainted with the state of the children of the Missionaries' it did not take long for them to become 'deeply convinced of the especial importance of a School for their Education, as well for the safety and prosperity of the Mission, as for their own sakes'.[24] The introduction of regional schools for missionary children would constitute the LMS's first concrete attempt to exert direct institutional control over the children of their missionaries, and thereby to incorporate them officially into the enterprise. As such, regional schools were initially planned in the South Seas, South Africa and India, all to be created under the auspices of the Deputation. In fact the South Seas Academy (SSA), on the island of Eimeo (later Moorea), just off Tahiti, would be the only (semi-)successful manifestation of this trend. What the LMS continually failed to realise was that missionaries were particularly precious about their parental autonomy and authority, spurred on by constant fears over the 'temporal and eternal good' of their children.[25] While the prescription for such fears seemed to be the separation of children from the local peoples (always a primary object of regional schooling), parents tended to prefer domestic sequestration, rather than collective education. The LMS's failure to recognise this, and to respond effectively to missionaries' familial concerns and anxieties, would shape the interactions between the Society and mission families throughout the 1820s–1850s.

In the South Seas, however, the Deputation was determined to carry through the Directors' wishes, and having 'met with various discouragements in efforts to establish the School for the Children of Missionaries', the SSA was, nonetheless, finally opened in March 1824.[26] The Deputation had insisted that the school should open before their departure for India, for if 'it is not accomplished before then', wrote Daniel Tyerman, 'I greatly fear it will fall to the ground'.[27] 'That the school, which proposes to afford your dear children a suitable and useful education, should have commenced its operations before we finally leave you, is to us highly satisfactory', they wrote on 21 May 1824.

> We have assisted you in placing it on the best principles, and under the most useful and efficient regulations; and we commit it to your guardian care, trusting that you will watch over it with an attention and an assiduity, which shall ensure, under the divine blessing, those benefits which it proposes to confer upon your numerous families, and perhaps on children yet unborn. Accept of this institution as a proof of the Society's affection for you, and its concern for the welfare of your rising families:- a more convincing proof it could not give you.[28]

The official stance of the SSM was one of enthusiasm: 'It is with no little pleasure and thankfulness we have learned that you, with us, see the great necessity of a school being established for the education of our children, and that you are anxious to carry that most important object into effect.'[29] This was not total, however, and individual families remained reticent. 'When I consider how much it is wanted, I am utterly astonished that so many difficulties should have been raised, and difficulties thrown in the way, and so little exertion made to remove them', wrote an exasperated Daniel Tyerman in November 1823.[30] The stakes remained high, for if the children continued to be so 'thoroughly neglected they may by and by prove a source of grief to their Parents, and a disgrace to the Mission'.[31] Despite the complaints of missionaries such as Hayward, who lamented that 'three years since I arrived in England, and represented their [the missionary children's]

Figure 15 The South Seas Academy by Rev. Simpson (1835).

case to the Directors, are now far advanced, and nothing effectual has yet ever been done for them',[32] individual missionaries continued to jealously guard that parental autonomy which they perceived as being under threat. Thus the school started with only two pupils: Charles Barff Jr (son of Charles Barff Sr 1817–64) and James Platt (son of George Platt 1817–65).

The key issue here seemed to be concern over the influence of other missionaries' children: 'You will not be displeased that we do not send our children to the public school at Eimeo', wrote William Crook in December of that year; 'we have kept them in subjection from their infancy and have watched over them with anxious care, instructing them daily and hourly ... We dread the idea of a public school especially where many of the young ones have ran wild among the natives and were never broke in.'[33] Indeed, one of the objects of the school was to iron out the type of irregular parenting that had led to the shocking debauchery of an earlier generation of missionary children. This generation had run off with unconverted locals, had produced children out of wedlock, and had turned away from the precepts of the church. Thus in November 1823 the Deputation wrote to the first superintendent of the SSA John Orsmond (1817–44) that, 'Under the strict regulations that you will doubtless lay down I *hope* you will be able to keep the children separate from their families, though you will all be in the same valley; if you can accomplish this, great good I trust will accrue to the children from the Institution.'[34] A more stinging indictment of missionary parenting is hard to imagine.[35]

Gradually parental concerns subsided, however, in the face of continued anxiety about their children's perceived cultural contamination in local environments.[36] By 1825 there were ten pupils in attendance at the school and the missionary parents found themselves 'convinced that under the blessing of Almighty God the Father, the Son, and the holy Spirit, the greatest good must arise from this institution to our children, and we hope to the Islands, and Mission in general'.[37] The SSA always had two main purposes: to socialise the missionary children into the normative morality of western evangelicalism, and to promote (and protect) the aims and objectives of the mission. To those ends the children were kept separate from the indigenous peoples, from their families, and from each other, an internal sexual segregation being implied by the positioning of the 'Mr and Mrs bedroom ... between the boys and the girls'.[38] They were not allowed any unsupervised contact with the local people, and were allowed to speak only English within the confines of the school. These basic principles formed the cornerstone of all the regional schools planned by the Directors, and were directly linked with the promotion and protection of mission objectives. When John Orsmond complained that his superintendence of the school was taking him away from his pastoral duties, the Deputation assured him that 'your employment as Tutor of the School, is Missionary work in the most important sense; and in no situation in these Islands, could you be more effectually accomplishing your Mission'.[39] The Directors also joined in these assurances.

> The good, resulting from an Institution like this ... may be expected ... not only to be visible in the further progress of the Mission, but also felt in the effects of a systematic and liberal education, upon civil society throughout the islands. We therefore strongly recommend, that ... you will continue to make the superintendence of the Academy your chief business; and although we by no means disapprove of your attempts to do good in the capacity of Pastor of a church, still we advise you not to extend your activity in this branch of missionary employment too far.[40]

The objections of the missionaries in India, however, proved harder to eliminate. There, more than in other regions, the missionaries clung to the precepts of juvenile repatriation to Britain. Inhabiting an increasingly colonial space, in which Anglo-Indian children were systematically sent 'home' in order to protect their health and morals, and the racial identity of their natal family,[41] missionaries too desired the fiscal and institutional ability to repatriate their children. Thus the early plans for a school in Madras had never materialised. The Deputation arrived in India in April 1826, and stayed (touring the various missions there) for just under eighteen months. Although they were unable to leave a school in India as they had done in the South Seas, their visit did rejuvenate the debate (which had grown stale in the intervening years), leading the Madras District Committee (MDC) to formulate a new school plan in November 1827.[42]

By this time, however, the Directors in London were beginning to back away from the idea of regional schools. Faced with controversy in the South Seas relating to the length of tenure at the Academy, London was increasingly uninterested in its earlier plans and had begun to incubate a brand new manifesto for missionary children. When the MDC finally got around to resolving that 'an application should be made to the Directors respecting the School for the Children of Missionaries' on 25 March 1829,[43] the Board in London was only four months away from its own resolution that 'the Directors ought not to contemplate the measure', owing largely to the 'diversity of opinion among the Missionaries themselves' and 'the great expense and trouble likely to result from carrying it into effect'.[44] This resolution was reaffirmed in November of that year, despite pleas from the

MDC, and the Indian school for missionary children never came into existence.[45]

The situation in South Africa was even less successful. There John Philip stood out against the plan, believing such a school was not necessary in Africa, where a good living could be made from the mechanical arts, and where 'Carpenters, Bricklayers, or Blacksmiths' could earn 'higher wages than the greater part of the Government Clerks in the publick [*sic*] offices'.[46] Philip was 'very much against the Society pledging its funds or its revenue for the support of large establishments' and urged that under his superintendence 'any thing of the evil I deprecated shall be avoided as much as possible'.[47] Despite this extremely negative reaction to the idea the Directors persevered. In January 1825 it was

> recommended to the Board to accept Rev Mr Foster … as the superintendent of the Institution at Hankey, South Africa, intended for the Education of the Children of the Missionaries and also the Instruction of pious and intelligent Hottentots, so as to qualify them for Native Teachers.[48]

Once again, the education of children was linked with native agency, that one remaining aspect of the integrationist principle: 'the *objects of the Institution* are to provide for the instruction of Native Teachers in such branches of learning as may best fit them for preaching the Gospel to their countrymen and to supply means for the education of the children of the Missionaries'.[49] The sum of £50 was immediately placed at the disposal of William Foster (proposed superintendent and South African missionary 1825–30) for the purchasing of an Academic Library and ultimate authority was placed in the hands of the reluctant John Philip.[50] Given his vehement disapproval of the plan it is perhaps unsurprising that the school never came off. Finding the arrangements totally unsuitable, Foster removed to Bethelsdorp where some of the missionaries' sons were briefly taken into his care.[51] This ad hoc experiment was also short-lived with Mr Foster focusing his attention on the African catechists, and returning anyway to England in 1830.[52] He was not replaced.

The SSA, then, was the only regional school for missionaries' children to be founded, despite the desperate need, on the part of LMS missionaries, for some kind of temporal and spiritual education for their children. The particular geographic and ethnographic specificities of the Pacific had added an urgency to its foundation, which had managed to overcome initial missionary concern about the erosion of their autonomy. Competing colonial trends in both India and South Africa, where alternative establishments for their children's education, a higher availability of class- and colour-appropriate occupations and, in India particularly, the colonial notion of juvenile repatriation, forestalled the successful implementation of regional schools in places of imperial activity. This is by no means to say that the SSA was a success, however. Concern about the school gave way to enthusiasm for its aims, but pessimism about its ability to fulfil them soon surfaced. It became increasingly clear that the Academy was insufficient. Very quickly after its foundation a controversy arose between the missionaries and the Directors over the length of tenure at the school. In August 1825 the Directors wrote to Charles Wilson informing him that the children were to be students at the SSA for no more than five years.[53] Orsmond was quick to respond, reflecting the general mood of the mission that five years was simply not enough.

> The two first years will be employed in casting off the sloth, and habits acquired in the first 9 years among the natives ... By far the greater part of the children have been so much neglected that by the time they will have to leave the school they will scarcely have attained the standing of those who are but seven years of age in England ... The memory has to be cleared of that lumber of notions facts and consequences which the adroit hand of ignorance and corruption had placed there.'[54]

In August 1826 Samuel Wilson, then aged 14 and thus soon to be ejected from the Academy, warned the Directors of the many 'temptations which beset us around on these shores. A person leaving this Institution at the time prescribed will be ruined except by the powerful Grace of God he is kept in subjection that vile and base affections of his sinful and licentious heart.'[55]

His comments spoke both to an inculcation of superiority and chauvinism, and to a high level of evangelical self-loathing (as well as poor grammar). More than this, however, they indicated a genuine fear about his own temporal future. What were his, and his peers', socio-economic prospects? Education was one thing, but in the Pacific context in particular the question of a career loomed large for the sons of missionaries. While in South Africa they could become 'Carpenters, Bricklayers, or Blacksmiths', and thus earn 'higher wages than the greater part of the Government Clerks in the publick [*sic*] offices' (leading John Philip to argue against the expense of a school in 1822),[56] in the South Seas, respectable opportunities were few and far between. James Hayward's initial comments in 1819 had equally stressed the importance of occupation for missionary children. It did not take long for missionaries and their children to begin to fret about these new issues, ones that had only been delayed by the founding of the SSA. What were to be the long-term plans for these missionary children? And how could the LMS and their parents 'promote their temporal and eternal good'?[57]

Permanent establishment

While implicitly the main reason for attempting to establish a series of regional schools for missionary children was to keep them separate from corrupting influences and inept parenting, ostensibly their foundation spoke to something much more practical. Their explicit function was to train the missionary children who would therein be fitted for useful stations in life. Missionaries across the enterprise were increasingly concerned that their children could have no future in the climates, both moral and physical, of their birth, at least without some assistance and guidance from the Directors. 'What will they be fit for, if they grow up in their present state? What will become of them, if I am removed from them?' lamented George Barker in 1825.[58] 'Our children are a great burden at times upon our minds', wrote George Platt in 1829, 'you cannot possibly form an adequate idea of the prospects before them nor to what they are exposed'.[59] The issue of post-school occupation had been delayed by the founding of the SSA, rather than resolved. Even the Academy's own students fretted about their prospects. 'Perhaps some of us will soon leave school and who can tell what shall be our situation. Some will perhaps have to endure very great hardships procuring their living among these barbarous and very revengeful peoples', they wrote to the Directors in 1828.[60] Missionaries thus increasingly appealed to the Directors to invest in their children's futures. The Directors meanwhile, continued to hold fast to the notion of parental responsibility embodied in the 1818 Resolutions: that they 'cannot take upon them the guardianship of the children of missionaries'.[61]

The issue of occupation was a highly gendered one. While the parents of both boys and girls lamented the lack of prospects for their children, there were at least some opportunities available for the sons of missionaries. In 1828 it was noted that William Henry Jr (son of South Seas missionary William Henry Sr, 1797–1842) and James Bicknell (son of South Seas missionary Henry Bicknell, 1797–1820) were apprenticed as shipwrights in the Colony (New South Wales); Charles Wilson (son of Charles Wilson Sr) was working for a draper and haberdasher there; Samuel Wilson (his brother) had been granted a free place at Dr Lang's school in New South Wales;[62] and in 1830 Charles Barff Jr was apprenticed, at the Society's expense, to a printer's in New South Wales under the agreement that he would return and work at the mission printing press after his training.[63] The only practicable option for missionary daughters meanwhile was respectable marriage. This was no easy objective in a racially and culturally isolated context where the only white men available for marriage were missionary sons (whose own financial situations made them less than practical husbands) or beachcombers, who were highly unsatisfactory in their moral laxity and dubious sexual and social habits.[64] 'We can form no virtuous connexions for our girls, nor can we put them into any situation where they may be useful to others', worried William Crook, as we have seen, in 1827.

Nonetheless, in a pleasing case of historical symmetry, the Directors affirmed their position expounded in the 1818 Resolutions, by passing a new set of Resolutions relating to missionary children in 1828. As shown at the start of this chapter, they had in that same year suggested to Crook that his daughters should become settlers in the islands, and through these 1828 Resolutions, the idea of 'the permanent establishment of the families of missionaries in the Island' was rolled out across the South Seas Mission. Again conforming to the idea of families as the primary agents of the civilising mission, the Directors noted that they were 'instrumental in introducing the Gospel' to the Islands 'and, at the same time, of advancing the progress of moral improvement, and social cultivation amongst the inhabitants'.[65]

> in furtherance of these views it is equally the interest and the duty of the Missionaries to devise and prosecute such measures as by the divine blessing may tend to promote the attachment of their children to the Islands and to provide for their comfortable maintenance in them.

In order to 'encourage the settlement of the Mission families in the Island the Directors will be ready at all times to furnish such assistance as the nature of the circumstance and the means of the Society will admit'. They extolled the missionaries, with their 'superior local knowledge', to reflect on what would be the best means of achieving this end, and asked them to submit 'a plan by which their families, on intermarrying with each other, may be provided for, either by Agricultural or mechanical pursuits'. Not having totally abandoned their integrationist hope that through intermarriage the mission might become self-sustaining, they reflected that the founding of the SSA itself had been 'greatly influenced by their views of its tendency to promote the improvement of the natives and the incorporation of the families of the Missionaries with them'. The LMS had shifted their ideal of racial and cultural integration down a generation, but ultimately continued to espouse the benefits of a racially mixed, but culturally homogenous society. As something of an afterthought it was proposed,

> That in those cases in which the Missionaries cannot settle their children in the islands and are thereby compelled to send them away, if they have friends in England or the Colony who would guarantee the guardianship

> of such children, without subjecting the Society to the responsibility or expense of providing for them – that the Society [would] furnish a small premium for their apprenticeship to some useful business, or grant a reasonable allowance for a limited period while the said children may be qualifying for a situation, in which they may provide for themselves.[66]

It was further resolved that £50 would be made available to those children sent home for apprenticeship, so long as the missionaries themselves paid for their passage home, the guardianship of that child be secured unto friends and/or relatives, that a report must accompany them from the majority of the missionaries at their station supporting the measure, and that no further monies whatsoever be requested or required of the Directors once the original £50 had been allocated. It is worth noting that in the financial context of the 1820s, during which decade the LMS were making frequent emergency appeals for funds, this was a generous allowance, even if it denoted the absolute limit of what the Directors were willing to invest. In the face of an internal financial crisis, however, the Board did affirm their primary wish for generational permanence, 'the missionaries be[ing] requested to exercise all the caution and prudence in their power in determining those cases which will require the aid of the Directors, and only to resort to the measure of removing the children to this country when it appears to be dictated by unavoidable necessity'.[67]

The Directors thereby expressed their hopes that the SSM would become a settlement of missionary families, expanding across the generations, mixing with the indigenous peoples, and creating that utopian and self-sufficiently integrated mission that they had hoped for from the beginning. While they were willing to allow some missionary sons to return to England, if absolutely necessary, on the whole, they pledged their support to a Christian settler community and an embodiment of 'commerce, Christianity and civilisation'. They promised that if the missionaries could formulate a practical plan to that end, they would 'do every thing in their power to enable them to carry it into effect'.[68] Meanwhile, they categorically denied any responsibility for the *guardianship* of missionary children, an issue that would return with some force during the Mills controversy in the 1840s.

The Directors wrote to the SSM on 10 January 1829 with a full exposition of the Resolutions thereby enacted.

> Whether we consult our own feelings towards you, or regard the subject as intimately connected with the welfare of the Mission itself, we cannot but feel an earnest desire to do all in our power to relieve you from anxiety on so tender a peril as the future condition of your children; so far as may comport with the nature and object of the undertaking in which you are engaged, and the means of the Society.

'In contemplating such dissemination of Christianity in the islands and such advancement in civilisation, the Directors could not but look to the rising and extending families of the missionaries', they continued.

> This natural and, as it appears to us, just expectation (which we could not doubt was also that of the Missionaries themselves) would of course lead us to cherish the hope, that the brethren would, in bringing up their families, constantly keep in view, the great importance of imparting to their children ... those kinds of instruction and training and habits which would ... qualify them for obtaining a maintenance or effecting a settled and permanent residence in the islands; and also assist in perpetuating and extending the benefit of religion and civilisation among the natives, with several capacities and situations to which the natural turn and talents of their children, or other circumstances, might direct.

The Directors ended their epistle with a gentle, but determined rebuke that 'the subject has not excited all the attention its importance demands' and once again reaffirmed the importance of considered reflection in taking up the offer of sending some few children home. The missionaries were reminded that those last resolutions:

> were adopted to meet special cases only, and by no means as the opening of a door for the removal of children of the mission families from the islands, where it is conceived ... they may be rendered, in a highly important respect, conducive to the formation and cementing and perpetuating of an improved state of civil society.[69]

The Resolutions of 1828 can be seen, in much the same way as the 1818 Resolutions, as a manifesto for mission families. They expounded the extent and limits of LMS responsibility for missionary children, yet at the same time made it clear that those children were to be incorporated into the missionary enterprise. The Directors were willing to take some limited steps to ensure that they remained in the regions of their birth, and through their lives and examples continued the work of their parents. Becoming a missionary was a contract of service that expanded horizontally across the missionary couple, and vertically down the generations.

Crook, as we have seen, had little patience with the Directors' plans. On the suggestion that his daughters become settlers on the islands, he replied with a mixture of exasperation and anger that 'the experiment has been fully tried by three married men ... Now if men who have traversed the ocean in every direction cannot succeed, how are such girls as ours to succeed as settlers'. The Resolutions seemed also to display a complete ignorance of the racial and cultural tensions on the islands. 'As to identifying themselves with the natives or making rope and canvas, there are things that cannot be mentioned here without exciting the most unpleasant feeling'.[70] The brethren in general were rather more considered in their reaction. They expressed their 'sincere thanks to the Directors for the great concern they have manifested for the future welfare of our children' and resolved to 'make the subject of the future settlement of the Children a matter of the most serious consideration'.[71]

Personal feelings continued to run high, however. Thomas Blossom (1821–44) noted that he thought 'the wishes of the Directors respecting a settlement might be accomplished' but that he was 'sorry to say, the greater part of the Brethren thought it impracticable'. 'But if something of the kind cannot be accomplished, and the present plan of transporting the Lads to Botany Bay, or any where else, And having the Girls on the Islands; Does not prove to be the ruin of all their families I am much mistaken; For take my word for it, if they cannot get White husbands, They will have Black ones, In spite of all they can do to prevent it.'[72] Indeed, the SSM as a whole ultimately concurred with Crook that the plan was utterly impracticable. Asserting their parental autonomy they concluded that, 'it will be best for each *Parent* to provide for his own children availing himself of the assistance kindly offered by the Directors as circumstances may require … It is a most trying thing to each Missionary to think of the future prospects of their families in these island[s].'[73]

By the 1830s then, a rather uneasy stalemate existed between the missionaries and the Board in London. Things were by no means resolved, and without the financial means to really secure the futures of their children, individual missionaries continued to fret and worry. The 1828 Resolutions highlighted a fundamental mismatch of ideas between the Directors and their missionaries in the field. For the latter, as expressed in George Barker's letter from South Africa in 1825, and in William Crook's letter from the South Seas in 1828, there seemed to be only one possible solution. '*I must beg of the Directors to furnish me and my family with a passage home, that my children may enjoy the privilege of British education and be trained up in British Society* [original emphasis]', pleaded Barker.[74] The Crooks, as we have seen, left the mission in disgust. Meanwhile, the LMS envisaged a generational mission based on a Christian settler community and a permanent establishment of missionary families. The two opinions could not have been more inimical to one another. As with the Widows and Orphans Fund in the 1820s, it was the missionary public who forced the issue, and broke the stalemate, ultimately introducing fiscal and practical provisions for missionary families that the LMS had been unable and unwilling to provide.

The mission schools in London

In the early 1830s, the provision for missionary children was clearly unsatisfactory. Such children had no prospects and little education. Unless their parents were stationed in the South Seas they had no educational establishment to attend, and while some could be shipped home to Britain for apprenticeships, grudgingly at the expense of the Society, most missionary parents could not afford British school fees. Nor, after a decade or more in a foreign clime, did they know where would be the best place to send their (often) under-educated offspring, and the problem loomed of what to do with the children during the school holidays, particularly 'when near relations of the absent missionary had died, or they were unable to take charge of his children, and but few friends would or could burden themselves with the responsibility of the little strangers'.[75]

Throughout the 1820s the LMS came up against a rising tide of opinion within the missionary field that children should be sent 'home' for their education. The South Seas Academy was an evident failure, with a number of students transgressing sexual and behavioural norms, despite the best efforts of the superintendent.[76] In other regions missionaries had to choose from a mixed bag of secular or religious schools with unknown reputations, and thus unforeseeable consequences. While the LMS tried desperately to interest its missionaries in schemes for the useful education and occupation of missionary children *in situ*, missionaries met these proposals with indifference at best. Increasingly, they wished to entirely remove their children from the sites of contamination, relieving their minds of anxiety even if at the same time filling their hearts with the pain of separation. While the LMS tried valiantly to ignore this trend, ultimately it was not one which could be brushed aside.

By the late 1820s talk in the SSM was of removing the Academy to New South Wales, where children would be extricated more effectively from corrupting influences, and where there was more potential for useful occupation once education had been completed. As early as 1826 the mission was a-buzz with news of Dr John Dunmore Lang's school in the Colony, which had been proposed to educate young evangelical men who wished to be schoolmasters, ministers or missionaries. While Dr Lang's establishment never materialised, the idea of educating the missionary children in the Colony had been planted in the minds of the younger missionaries in particular, who began to discuss the removal of the SSA to that more appropriate location While they 'who have increasing families' would prefer that the Institution be removed, the older brethren 'would *now* prefer keeping their children, to sending them to any place from under their own eye as their families are on an average too far advanced in years to benefit much by the contemplated change'.[77] As such the issue fed and reflected a broader generational tension that marked the SSM out in these years.[78] More generally this discussion flowed into a much larger debate on the issue of the total removal of missionary children from the regions of their birth. Increasingly, this was seen as the most appropriate option for their education. The notion of sending children 'home' to Britain had been a consistent undercurrent in all the debates surrounding the establishment of regional schools, and one which the Directors had attempted to forestall through their own mechanisms of familial permanence. In response to the Madras District Committee's plan for the Indian school in 1827, two of the five respondents had noted that an English education would be far preferable. The proposed school was, after all, 'still [in] an Indian climate' and 'Whatever the advantages might be, they could not be equal to an English Education, and the climate of England. Therefore if we must send our children away, we would rather send them to England'.[79] The climatic and moral conditions in India, as well as the example of the Anglo-Indian community, made the missionaries there early proponents of sending children home. In due course their voices would be echoed by their brethren across the globe.

Nonetheless, the Directors remained firm, adhering with vehemence to the relevant passage in the 1818 Resolutions that

> the Directors, in addition to the Duties they have to fulfil, cannot take upon them the guardianship of the children of missionaries whose Parents or Parent may be desirous of sending them to England for education and therefore can give no countenance to the sending of their children for that purpose unless they have relations in England to take that charge entirely upon themselves. Nor will the duty which they owe to the Secretary in the application of its funds allow them to incur the heavy expenses which such a practice would occasion.[80]

But the calls of the mission community were difficult to appease. As with the Widows and Orphans Fund of 1824, it was through the involvement of the missionary public that a compromise was ultimately formed. In July 1837 a notice was placed in the *Evangelical Magazine* proposing the establishment of a school for missionary children in Britain:

> In an age of growing and enlightened Christian benevolence, like the present, I am not surprised to find that the impression has become very general, and it will prove, I doubt not, equally permanent, that some more specific and systematic efforts are demanded to secure *an appropriate and liberal education of the children of missionaries* [original emphasis].[81]

Such an establishment needed to be 'specifically adapted for the peculiar circumstances of the case',[82] and not only must its cost meet the means of missionary parents, who 'are understood to receive from the Society no more than is absolutely necessary for their own support',[83] but it also needed to be more than an educative establishment, in fact a home away from home: the 'great desideratum is a home for the Missionaries' offspring, and such a home as would give entire confidence to the minds of the anxious and far-distant parent'.[84] Such an institution should 'take the entire care of the children, including board, clothing, and education'.[85] This would 'render the institution, so far as practicable, the "parents' substitute" ... It is wished that the establishment should assume an entirely parental character; that it should be the home of the children while under its care, providing for all their personal wants, caring for their health, and regarding, with a watchful eye, their individual characters.'[86] Its ultimate purpose was to be generational vocational replication: the 'education, embracing what is manual, as well as mental and religious, should be specifically directed with a view to ultimate foreign service'.[87]

'The Institution for the Education of the Daughters of Missionaries, at Walthamstow' (later Walthamstow Hall, in Sevenoaks, Kent) was founded through private philanthropy in November 1838.[88] 'A large number of ministers and other friends met on the occasion, and were much gratified by the highly encouraging aspect of this new and important object of Christian benevolence'.[89] The school opened with eight students, and the number quickly grew so that by December 1840, with thirty students in hand, the school was forced to appeal for funds to build a new wing, in order that it might accommodate fifty.[90] By January 1841 they had raised £200, by February £300, by April £400 and by August, with £508 having been raised (though £260 still required), the school was re-opened with twenty-eight students (two having completed their studies), and eight more on their way 'from the East'.[91]

Even before the Girls' School was opened there were calls for a boys' school to follow. 'That such an establishment would be hailed with feelings of grateful delight by missionaries in every part of the world, I think there can be no doubt', wrote John Williams, 'and this feeling would be greatly enhanced if it embraced a department for the sons also'.[92] This call was echoed at the Second Annual Meeting of Walthamstow Hall in 1841. 'A strong feeling was manifested at the meeting, in favour of a similar institution for the sons of missionaries, or a department of the same institution, on a separate establishment', and an appeal was made that if enough interest was provoked on its behalf, such an institution would be opened.[93] In July, 1841 Samuel

Dyer (missionary in Asia, 1804–43) pressed the issue further, writing in the *Evangelical Magazine* to express his thanks for the school now opened, and his hopes for an additional institution.

> I think I may venture to express on behalf of my brethren and myself our gratitude for the institution at Walthamstow. It meets the case exactly, and if we must be separated from the little objects of our affection, if we cannot longer enjoy their fond caresses, if we cannot pronounce over them from day to day the morning and evening benediction, we feel that we can with the fullest confidence commend them to the care of our friends at Walthamstow.

'If we could have a similar institution for our boys it would indeed relieve our anxiety on their behalf'.[94] The boy's school (later Eltham College) was opened, also at Walthamstow, on 22 February 1842.

The boys' school was not a success, however, failing to capture the imagination of the philanthropic public. By 1846 it had been unable to clear the original debt incurred in its foundation, and found itself having to launch an emergency appeal for funds.

> In the present state of the school ... additional pupils cannot be received. The house is quite full. The demands already made upon the institution have so far exceeded its resources, that the funds, which were never adequate, are more than exhausted ... Extension is, therefore, impossible. Under these circumstances the managers are compelled to make an immediate and earnest appeal to the friends of mission, entreating assistance.[95]

While the girls' school had successfully raised over £500 in 1840, the appeal of the boys' school was not a success, leading Jonathan Morison, one of the school's directors, to express his 'surprise and grief, that the kindred institution for the sons of missionaries, though equally needed and equally deserving of public confidence, has not met with the amount of patronage to which it is fairly and honourably entitled'. Morison was left pondering whether 'the sons of missionaries [have] a less substantial claim upon the churches of Christ then their daughters',[96] and with £900 of debt still outstanding, the school was forced to close, its students dispersed to various suitable schools in and around London.[97]

While the boys' school ultimately reopened in 1852, having finally been able to raise the necessary funds,[98] the relative success of the two schools reflected the gendered nature of philanthropy in the mid-nineteenth century, and the particular difficulties facing missionaries in disposing of their daughters.[99] Though the institution that had been proposed in 1837 was to be for both sexes, it was the girls' school which opened first, due in no small part to the initiative of its founder, Dorothea Foulger, and the gendered nature of the charitable philanthropy on which it relied. Foulger was very familiar with the real plights of missionary parents, having lived many years (with her merchant husband) in the Cape, and having been part of a vibrant evangelical circle there. During their time in South Africa, the Foulgers had had extensive contact with the South African missionaries, and knew well their difficulties in disposing of their children, and particularly their daughters.[100]

Upon the Foulgers' return to London, too, Dorothea ran her home as the centre of an evangelical network for missionaries returning or visiting from the field. As such she was well placed to understand missionaries' anxieties about their daughters in particular, and how to secure their temporal, material and spiritual prosperity. It was her persistent initiative that led to the founding of Walthamstow Hall, and thus provision for missionary daughters that would not exist for their sons until four years later.

The creation of Walthamstow Hall also adhered to a conception of woman's work and female public and private philanthropy, particularly in the middle-class and evangelical sphere.[101] That the school was founded was due to the efforts of 'several excellent and influential ladies' who campaigned for funds and recognition on behalf of the institution.[102] Public female philanthropic action was often directed at women, a way of maintaining respectability and notions of separate spheres and woman's work for those ladies thereby active in the public, and so-called male, sphere. Female education was also very much in the air at this time, with Cheltenham College being founded just two years later, in 1840. So-called 'formal' secondary and higher education for women was still in its infancy, the North London Collegiate School was opened in 1850 and the Camden School for Girls in 1871. Meanwhile, at university level Bedford College (University of London) was founded in 1849, Girton College (Cambridge) was founded in 1869 and Newnham College (Cambridge) in 1871.[103] On a more practical level, it was noted in October 1837 that the school for the sons of ministers and missionaries in Silcoates, Yorkshire, already offered an education for missionary sons, at the rate of £15 per annum,[104] but there was no such provision for missionary daughters. Within this climate of gendered philanthropy, and an increasingly competitive philanthropic marketplace, the girls' school would always have a higher claim on the charitable public, when 'even the most liberal should sometimes be tempted to grow weary in well-doing'.[105]

Despite these ups and downs, both mission schools were ultimately a great success (and survive to this day). Their foundation was, in some literal sense, a godsend to the LMS. Their establishment seemed (at first) to completely neutralise the difficulties arising between London and the field over the issue of juvenile repatriation, and at no extra cost to the Society itself. The schools were run entirely as charitable institutions, with missionary parents paying half the costs (of education and board), and the other half being raised by subscriptions and donations from the missionary and philanthropic public. Nonetheless, in their foundation, the schools had not had an easy relationship with the Board of Directors, who were perhaps wary of what financial contribution they may be expected to make. As L. E. Lauer has noted in Foulger's entry in the *Oxford Dictionary of National Biography*, in

> April 1838 she pressed the home secretary of the London Missionary Society, John Arundel, for an opinion about the feasibility of opening such a school. When Arundel replied that the society thought it better to educate girls at existing schools (at reduced rates to the society), Mrs Foulger and her committee politely ignored him.[106]

Nonetheless, the LMS soon embraced these institutions which would so relieve them of both anxiety and expense. In April 1838 it was decided that the Society would systematically send their missionaries' daughters to Walthamstow Hall, and missionary sons were also soon systematically dispatched to their equivalent. Despite the fact that these institutions quite self-consciously flew in the face of the LMS's plans for permanent establishment,[107] the Board members were happy to embrace them and lend their 'decided encouragement' to the scheme.[108]

What neither the LMS, nor the schools anticipated was the response from missionaries in the field. While many of them welcomed the aid of these charitable institutions, concerns soon surfaced concerning parental autonomy, authority and care. In their very foundation, the schools at Walthamstow had been designed to be more than educative establishments. Missionary parents needed to be assured that their children would receive the type of care they could provide: emotional and physical. Yet in so doing the schools trod an emotive line between benevolent parental proxy, and seeming to deny missionary parents their autonomy and importance. Missionaries felt strongly that their parental independence should not be eroded as a result of the practicalities of their domestic situation.

John Orsmond, on sending four of his daughters to the new school for missionary daughters in 1843, wrote with caution, but confidence in the judgement of his employers. 'To a public education I am no friend, but to such a school, under such managers, with such Tutors I readily entrust my children.'[109] But reports of the reception of William and Lillias Mills in 1847 soon reverberated around the SSM, feeding into emerging fears about how well the missionary children would be cared for in Britain, how far the missionaries could trust the educative choice of the Directors, and to what extent parents could still exert their autonomous authority in the face of their fiscal impotence.

The Mills's arrival, with six (though reported to be twenty) missionary children (as described in Chapter 2) coincided with the fiscal crisis in the boys' school mentioned above. This was a tender moment for missionaries who had just dispatched their children into the care of the Board for the first time, and the Directors' response did nothing to diffuse an already tense situation. Disturbed that this apparent godsend (i.e. the charitable schools) was now directly contravening the principle of non-devolvable parental responsibility (not to mention incurring unforeseen cost, with £15 per child per annum being promised to missionary parents for their education in 1848),[110] members of the Board lashed out in exasperation at William and Lillias Mills. 'I wonder', the Chairman observed, 'that the Missionaries should send their children to us, and that they cannot themselves educate their children.' Lillias Mills

> understood the language to mean, as plain as language could mean, that the Missionary in sending home his children, had no other object than to cast his cares on others. If the Chairman implied that we ought to train up our children in the Islands – I say, with the examples we have at other groups, God forbid that we should.[111]

It was not long before news of the 'unlovely spirit and unkind remarks'[112] of the Directors had raged across the Samoan mission.[113] 'The conduct of some members of the Board on that occasion appears to have been the reverse of which might have been expected under the circumstances from Christian men', remarked Samoan missionary Archibald Murray.[114] The official response of the mission was no less wounded.

> We are much surprised and deeply grieved that the reception of Mr and Mrs M[ills] by the Directors, as well as subsequent procedure towards them and the children was such as to produce on their minds the painful impression that they, but especially our beloved children, were far from being welcome to the Directors … The greatest trial of our missionary life is separation from our children, and unless arrangements are made more satisfactory than now exist to secure careful and affectionate attention to these dear objects of our solicitude on their arrival in England, and during their educational years it will be impossible for us to part with them.[115]

The Directors soon had a serious problem on their hands. The missionaries in the South Seas began to argue that if the Directors could not be trusted to care for their children, and to promote their moral and practical education as well as their emotional and physical well-being, then they should themselves be furnished with the means to secure a British education for their children (particularly relevant at a time during which the boys were being dispersed across London). The Mills controversy had eroded the missionaries' trust in the Board, and consequently in the schools that the Board chose for their children. Arguing from their rights as parents, they sought to re-establish their own autonomy by using the £15 per annum allowed for the education of their children to choose their own schools (and guardians).

> We are still willing and still earnestly desirous to consecrate every moment of our time, – to spend and be spent in the service of Christ among the heathen, and while this is the case we think that it is unquestionably the duty of the Directors to relieve our minds on this point either by receiving our children on their arrival in England into an Institution in which we can all have *the utmost confidence* [original emphasis], or furnish us individually with the means of paying for their board and education under the care of some other parties we may see fit to select.[116]

The missionaries had (in particular) lost faith in the Directors' guardianship, as a direct result of the Mills controversy:

> could they but enter into our feelings every day as we attempt to anticipate their future life, it may be as missionary orphans – I think they would feel it impossible to talk as they did respecting being 'Grandfathers to all these children' – It was the cause of much suffering to many parents['] hearts when we heard of these things – We ask not *such* to be either Grandfathers or Guardians to them – We commit them to those who have their speech under the control of the law of kindness and in whose heart the love of Christ reigns.[117]

The issue crystallised over missionary demands that they be allowed to send their children to schools near close family or friends, people more personally connected with the moral, physical and emotional well-being of their children, and who would respect the authority of the parent in decisions relating to their children's mental and spiritual growth. 'Were we to send our children to the mission schools, we have no relative or special friends in the neighbourhood whom we could ask to act as guardians to the dear little ones while thus far away', wrote South Seas missionary Henry Nisbet.[118] 'To send them in such circumstances we think very undesirable unless obliged to submit to it as a matter of dire necessity!'[119]

Missionary reticence about the mission schools in England also reflected a concern that by their very nature they 'neutralised to a considerable extent one great object which we have in view in parting with our children, viz that they should be associated with children who have been brought up in civilised life'.[120] Missionary parents worried that the mission schools were 'collecting too many children from heathen lands, without them having the advantages of mixing with other society'.[121] Yet at the same time, it was considered 'a settled question that these islands are not in a condition to enable us to train up our children here'.[122]

As has been clear throughout this chapter, missionary parents were divided in their own minds between wanting their children to be removed from regions of moral and physical contamination, and suffering the emotional consequences of separation. The South Seas missionaries in the 1840s and 1850s sought to accommodate this internal disquiet by reasserting their rights as parents, and reaffirming their autonomous parental authority.[123] There needed to be a 'plan which appears to offer the greatest advantages to our children and enable us without over-anxiety to pursue our work at our appointed stations'.[124] For the South Seas missionaries such a plan had to involve financial support for parental choice.

> there are some cases where brethren strongly prefer committing their children to the care of private friends in England or the Colonies, – and we further beg that the Directors will meet their wishes as well, and allow them to draw per annum for each child a sum not less than Twenty pounds, to cover the expense of board and education, and that they too have the privilege of drawing that sum for their children under the care of private friends annually, for a term of not less than six years, provided that during that time, the children are strictly under instruction.[125]

While they sought to re-establish missionary trust in the Board, the Directors did little to alleviate parental anxiety. Having already been forced by circumstance to allow £15 per annum for the education of each child between the ages of 7 and 14 (a cumulatively massive investment for the LMS at a time when missionary families across the globe averaged four living children),[126] they absolutely refused to countenance raising the allowance, extending the tenure of education, or allowing missionary parents the level of control they had demanded. Missionaries would only receive the allowance if their children attended the (charitably subsidised) mission schools in London.

With the LMS hierarchy in London seemingly unmoved by their demands, the South Seas missionaries again drew the Board's attention to the potentially damaging consequences of refusing their requests. Noting the potential of missionary children to bring 'disgrace on the Missionaries generally',[127] and stressing the obstacles to efficiency being placed in their path, they began to threaten withdrawal from the mission itself.

> If the Directors knew but the half we could tell them of the wreck and ruin of neglected mission families, – neglect occasioned, to a great extent, by the inadequate provisions made for their education, – and if they knew by half of the anxiety which we have while this question is either unsettled, or settled in an unsatisfactory manner, we think they would not allow so many years to pass without setting our minds entirely at rest on the question, and enabling us to go on with our work without this harassing hindrance.[128]

South Seas missionary George Turner expressed a wish to 'be enabled to go on with my duties without these embarrassing hindrances',[129] while Nisbet reminded the Directors that 'you are as much convinced as I am of the importance of a minister or missionary having his mind as free as possible from corroding care, so that he may be able to devote his undivided energies to his peculiar work'.[130] The SSM's official response made the situation clear. 'The consequences [of being unable to repatriate their children] are obvious, and will be painful to us as well as to the Directors, but we do not think that for these we shall be responsible.'[131] The worst nightmares of those early LMS Directors, that missionaries could not be both effective ministers and fathers, were finally coming true.

Conclusion

Despite these threats, however, the Directors remained unmoved. The allowance for the education of missionary children remained at £15 per annum (the cost to missionaries of their children's attendance at the mission schools). While the missionaries had failed to exert their complete parental authority the LMS had nonetheless been forced to financially invest in the education, and repatriation (costing £25 per child),[132] of missionary children. An uneasy equilibrium eventually returned to the SSM, with most parents deciding to send their children to the appointed schools in London. The 1840s and 1850s had marked the end-point of two decades' worth of negotiation and debate about the terms of missionary families' existence in the field. Flying in the face of permanent establishment and incorporated labour, missionary parents refused to consign their children's spiritual, moral and physical condition to the temporal realities of their vocational choice.

> while the Christian Missionary feels constrained by the love of Christ to go forth and dwell among the heathen, expatriating himself from his native land, it does not necessarily follow that he is required to expatriate also his offspring. This should be as voluntary an act on their part as on his.[133]

The Mills controversy once again marks a watershed in familial ascendancy, however. Just as Mrs Mills had severely troubled LMS expectations of her professional agency, so too were they troubled by the fiscal, material and practical consequence of missionaries having families. The years of familial ascendancy had been continually fraught with difficult tensions within the enterprise, and often bitter and emotive arguments between the missionaries and London. By the 1840s it was clear that the LMS would have to incur the financial costs of juvenile repatriation, despite their best efforts to avoid it. At the same time, family structures in the field, disrupted by separation, problematised the notion of the normative Christian household, upon which the civilising mission had come to depend. The single female missionary became an antidote to all these problems, as well as the means of extending mission into the increasingly prized female sphere. Cheap, professional and single-minded, lady missionaries embodied everything the LMS had desired from its pious mechanics, and more. The exact dynamics of the changeover between missionary families and the lady missionary must remain the content of another project, but her ascendancy, and the ideological 'feminisation' of the mission endeavour, cannot be fully understood without understanding how her presence solved so many of the internal contradictions and tensions in the missionary family.[134]

The 1820s–1840s were years of ultimate consolidation for the missionary family, despite deep institutional questioning. The 1818 and 1828 Resolutions, the founding of the Widows and Orphans Fund in 1824, and the grudging acceptance and facilitation of the mission schools in the 1840s, had all incorporated the mission family into the enterprise despite continued institutional ambivalence. Once the LMS had accepted that missionaries would have white wives, whatever policies they attempted to institute to the contrary, it naturally followed that some kind of official provision would have to be made for their children. Their bi-cultural identity, worrying propensity for misbehaviour, and potential to undermine the mission from within, meant that they were an element of the missionary enterprise which could not be ignored. At the same time, they had the potential to form a fundamental aspect of mission, and could be effectively integrated into a mission theory based upon the precepts of 'Christianity, commerce and civilisation'. By the late 1820s the LMS had absolutely come around to this way of thinking, and had decided that mission had the potential to be both generational and once again self-sustaining. Missionary children, upon intermarrying, could settle in the regions of their birth, creating thereby a permanent establishment of evangelically- and missionary-minded families who, by both their nature and their active engagement with a notion of mission based on domestic normativity, could ultimately achieve that object so desired by all mid-nineteenth century missionary societies: a self-sufficient, self-sustaining and self-propagating mission.

Missionary parents, we have now seen, had other ideas. Wracked with anxiety and concern about the moral, physical and spiritual welfare of their offspring, they continually looked to the Directors in London to invest in the futures of their children. Aware of the potential for both harm and good within their children, missionaries began to judge that the LMS had a moral (and temporal) responsibility towards the next generation, and were willing to compromise the basic tenets of their vocation in order to secure their future well-being. At times, this meant engaging in open conflict with the Directors, even threatening the abdication of their vocation if their demands were not met. They expected the institution that sustained them to implement mechanisms of investment into their children, and anachronistically expected an institution to involve itself in the intimacies of family life. At the same time, however, they jealously guarded their autonomous parental authority, even as it was continually undermined by their fiscal impotence.

Neither the dream of permanent settlement, nor of parental autonomy would be fulfilled within the missionary enterprise. Rather, an uneasy compromise was reached, mediated by the missionary and evangelically philanthropic public. Thus it was that the most powerful recurring motif of the missionary experience came into being: the sending 'home' of missionary children to be educated in Britain. Persistently regarded as an absolute necessity in the missionary enterprise, it was a process of juvenile repatriation that provoked intense emotional suffering among missionary parents (and children), and yet remained an integral part of the nineteenth-century mission experience. This was one of the many contradictions embedded within the enterprise when it came to families, marriage and parenting. It is to the latter of these, missionary parenting, that we now turn.

Notes

1 'Biographical Sketch of the Life and Labours of the Late Rev. William Pascoe Crook', *The Melbourne Argus*, 14 August 1846, p. 6.

2 Ibid., p. 8.

3 Crook to London, 1 May 1829, South Seas Incoming Letter (hereafter SSIL) 7/2/C.

4 Ibid., 28 December 1827, SSIL 6/3/D.

5 Ibid., 24 January 1828, SSIL 6/5/A.

6 Ibid.

7 London to Crook, 23 September 1828, Western Outgoing Letters: South Seas (hereafter WOL:SS) Box 1.

8 Ibid.
9 Crook to London, 1 May 1829, SSIL 7/2/C.
10 John Orsmond to London, 1 January 1829, SSIL 7/1/A.
11 See Crook to London, 1 January 1830, SSIL 7/5/A and 23 October 1830, SSIL 7/6/D.
12 LMS Board Minutes (hereafter BM), 27 October 1828, p. 396.
13 BM, 27 October 1828, pp. 396–7.
14 Crook to London 24 January 1828, SSIL 6/5/A
15 James Hayward's Answers to Queries, 1819, SSIL 3A/1/B.
16 BM, 20 November 1820, pp. 134–5.
17 BM, 15 January 1821, pp. 188–93.
18 Ibid., pp. 192–3.
19 This idea is developed in Chapter 6 (pp. 162–4).
20 William Loveless to London, 30 June 1821, South India (Tamil) Incoming Letters (hereafter SI(T)IL) 1/3/A.
21 Ibid.
22 John Philip to London, 14 April 1822, SAIL 8B/4/C.
23 Daniel Tyerman and George Bennet, *Journal of Voyages and Travels by the Rev Daniel Tyerman and George Bennet, Esq, deputed from the London Missionary Society to visit their various stations in the South Sea Islands, China, India etc. between the years 1821 and 1829 compiled from original documents by James Montgomery*, vol I (London, 1831), pp. vi–vii. See also Neil Gunson, *Messengers of Grace: evangelical missionaries in the South Seas, 1799–1860* (Melbourne and Oxford: Oxford University Press, 1978), pp. 123–4 and Tom Hiney, *On the Missionary Trail: the classic Georgian adventure of two Englishman, sent on a journey around the world, 1821–1829* (London: Vintage, 2001).
24 Deputation to London, 11 February 1824, Home Odds Box 10.
25 Charles Barff and George Platt to London, 21 April 1834, SSIL 9/5/B.
26 George Bennet to London, 21 May 1824, Home Odds Box 10.
27 Tyerman to Orsmond, 18 November 1823, Home Odds Box 10.
28 Ibid.
29 SSM to the Deputation, 12 November 1823, Home Odds Box 10.
30 Tyerman to Orsmond, 18 November 1823, Home Odds Box 10.
31 Hayward to London, 16 August 1822, SSIL 3B/8/A.
32 Ibid.
33 Crook to London, 4 December 1824, SSIL 3B/5/B.
34 Bennet to Orsmond, 14 November 1823, Home Odds Box 10.
35 It is interesting to compare the treatment of missionary children and indigenous children. See Patricia Grimshaw, 'Faith, Missionary Life, and the Family', in Philippa Levine (ed.), *Gender and Empire* (Oxford: Oxford University Press, 2004), pp. 26–280, 272; Margaret Jolly, '"To Save the Girls for Brighter and Better Lives": Presbyterian Missions and Women in the South of Vanuatu, 1848–1870', *Journal of Pacific History* 26:1 (1991), 27–48; Deborah Gaitskell, 'Race, Gender and Imperialism: A Century of Black Girls' Education in South Africa', in J. A. Mangan (ed.), *Benefits Bestowed: education and British imperialism* (Manchester: Manchester University Press, 1988), pp. 150–73.
36 Elizabeth Buettner has discussed this in her *Empire Families: Britons and late imperial India* (Oxford: Oxford University Press, 2004); and 'Problematic spaces, problematic races: defining "Europeans" in late colonial India', *Women's History Review* 9:2 (2000), 277–98.
37 David Darling to London, 2 April 1825, SSIL 5A/2/A.
38 Ibid.
39 Tyerman to Orsmond, 17 March 1824, Home Odds Box 10.
40 London to Orsmond, 20 February 1827, WOL:SS Box 1.
41 Buettner, 'Problematic Spaces'.
42 Printed Plan for the School for Missionary Children, 1 November 1827, SI(T)IL 2/3/C.
43 Annual Report of the Madras District Committee, 30 June 1829, SI(T)IL 3/2/C.
44 BM, 20 July 1829, pp. 522–3.

45 BM, 16 November 1829, p .625.
46 Philip to London, 14 April 1822, SAIL 8B/4/C.
47 Ibid.
48 BM, 10 January 1825, p. 7.
49 BM, 20 June 1825, p. 138.
50 Ibid., pp. 138–41.
51 Foster to London, 19 June 1826, SAIL 10/1/C.
52 *Annual Report* (1831), p. 76.
53 London to Charles Wilson, 22 August 1825, WOL:SS Box 1.
54 Orsmond to London, 1827, SSIL 6/1/A.
55 Samuel Wilson to London, 4 August 1826, SSIL 5B/6/B.
56 Philip to London, 14 April 1822, SAIL 8B/4/C.
57 Barff and Platt to London, 21 April 1834, SSIL 9/5/B.
58 Barker to London, 4 August 1825, SAIL 8B/3/C.
59 Platt to London, 1 April 1829, SSIL 7/2/A.
60 SSA Students to London, 13 March 1828, SSIL 6/5/C.
61 BM, 18 May 1818, pp. 188–93.
62 Dr Lang, who planned to establish a Non-Conformist school in Sydney, had offered the missionaries two free places for their sons. The school did not in fact come off. See D. W. A. Baker, 'John Dunmore Lang', *Australian Dictionary of National Biography* and John Dunmore Lang, *An historical and statistical account of New South Wales* (London: Cochrane and M'Crone, 1834), Chapter XII.
63 SSA Students to London, 13 March 1828, SSIL 6/5/C and BM, 15 March 1830, pp. 693–4.
64 H. E. Maude 'Beachcombers and Castaways', *Journal of the Polynesian Society* LXXIII (1964), 254–93; James Wightman Davidson and Deryck Scarr (eds), *Pacific Islands Portraits* (Wellington, Auckland: A. H. & A. W. Reed, 1970); Jonathan Lamb, Vanessa Smith and Nicholas Thomas (eds), *Exploration and Exchange: a South Seas anthology, 1680–1900* (Chicago, London: Chicago University Press, 2000), pp. 117–273; Deryck Scarr, *A History of the Pacific Islands: passages through tropical time* (Richmond: Curzon, 2001), part four, pp. 87–126. See also Catherine Hall, 'Missionary Stories: gender and ethnicity in the 1830s and 1840s', in Catherine Hall, *White, Male and Middle Class: explorations in feminism and history* (Cambridge: Polity, 1992), pp. 205–55, pp. 211–14 in particular.
65 BM, 27 October and 24 November 1828, pp. 388–95.
66 Ibid.
67 BM, 8 December 1828, pp. 396–8.
68 BM, 24 November 1828, pp. 393–4.
69 London to SSM, 10 January 1829, WOL:SS Box 1.
70 Crook to London, 1 May 1829, SSIL 7/2/C.
71 SSM to London, 7 April 1831, SSIL 8/1/B.
72 Thomas Blossom to London, 25 April 1831, SSIL 8/1/C.
73 David Darling to London, 28 October 1831, SSIL 8/2/D.
74 Barker to London, 4 August 1825, SAIL 9/3/C. In fact, George Barker did not retire from the service of the LMS until 1856.
75 'An Appeal to the Pastors of our Churches on Behalf of the Institution for the Education of the Daughters of Missionaries', *Evangelical Magazine* (hereafter *EM*) (February, 1848), p. 94.
76 Chapter 6 (pp. 166–8).
77 Alexander Simpson to London, 10 November 1840, SSIL 13/2/D.
78 Gunson, *Messengers of Grace*, pp. 107–217.
79 Responses to the Plan, November 1827: M. J. Adam, 10 December 1827 and Robert Morrison, 14 June 1828, SI(T)IL 2/3/C.
80 BM, 18 May 1818, pp. 188–93.
81 'Education for the Children of Missionaries', *EM* (July 1837), p. 300.
82 'Institution for the Education of the Children of Missionaries', *EM* (December 1838), p. 599.

83 John Williams, 'Education of Missionaries' Children', *EM* (January 1838), p. 31.
84 'Institution for the Education of the Children of Missionaries', *EM* (December 1838), p. 599.
85 'Education of the Children of Missionaries', *EM* (July 1837), p. 300.
86 'Institution for the Education of the Children of Missionaries', *EM* (December 1838), p. 600.
87 'Education of the Children of Missionaries', *EM* (July 1837), p. 300.
88 'Institution for the Education of the Daughters of Missionaries', *EM* (Supplement, 1838), pp. 652–3.
89 Ibid., p. 653.
90 'Appeal to the Children of Christian Families in Great Britain', *EM* (December 1840), pp. 605–6.
91 'Mission School, Walthamstow', *EM* (January 1841); (February 1841); (April 1841); (August 1841).
92 John Williams, 'Education of Missionaries' Children', *EM* (January, 1838), p. 31.
93 'Second Annual Meeting of the Mission School at Walthamstow', *EM* (June, 1841), p. 294.
94 'Proposal for the Sons of Missionaries', *EM* (September 1841), p. 460.
95 'Missions Schools at Walthamstow, for the Sons of Missionaries', *EM* (June 1846), p. 320.
96 Ibid., pp. 319–20.
97 See 'Home and School for the Sons and Orphans of Missionaries', *EM* (April 1852), pp. 216–7.
98 Ibid.
99 See Elsie Pike, *The Story of Walthamstow Hall. A century of girls' education. Material collected by E. Pike and Constance E. Curryer* (London: Carey Press, 1938); and Clifford Witting, *The Glory of Sons. A history of Eltham College school for the sons of missionaries* (London: Board of Governors, Eltham College, 1952).
100 L. E. Lauer, 'Dorothea Foulger', *Oxford Dictionary of National Biography*.
101 F. K. Prochaska, *Women and Philanthropy in Nineteenth-century England* (Oxford: Clarendon Press, 1980); Mary Clare Martin, 'Women and philanthropy in Walthamstow and Leyton, 1740–1870', *London Journal*, 19/2 (1995), 119–50; Mary Clare (Hewlitt) Martin, 'Children and religion in Walthamstow and Leyton, 1740–1870', PhD Thesis (University of London, 1997).
102 John Williams, 'Education of Missionaries' Children', *EM* (January, 1838), p. 31.
103 On female education see Joan N. Burstyn, 'Women's Education in England during the nineteenth century: A review of the literature, 1970–1976', *History of Education* 6:1 (1977), 11–19; and Joyce Senders Pedersen, 'The Reform of Women's Secondary and Higher Education: Institutional Change and Social Values in Mid and Late Victorian England', *History of Education Quarterly* 19:1 (1979), 61–91.
104 'Education of Missionaries' Children', *EM* (October 1837), pp. 462–3.
105 'An Appeal to the Pastors of our Churches in Behalf of the Institution for the Education of the Daughters of Missionaries', *EM* (February, 1848), p. 93.
106 Lauer, 'Dorothea Foulger'.
107 See 'Institution for the Education of the Children of Missionaries', *EM* (December 1838), p. 600.
108 BM, 2 April 1838, pp. 417–18.
109 Orsmond to London, 15 February 1843, SSIL 16/1/A.
110 BM, 30 October 1848, p. 14.
111 William Mills to London, 16 July 1850, SSIL 23/5/C.
112 Archibald Murray to London, 9 June 1848, SSIL 21/4/D.
113 William Mills to London, 16 July 1850, SSIL 23/5/C.
114 Murray to London, 9 June 1848, SSIL 21/4/D.
115 George Stallworthy to London, 3 July 1848, SSIL 21/5/A.
116 Ibid.
117 William Harbutt to London, 7 August 1848, SSIL 21/5/A.
118 Henry Nisbet to London, 30 January 1854, SSIL 25/7/B.

119 Ibid.
120 Harbutt to London, 14 December 1854, SSIL 25/8/E.
121 William Mills to London, 20 November 1854, SSIL 25/8/E.
122 Nisbet to London, 30 January 1854, SSIL 25/7/B.
123 This reassertion of parental rights also took place in the context of scandals related to the SSA which surfaced in 1842. See Emily J. Manktelow, 'Rev. Simpson's "Improper Liberties": moral scrutiny and missionary children in the South Seas Mission', *Journal of Imperial and Commonwealth History* 40:2 (2012), 159–81; and Chapter 6, pp. 168–74.
124 Nisbet to London, 30 January 1854, SSIL 25/7/B.
125 Murray to London, 5 July 1851, SSIL 24A/5/B.
126 This figure comes from statistical work carried out with the LMS's Register of Missionary Children.
127 Charles Barff to London, 21 October 1843, SSIL 16/3/D.
128 Murray to London, 5 July 1851, SSIL 24A/5/B.
129 Turner to London, 1 October 1856, SSIL 26/7/E.
130 Nisbet to London, 17 July 1854, SSIL 25/7/E.
131 Stallworthy to London, 3 July 1848, SSIL 21/5/A.
132 BM, 30 October 1848, p. 12.
133 'Institution for the Education of the Children of Missionaries', *EM* (December 1838), p. 600.
134 Rhonda A. Semple, *Missionary Women: gender, professionalism and the late Victorian idea of Christian mission* (Woodbridge: Boydell, 2003).

CHAPTER FIVE

Missionary mothers and fathers

> No parent is able efficiently to attend to his family and the duties of the station too. The children will therefore have learned every thing that is vile before they come here ... Here is all to tempt and few if any barriers to gratification. It is therefore of the highest importance that the children be taken as soon as possible away from the gross absurdities of the peoples and from a sight of those base practices to which the younger part of the community are addicted.
> (South Seas missionary John Orsmond on the state of missionary parenting, and missionary children, 1826)

In Chapter 3 we saw how the personal and professional lives of male and female missionaries were structured around marriage, and if they were lucky, companionate marriage. Somewhat inevitably missionary marriage led to missionary children, and large missionary families were the norm for most of the nineteenth century. Children could be a source of great joy and happiness for missionary parents – be they playing with their home-made toys, engaging in precocious disquisitions on the nature of eternal life (for that story, you will have to read on), or acting as a source of consolation to a grieving heart (as in the case of George Barker). But they could also be a source of great anxiety and concern. Their spiritual and temporal lives had to be safeguarded from all the dangers of the missionary field – physical and moral – and missionary parents expended a great amount of time and energy on both aspects of their children's upbringing.

It is surprising then, that mission history has not been particularly good at engaging with the missionary as parent. Given that from the early nineteenth century the missionary couple, and thus the missionary family, became the building blocks of evangelical mission – serving not only as a base from which missionaries undertook their work, but as an integral part of the spiritual and civilising mission itself – it would seem that we, as historians of Christian mission, have been remiss in not giving them more of our attention. This chapter explores the dynamics of parenting in the missionary context, and how missionaries conceptualised and understood their role as parents. Chapter 6 considers missionary children themselves. Male and female missionaries on the spiritual frontier had to deal with the all the difficulties and delights of parenthood in a state of perceived racial and cultural isolation, often as a family alone in a sea of foreign, if not hostile, people. At the same time, where missionaries could have tapped a pool of communal indigenous support in the raising of children they usually did not, fearing above all else their offspring's cultural contamination in bi-cultural contexts. Even children's access to servants, converts, and other children, was tightly circumscribed and monitored. Parental anxiety was a constant undercurrent to missionary activity.

While the complementarity of missionary parenting ultimately defies neatly gendered encapsulations, meanwhile, this chapter puts forward the argument that there developed in mission practice a broadly gendered understanding of missionary parenting. While mothers were more concerned with the day-to-day practicalities of life, fathers fretted about their children's long-term spiritual and economic prospects. Or, to put this another way, mothers and fathers found it easiest to express their anxieties and concerns within gendered paradigms of both parenthood and work. Both of these parental priorities emanated from the gendered nature of vocational concerns and thus the self-imposed limits of expression imposed upon them by total personal and professional immersion in the vocational context. What this amounted to was complementary parenting, and a gendered division of worry which ultimately impacted upon every aspect of mission family life.

Yet, at the same time as parenting was cooperative (an argument which pays particular attention to male missionaries as fathers, arguing against an assumption that their identities were primarily professionally and spiritually defined), it was also another important site at which the fractures in mission familiarity became evident. One of the most common mission-family experiences was separation occasioned by juvenile repatriation: that is, sending children 'home' (to Britain) to be schooled. Missionary parents dealt with this separation in a variety of ways, but most especially by creating a metaphorically and theologically defined shared space, through detailed letter writing (which continued to orient missionary children in the places, people and experiences of the mission community), and coordinated prayer, which sought to heal temporal ruptures through eternal and transcendental communion. Separation from their children was 'the greatest trial of ... missionary life'; yet one deemed absolutely necessary by the racial, cultural and moral context of the mission field.

For if broken families caused missionaries emotional pain and distress, having one's children with one in the field could be equally trying. Normative domesticity meant that juvenile actions took on added importance to mission communities constantly subject to indigenous scrutiny. The local people were by no means a passive backdrop to missionary action, but rather interacted with mission in a variety of ways. This was, of course, the very point of evangelical mission, but became a particular problem for missionaries when they became parents. Missionary parenting was subject to a form of communal scrutiny that was embedded within the theory and practice of mission. Perhaps the biggest fracture in the missionary experience – between evangelical universalism on the one hand, and mission racism on the other – was often structured around missionaries' reaction to the presence of their children in 'contaminating' contexts, and the subsequent need to segregate their offspring from the local people, particularly when even 'the indiscreet and excessive kindness of the *converted* natives' could be a danger.[1] Parenting came, unexpectedly, to be at the heart of the missionary encounter – dictating and reflecting evangelical missionaries' reactions to physical, cultural and moral difference on the spiritual frontier.

Pregnancy and birth

Before a missionary couple could become a family, the trauma, pain and joy of childbirth had to be endured. It was during pregnancy and birth that missionaries stood on the brink between spouse and parent, and during which male missionaries in particular straddled the cusp of their husbandly and fatherly responsibilities, the two roles becoming mutually reinforcing at that most tender of times. Male missionaries proved themselves as good husbands by being good fathers, and good fathers by ensuring the health and happiness of their wives. How husbands dealt with pregnancy and birth could set the tone for their marriage. In the case of Ann Hamilton, it seems likely that a traumatic experience when having her first child was at the root of her subsequent estrangement from her husband. Her refusal to 'again be united to Mr H as his wife',[2] and her subsequent disconnection from the church and separation from the mission can all be traced back to this defining moment in their shared experience.[3] Separation from the church was a dire consequence for a woman of faith, one which 'cut her to the heart' and demonstrated her strength of feeling about sexual contact and its consequences.[4] She was willing to endure the spiritual and temporal ramifications of separation in order that Mr Hamilton 'should never father another child by her'. While some of her rejection of motherhood can be attributed to a stridently active vocational desire (hindered by the arrival of children), the vehemence of her rejection indicates something more than spiritual frustration.[5] In explaining her determination she mentioned three occasions which I think were directly related to her first pregnancy and experience of child-bed that had shaped the nature of her marriage.

> When interrogated why she called Mr H *brutish* &c to prove his brutality she replied that he did not pay her sufficient attention on board of ship. He left her while sickly at Griqua Town and went on a journey to Latakoo and thirdly he fell asleep 'and snored like a Hog' while a person was praying for her when she was considered in a dangerous state.[6]

While Robert Moffat, in the above account, is dismissive of her reasons, it seems likely that there is a deeper and consistent thread running through these charges of brutality. The first probably referred to Ann's difficulties in coping with the early stages of pregnancy while travelling to South Africa. It was common for missionaries' wives to become pregnant en route to the mission field. This was a time of marital assessment for both parties (particularly if previously unknown to each other), in terms of personality, spirituality and the levels of comfort and sympathy they could expect from their new spouse, even how successful the marriage would be. A husband's attentiveness to the discomforts and difficulties associated with morning sickness exacerbated by seasickness could bode ill or well for the marriage to come.

The second charge levied against Robert Hamilton was that he had journeyed to his mission station (Lattakoo, later Kuruman) while she was 'sickly'. Sickliness being a frequently-used euphemism for pregnancy and confinement, it seems likely that Ann's objection related to his seeming indifference to her condition. While we know that male itineration and mission priorities were the norm in missionary marriages (see Chapter 3), for a new wife facing the fears of pregnancy and birth for the first time, in an alien and frighteningly disconnected context, her husband's seeming indifference towards her emotional and physical health would not have augured well for their marriage and her future happiness. Finally, when she was brought to bed of a daughter (Rebecca), it seemed that her early concerns had been realised. Having suffered complications she was 'in a dangerous state'. Again her husband's indifference, exemplified by his ability to sleep so soundly as to snore 'like a Hog', did not bode well for her future comfort or happiness as a missionary's wife.

It seems then that Ann Hamilton had suffered a traumatic experience in childbirth, separated from a husband whose indifference was both emotionally hurtful and physically dangerous. Ann's determination not to return to the marital bed was directly linked to these experiences, and her husband's failure to successfully juggle his multiple roles as missionary, husband and father. After a short reconciliation however, a second child, William, was born in 1818. This spelled the end of the Hamilton's marriage. 'She then finally determined that Mr H should never father another child by her.'[7] Jeffrey Cox has stated that Ann 'appears to have refused to sleep with her husband on the grounds that children were interfering with her missionary work'.[8] As a determined missionary this is certainly likely. Their marital incompatibility and the *uncompanionate* nature of their marriage certainly did not help matters.

Ann Hamilton was certainly not the only wife to face difficulties in balancing vocation with family life; but it was the intimacies of her personal experience and her treatment by the mission community that led to her ultimate rejection of that vocation entirely. Ann's response was highly unusual, and as discussed in Chapter 3, most women accepted the prioritisation of mission over family. However, *Robert* Hamilton's actions may also have been unusual. There is some evidence to suggest that when it came to a missionary couple's first child, these priorities were as yet undrawn, and that missionary husbands fretted about leaving their wives during confinement. When Ann Hamilton asked George Barker to join her and her husband's mission in Lattakoo in 1818, he refused, citing numerous concerns about the condition of his wife, who was 'near being confined', and the health and safety of both her and the child, once it was born.[9] Even David Livingstone experienced some inconvenience in refusing to leave his wife at the time of their first child's birth. Embroiled in bitter disputes with both William Ross (South African missionary 1841–63) and Roger Edwards (South African missionary 1823–74), David nonetheless refused to travel to Kuruman for the District Committee, though this would have afforded him an opportunity to rebut their criticisms: 'The probable circumstances in which my dear partner will then be placed [Mary was expecting a child in December] convince me that I need no revelation from heaven in order to pronounce that it is clearly not my duty to go out.'[10]

Missionary husbands also fretted internally about the health and well-being of their wives and children. Rowland Hassell, upon arriving at the SSM (where he was a missionary 1797–98), had been extremely worried about the health of his wife and new child, particularly once the mission surgeon had determined to leave the station. 'I had a thousand fears through the Dr leaving and Returning home', he noted in his journal of 1798, 'yet the Lord was so kind as to spare Both Root and Branch and caused her to have as good a time as ever before

... I have reason to call on all my friends, or powers, to Praise and adore the God of our Salvation.'[11] The 'thousand fears' of Rowland Hassell eloquently remind us that it was not just women who faced the possibly fatal consequences of childbirth in this era. Husbands too worried about the fate of wives and children. While their voices in this vein can be harder to evince, their relief when children were delivered safely, and their grief when they were not, speak to their pre-natal hopes and fears. When Mary Sass died in South Africa in 1814, her husband Christopher described her death to his mother-in-law.

> About two o'clock yesterday morning she was taken ill: the pain of labour commenced; and she had to suffer as a martyr till about seven last evening, when the Lord saw fit to take her from my arms to his eternal embraces. We were both looking forward to the enjoyment of our offspring; but alas! both are cut off, and I am left to traverse this desert alone!

The sense of both husband and wife excitedly awaiting the birth of their child and planning their future together is extremely poignant. Yet, it is also clear that the Sasses had both been prepared for the possibility of a tragic end. 'The Lord had, in a measure, prepared us for the scene. She was familiar with death, and talked often about it.'[12] Large numbers of missionaries' wives died bearing children and though these are often silent deaths in official records, they are noisily present and moving in more personal accounts.

Women, meanwhile, tended (in their writings at least) to experience the anticipation of childbirth and the event itself as a crystallising moment in their faith. In the context of a lived and vital faith, confinement and delivery were often understood as a spiritual test. For Hannah Crook, the experience of her youngest daughter's birth in 1821 was saturated with spiritual significance and trial.

> April 10 Lydia born. The Lord was better to me than all my fears. Having suffered much for many months past, my unbelieving heart told me I should not survive this trial. But behold here I am still spared to praise the Lord for his loving kindness, to so poor a sinner and to my dear infant a fair female baby my ninth child. Praise the Lord Oh my soul and all that is within me, praise his holy name.[13]

Her 'unbelieving heart' had been afraid of death, a spiritual transgression on two fronts; first in not having faith in God's protection, and second in fearing what should have been divine – death in the Lord.

Geographical and material specificity were also crucial to women's experience of pregnancy and birth. When Hannah was expecting this ninth child, she already had five daughters aged ten and over, two of whom were nearing adulthood at 17 (Mary) and 15 (Hannah Jr). For this reason, she determined that she would not require the aid of any of her brethren during her confinement, but 'chose rather to trust to providence and the assistance of my own family'.[14] In South Africa meanwhile, Sarah Barker had both older daughters and the aid of other women. 'At twelve o clock Mrs B[arker] awoke Sarah [Jr] saying she was ill and while standing with her alarming symptoms disclosed her dangerous situation. The women were called and Sarah prepared sending for me.'[15] Mrs Bourne (wife of South Seas missionary Robert Bourne, 1817–27) in contrast, was less well positioned materially. Unlike Crook (and Barker) she had no older daughters, and instead had two young children (aged 4 and 2) to look after. Though Hannah had decided to rely upon her family's assistance, 'Mrs B had made up her mind to come and lie in here[;] she determined to come before the time that she might be with me.'[16] Given that the Bournes's daughter was born on 24 April, just two weeks after Lydia Crook, it seems evident that Mrs Bourne had sought Hannah's assistance as much as she proposed to lend her own.

In travelling to be with Crook at the time of her confinement, Mrs Bourne was conforming to a tradition of mutual assistance in childbirth. The Directors themselves had obliquely encouraged this. 'We suggest also, that no settlement of married persons should consist of less number than three families', they counselled in 1798, for 'in the event of the death of a married Brother, the widow would be placed in a very distressing situation if she had not the consolation of a female friend at hand'.[17] One can suppose that female support networks were also envisaged as important for confinement and birth. This network of support was very swiftly put into effect when the first missionaries arrived at Tahiti in 1797. There Sarah Henry gave birth to a daughter 'just 10 weeks after our arrival', having been 'very carefully attended by the Surgeon and our women'.[18] By January 1798 (some seven months later) the surgeon had left the mission, and when Jonathan Hassell was born at the end of that month it was Benjamin Broomhall (former buckle and harness-maker) who had 'spared no pains to obtain a knowledge in surgery that he Might be Useful'.[19] Given his inexperience it seems likely that 'our women' were the more helpful on that occasion.

Indeed, male interference in childbirth was not always welcome. Mrs Ross in South Africa certainly did not esteem the presence or actions of David Livingstone despite the fact that he considered himself 'the means of saving its [the baby's] life as clearly as anyone could be'.[20] While her later comments undoubtedly reflected their long-standing feud and dislike of one another, it is nonetheless rather surprising that the presence of a qualified doctor would not have been more welcome. Instead, he received opprobrium from the Rosses for trying to 'make her afraid' and doing 'nothing at all but pretend that the child was in danger, in order to take credit'.[21] For most missionary women a female-centric birthing ritual was much preferred.

Other women were not always available at the needful moment, of course. Most male missionaries on the spiritual frontier knew that they would be the only source of assistance for their wives during childbirth, undoubtedly heightening their anxiety. While Bessie Price had enjoyed the aid of Mrs Mackenzie (wife of John) at the birth of her first child, when their second arrived, 'Roger and I were quite alone to welcome him.'[22] It was at these times in particular that male missionaries proved themselves as husbands and fathers in a mutually reinforcing role-fulfilment. Evan was their second child, and while Roger had been 'quite jubilant' at the birth of their first,[23] it was after Evan's birth that his multiple roles as father and husband came to the fore. 'Roger was my faithful nurse, doctor, friend and cook. He tended me and my wee thing in the most tender way.'

> I wonder whether you would most admire to be amused at my good Husband as, arrayed in the flannel apron, he would take my wee thing and undress and wash and redress it just like any old nurse – *so* beautifully – leaving not a single thing undone of all those innumerable delicate performances required in the dressing of a baby. It was always a rich treat for me to receive my sweet little thing fresh and comfortable from its bath.

'At first I used to tremble a little and shut my eyes for fear', remarked Bessie on the above scene, 'but soon was quite able to trust R[oger] and watch him with delight and gratitude'.[24] Isolated from female support networks missionary couples were interdependent in the most profound of ways, and missionary husbands in particular proved their familial mettle at this most precarious of times.

But what of indigenous women and midwives? Was it not better to have the aid of the local women, rather than rely solely on the oftentimes non-existent expertise of missionary husbands? It is near impossible to answer this question, and is certainly something that rarely appears in the available sources. Ann Hamilton seems to have received a large amount of scorn for the fact that when she apparently miscarried in 1821, she 'had only called in a Hottentot woman who I believe is one of her confidants'. Indeed, the sole presence of an indigenous woman, in addition to the general dislike of Ann, led the Moffats to disbelieve a miscarriage had occurred. 'She and her husband had then been a month united – we did not believe it for she had no proof for what she advanced and had only called in a Hottentot woman.'[25] It is difficult to draw broader conclusions from this one case. Was the fact that Ann had called in an African friend indicative of a wider use of indigenous midwifery and support than might previously have been imagined? The aforementioned Mrs Ross had the assistance of Rachel, a Cape Coloured convert. Did her mixed race origins and spiritual and cultural status as a convert remove any stigma associated with indigenous involvement? Or does her presence suggest again a broader communal presence at mission childbirth? Was Ann Hamilton's case worthy of mention because of its peculiarity and if so, was it peculiar because her confidante was a 'Hottentot', rather than a noted (and named) convert like Rachel? Were the Moffats particularly sensitive to the idea of indigenous involvement? They were, after all, the standard-bearers of the new civilising mission. When Sarah Barker went into labour in 1836, who were 'the women [who] were called'?

It is frustrating that we cannot answer these questions, but the general missionary view of indigenous medicine (and indeed cleanliness), plus the more common expressions of being 'alone' to greet newborn babies, seems to indicate that local women were not extensively involved in mission births. Having said that, however, missionary women were certainly involved in indigenous births. The 'Queen' of Tahiti (wife of Pomare II) requested that Hannah Crook visit her regularly during her confinement, and be present at the birth, so 'that the child might be attended to'.[26] On 21 June 1819 she was 'sent for in haste to attend the queen who was in labour. I went and found her attended by her sister and two of our women[;] as she was not very bad we read, conversed and prayed – I conceived that it would not be over soon and proposed returning home and coming again but she was unwilling I would leave her'. When the king arrived, 'his countenance was gloomy and I began to think he was not pleased with my being present[,] but as soon as the child was born his countenance brightened and he called out to the queen's sister ["]leave the entire management of these things to Mrs Crook["] ... I dressed the young prince in clothes which I brought with me for that purpose.'[27]

This story, of course, fits neatly within a mission power dynamic that missionaries were comfortable with (particularly in the dressing of the infant),[28] but the early years of the Tahitian mission, at least, did witness more cross-cultural involvement than would later be seen as permissible, speaking to the changes in the missionary encounter over time. Sarah Henry's baby had frequent intimate contact with the local peoples. 'The natives are exceedingly fond of the child and are highly gratified when they get her to nurse', noted William Henry in his diary. 'The Chief's wife of the District in which we live, calls her her daughter, and takes her sometimes to her own house when she feeds her well with a kind of Pudding they make of Plantains and

Breadfruit … on which, together with the breast, she feeds Eagerly and thrives well.' The local people felt so connected with the Henry's baby that they were 'exceedingly well pleased when we allow them to call her, Mydidde no Otaheite, which signifies, a Child of Otaheite'.[29] Later missionary parents were much more wary about such interracial and cross-cultural contact.

Later generations of missionaries were also not entirely disconnected from the medical practices of the local people, however, though how far we could scale this up to intimate personal involvement is unclear. Bessie Price was certainly desperate for the advice of her female servants when baby Evan became seriously ill shortly after his birth. 'I used to question them about this and that symptom and enquire as to their modes of proceeding in sickness &c. – yearning for advice and help', despite the fact that they were 'pure heathens … in thorough native style, with dirty skins and greasy bodies'.[30] Nonetheless, Bessie Price also gives strong evidence that indigenous women were *not* involved in missionary births. She and Roger had been alone at the birth of their second child, seemingly disconnected from any indigenous female support networks that may have been available to them. As with many issues relating to missionary interactions with indigenous peoples, this could speak more to change over time and differences in geographical location, as well as personal preference, than to any definitive answer to this perplexing question. For now, the extent of indigenous involvement in missionary births will have to remain questionable, and hopefully a site for future research. What can be said is that it seems highly likely that missionary husbands were frequently the sole midwives at the birth of their children. At this fragile moment in the missionary experience, all eyes were upon the male missionary to fulfil the multi-layered expectations of a man in his personal and professional position.

Missionary parenting

Birth was a cooperative process eliciting fear and anxiety in both husband and wife. Parenthood too was cooperative, though in some ways involving the mother more than the father. This was both practical and ideological. The male missionary was, after all, the employee of the LMS, and as such had to fulfil his mission commitments, which often included work that took him away from the domestic sphere, both during the day, and at times for longer periods of itineration. Fathers could not, nor would want to, abandon their vocational responsibilities in the face of familial ones, however tender the ties of family had recently become.

At the same time, certain functions of parenthood fell clearly and practically within the female sphere – for example breastfeeding. The first few weeks and months could be particularly difficult, undoubtedly for both parents, as the birth of a new child always disrupts family life, but most physically so for the mother. 'Thomas is a fine strong child, in no way troublesome, for which although none of the trouble falls on me I thank him sincerely', wrote David Livingstone at the birth of his third child in 1849.[31] Self-consciously reflecting that as a father the impact of the new baby was somewhat lessened, he seems to have nonetheless worried about the impact on his wife (now with three young children in as many years) and was thankful if that burden could be reduced by the temperament of his son. Bessie Price found the early years of motherhood deeply trying. 'Jeanie if you saw my dreary monotonous life here in the wagon, where I do little more than turn round and round with my babes within a space of about 2 yards.'

> I am a fixture to the wagon – in fact to the bed therein – nursing my little lassie, and if she sleeps a bit, I just tug about and put bundles and bags in order, and take pity on my Roge[r Jr], all dirty and cross, to clean him, and let him play about and wake Baby again – and the day strides on I don't know how when I seem only just to have got up, washed my babes, made the bed and wagon right, had dinner, and nursed a bit – or all the while, rather – and it is time ... to put the babes to bed again, to have supper and hear R's news and dot it all down here and then go to bed myself!

Nursing in particular was physically tiring, and mentally boring. 'This cramped up position in which I sit all day makes my evening one of weariness and fatigue', wrote Bessie, '... simply sitting in a stooping way, nursing'.[32]

When it comes to missionary parenting, mothers and fathers experienced and expressed their anxieties and fears in particular ways. Most mothers were more involved in the daily lives of their children; the day-to-day dynamics of the mission household were usually run to the rhythm of the mother-figure who woke, fed, bathed and bedded the children, as well as looking to their day-to-day education and socialisation. Thus their fears and concerns tended to be more rooted in the immediate, and the everyday. Fathers, meanwhile, while by no means necessarily distant figures, tended to express themselves as more concerned with the long view: 'formal' education, life-cycle events and long-term materiality, spirituality and prosperity.

For missionaries their style of parenting emanated from the form of their vocation. Female vocation, as has been seen, was rooted in the normative household, exemplifying domesticity and family in its most 'natural' and godly form. Central to this was the treatment of children and their accommodation in a hostile environment. In that vocational context, it is unsurprising that it was women who felt themselves more occupied with the day-to-day challenges of parenthood. Male missionaries, meanwhile, fulfilled their vocation in preaching and teaching, two activities that by their nature looked to the future, and indeed relied upon a vision of future spirituality and temporality justifying present hardship or difficulty (as in the often disconnected and ostracised life of the convert). Their professional lives dictated that they held a long view. In *that* vocational context, it is little wonder that they concerned themselves with the long-term prospects of their children. William Crook drew the line explicitly. 'In your printed instructions ... I perceive an important omission, the family of the missionary. He ought to be instructed how to bring up his children and how to dispose of them, for if a man know not how to rule his own house, how shall he take care of the church of god.'[33]

Thus for female missionaries, whose spiritual agency was fulfilled through the minutiae of daily life, so parenting was a practice rooted in the everyday. In the early years of her marriage and motherhood, Bessie Price developed numerous neuroses based around the daily physical dangers presented to her children by their local environment. 'A wretch of a scorpion was seen crawling over my baby's basket! (the night the lion killed an ox) on the tent of the wagon – so that any minute the reptile might have fallen in where he lay sleeping', she noted in 1862.[34] Her unconscious linking of the scorpion incident with the much larger danger to the homestead being posed by the lion speaks to her fear of domestic penetration by foreign bodies, also implicitly linked with the landscape and the environment in which she found herself. 'They [spiders] are *very* numerous at the Bamanguato because of the rocks surrounding us and after rain the creatures come in at the windows so that we kill them systematically, lifting the curtains after rain and searching – R. and I together.' Somehow, Bessie felt she could not accustom herself to these ever-present dangers. 'I am well known as a *coward* of *oxen* and *reptiles*. Over the fear of these somehow I cannot get as others [do].' For Bessie her persistent fears were explicitly linked with the safety of her children.

> I long to sleep once more under a nice sealed roof with my bairns, for my last waking moments at night are full of tormenting thoughts about these creatures and the possibilities of their falling upon us. O fancy a babe stung by a scorpion! Indeed, when I commit myself and loved ones to the care of Him who never slumbereth not, I think no little of these dreadful reptiles – snakes of course included. Of *maniacs* and robbers I never dream! and much less of murderers ... *Fear* is one of the most terrible things in this world to me. It is worse than pain I think – the fear

> of one of these reptiles creeping over me or my child is worse and has more torment than the pain would be to either of us, if it stung without my seeing it.[35]

Missionary motherhood on the spiritual frontier took the form of a constant battle with the local landscape: its dangers and discomforts. 'I never get down from the wagon to sit outside, because the glare is too much for my little lassie's sore eyes. I am just too glad to keep her within the green-curtains', explained Bessie in 1866.[36] The Prices, while at Molepolole, had terrible trouble with flies:

> the glare and heat excessive and the *flies*! Jeanie! I *never* never saw anything like it ... Our hut ... is *swarming* ... those three fierce midday hours (fr. 12 to 3) when we shut ourselves in with the children for rest and sleep – the flies defy us to sleep, altho' we shut out all light as much as possible. I spent my time in brushing away flies from the bairnies and R – and today Roger did it, but the idea of any one trying to brush away flies while I slept drove all sleep from my eyes. I give up in despair – and just think that to lie resting beside the children, brushing away the flies, is my best and happiest employment for those 3 hours.[37]

However modest, the home was a place of physical and social shelter from the indigenous landscape. For Bessie Price, leaving the security of the domestic space (even if just a wagon) could be a frightening experience. As always, her fears were articulated with reference to her children and their safety in the wild.

> Roger and I had a beautiful long walk this evening ... He carried 'Rora' [Roger Jr] and I the Babe [Isabella], and he allured me away over stones and rocks and past the fountain into a charming place, but awfully wild – and it was to me a mixture of sheer terror and pleasure, for I imagined every rustle among the bushes to be some crouching tiger intent upon one of my precious babes. Indeed I *enjoyed* it all *too* but now that the darkness has closed in upon us – I cannot imagine how ever I could have dared to take my babes into such a place ... My old horror of wild beasts is as great as ever – always intensified by my having sweet, tender, helpless babes in my charge. My imagination is too active on such terrible subjects. Roger of course says 'Tuts!'[38]

The physical space of the wagon provided the opportunity to draw the children into its shelter, and remove them from the pernicious physical and social landscape.

> This afternoon a number of women went past our wagons quite drunk – and one, catching sight of me and my babes, came and danced to me in the most ludicrous insane manner imaginable ... Lamucha [nurse-maid] and I laughed so (*behind the curtains*) [my emphasis] that the woman thought she was delighting us and got worse and worse ... I found

> presently that the object of attraction was a string of beads which Roge was playing with and which he (laughing merrily) held out every now and then to her – for seeing this to be the cause, I nipped them out of his little hand and drew him inside the curtain with me.[39]

Even at its most exposed, the mission home at least afforded some limited ability to screen the missionary, and the mission family, from the outside world. When the Prices arrived in Logagen (later, Molepolole), Bessie contrasted the privacy available at that place, with the constant supervision they had endured at Shoshong: 'it would be miserable if they thronged us as at Sekhomi's they used. How well I remember it ... when I used to go to the far corner [of the wagon] to eat my morsel in secret, and then always wipe my mouth before I turned round to the gazers in front.'[40] This serves as a neat reminder that every act of the mission family was deemed exemplary. Bessie ensured that the local people did not see her in any disassembled state, to the extent of wiping her mouth before turning around. Missionary mothers' preoccupation with the daily battle against the local environment, and the way in which this was articulated in reference to their role as mother, was an extension of their broader centrality in the daily maintenance of respectability. Their vocational agency determined their personal parenting and family interaction and, indeed, vice versa.

In line with the long view of their vocational activities, meanwhile, missionary fathers articulated their parental fears in terms of the long term and concerned themselves with the enduring effects of moral exposure, and the unstable economic, material and spiritual prospects of their children. As John Tosh has noted for the British context, fatherhood was 'primarily a duty performed in relation to the outside world'.[41] 'One does not know how our children may turn out', wrote David Livingstone, tussling with the consequences and difficulties of having children in Africa. 'Ours are surrounded by heathenism. It is very difficult to keep them from contact with it, and then we know that the soil is more favourable for that seed than for the good seed of the Word. We shall be obliged to send them home, and then that will be like orphanising them.'[42]

Male missionaries in particular directed their long view at the economic and material future of their offspring. David Livingstone often fretted about the future security of his children.

> I have no money to leave you. Each of you must work for himself in the world ... You will have need of brave purposes and preparation for the battle of life. There is none better than learning, learning of all sorts, and the sooner you learn the better, for you will get into the habit and then it will no longer be irksome.[43]

No doubt thinking about his own childhood prospects, and how hard work and learning broke him free from that life, he consistently urged his children to work hard, so that they might make something of their own lives. When Thomas (Tau), was withdrawn from school, David expressed a deep concern. 'Am very sorry to learn that poor Tau cannot study. I would not have agreed to it, for he has nothing else to depend upon but the divine blessing on his learning and abilities.'[44] David was not alone in his concerns about the future material security of his children. It was on the issue of their children's prospects that male missionaries were willing to invert the usual hierarchy of priority, and put their families' welfare above their vocation and the mission. Missionary fathers entered into protracted battles with London in order to secure their children's economic future, while some as we saw in Chapter 4 ultimately severed their connection with a society they felt did not afford their concerns enough attention.

Of course, there can, in fact, be no clear-cut and straightforward gender division in missionary parenting, and the clean explanation proposed here can be troublesome on various levels. Fathers often found themselves concerned with the daily lives of their children, materially and emotionally. 'There is abundant evidence of fatherly concern and involvement with the day-to-day raising of children', writes Tosh of the British context.[45] This was certainly true in the mission context also, if not heightened in fact by the permeable boundaries of the mission home (particularly when it resulted in fathers working from home), and the lack of nursemaids and servants to spirit the children away. Family life in the mission context was an all-embracing concern. Rogie Price, for example, had 'a wagon made by his Papa notwithstanding all his work (a box with 4 little wheels and a disselboom) and in this he rides about to his heart's content'.[46] George Barker found himself very much involved in the making of toys for his children, even if it was originally their own design, 'in fact, when the thing is determined on, I must be the principal agent'.[47] After the death of his wife, George frequently informed his sister in England of his families' evening amusements. 'We endeavour to amuse each other by cheerful conversation, reading and singing[,] in fact some one is almost always singing.'[48] It seems unlikely that this was an innovation occasioned by the death of his wife, and more likely that family singing had always been a part of their family routine. 'Singing is a favourite pastime and always in two parts. Sarah used to play the [word missing] but we have not one now. I often join [word missing] and the house rings with the noise.'[49]

We have already seen that Roger Price fulfilled his role as both husband and father by nursing his wife and newborn son in 1863. This was by no means the extent of his parenting, and although he continued to put his mission duties at the forefront of his priorities, he nonetheless frequently concerned himself with the day-to-day happiness and health of his children, from joining his somewhat neurotic wife in her daily spider-hunts, to fretting over the health of his young children on a daily (and nightly) basis. 'My darling Roge was very poorly and we had to lance his gums … In the middle of the night, Roger woke me suddenly to listen to the poor little fellow – how wildly he talked and acted – half-asleep.'[50] It is easy to imagine Bessie Price lying awake worrying about the safety of her children (which she then proceeded to do, preoccupied with the thought of a mouse gnawing its way in – 'and mice are my terror with babes or children'), but this reminds us that Roger too was anxious about the physical well-being of his son. David Livingstone, meanwhile, worried about his children's day-to-day existence while they were living in Scotland (his wife, after all, having been brought up in Africa). 'Tell Mamma that she is to buy plenty of meat for you in cold weather to make you warm, and you must take care and not get wet.'[51]

Nor did mothers neglect the long-term prospects of their children. It is in mothers' concern with juvenile spirituality that neat demarcations between mothers and fathers really fall apart. While Tosh has talked about competition between the 'masculine' (or patriarchal) family prayer and the more intimate (and feminine) bedside prayers, it is clear in the mission context that both mothers and fathers were intimately involved in the burgeoning spirituality of their children, and both cherished high hopes that they would one day follow them in the service of God.[52] Inculcating, guiding and encouraging juvenile spirituality was a cooperative concern. For male and female missionaries, the replication of their own piety and vocation was the ultimate sanction and blessing upon their parenting. Parental attempts to inculcate religiosity implicated fathers in the daily domestic scene (in terms of family worship) and mothers in their children's long-term prospects (in the sense of spiritual education). 'Now is the time that you should employ in laying up a stock of knowledge to fit you for future usefulness', wrote Jane Philip to her son Wilberforce in 1838.[53] David Livingstone, meanwhile, intimately concerned himself with the religiosity of his children, to the extent of continually barracking them on the issue in his letters to Britain during their years of separation.

> I wish you to be brave servants of Jesus. I wish you not to be afraid to own him. If others are ashamed to say, 'I won't sin because I love Jesus', my brave ones must say, 'I am his, I am the child of a king, I fear to sin against him.' There are many naughty boys and girls who will laugh at you if you fear to sin or do and say naughty things, but never fear a laugh or mocking. Brave ones don't care who laughs if Jesus smiles.[54]

Indeed, for Livingstone, religious education was part of a broad parenting package. His letters covered everything, from the basic rituals of religiosity ('When we ask things from him, that is praying to him'),[55] through analogies that made religion real to his children ('You see little Zouga [William Oswell Livingstone] is carried on mamma's bosom. You are taken care of by Jesus with as much care as mamma takes of Zouga. He is always watching you and keeping you in safety'),[56] to more stern and complex messages relating to punishment and sin ('No one can put you in chains unless you become bad. If, however, you learn bad ways … Satan will have you in the chains of sin … till you are put into the dreadful place which God hath prepared for him and all who are like him. Pray to Jesus to deliver you from sin, give you new hearts, and make you His children').[57]

Spiritual education was thus fundamental to parental responsibility, family worship, for instance, punctuating the daily schedule. More generally, parents nurtured their children's burgeoning piety. When filling out their applications to the LMS, second-generation missionaries (who receive more attention in the Epilogue) often referenced the spiritual education they had received from their parents. 'My first religious impressions were produced … through an address given by the Rev John Williams', wrote John Barff (son of Charles) in 1838. 'His address together with the parting words of my dear mother, have since my arrival in this country, been brought forcibly to my mind, and have I trust proved as the seed sown in good ground.'[58] For William Philip it was 'almost needless to say that from my childhood I have been favoured with religious instruction, and with many prayers … I owe more to the prayers of my Parents and friends than to my own.'[59] His brother echoed these sentiments some twenty years later. 'Being the son of pious parents I was early instructed in religious Truth, and brought under the influence of powerful persuasions',

> but the pleasures as well as the bustle of life soon effaced them and I was not seriously concerned about my soul's welfare till the year 1847. In that year after an absence in England of about three years I rejoined my Parents at the Cape; My mother was in bad health and had no expectation of recovery, but the intercourse I was permitted to hold with her the few months before her death were of the greatest benefit to me and led me by Divine grace to see my own sinfulness and the necessity of faith in Christ for salvation.[60]

Missionary parents themselves derived immense satisfaction from their children's piety, and felt severe pain if any of their children did not declare themselves for God. George Barker found great comfort in his children after his wife's death. 'Besides I have a lovely family, the elder Girls inherit something of the prudence of their dear mother, and the two eldest have already declared for the Lord and are both members of the church.'[61] His children, and their spiritual conversions, were a 'cause of gratitude'.[62] Not all missionary parents were so lucky. The Barffs in the South Seas had severe problems with their sons, but, 'Our daughters have all given us much pleasure as affectionate, obedient, and consistent. I wish I could say also truly pious.'[63]

Missionary parents also exercised a constant vigilance against their children's social interaction with indigenous people. Bessie Price's physical removal of her children from instances of 'pernicious association' (by drawing them physically into the wagon) has already been noted. Missionary children were 'spatially quarantined',[64] (particularly in the South Seas) pushing missionary women further into the domestic space (as guardians of physical, social and moral boundaries), promoting the formulation of a domestic mission theory, and thereby shaping the very history of mission itself. Fathers channelled their concerns about the social interactions of their children into calls for educational establishments in Britain for missionary children, which were seen as the most effective way to forestall intercultural contact. While still present on the mission station, however, *both* mothers and fathers guarded the boundaries of the home and exerted control over juvenile socialisation. When it came to expressing their parental fears, however, male missionaries spoke the language of *longue durée* and anxieties about their children's future. Female missionaries, meanwhile, fretted about the daily aspects of life in foreign climes. For both male and female missionaries, parenthood was inextricably interwoven with the notion of sheltering one's children from indigenous physicality, sociability, and morality.

Racial segregation was crucial to domestic separation. Some level of social interaction was inevitable, particularly as many missionaries had servants, and, in the words of Gunson, 'however carefully they were guarded, they [missionary children] seemed to have an easy access to the native mind'.[65] It was this realisation that gradually led to missionary chauvinism transfiguring into missionary racism. Contact, conversation, and example were the keys to conversion. Yet missionary parents rejected these fundamental tenets of mission theory when faced with the possibility of the cultural and spiritual contamination of their children. Not only did parenthood result in missionaries battling against the LMS on official policy, even at the risk of their vocations, but it fundamentally shaped their understanding of mission itself, and resulted in the gradual corruption of humanitarian universalism as missionaries increasingly slid into a racialised rhetoric of difference.

But we should not forget that missionary families were also loving environments, and there can be no doubt that missionary parents, mothers and fathers, adored their children. Even David Livingstone, that most gruff of Scotch missionaries, spoke lovingly of his children. His pain at parting with them reflected a deep affection that should not be obscured by the pragmatic and gruff nature of his correspondence. 'I should like to see you much more than write to you, and speak with my tongue rather than with my pen; but we are far from each other – very, very far.'[66] Missionary fathers' love for their children is most easily evinced at points of disconnection: separation and death. 'It is wonderful how soon the affections twine round a little stranger', noted Livingstone upon the death of his daughter Elizabeth in 1850. 'We felt her loss keenly.' Indeed, David found himself haunted by little Elizabeth's illness and death. His frustration at being unable, in his capacity as a doctor and a father, to save her saturated his writing:

> We administered quinine with the barely formed hope that she might come through, but yesterday evening the beautifully formed countenance began to set in death ... at one o'clock she opened her beautiful eyes and screamed with a great effort to make her lungs work, and instantly expired. That scream went to our hearts, and will probably not be forgotten in Eternity.

'She is home now, yet it was like tearing out one's bowels to see her in the embrace of the King of Terrors.'[67] It is extremely difficult not to be moved by such a description. To see only Livingstone's 'apparent equanimity' at the loss of his child, evidenced by his (guilty?) observation that the death was 'just as likely to have happened if we had remained at home' seems wilful blindness at best.[68]

David Livingstone was, of course, not the only male missionary to love his children, and with some effort, glimpses of tender scenes between missionary fathers and their children can be perceived within existing records. That these moments appear at points when missionary mothers were indisposed or absent reflect more the inability of the male missionary to find space in his *writing* for his children, rather than a difficulty in finding them space in his life. Male missionary writing, though often voluminous, was more often than not professional, and had little conceptual or practical room (given the price and scarcity of paper) for scenes of family jollity. Their daily involvement in family life was not always something they could conceptually accommodate in their idea of themselves as missionaries, and as such, often fell by the wayside in both their personal and professional writings. At the same time, however, there are interesting tensions and ambiguities in missionary fatherhood that chime with more broadly shifting patterns in work and home life.[69] Bessie Price, writing after the death of her first child Moffat in 1863, drew a distinction between her husband's evening 'hour with his son' and his smithing work in the house ('to the amusement and delight of his little son').[70] In so doing, however, she draws our attention to the fact that missionary fatherhood, as much as motherhood, on the spiritual frontier was an all-embracing concern. If male missionaries were implicated as much as female missionaries in creating the exemplary home (as shown in Chapter 3), then an intimate male presence in and around the home was inevitable. Roger Price thus brought his smithing work home. This both reflects and highlights some of the emerging tensions between home-based (male) work, and what John Gillis has called 'family time'.[71]

Missionary fathers, like evangelical fathers in Britain, were often actively involved in the lives of their children. As Davidoff and Hall have noted, 'local sources more often point to an intense involvement of men with their families, and a loving interest in their children's lives'.[72] As we have seen, taking on the familial narrative role after the death of his wife, George Barker described the amusements he shared with his children. 'Crying or scolding is seldom heard in our house, and yet the house is never quiet after school hours unless they are reading. Singing is a favourite pastime ...'[73] Barker even turned down numerous opportunities for visiting England after his bereavement (a course advised by John Philip) because he could not bear to part with them. 'My Dear children twine round my heart, I could not think of leaving them to see my mother.'[74] Livingstone was not always at his most voluble when discussing his children, to the extent that his sister Janet wrote asking him to say more about them,[75] but when he did mention them, it was with some tenderness. 'The children enjoyed paidling [*sic*] in the river much. Took to it as if they had been ducks, laughing and shouting.'[76] Bessie Price frequently referred to Roger as a doting and loving father. Speaking of their daughter Isabella, Bessie remarked, 'I am always poking her up into Roger's face and saying "There! is not she beautiful?" – and you can imagine how *he* dotes on her now that she crows and talks and laughs.'[77] Roger himself wrote to his elder children upon their separation in 1879, 'We shed many tears on that day and we were very sad, because we had to part from one another ... the thought of being separated ... for a long time was too much for our poor hearts.'[78] In the mission context it seems that the most common form of fatherhood (to use Tosh's categorisations) was the 'intimate father'. Absence, tyranny and distance could not be sustained within such a context of absolute interdependence, the unfeasibility of public/private divides (practically and conceptually), and the mutual imbrications of family life.[79]

Juvenile repatriation

The best evidence of how much missionary parents loved their children, however, lies in their actions. For it was on the point of their children that missionary parents were willing to endanger and compromise some of the deepest ethical tenets of the missionary enterprise. Not only were mission parents, in particular, willing to come to blows with the LMS in London over the financial, material and emotional care of their children, in the field and at 'home', but in sending their children home in the first place, they were undercutting the basic principle of mission: the belief in the power of conversion. In removing their children from indigenous environments, they were signalling their lack of faith in the conversionist principle, and demonstrating that indigenous peoples remained a dangerous influence over their children, even to the point of bemoaning 'the indiscreet and excessive kindness of the *converted* natives'.[80] It is interesting to consider that it was on the point of their children that missionaries became their most culturally and racially chauvinistic, underlining the importance of a thorough understanding of the missionary family context to a deepened understanding of mission itself. The desire to send children home to be schooled both reflected and constituted a change in ideology from one of cultural tolerance, to one of cultural chauvinism, and as such challenged the very nature of the missionary enterprise itself.[81]

'The greatest trial of our missionary life is separation from our children', wrote George Stallworthy speaking for the whole Samoan mission in the middle of the Mills controversy in 1848.[82] Once the schools for missionary children in England opened their doors, parent–child separation became an integral part of the missionary enterprise, and the most effective, if painful, way for missionary parents to ensure the physical, social and moral protection of their children. Separation formed a painful commonality among mission communities.[83] It was the most difficult aspect of missionary parenting, and yet remained the most basic shared experience of missionaries in different corners of the globe. Separation marked a rupture in missionary parenting that was gradually re-established through the writing of letters, which became points of connection on a shared map of experience and existence.[84]

The painful difficulties of separation leap out from missionary letters and journals, and speak most eloquently to the bonds of love and affection that existed between missionaries and their children. In the Pacific, the mission community spent years vacillating between an anxious desire to send children home for their schooling, and an equally anxious concern about separating from their children. In many ways this was a generational conflict, between an older cohort of missionaries who could not bear the idea of separation, and who could not see its use anyway; and a newer generation whose profound belief in its utter necessity was itself created and shaped by their contact with a seemingly debased generation of former missionary children. Thus, though it was a painful one, separation became a duty for missionary parents in the South Seas, and elsewhere. In 1830 Mary Moffat prepared to part with her two oldest children, Mary and Ann, then aged 9 and 7, 'as keeping them at home is beyond all doubt highly improper'.[85] Her journey on this errand was articulated not as one of benefit conferred, but of a duty imposed. The material and moral context of their home at Kuruman necessitated the change in their familial dynamic. 'Hence you will perceive that we are entering on a new sort of trial.'[86]

Missionary parents experienced deeply conflicting emotions about sending their children away to be educated. On the one hand, they were anxious that this separation should occur, and that their children should therefore be protected from the 'heathenish' environment into which they were born. On the other, they knew that separation would be painful and difficult, and further fretted about the physical and emotional well-being of children removed from parental care. Some ten years after the above incident, Mary took her three youngest children (John, 12; Bessie, 8; and Jeanie, 7) to the Cape in order that they too might enjoy a formal education. John later remembered that journey with some tenderness in 1885.

> The journey to Cape Town, extend[ed] over a period of two months … but to the mother the time seemed all too short. She felt that it was the last she would ever have with her young children about her. Her heart never got hardened to these partings, one of the severest crosses incident to the missionary calling. The children, too, were not so young that they could not feel the shadow of the impending change. During those few weeks of lonely wilderness life, the members of the little group were all in all to each other. There was a pathetic tenderness in the interest which the mother took in the wild flowers and curious pebbles which the children gathered on the hill-sides and in the stony river-beds; and the gentle and homely counsel and warnings given are not forgotten even now, nearly forty years after.[87]

When the opportunity for an English education arose, though, her 'heart was heaving with anguish, I joyfully and thankfully acceded forthwith'.[88] 'On the 10th of February they embarked [upon the ship bound for England], and after stopping the night on board, I tore myself from my darlings to return to my desolate lodgings to contemplate my solitary journey, and to go to my husband and home childless.'[89] Thirty years later, in 1879, Mary's own daughter Bessie experienced the same pain of separation. 'Oh how sad I felt last night when I went on deck, and sat in the cool balmy air so soft and sweet and fresh. How I thought of you all our beloved ones in that isle of mist and fogs ... My heart aches every time I enjoy that lovely air on deck with the longing for you all to enjoy it also!'[90]

For missionary mothers there was something particularly poignant about the empty home. As young mothers, their vocational activities were dictated by the needs and timetable of their children. 'My class, consisting of spellers and alphabet*ers*, has to sit and wait my time irregularly, according to the will of my little son – and his morning sleep is generally my hour for taking them,' noted Bessie.[91] At times frustrated in their desire to undertake missionary work, women found comfort in providing a merry and joyous home for their husbands to return to, thereby rejuvenating *him* for his missionary labours.[92] The empty mission home, by contrast, could be a comfortless place. Missionary mothers often, therefore, articulated their own pain upon separation with reference to this sense of the empty house or the childless father. Thus Mary Moffat wrote to her son John in 1848 of her reunion with Robert having seen the children off to England:

> we had soon a joyful and sorrowful meeting: joy, because of all the goodness and mercy of God to the whole family during our separation, and sorrow, or rather tender regret, for the absence of the three younger children. Yes, it was trying for papa to see me alone, with not the little prattler. But these feelings were quickly swallowed up in thankfulness and praise.[93]

This pain was of course magnified when the separation was occasioned by death, but was nonetheless expressed in similar ways. 'There is an indescribable loneliness in our wee home – caused by our darling's absence from us', noted Bessie Price after the death of their first son Moffat in 1863, 'most of all at the twilight hour when the work and bustle of the day is over and my poor hands are empty'. She too articulated her own grief in terms of the empty and cheerless home she was forced to present to her husband, remarking:

> Then I sit down in the lone, still bedroom – just as the time when I used to bathe and dress him in his wee white night dress and spread his *evening* bed in the parlour and then sit waiting with him – my bright, beautiful boy – for Papa! That used to be Papa's hour with his son – and now we sit so lone and sad. Sometimes 'tis tho' we cannot speak for it – and I never seem able to greet and welcome him home as I used to – only my lone, sad self, in my black dress – no sweet, smiling dancing cherub in my arms![94]

The grieving parents found facing the domestic space so emptied an extreme trial.

> We came – he and I – and courage failed that first day to unbolt the little door and look in – so utterly desolate was the appearance of everything outside – the verandah or shade beneath which I used to sit with my wee thing – the corner where Papa used to do his smith's work and hammer away to the amusement and delight of his little son – the dilapidated condition of the walls here and there and the *desolation* all around us – *because we had not 'our wee thing'*! Dear R. and I walked together round and round, but could not utter a sound. It was so unutterably *sad*![95]

Of all the things that the mission home was (exemplar, classroom, workshop), it was fundamentally a familial place. Once that aspect was stripped away, missionary parents felt the pain of the absence, be it from death or temporal separation. When the Prices returned to Molepolole in 1879 they reinhabited their old home, having this time left their four elder children alive and well in England. 'It *cannot* be quite its own self without *you*, my absent darlings – that I am fully alive to.'[96]

However difficult it may have been, separation had, by the 1840s, become an integral part of missionary life. 'But we know it is better for you all to remain in England to get such education as we could not give you at our home in Africa with all our own work about us', wrote Roger Price.[97] Missionary parents were forced (through their own cultural and racial chauvinism, as well as their children's propensity to 'bad behaviour' – see Chapter 6) to develop coping mechanisms in the face of separation. As in all things, the first was faith, and trust in God.

> But the same loving God who has always taken care of us when we were together will take care of us still … [and you can] ask Him to take care of us and for us to ask Him to care of you. And He will do so, for He loves us more than we can love one another. It is this that makes mamma and me happy when we think of you our precious ones as far away from us.[98]

Missionary parents, separated from their children, turned to God not only to justify that separation, but to soothe the distress and anxiety that it caused. 'How happy are we, my dear friend, to have a covenant God to go to in all these straits and difficulties. Nature has its struggle, but we are not to confer with flesh and blood', wrote Mary Moffat when first separated from her children in 1830.[99] David Livingstone frequently noted to his children that he had given them back to Jesus: 'But though I call you my children it is from custom, for you are now the children of Jesus. I have given you back to him, and you are in his care. He is your father, and a kinder better father never was. But you yourselves must look up to him to be your Father and guide.'[100] Whether the children found this notion particularly comforting is debatable, but it clearly gave their father comfort. Having knowingly 'orphanize[d] them',[101] he derived some consolation from the idea that he had consecrated them to God and to Jesus, who could guide them better than he ever could.

Livingstone not only understood his faith as a source of comfort in those difficult years of separation, but as a shared point of contact between himself and his children that could transcend the physicality of their separation.

> My dear Children, I write another little letter for you, but … a shorter way of sending to you … is by praying our Father in Heaven to send you down a blessing, and though I am far away from you he hears me, and he can send you down His blessing at the very time I pray for it. Is this not a good way?[102]

For Livingstone, mutual spirituality with his children was a pathway to connectedness, more efficient and effective than the letter-writing that his young children were unable to perform. Having said that, it was also clear that Livingstone yearned for the day when his children *would* be able to write to him. His constant nagging about education can be seen not only in the context of a self-made man wishing the same for his children, but in the additional context of a man sorely missing daily interaction with his children.

> My dear Tau, Is it very cold in Scotland? When will you be able to write and tell me about all the things you see? … you must learn to read soon. Ask Robert to give you a lesson. See how nice it is to be able to write. I can speak to you by this little bit of paper, though I am sitting in Grandma's house in Kuruman and you are perhaps in Grandma's house in Scotland.[103]

Until his children could learn to read and write, David had to rely upon second-hand reports from his wife, from whom, due to the vagaries of nineteenth-century international postage, he heard little. 'I hope Robert, Agnes and Tom are each learning as fast as they can. When will they be able to write a letter to me? How happy I shall be to meet them and you again!'[104]

Letters became the primary means for parents to stay linked with their distant offspring. Missionary parents used letters to create a communal space inhabited by both themselves and their children. Though separated in physicality, they could be united in concern. The primary way of achieving this was to keep children up to date with news of the mission; not necessarily the sort of news that would have sustained the mission community, relating to success rates, school attendance and the like, but more personal news which maintained a connection between the everyday realities of mission life, and the youngest members of that community from whom it had been severed.

'In the constant flow of letters they built a common share in their everyday lives', notes P. Pedersen.[105]

> Here are Seipone, and Meriye and others who saw you as the first white children they ever looked at. Meriye came the other day and brought a round basket for Nannie [Agnes Livingstone]. She made it of the leaves of the Palmyra. Others put me in mind of you all by calling me Rananee, and Rarobert, and there is a little Thomas in the town, and when I think of you I remember, though I am far off[,] Jesus, our good gracious Jesus, is ever near both you and me.[106]

Bessie's letters were also crowded with people and places she wished to keep alive in the minds and memories of her children. This not only served to maintain their interest in the mission that their parents hoped they would one day serve, but the constant interchange of letters was, as Pedersen notes, 'also an end in itself, a way of creating order and reducing anxiety, or, in short, *a ritual*'.[107] The act of letter writing was as important as the content, and served to assure the recipient that the writer was alive and well in a context of ever-present danger. 'It occurs to me, my dearest Mary, that if I send a note from different parts on the way through this colony, some of them will surely reach you; and if they carry any of the affection I bear to you in their composition, they will not fail to comfort you', wrote David Livingstone in 1854.[108] Letter writing could provide comfort; but it could also be the means of increasing anxiety, particularly when the flow of letters was interrupted. 'The post has arrived, but nothing for us from you, altho' the Sykes ... have letters from their children in England ... Still we make up our minds now to this sort of disappointment, and hope it is all right – for, as they say, "no news is good news".'[109]

Juvenile repatriation was difficult and trying for missionary parents. It also fractured the missionary family, and undercut the civilising mission's normative domesticity. Nonetheless, while separation could be painfully difficult for parents (and children), having their children with them could also be a trial for missionary parents. Missionary children were by no means always the pious and well-behaved Christians their parents desired. Missionary parenting was undertaken amid a climate of scrutiny that pervaded mission communities, and it is on that thought that this chapter concludes.

Scrutinising the missionary parent

Missionary parenting was fraught with anxiety and concern: temporal and eternal, material and spiritual. While mothers articulated their parenting as a constant battle against the physicality of the indigenous landscape, fathers understood their role as one of securing the long-term economic prospects, and behavioural morality of their children. Parental concerns converged over social contact between missionary children and indigenous peoples, and over the daily and long-term spirituality of the next generation. Their personal and mutual concerns reflected the realities of their own lives, and the specificities of their mission context. From pregnancy and birth onwards, parenting was a cooperative process, and one that would become a defining aspect of the missionary as a professional agent. Across the first half of the nineteenth century the idea that effective missionary parenting was crucial to the missionary enterprise was gradually codified, resulting in the 1840s in a series of resolutions by the LMS regarding missionary parenting, which was increasingly subject to the scrutiny of the community.

Indeed, missionary parenting was subject to two forms of scrutiny (as were their children): official and informal. Official scrutiny evolved slowly over the course of mission experience. Certain figures in the missionary community were given formal sanction to catalogue and judge missionary parenting: the superintendent of the mission, the district committee, and the superintendents of mission schools. Overarching these varied forms of official scrutiny was the ever-present, if second-hand, supervision of the LMS in London who, through reports from its missionaries, and from other interested or disinterested parties (traders, sailors, travellers) could both learn about and exercise control over various mechanisms of parenting in the mission context. The scrutiny of mission parenting was always conceptualised through an understanding of mission life based on the power of example. The children had a profoundly important role in this exemplary model of conversion. Not only were they directly used as tools for the missionary enterprise, but their very presence denoted a normative conception of the Christian family. Bad parenting could fundamentally endanger the success of the mission through the supposed power of example: be it good, or bad.

It was the liminality of missionary children meanwhile – the fact that their 'whiteness' had to be both learned and earned – that caused such parental anxiety for missionary parents.[110] Rather than being a biologically determined social identity, 'whiteness' was fluid and constituted a contested space in colonial and non-colonial frontiers.[111] If the 'heathen' could be 'civilised', a fundamental mission tenet, then missionary children could be 'heathen-ised' in an environment of negative example and reinforcement. The importance of the mission family to 'civilising' the 'heathen' through positive example and anticipated emulation was a process which could easily fall into reverse.

Negative examples of indigenous sociability and domesticity could lead missionary children astray. Cultural permeability was here a bi-directional process in the most alarming of ways. James Hayward noted in 1819 that 'as things now are, the native children are likely to corrupt the children of the mission – instead of the latter becoming patterns for imitation to the former'.[112]

Formal scrutiny of missionary parenting thus became embedded into the missionary enterprise. In the SSM from 1824, the superintendent of the South Seas Academy (SSA), became the formal scrutinising agent of the missionary community. John Orsmond was dismayed at the bad behaviour and habits of the children under his care, but knew distinctly where to place the blame.

> No parent is able efficiently to attend to his family and the duties of the station too. The children will therefore have learned every thing that is vile before they come here ... Here is all to tempt and few if any barriers to gratification. It is therefore of the highest importance that the children be taken as soon as possible away from the gross absurdities of the peoples and from a sight of those base practices to which the younger part of the community are addicted.[113]

'By far the greater part of the children have been so much neglected that by the time they will have to leave the school they will scarcely have attained the standing of those who are but seven years of age in England ... all is wild; briers only thrive; the book is viewed as an enemy; constraint is worse than death; while the fond parent calls discipline cruelty!!!'[114] While moral and behavioural neglect were undoubtedly the most worrying of the mission parents' transgressions, the physical neglect of missionary children was also remarked upon. 'The missionaries not only send their offspring to the academy, but they send them in such a way that we have to mend all their clothes ... The parents neither come to see them nor to ask if they can help them[;] they neither send buttons, patches nor thread.'[115]

Physical, emotional and moral neglect could all be imputed to the missionary parents of the SSM, with distressing and irreversible consequences. 'It is therefore for the good of the Mission generally, for the comfort of the parents particularly and for the interest of the youths especially that they be removed from their parental roofs as soon as possible.'[116] Orsmond's successor to the post of superintendent (Alexander Simpson, SSM 1827–50) continued to lay the blame at the parents' door. 'It has been the opinion of Mrs Simpson and myself from our landing on the Island to the present moment that the great predilection in our children to native habits, has a prior existence to their entering the school.'[117]

Ultimately the LMS in London also drew a direct line between bad juvenile behaviour and bad parenting. In 1845 William Henry (SSM 1797–1845) was informed that because of the 'the accounts we have received of the gross misconduct of several members of your family', it had been rendered 'imperative that we should mark our sense of it in a way that will clearly prove both to the friends and enemies of our holy cause that such proceedings must be utterly discountenanced by the Society'.

> We are exceedingly concerned that the sad disorders of your family should thus be reflected back upon yourself. Taking into consideration the flagrant character and conduct of your elder children, and the almost certain risqué [*sic*] of the younger ones being contaminated by their example, and that the evil influence will thus be extended, we consider there is no alternative but your return with those of your household who [are] under your control, to the Colony of New South Wales ...

Henry was informed that 'the future support afforded by this Society must depend on his immediate removal from the Island with those of his Children who are dependent on him'.[118] More generally the Directors, having

> learnt with the deepest sorrow that the children of several of the missionaries ... are notoriously guilty of gross and profligate habits, by which the Christian character of the Parents have been dishonoured and the influence of their labour counteracted, ... cannot suppress the painful conclusion that such instances of delinquency are at least in some cases, to be acquitted to the absence of proper control and discipline in the missionary families.

Thus they concluded that 'should any missionary decline to withdraw his countenance and support from any member of his family guilty of open and habitual vice, the Directors will feel under the painful necessity of withdrawing their support and confidence from such missionary'.[119] In so doing the Directors made clear that bad parenting equalled a bad missionary. Good parenting thus became an implicit and fundamental part of missionary professionalism. William Henry's response is most moving in its pained acquiescence and shame.

> your letter ... has overwhelmed me with grief and distress. How can I bear the thought that after being employed and labouring in the society's service for nearly half a century ... I should ... be represented to the world as banished like a criminal from the Islands of my labours? O the thought how distressing![120]

His disbelief that after fifty years of successful missionary activity he could be so treated because of his *parenting* undoubtedly caught the mood of the missionaries. It would seem that the LMS had been correct to worry, all those years earlier in 1797, that if a missionary had a family, 'he would neglect the formation of the morals of his own children, for which nature and Providence has made him almost the guarantee' and that God 'has not placed an essential duty [fatherhood] in a state of variance with another [mission]'.[121] What they had not quite realised until the 1840s, was the level to which parenthood and vocational ability would be so inextricably linked and mutually reinforcing. In short, by 1845, being a good missionary meant being an effective parent also.

Notes

1 My emphasis. 'An Appeal on Behalf of the Institution for the Education of the Daughters of Missionaries', *Evangelical Magazine* (hereafter *EM*) (October 1847), p. 547.
2 Robert Moffat Journal, 31 July [undated], National Library of South Africa (Cape Town) (hereafter NLSA(CT)) MSB 858 LMS Miscellaneous, 1(2).
3 Karel Schoeman, *A Thorn Bush that Grows in the Path: the missionary career of Ann Hamilton, 1815–1823* (Cape Town: South African Library, 1995).
4 Robert Moffat to John Philip, 12 September 1821, South Africa Incoming Letters (hereafter SAIL) 8B/3.
5 Robert Moffat Journal, 31 July [undated], NLSA(CT) MSB 858 LMS Miscellaneous, 1(2).
6 Ibid.
7 Ibid.
8 Jeffrey Cox, *The British Missionary Enterprise since 1700* (London: Routledge, 2008), p. 110.
9 In Schoeman, *A Thorn Bush that Grows in the Path*, p. 34.
10 David Livingstone to Robert Moffat (hereafter Livingstone to Moffat), 6 June 1845 in David Livingstone, *Family Letters, 1841–1856* 2 vols. *Edited with an introduction by I. Schapera* (London: Chatto & Windus, 1959), vol. 1, p. 125. On the disputes Livingstone was involved in see Tim Jeal, *Livingstone* (New Haven and London: Yale Nota Bene, 2001), pp. 35–6 and 63–6.
11 Diary of Rowland Hassell, 31 January 1798, South Seas Journals (hereafter SSJ) 1, p. 6.
12 'Obituary of Mrs Saas [*sic*], wife of Mr Saas [*sic*] of South Africa', *EM* (October 1814), p. 395.
13 Journal of Hannah Crook, 10 April 1821, National Library of New Zealand (hereafter NLNZ) Micro-MS-0726, p. 182.
14 Ibid., 5 March 1821, NLNZ Micro-MS-0726, p. 180.
15 George to Thomas Barker, 7 January 1837, NLSA(CT) MSB 57, 1 (14).
16 Crook Journal, 5 March 1821, NLNZ Micro-MS-0726, p. 180.
17 'Letter of Instructions from the Directors of the Missionary Society to Captain Robson of the Missionary Ship, Duff', *EM* (January, 1799), p. 9.
18 Diary of William Henry, Tahiti 1797, SSJ 1.
19 Diary of Rowland Hassell, 31 January 1798, SSJ 1, p. 6.
20 Livingstone to his parents, 13 July 1842 in Livingstone, *Family Letters*, vol. 1, p. 60.
21 Livingstone to Moffat, 11 February 1846 in Livingstone, *Family Letters*, vol. 1, p. 168.
22 Elizabeth Price to Jane Moffat (hereafter Price to Moffat), 23 November 1863, in Una Long (ed.), *The Journals of Elizabeth Lees Price: written in Bechuanaland,*

Southern Africa 1854–1883 with an Epilogue: 1889 and 1900 (London: Edward Arnold, 1956), p. 138.
23 Price, 'Reminiscences' in Long, *Journals*, p. 80.
24 Price to Moffat, 23 November 1863 in Long, *Journals*, p. 139.
25 Mary Moffat to Jane Philip, 12 September 1821, SAIL 8B/3.
26 Crook Journal, 24 May 1819, NLNZ Micro-MS-0726, p. 136.
27 Ibid., 21 June 1819, NLNZ Micro-MS-0726, pp. 139–41.
28 Anna Johnston, *Missionary Writing and Empire, 1800–1860* (Cambridge: Cambridge University Press, 2003), pp. 147–55.
29 Diary of William Henry, Tahiti 1797, SSJ 1.
30 Price to Moffat, 23 November 1863 in Long, *Journals*, p. 140.
31 David to Janet Livingston, 20 April 1849 in Livingstone, *Family Letters*, vol. 2, p. 33.
32 Price to Moffat, 24 June 1866 in Long, *Journals*, pp. 181, 178–9 and 182.
33 Crook to London, 14 May 1829, South Seas Incoming Letters (hereafter SSIL) 7/2/C.
34 Price to her sister Helen, 21 November 1862 in Long, *Journals*, p. 93.
35 Price to Moffat, 17 October 1866 in Long, *Journals*, p. 243.
36 Price to Moffat, 24 June 1866 in Long, *Journals*, p. 181.
37 Ibid., 17 October 1866 in Long, *Journals*, p. 242.
38 Ibid., 24 July 1866 in Long, *Journals*, pp. 202–3.
39 Ibid., 24 June 1865 in Long, *Journals*, p. 182.
40 Ibid., p. 179.
41 John Tosh, *A Man's Place: masculinity and the middle-class home in Victorian England* (New Haven, CT and London: Yale University Press, 1999), p. 86.
42 Livingstone to his parents and sisters, 9 February 1851 in Livingstone, *Family Letters*, vol. 2, p. 122.
43 Livingstone to his children, February 1853 in Livingstone, *Family Letters*, vol. 2, p. 206.
44 David to Mary Livingstone, 14 September 1855 in Livingstone, *Family Letters*, vol. 2, p. 268.
45 Tosh, *A Man's Place*, p. 86.
46 Price to Moffat, 17 October 1866 in Long, *Journals*, p. 236.
47 George to Elizabeth Barker, 5 May 1838, NLSA(CT) MSB 57, 1 (14).
48 Ibid., 20 December 1837, NLSA(CT) MSB 57, 1 (14).
49 Ibid., 17 October 1838, NLSA(CT) MSB 57, 1 (14).
50 Price to Moffat, 24 July 1866 in Long, *Journals*, p. 192.
51 David to Thomas Livingstone, 26 November 1852 in Livingstone, *Family Letters*, vol. 2, p. 192.
52 Tosh, *A Man's Place*, p. 91.
53 Cited in Natasha Erlank, 'Jane and John Philip: partnership, usefulness and sexuality in the service of God', in John de Gruchy (ed.), *The London Missionary Society in Southern Africa: historical essays in celebration of the bi-centenary of the LMS in Southern Africa, 1799–1999* (Cape Town: David Philip, 1999), p. 91.
54 Livingstone to his children, February 1853 in Livingstone, *Family Letters*, vol. 2, pp. 204–5.
55 David to Agnes Livingstone (Nannee), 18 May 1852 in Livingstone, *Family Letters*, vol. 2, p. 183.
56 Livingstone to his children, 2 October 1853 in Livingstone, *Family Letters*, vol. 2, p. 230.
57 Ibid., p. 230–1.
58 John Barff's Answers to Printed Questions (hereafter AtPQ), 2 May 1838, Candidate Papers (hereafter CP) 1/29.
59 William Philip to London, June 1836, CP 13/22.
60 Wilberforce Buxton Philip's AtPQ, 26 June 1855, CP 13/23.
61 George to Thomas Barker, 7 January 1837, NLSA(CT) MSB 57, 1 (14).
62 Ibid.
63 Charles Barff to London, 9 September 1845, SSIL 18A/4/B. See Chapter 6, pp. 162 and 167.

64 Lee Wallace, 'A House is not a Home: gender, space and Marquesan encounter, 1833–34', *The Journal of Pacific History* 40:3 (2005), 265–88. Quote on p. 273.
65 Neil Gunson, *Messengers of Grace: evangelical missionaries in the South Seas, 1799–1860* (Melbourne and Oxford: Oxford University Press, 1978), p. 159.
66 Livingstone to his children, 2 October 1853 in Livingstone, *Family Letters*, vol. 2, p. 229.
67 Livingstone to Moffat, 18 September 1850 in Livingstone, *Family Letters*, vol. 2, p. 104.
68 Jeal, *Livingstone*, p. 96.
69 Tosh, *A Man's Place*, p. 79.
70 See below, pp. 151–2.
71 John Gillis, 'Making Time for Family: the invention of family time(s) and the reinvention of family history', *Journal of Family History* 21:1 (1996), 4–21. How this may have changed in the face of mission institutionalisation (predominantly outside the chronological boundaries of this thesis), and thus male missionaries spending more time away from home, is interesting to consider.
72 Leonore Davidoff and Catherine Hall, *Family Fortunes: men and women of the English middle class, 1780–1850* (London: Hutchinson, 1987), p. 329.
73 George to Elizabeth Barker, 17 October 1838, NLSA(CT) MSB 57, 1 (14).
74 George Barker to his brother [unnamed], 4 April 1838, NLSA(CT) MSB 57, 1 (14).
75 Jeal, *Livingstone*, p. 76.
76 Livingstone to his parents and sisters, 28 July 1850 in Livingstone, *Family Letters*, vol. 2, p. 97. See also pp. 118–19.
77 Price to Moffat, 22 September 1866 in Long, *Journals*, p. 231.
78 Roger Price to his children, 13 January 1879, Cory Library, Rhodes University (hereafter CLRU) MS 5812.
79 Tosh, *A Man's Place*, pp. 93–100.
80 My emphasis. 'An Appeal on Behalf of the Institution for the Education of the Daughters of Missionaries', *EM* (October, 1847), p. 547.
81 See Chapter 6, pp. 174–5.
82 George Stallworthy to London, 3 July 1848, SSIL 21/5/A. See Chapters 2 and 4, pp. 44–8 and 118–20.
83 And colonial families: see Elizabeth Buettner, *Empire Families: Britons and late imperial India* (Oxford: Oxford University Press, 2004), pp. 110–87; and 'Parent-child Separations and Colonial Careers: the Talbot family correspondence in the 1880s and 1890s', in Anthony Fletcher and Stephen Hussey (eds), *Childhood in Question: children, parents and the state* (Manchester: Manchester University Press, 1999), 115–132.
84 See P. Pedersen, 'Anxious Lives and Letters: family separation, communication networks and structures of everyday life', *Culture and History* 8 (1990), 7–19; Buettner, *Empire Families*, pp. 130–8.
85 Mary Moffat to Elizabeth Lees, 15 September 1830 in John Smith Moffat, *The Lives of Robert and Mary Moffat* (London: T. Fisher Unwin, 1885), p. 168.
86 Ibid.
87 Ibid., p. 260–1.
88 Mary Moffat to her father, 17 March 1848 in Moffat, *Lives*, p. 264.
89 Ibid.
90 Price to her children, 17 January 1878 [*sic*], CLRU MS 5844.
91 Price to 'Dear friends', 15 December 1863 in Long, *Journals*, p. 155.
92 See Chapter 3, pp. 62–9.
93 Mary to John Moffat, 21 April 1848 in Moffat, *Lives*, p. 269.
94 Price to Moffat, 17 July 1863 in Long, *Journals*, pp. 128–9.
95 Ibid.
96 Price to her children, 28 May 1879 in Long, *Journals*, p. 355.
97 Roger Price to his children, 13 January 1879, CLRU MS 5812.
98 Ibid.
99 Mary Moffat to Elizabeth Lees, 15 September 1830 in Moffat, *Lives*, p. 168.

100 Livingstone to his children, February 1853 in Livingstone, *Family Letters*, vol. 2, p. 204.
101 Livingstone to his parents and sisters, October 1851 in Livingstone, *Family Letters*, vol. 2, p. 144.
102 David to Robert, Agnes and Thomas Livingstone, November 1852 in Livingstone, *Family Letters*, vol. 2, p. 191.
103 David to Thomas Livingstone, 26 November 1852 in Livingstone, *Family Letters*, vol. 2, pp. 192–3.
104 David to Mary Livingstone, 25 October 1854 in Livingstone, *Family Letters*, vol. 2, p. 250.
105 Pedersen, 'Anxious Lives and Letters', p. 9.
106 Livingstone to his children, 2 October 1853 in Livingstone, *Family Letters*, vol. 2, pp. 229–30.
107 Pedersen, 'Anxious Lives and Letters', p. 17.
108 David to Mary Livingstone, 25 October 1854 in Livingstone, *Family Letters*, vol. 2, p. 248.
109 Price to her children, 3 July 1879 in Long, *Journals*, p. 359.
110 See Buettner, *Empire Families*, pp. 72–110; Catherine Hall, 'Missionary Stories: Gender and Ethnicity in the 1830s and 1840s', in Catherine Hall, *White, Male and Middle Class: explorations in feminism and history* (Cambridge: Polity, 1992), pp. 205–55; Ann Laura Stoler, *Race and the Education of Desire: Foucault's History of sexuality and the colonial order of things* (Durham, NC and London: Duke University Press, 1995), pp. 98–9; and Ann Laura Stoler, 'Cultivating bourgeois bodies and racial selves' in Catherine Hall (ed.), *Cultures of Empire: colonisers in Britain and the Empire in the Nineteenth and twentieth centuries* (Manchester: Manchester University Press, 2000), pp. 87–119.
111 Stoler, *Race and the Education of Desire*; Mrinalini Sinha, *Colonial Masculinity: the 'manly Englishman' and the 'effeminate Bengali' in the late nineteenth century* (Manchester: Manchester University Press, 1995); Pamela Scully, 'Rape, Race, and Colonial Culture: the sexual politics of identity in the nineteenth-century', *The American Historical Review* 100 (1995), 335–59.
112 Mr Hayward's Answers to Queries, 1819, SSIL 3A/1/B.
113 John Orsmond to London, 1 June 1826, SSIL 5B/6/A.
114 Ibid., 1827, SSIL 6/1/A.
115 Ibid., 17 December 1827, SSIL 6/6/C.
116 Ibid., 1 June 1826, SSIL 5B/6/A.
117 Simpson to London, 18 May 1833, SSIL 9/1/D.
118 London to William Henry, 16 January 1845, Western Outgoing Letters: South Seas (hereafter WOL:SS) Box 3, pp. 338–9.
119 London to Darling, 15 January 1845, WOL:SS 3, pp. 327–8.
120 Henry to London, 9 October 1845, SSIL 18A/4/D.
121 *Annual Report* (1797), pp. xi–xii.

CHAPTER SIX

Missionary children

> Our sons Charles and Richard who have gone astray, have ceased to live with us since they acted so improperly. Every effort has been used to produce (under the blessing of God) a reform – conversation, prayer, writing, presentation of good books etc. and tears frequently flow when brought into conversation with us. Until about 3 or 4 years ago they were both hopeful characters, but on entering, in their little way, the commercial world, they were brought into contact with evils and characters they were unable to withstand ... and their conduct since has given us extreme pain.
> (South Seas missionary Charles Barff, 9 September 1845)

As we have seen throughout this book, then, the London Missionary Society (LMS) was constantly and consistently preoccupied with issues relating to missionary families, a situation forced upon them by missionaries in the field, who fretted anxiously about their children's futures, and by a philanthropically- and evangelically-minded missionary public. The LMS found itself embroiled in the intimacies of family life: from regulating and interfering with marriage, to monitoring missionaries' effectiveness as parents, and adopting an institutionally parental stance towards missionary children. Amid the debate, missionary children themselves can seem somewhat invisible, relatively silent, if not rendered speechless by the vagaries of institutional bookkeeping and historical accumulation. Nonetheless, by this stage in the book it has become clear that the LMS was continually forced to institutionally and formally interact with them, to the extent that missionary children, their presence and experience, fundamentally shaped the evolution of mission itself.

Mission theory had to respond to the presence of both missionaries' wives and children, and both can be seen as deeply involved in the civilising mission. Simultaneously, missionary parents were also preoccupied with their children's welfare, with the result that their understanding and practice of mission was also heavily influenced by their roles as parents. This chapter unpacks the duality of missionary children, how their good and bad behaviour could actively shape the mission experience, and even more profoundly, how parental responses to the presence and absence of their children shaped missionary prejudice. For it was parental anxiety about the moral, spiritual and material prosperity of their children that often elicited the most prejudiced responses from missionary parents, whose concerns increasingly shifted from cultural chauvinism to concerns about racial contamination and contact, and thus ultimately the increased racialisation of missionary discourse.

Third culture kids

All of the policies implemented by the LMS to consolidate the position of missionary families (from regional education to permanent establishment), and all of the parental strategies explored in Chapter 5 (from domestic sequestration to juvenile repatriation) were rooted in the notion that missionary children could either be an asset to the mission, or a hindrance. Embedded within their bi-cultural existence was the potential to seriously harm the mission, particularly as it became more extensively associated with the power of example, and the precepts of the civilising mission. Missionary children existed on the boundaries of two distinct, and mutually exclusive, cultures and societies. Their slippery social identities caused great anxiety to missionary parents, and to the London hierarchy of the LMS. Owing to the nature of their environment, they had the potential to cross both conceptual and social boundaries. Contact with local people, in relationships of both power and friendship, endangered their social identities and had the potential to compromise their racial and cultural status. Fears over 'contamination' through contact with indigenous peoples were at the root of policies of separation, from the role of the missionary mother as guardian of domestic boundaries, through the foundation of regional schools based upon the rubric of segregation, to the systematic introduction of juvenile repatriation. When Alexander Simpson, superintendent of the South Seas Academy (SSA) 1831–*c.*1840, 'built at my own expense, a wall six feet high and four thick enclosing nearly 5 acres of land' around that school in 1833, he was physically inscribing the social boundaries of segregation on to the spatial architecture of the Academy itself.[1] Contamination, separation and moral contagion became the ciphers through which missionary families' interactions with indigenous peoples were understood.[2] As such, the presence of missionary children often brought out the most chauvinistic and judgemental aspects of the missionary personality, informed by an ever-present anxiety about their racial, cultural and spiritual status.

Because of these difficulties in racially, culturally and socially positioning missionary children, they have been defined, along with other children of expatriate communities, as 'third-culture kids', a term originally coined by John and Ruth Hill Useem in the 1950s, and subsequently developed in sociological and educational circles, joined by the term 'global nomads,' more commonly used by followers of Norma McCaig and Barbara Schaetti.[3] The term originally denoted children raised in an interstitial atmosphere, whose social ties were linked with both the home culture of their parents, the regional culture in which they lived, and the third (or hybrid) culture in which they felt themselves to be situated. As such their position was an interstitial one; caught between, but also connecting, two cultural manifestations. While much of the work on these 'third-culture kids' (TCKs) relates to international children and families in the twentieth century, and is rooted in sociological investigations rather than historical examinations, the notion of children flowing across and between cultural boundaries is potently relevant to the lives and experiences of missionary children. What brings the importance of boundaries more to the fore in this instance is the fact that for missionaries, social and behavioural transgressions were entirely prohibited, viewed as temporally and spiritually dangerous, and seen to be indicative of a much broader and more worryingly intimate engagement with corrupting indigenous cultures. In the case of missionary children, their interstitial engagement with evolving cultures was less a point of connection and more a rift of division, hardening attitudes of separation among missionaries, and promoting an understanding of interracial contact (as dangerous) that was fundamentally inimical to the precepts of mission.

The children themselves, meanwhile, were understandably curious about the world around them, and whatever missionary parents tried to do to prevent it, often had relationships of varying sorts with the local people. Indeed, as in colonial settings more generally, while missionaries tended to think of themselves as isolated, their lives were structured around interracial and intercultural contact. They shared both their domestic and social spaces with the local community: from servants and visitors, to friends and converts. As has been discussed already, the mission home operated within permeable boundaries, and was a site for the public consumption of the civilising mission. For every story like Bessie Price's withdrawal of her son Rogie into the safety of the wagon 'inside the curtain with me',[4] there is another like that of Mary Moffat, who 'invite[d] them [the local women] in ... so that they might sit and become friendly'.[5] Contact with indigenous people was fundamental to the missionary endeavour, and it would be naive to imagine that children were not a constant part of it.

Thus, while the presence of missionary families could harden the racial attitudes of the missionaries, their children were often more open to interracial and intercultural contact. Unfortunately for missionary parents, this seemed at times to manifest itself in a juvenile propensity for misbehaviour, the children having picked up the seeming worst aspects of behaviour from their host cultures. The threat posed seemed redoubled in areas where local customs came across as peculiarly inimical to evangelical culture, such as in the Pacific where the 'temptations, inhibitions and opportunities for sexual experiment were more real for them than for children in other spheres'.[6] Missionary children were in a particularly difficult position. 'The mission children suffered considerably', notes Neil Gunson with some sympathy, 'for they could not be the children of both cultures and be happy'. In any form of social contact with the indigenous peoples they 'became estranged from their proper social community', ostracised and disconnected from their natal belongings.[7] For missionary children in the Pacific sexual transgressions were particularly prevalent, with one family in particular blazing a trail of sexual misconduct across the SSM. William Henry, a native Irishman who sailed to the Pacific with the first fleet of missionaries in 1796 and remained at the mission for fifty years (until 1847) had a 'large and frequently wayward family', whose multiple transgressions seriously undermined both his own career, and the mission itself.[8]

It was in fact to William and his first wife Sarah that the first child of the mission community was born, just ten weeks after the missionaries' arrival at Tahiti in 1797. In Sarah Henry Jr was signified both the great benefits that could accrue from missionary families and the first inklings of the dangers. Her presence signified the peaceful intentions of the missionaries, and united both the people and the local 'Chiefs' in an empathetic enjoyment of her presence: 'We are almost daily visited by strange natives, who come designedly to see her, and express no small astonishment at her principally because of her dress; and are exceedingly well pleased when we allow them to call her, Mydidde no Otaheite, which signifies, a Child of Otaheite.'[9] Their affection and indulgence of the young baby, however, both foreshadowed that 'excessive kindness' feared by missionary parents,[10] and indicated the potential linguistic, cultural and physical intimacy between missionary children and indigenous people that would later be deemed so unacceptable, owing to its potential subversion of a strictly evangelical culture. In naming her *Mydidde no Otaheite* (child of Tahiti), they were both transgressing later linguistic boundaries, and situating her firmly in their own social, cultural and regional context.

And of course this is the important point. The lives of missionary children were in fact forged through encounter. While parents attempted to socialise children into uncomplicated western norms, this was both impossible and impractical. Cultural hybridisation was an inevitable consequence of mission, particularly on the spiritual frontier, whether missionaries liked it or not. This hybridisation could be manifested in numerous ways. Even the Moffats, sometimes seen as the paragons of colonial values, as well as missionary values, found their home and bodies shaped by local custom. When Mary first heard of the practice in southern African of smearing one's floors with cow-dung, she exclaimed, 'I'll do without that dirty trick, or I will try hard [...] However, I had not been here long but was glad to have it done ... It lays the dust better than anything, [and] kills the fleas ... I now look upon my floor smeared with cow dung with as much complacency as I used to do upon our best rooms when well scoured.'[11] Even clothing, which so often in the missionary and colonial world stood as a cipher for western 'respectability' and 'civilisation', was subject to hybridisation on the spiritual (as the colonial) frontier. 'I often wear a Bichuana cap made of fox skins', wrote Robert in 1823, 'trousers of a prepared antelope skin, and my shoes are of my own manufacturing, entirely of leather, without either hemp or nail, and, if neatly made, quite resemble English shoes but in their native colour. Last winter I had a waistcoat and tucket made of tiger skin for the cold weather.'[12] Missionaries on the spiritual frontier engaged in a constant process of adjustment, so that their homes and bodies became nourished by the customs around them. On describing the 'thick milk' they drank in southern Africa, Mary Moffat noted that, 'I did not fancy it at first, but probably it was on account of its being brought in their dirty vessels. I have now got over that, and eat it with relish.'[13]

Pragmatism entailed hybridisation; but when it came to their children, missionaries tended to do all they could to mitigate against this legacy of encounter. It was Mary Moffat who had been 'tempted in thought to tie the little one on to her back as safely and comfortably as possible', but had concluded that 'with these women all round her doing the same ... it was too heathenish in appearance if not in reality'.[14] The dynamics of missionary families were forged in the history of encounter, whether through actual hybridity and change, or through the stubborn refusal to adjust to local pragmatism. 'The story of the first Henry ménage', meanwhile, argues Gunson, 'highlights many of the problems of adjustment' for missionary families on the spiritual frontier. The daily intimacy between the Henry children and the Tahitian people, including nursemaids and other servants, was something later stigmatised in a local context where 'fertility rites were practised ... human sacrifices were offered ... [and] sexual subjects were a constant topic of adult conversation'.[15] The history of the Henry children is one of sexual misconduct, marital breakdown, illegitimacy, cultural transgression, and immorality painted with broad strokes.[16] They were considered a great danger to the mission, and it is no coincidence that it was William Henry who suffered the first official wrath of the Directors when in 1845 effective missionary parenting was enshrined into missionary professionalism.[17] Yet the Henry children were by no means unusual, and the immorality of missionary children was a constant problem for the SSM (in particular). In 1829 Samuel Crook and Charles Wilson (Jr) were taken home from the SSA by their parents having received 'the sign of native circumcision'; in 1831 Adam Darling and Andrew Bicknell were expelled from the same institution 'for immoral conduct'.[18] 'Tears frequently flow' noted South Seas missionary Charles Barff on the topic of his wayward sons. 'Every effort has been used to produce (under the blessing of God) a reform – conversation, prayer, writing, presentation of good books etc ... Until about 3 or 4 years ago they were both hopeful characters, but on entering, in their little way, the commercial world, they were brought into contact with evils and characters they were unable to withstand ... their conduct since has given us extreme pain.'[19]

Nor was it just the boys who manifested such misbehaviour; 'some of the girls [also] show bad dispositions'.[20] The Misses Darling (daughters of David Darling) were accused of fornication, when the 'face of a native man ... [was] ... discovered under the bed'; Harriet Platt (daughter of George Platt) had been found with a local man in her bed, causing her mother to fall 'down in a fainting state'; and even John Orsmond's home came into question when a 'native was also found in her [his daughter's] bedroom but escaped through the thatch of the house'.[21] 'It is a well known fact to you', wrote Simpson to the Directors, 'that many of the children of missionaries in this section of the field are awfully depraved'.[22]

Missionary children rebelled in highly gendered and psychologically potent ways, with the active involvement of the indigenous peoples they were supposed to avoid. The sexual liaisons of the missionary daughters clearly involved indigenous men actively crossing the boundaries of mission-parent supervision, and intimately rejecting the cultural and racial mores of the mission community. More generally, the indigenous community at large, and important (and powerful) elements within it, were actively involved in the deviance of missionary children.

> Samuel Crook was taken home last month. It has come to light that on occasion he and Charles Wilson went over the play ground on a Saturday afternoon, went through our large garden, over its fence, and over by the side of the river under some trees received from the hand of a Hutae auri [i.e. a member of the religious Arioi society] the sign of native circumcision.[23]

Indigenous complicity was a clear element to this juvenile delinquency. The *Hutae auri* who administered the mark of native circumcision was actively engaging in a moment of serious spiritual and cultural transgression on the part of the missionary sons involved. This is suggestive of striking at the heart of missionary culture, and emotive resistance to missionary incursions into traditional practices and cultural life.

While missionary daughters collaborated in indigenous incursions on missionaries' private domestic space, then, sons of the mission tended to escape (rather than subvert) the physical and spatial boundaries of the mission, in order to engage with either indigenous custom or indigenous women. Simpson, in his narrative above of the deviance of Samuel Crook and Charles Wilson, seems to have dwelt more on the escapology of the children, than their actual deviance. They 'went over the play ground on a Saturday afternoon, went through our large garden, [and] over its fence' in a clear rebellion against the physical and moral boundaries erected around them. Simpson seems to have found this to be a particularly troubling aspect of their deviance, he having been the one to build the Academy's wall, designed specifically to keep 'improper characters at a respectful distance from the school'.[24]

Missionary children's deviancy undermined the moral legitimacy of the mission from within, and powerfully contravened the basic tenets of evangelical respectability. But the lives of their children were shaped by the politics of encounter. What they needed was to be sequestered, scrutinised and socialised into an understanding of cultural superiority. The lives of missionary children were shaped by their part in the missionary endeavour (for good or ill), but at the same time their influence over that endeavour was also important. Missionary children were an integral part of mission; their presence like their absence both shaped and undermined the nature of mission itself.

Moral scrutiny

Missionary children, from early in the missionary enterprise, were subjected to the intense and intimate moral scrutiny of the mission community. Their thoughts, words and deeds were all monitored and judged against a standard of evangelical morality that many of the missionaries themselves did not meet. While adult missionaries could be formally absolved or forgiven for their various (and numerous) transgressions, however, their children's psycho-sexual development was the most jealously guarded element within the missionary enterprise, one which would ultimately lead to the LMS formally instituting policies of moral scrutiny that infringed on the most intimate aspects of missionary childhood and adolescence. Moral scrutiny was generationally uneven, but stringently intense for missionary children. Nothing illustrated this more effectively than the case of Alexander Simpson, and his 'improper liberties'.

In the context of the SSM, moral scrutiny operated at a number of different levels, from the mission home and family, to the SSA, and ultimately to the mission committee. It was the mission families' apparent inability to effectively scrutinise their own children (as shown in Chapter 5) that led to this multi-layered approach, and as the second superintendent of the SSA, Alexander Simpson was a proud proponent of scrutinising strategies. When Adam Darling was accused of 'annoying the young women when in the house of God', Simpson 'reproved him sharply for his conduct, and henceforth narrowly watched his behaviour'.[25] Indeed, 'knowing the liability of those entrusted to our care to fall in the snares of bad men, we used parental watchfulness over them',[26] Simpson assured the Directors in 1844. As superintendent of the SSA, and therefore an 'official' or 'formal' scrutiniser of missionary children, Simpson involved himself in the absolute intimacies of the children's daily lives, including inspecting their dress and hygienic cleanliness, and even monitoring the girls' menstrual cycles.

> If it be indecent when I see a young woman placed under my care in a white dress, with *large 'stains'*, behind, of no doubtful character, I tell my wife of it, in order that the individual may know, be 'indecent language', [then] I plead guilt to the charge.[27]

The irony here is that in 1843 Simpson himself became subject to the scrutiny of his peers, having been accused of 'taking liberties of an indecent nature with the girls when at school and under his care'.[28] The two-day meeting to which the accusations against Simpson were presented proceeded with the letters of various of the missionary daughters being read to the assembled brethren, the young women themselves being absent. Simpson had five main charges brought against him, the details of which are worth quoting at some length.[29]

1. The case of Elizabeth Bicknell: 'Eliza Pritchard, Elizabeth Bicknell and myself [Harriet (Platt) Johnston] were one night sleeping together in one bed in the spare bed room … I was sleeping in the middle, and Elizabeth Bicknell on the side next to the door. I had not been

asleep long when Elizabeth Bicknell awoke me by pushing me with her elbow and making a noise with her mouth as if suffering pain. I turned round immediately and saw Mr Simpson lying upon Elizabeth Bicknell. Mr Simpson had only his night shirt on. I roused Eliza Pritchard and then Mr Simpson jumped off the bed and began to pull our toes. Eliza Pritchard cried out, oh! you hypocrite and then Mr Simpson left the room ... We had no sleep that night and lay thinking and talking about it till morning, and Elizabeth Bicknell positively declared to me and Eliza Pritchard that Mr Simpson had tried to violate her person, and had nearly succeeded, but for our disturbing him she thought he would have done it.'[30]

2. The case of Jane Barff: 'Jane Barff also told me [Eliza Darling] that Mr Simpson came to her bed during the night.'[31]
3. The case of Eliza Platt: 'Eliza Platt then related to me [Eliza Darling] as follows, during the day which was Tuesday, Mr Simpson winked at her, and asked her in Tahitian if she was a "*cahavai*" which means a chatterbox, to which she replied no she was not ... he said nothing more to her during the day, at midnight she awoke and was startled by hearing some one coming to her bed, and saying to her *E Raita E Raita* she got up in a fright to get out of bed, he pulled her back and said ... *Eiaha e natam** [*Do not fear], he then got under the clothes and she turned towards the wall and got her bed gown tightly round her, he then began to pull her about and to feel her bosom, and attempted to violate her person. She said to him Go away Sir, and was going to scream out, he then got up to go away, before he went he said to her *Eidia e farante ite man tamaline** [*Do not tell it to the girls], she thought he was under the influence of liquor, as he smelt very strong of spirits ...'[32]
4. The case of Louisa Barff [later, Thomson]: 'One Sabbath afternoon Mrs Simpson sent me to the boys room to awake Mr Simpson who was asleep upon one of the boy[']s beds ... instead of getting up, he invited me to lie down beside him, which I declined doing and drew back, when he said "Why not; there is no heaven unless we are under the clothes"!'[33]
5. The cases of Charlotte Wilson and Eliza Darling: 'I [Charlotte Wilson] ... did think that Mr Simpson used too much freedom with my self and the young ladies at school. The freedoms to which I refer were coming into our bed room where we have been but partly dressed, tickling us ... also coming into the bed room at night'.[34] ' ... we [Mary and Eliza Darling] are sorry to be obliged to say that we have frequently thought Mr Simpson's conduct improper and unbecoming such as coming in the girls bed room when we have been washing, coming in at night when we have been undressed and pushing us about ...'[35]

On top of this, Simpson was also accused of indulging in apparently lesser 'improprieties', including 'too great [a] freedom with the bottle' and 'adultery with native girls and women'.[36] He denied all the charges and challenged the validity of both the evidence brought forward, and the fact that his accusers were not present at what amounted to his trial.

Despite what seemed to be the overwhelming evidence of indecent behaviour, including at least two charges of serious sexual assault, Simpson was not removed from his post and the majority of the brethren merely resolved,

> That the Rev A Simpson has subjected himself to the severest censure of this Committee by his past conduct and its members hope he may be led to humble himself before God, at the same time they assure him that should his future conduct again render him subject to an investigation his conviction will occasion his separation from the Mission, but should his course become such as we desire he will be admitted into our fullest confidence.[37]

While 'Simpson manifested unendurable calmness on the occasion and received the resolution of the Brethren with every appearance of a good spirit, confessing nothing more than imprudencies',[38] it soon emerged that the mission was deeply unhappy with this conclusion. Missionary John Jesson was said to have told Mr Simpson that, 'Yea could we prove half these reports about the dear young ladies, children of the venerable Missionaries; you ought to hang by the neck',[39] and a number of the missionaries wrote to London expressing their unhappiness with the censure passed upon their colleague.[40] Scandalised by the implications of the case, but at the same time unable to effectively cope with its deeply emotive subject matter, the SSM opened itself unashamedly to the 'impartial though rigid' scrutiny of the LMS Directors in London,[41] that they 'may be able to form a judgment of their own independent of our decisions'.[42]

Many fascinating and important points and details arise from this case, and the many papers that flowed back to London in relation to it,[43] but two stand out in importance for this chapter, and this book. The first is that moral scrutiny was a pervasive and fundamental aspect of mission community life; the second is that such scrutiny was asymmetrical, directed far more at the children of the community, than at the adults. Indeed, the secretary of the mission Thomas Joseph freely admitted that 'nothing has been done in regard to the reports relative to the native women', and that he was thus 'not at liberty to say anything officially in regard to them'.[44] As for the alleged victims, however, only three of the missionaries 'receive[d] the statement[s] of the young ladies to their fullest extent'. Mr Simpson, meanwhile, 'had a large share of our sympathy on the occasion and we started the enquiry with the express understanding that he would have the benefit of every doubt'.[45]

On top of flatly denying the more serious charges, Simpson also called forth a defence of parental care by proxy, arguing that his monitoring of the missionary daughters was purely paternal, and further that he only ever undertook this responsibility (his usual monitoring duties being directed at the boys in the school) 'during the illness of Mrs Simpson',[46] or when the girls were unwell, 'but then always with a light'.[47] It was through this defence that he has left a revealing account of parental (and quasi-parental) moral scrutiny to us as historians of Christian mission, even though it was ultimately concluded that his parental scrutinies had crossed the boundaries of acceptable behaviour, he having been 'found in the bedrooms of the young ladies under mysterious circumstances'.[48]

For missionary children, moral scrutiny started at the most basic level. All aspects of their lives had a moral dimension, and required the strict implementation of scrutinising strategies to mitigate against moral contamination. Language in particular was a key site of moral policing. While the children were educated in, and socialised into, English, they could still 'converse in the Tahitian as well as in the former language'.[49] In the missionary context there was a strong moral dimension to linguistic adherence and contravention. Etymological facility denoted cultural fluency, and behavioural fluidity. As Ann Stoler has argued, 'language was seen to fix the parameters of children's perceptions, enabling them to think certain sentiments and not others'.[50] Language was the gateway to 'the native mind', for if they understood the linguistic markers of cultural practices, there were few boundaries to their involvement in indigenous behaviours. 'Language, then, is a nodal point of mutual imbrication at the most personal, subjective level. Linguistic exchange threatens to destabilise foundational assumptions about selfhood and cultural integrity.'[51] In short, the Tahitian language unlocked those aspects of Tahitian culture not easily linguistically or culturally translated, and fluency in Tahitian for missionary children was the most obvious marker of moral corruption, with worrying undertones of sexual deviancy, rejection of Christian spirituality, and adherence to local culture and custom. These complex links were noted by Richard Lovett when writing his history of the LMS in the 1890s.

> The missionaries soon discovered that for their children to acquire the language, and hear it daily spoken, in which almost every colloquial sentence contained indecencies too gross for description, was a most hurtful moral influence. The fact of living in the midst of a heathenism whose daily and outward practices were of the most foul and debasing character inevitably blunted, and that very early, the moral perceptions of these unhappy children. Some of the saddest pages in these early records

> are those which tell of the grievous moral lapses of both boys and girls who, carefully watched over by their parents, the children of earnest, fervent, continuous prayer, yet could not be kept from the deadly pollution of the heathenism amidst which their childhood was passed.[52]

'In no instance are the boys, or girls, allowed to converse with native adults, or children, unless in our presence, and at our request,'[53] wrote Simpson in 1833. Despite the practical utility of bi-linguality, the language of the SSA was proscriptively English. 'In the case of Eliza Platt who said I spoke to her in Tahitian [that is] a thing very unlikely as I always spoke to them in English.'[54]

For missionary children (as indeed for indigenous converts) materiality was also a moral issue. Linguistics, hygiene, and the practical intimacies of daily life were infused with moral meaning. 'We had *often* to reprove a *want* of cleanliness in their persons', remarked Sarah Simpson at the height of the case against her husband.[55] While this was not necessarily unusual in nineteenth-century dealings with adolescents and children, in the South Seas (or global) context material-moral elements of life stood as ciphers for deeper concerns; and transgression from Western materiality was embedded with a worrying potential for a more pervasive cultural contravention of Western norms and standards. On the issue of insufficient hygiene, represented earlier by menstrual 'stains' on the girls' clothing, the Simpsons again pointed out the girls' moral failings through material circumstances. In mission and colonial contexts, deep-rooted moral and spiritual corruption were evidenced by outward signs that required a vigilant scrutiny, so that restorative measures could be enacted before the child was lost to a more profound infringement of respectability.

Simpson, meanwhile, was not found guilty of sexual assault, despite what seemed overwhelming evidence. The young ladies' testimonies were fatally corrupted by their liminal racial and cultural status, and the mission refused to implement the unfettered scrutiny of their missionary colleague required by such a case. It was questioned, however, how far a non-parent could be charged with the scrutinising strategies required of missionary parents. The District Committee did conclude that: 'Mr Simpson has been found in the bedrooms of the young ladies under mysterious circumstances and that the charge of indecencies is fully borne out.'[56] Simpson's failure to convince in his defence of parental care by proxy re-drew the lines of parental (over communal) responsibility and scrutiny. In so doing, however, it also implicated missionary parents in the deviancy of their children. Thus it was in the context of this case that effective parenting was inscribed into the missionary's professional duties and identity: 'should any missionary decline to withdraw his countenance and support from any member of his family guilty of open and habitual vice, the Directors will feel under the painful necessity of withdrawing their support and confidence from such missionary'.[57] With extra parental rights came additional parental responsibilities. While the linking of missionary parenting with missionary professionalism was a result of adult deviancy, its primary ramification was to formalise the (official, if not intimate) moral scrutiny of missionary children: 'the Missionary Committees are expressly required to report to the Directors every such case [of deviancy] that may unhappily occur in any mission family'.[58]

Socialisation, superiority, and vocational replication

Separation, moral scrutiny, and juvenile repatriation were all very well, but to some extent attempted to lock the door after the horse had bolted. Missionary children needed to be socialised into the normative cultural relationships upon which evangelical mission respectability was based. Healthy relationships with indigenous peoples needed to be mapped on to a stadial hierarchy, in order that missionary children could instinctively assert their own moral superiority and thereby avoid the contaminating influences involved in interracial and intercultural contact. Inculcating this embedded hierarchy of relationships became a crucial aspect of missionary parenting. Their superiority, in the eyes of the mission, needed to be established from a young age, as did the dangers involved in too much contact with indigenous peoples. Missionary children, like their colonial counterparts, had to learn the 'right social affiliations'.[59] If they could be correctly socialised, contaminating influences would simply spin off a barrier of respectability, faith, and hierarchical pre-eminence.

At the same time, of course, the instillation of some fusion of racial and cultural authority into missionary children fundamentally undermined the humanitarian universalism that formed the ideological basis of the missionary enterprise. The presence of children in the mission elicited responses from the mission community that were dialectically opposed to its basic ethical tenets. Colonial historian Richard Price has recently described the 'closing of the missionary mind'.[60] Contact with indigenous peoples and their refusal to conform to new mission or Christian identities, as well as the nature of their cultures and how these were understood by missionaries steeped in their own cultural baggage, meant that the 'optimistic and hopeful missionary culture of the evangelical revival was steadily eroded, to be replaced by a volatile, pessimistic despair'.[61] While rather reductionist in its homogenising of 'the missionary mind', this is a powerfully eloquent way of describing a process implicit in many understandings of mission history. This chapter suggests a new element in this process of erosion: missionary children. The dynamics of missionary racism and cultural chauvinism, linked with the evolving importance of the civilising mission, cannot be disentangled from that most intimate of life-states: parenthood.[62]

This is not to impute racism to missionary children themselves. The parental responses that the presence of the children educed were based on anxious fears about the influence of mission contexts and environments on missionary children, and how contact with indigenous peoples could contaminate juvenile members of the mission community. After all, 'bad native habits are so exceedingly contagious for young people', wrote Simpson.[63] This concern about missionary children being 'heathenised' bubbled over into hints (if not overt statements) of biological essentialism and fears about juvenile contact with indigenous converts which were entirely contradictory to the universalist principles of mission itself. This was not necessarily a conscious or overt process, but rather flowed from the presence and parental socialisation of missionary children. Missionaries had no vested interest in ideologically undermining their own vocation, which *had* to be based upon universalism; but they did have an interest in safeguarding the temporal and eternal futures of their children.

This was most evident in the socialisation of children into superiority, something which became an implicit and unconscious part of a much broader and more self-consciously positive education on what it meant to be a missionary. While the ultimate purpose for missionary parents of this social instruction was to create a new generation of missionaries, it also served to socialise children into an understanding of indigenous contact based on moral, cultural and at times even racial pre-eminence. It was the earnest desire of missionary parents that their children would become missionaries. 'Were I a mother', wrote Mary Moffat to her mother in 1818, 'I should esteem it the greatest honour which could be conferred on me or my child' that they should be a missionary.[64] She reiterated the notion in 1860. Referring to a period of illness occasioned by the birth of her son John in 1835 she noted,

> How little did I then think that the very babe who sat before me on his nurse's lap was destined to go to that savage people to hold before them the lamp of eternal life ... Now ... those sweet infant smiles so tenaciously held in my remembrance seem to have had language. Methinks they said, 'cheer up, dear mother; though you think your course is nearly finished, I am destined to live to fulfil your heart's desire. I shall yet become a missionary to that very people for whom you have so cheerfully parted with him who could, better than any one else, have succoured and cherished you in the season of debility and weakness.[65]

For Mary Moffat the sense of importance imputed to ensuring a recurrence of the missionary vocation within her own family remained an undercurrent to her parenting throughout her life. Four of her seven children who lived to adulthood were missionaries; and this not including Jane (who remained with her parents, facilitating and contributing to their mission activities until their respective deaths), nor Robert Jr (who before his death had apparently 'promised to be not only a help to the mission, but a stay to them [his parents] in their declining years').[66] Mary Moffat was not the only missionary mother to instil a sense of vocation in her children. 'Jane Philip's children and grandchildren were constantly being admonished to be useful',[67] and missionary parents throughout the enterprise sought to bequeath both religiosity and vocation to their children.

Nor was it just missionary mothers who cherished hopes that their children would become missionaries. Missionary fathers cherished similar hopes for their offspring. Parental desire for vocational replication may well have been a feature of the professional classes more generally. For missionary families this had a religious and eternal dimension linked not only to the individual soul, but to the souls of thousands of 'perishing heathen'. 'Now you are little, but you will not always be so, hence you must learn to read, and write, and work', wrote David Livingstone to his children in 1853.

> All clever men can both read and write, and Jesus needs clever men to do His work. Would you not like to work for Him among men? Jesus is wishing to send His gospel to all nations, and He needs clever men to do this. Would you like to serve Him? Well, you must learn now, and not get tired learning. After some time you will like learning better than playing, but you must play too in order to make your bodies strong and be able to serve Jesus.[68]

The desire to replicate parental vocation had to be socialised into children and encouraged from an early age. 'The bell has just been rung, and I am alone with Jim [aged five] and Jack [aged three]', wrote Robert Moffat in 1838, 'the one on my right hand, and the other on my left, talking and questioning with no little volubility.'

> I had scarcely finished [my] work when he [Jim] perched himself at the end of the table and stood in the attitude of a Grecian orator, and questioned me about the resurrection from the dead. The conversation, or rather the contention, lasted for more than half an hour, while Jack stood with his hands crossed behind his back wondering and sometimes repeating Jim's enquiries. Never in my life was I so delighted with the questions of child. 'Will these hairs,' laying his hand on his brow, 'also come out of the dust on that day?' 'Could the naughty children who have died come back and hear preaching they would not be naughty again'.

> 'How can that which has decayed become alive again?' 'I know mamma says that God is a very, very great God; will He make the dead come out of their graves?' I gave a few simple hints about the coming of Christ.[69]

Children are hard-wired to mimic their parents (and other adults) as a tool to learning, and the primary mechanism for this socialisation into missionary norms was the power of example. Young Jim Moffat, in his exposition, was both mimicking his father, and exploring a missionary understanding of the world around him. 'When I asked where he had heard of Christ coming in flames of fire, he said, "Do not you teach the people that He will come in that way?"' Robert was clearly enchanted by the connections his son was drawing between the temporal and the spiritual. The 3-year-old Robert Livingstone also mimicked his father's professional activity.

> Robert is just beginning to understand matters. A great imitator. When just beginning to walk he was fond of doctoring the Natives and himself. Butter is his great remedy. After having the rod applied to his tail, he applies a piece, and thinks all right. Any one with a wound coming past may get it mollified if Robert sees it. He shewed his faith in butter long before he could speak.[70]

There was parental direction behind this mimicry, however, and missionaries explicitly promoted the connections between emulation, and educative socialisation into missionary activity.

> Janet and Agnes will be amused by one of Robert's ideas. Having spoken to him in private about praying, a few days after he had seen me baptising the little one who was removed from us, he went out and came in again with some water on his face and said, 'Papa, I have baptised myself'!! We desire above all things that they may be on the Lord's side, as we have dedicated them all to Him and His service.[71]

The links between education (David having taught his son about prayer) and emulation (Robert having recently witnessed his father baptising his sister) are clear. That David himself saw a logical connection between this and cherished hopes of vocational continuity speak to the socialised nature of young Robert's missionary attitude.

While Robert Livingstone's use of butter as a medical panacea is clearly simple mimicry (and a way for him to alleviate pain), there is something deeper in Jim Moffat's rhetorical exposition on theology. At the age of only five, and with some recognition that Robert's transcription of the event probably contained editing and exaggeration, he was isolating the key questions relative to the missionary enterprise: existentialism and the materiality of the soul, the power of the Word, and the imponderability of the resurrection. The conscious ascription of meaning and content to such action and engagement most likely evolved over time, under parental direction. Facing the questioning mind of his son, Robert Moffat did not expound on deeply theological answers to these questions. He merely 'gave a few simple hints about the coming of Christ', and took pride in his son's ability to ask the right questions. A deeper understanding would come with time.

Religious (and cultural) socialisation was crucial to missionary parenting. After all, while ('bad') children could be harmful to a mission's moral authority ('good') children could also be a great bulwark of mission, and not just as examples in its 'civilising' aspect. Male and female missionaries utilised their children in the mission context, implicitly and explicitly. Implicitly, effective parenting and the correct treatment of children were central to the normative Christian household. When Bessie Price noted that she could not teach Bantsan (one of Chief Sechele's daughters) English because of her familial commitments, Bantsan replied,

> 'My children! Besi! do I know them? – do you suppose I nurse and follow them about as you do yours? Not I! – I never see them – this one and that one nurses them – but I don't have anything do [to] do with them!' Whereupon I shook my head very sadly at her.[72]

While parental neglect was clearly problematic, over-indulgence was equally discredited (and ridiculed). Hannah Crook noted with some exasperation the over-sensitivity of 'her women' towards their children. 'One woman came to us the other day in tears to tell us she had whipped her child and was in great trouble about it though the child was with her and playing about as if nothing had happened.'[73] The key to a mature fullness in Christ was balance within family life, and knowing that a Christian household had space for both kindness and discipline. The parent was, after all, like God: firm yet loving.

More than this implicit example, however, missionaries used their children as tools within the missionary enterprise, from practical involvement, to active engagement.

> Little Rogie has become quite active in bestowing the spelling books, for when I have stitched and cut it, I give it to him always and he just goes straight to the door and gives it to the eager supplicant, who loads him with thanks – 'Ah my little friend! my Father! you have indeed enriched and blessed me!!!'[74]

In involving her young son in this aspect of the missionary enterprise, Bessie Price was not only providing a bored toddler with fun activities, but was implicitly socialising him into missionary behaviour, and inculcating in him a sense of beneficent superiority, as exemplified by the apparently excessive gratitude of the local people. This socialisation into superiority was the darker side of missionary parenting: the bequeathal of cultural, and even racial, chauvinism.

Domestic normativity itself also involved the familial performance of cultural superiority. When Hannah Crook took her children with her on what transpired to be an inspection of the local people's houses, her comments drew a line between correct familial relationships, household normativity, and what form of domesticity was appropriate for Christian children. She made explicit the implicit normativity of the missionary household in taking her daughters to visit the local houses. In so doing, she was both involving them in missionary visitation, a key tool of the female missionary enterprise in particular, and utilising them to reference the normative Christian household.

> Today I took a walk with the children my intention was to see if I could stir up the people to be more cleanly in their houses ... I went on looking into several houses ... I said these houses are dirty. We cannot go into them for the fleas will torment us. You like to talk to me at our house, do you not like us to come and talk to you at your houses. Show me I said but one clean house that I may go in and sit down.[75]

Crook's children thus became a test of respectability and decency. They, being constructions of exemplary familial relations and Christian respectability, as well as promoting an ideal of Christian childhood, could not even find a suitable place to sit. How could the local baptised people effectively raise their Christian children in a domestic setting which the missionary's children could not even visit? It is not difficult to imagine how such an episode could have inculcated a sense of superiority in these missionary daughters. The fact that these were baptised people rather than simple 'heathens', began to blur the line between cultural chauvinism and racial prejudice.[76]

This sort of missionary-supervised contact between children and indigenous peoples often involved elements of superiority and normativity. The social intercourse between missionary children and indigenous peoples was extremely circumscribed, and missionaries sought to ensure that such association as did occur made clear the hierarchical authority of their children within the minds of the children themselves, and within the minds of the indigenous peoples who were taught to look to missionary families as exemplars of Christian domesticity. Thus, Hannah Crook managed the contact her children had with the local baptised people, and in the SSA too, legitimate contact was supervised, highly staged and demonstrably performative. On the Sabbath they 'attend[ed] the preaching to the natives morning and afternoon', and on Wednesdays 'all attend the morning lecture to the natives'.[77] It seems likely that both such activities would have involved potent displays of performed missionary superiority, probably including religious exhortations, tirades against 'debased' indigenous behaviours, and the consistently staged inferiority of indigenous culture and custom.

All in all, missionary children were socialised into two contradictory principles: on the one hand to love and cherish indigenous peoples as children of God ripe for conversion (the missionary principle); on the other, to fear and loathe them as degraded and debased creatures of devilish desires (the principle of superiority). In expressing their gratitude to the Directors for founding the SSA, the female students of that institution expressed this essential dichotomy in succinct form: 'To be kept from the filthy communications of the ungodly natives, from those unblushing sights which shock our modesty; to be associated with those who while they seek to store our minds with useful knowledge aim to point us to the Lamb of God for life and peace are certainly some of the greatest blessings.'[78] On the one hand then, missionary children were educated into an all-embracing Christianity, and a missionary enterprise that *had*, by its very nature, to see indigenous peoples as equally capable of salvation; on the flipside they were constantly warned of the dangers of 'pernicious association',[79] and upbraided to be grateful for their enforced separation from the local peoples. 'Some of us will soon leave school as our time is up', wrote Samuel Crook when faced with leaving the SSA in 1827, 'and we shall be left to get our living as well as we can by ourselves in a land that is full of revengeful, jealous, and ill natured Tahitians.'[80]

Informal missionaries

By adolescence, many missionary children were active participants in the missionary enterprise, to the extent of blurring the lines between official and unofficial involvement. At adolescence, missionary children stood between childhood participation, and adult vocation. Hannah Crook found the assistance offered by her two eldest daughters indispensable in the later years of her mission. 'In conversing with the natives I always have one or both of them with me as assistants in the language as they are well acquainted with it.'[81] When Hannah started a women's meeting designed to encourage and inculcate indigenous philanthropy (through the visitation of the sick), Mary was to 'keep our accounts and Hannah [Jr] is to be overseer of the property'.[82] By 1824 both girls were actively engaged in the missionary work of their parents, causing their father to reflect that, 'God has given us his blessing. The two eldest girls have given decided evidence of their piety and have joined the church. They are also of great service to me in teaching and governing the young ones ... I take the principal class of men and Mary and Hannah [Jr] the two principal classes of women, the rest are arranged under native assistants.'[83] At 20 and 18 years of age respectively, Mary and Hannah (Jr) were both occupied in mission teaching and the governing of their younger sisters (aged between 4 and 17). This was the result not only of their own active faith,[84] but of the tuition they had received from their parents: 'We have carefully educated our daughters to fit them for the Lord's service in this world, and for happiness in the world to come.'[85]

The Crook girls thus conformed to a steady trend in missionary circles, and one with which historians of Christian mission will be familiar: adolescent mission activity. What we can see here is that such activity flowed directly from the desires and designs of their parents. The Moffat girls too were socialised into mission activity from an early age. When later talking about her post-education return to Kuruman aged 15, in 1854, Bessie Price described how on their journey home, her mother had shared the principal events of her life, including her childhood, but most notably told through the rubric of her mission experience.[86] For Mary and Bessie, this was the beginning of a period of apprenticeship during which Mary taught her daughter how to be both a woman and a missionary.

> When I reached Kuruman and began learning all my little home-duties, I was quite shocked to find that I could not sew half as well as my Mother's servants and pupils could ... My Mother said very little about it, but she cut me out half a dozen calico shirts for my father, and bade me learn on those, 'for' she said, 'a shirt has in it every kind of needle-work' ... Next I learnt how to starch and iron a shirt – blundering a good deal at first, but succeeding at last ... and I then learnt the same process with my mother's Caps ... I can remember one occasion on which my mother reproved me saying – 'Bessie! What a spectacle you have made of this Cap this week.' How I winced under it. But my Mother taught me very kindly. I remember saying to her one day 'Every thing seems easy to learn out here with you' and I meant it – for there was a sense of ease about her teaching altho' she was sometimes a bit hasty, but t'was like a flash and out in an instant, excepting when I said anything at all heterodox – then she became severe – and could not get over it for awhile.[87]

The practicalities of women's work in the South African context were the first order of business in this apprenticeship, though there is a suggestion that some element of religious training was also involved, for when she said 'anything at all heterodox' her mother would become 'severe'. More explicit missionary training was also involved.

> I remember on one or two occasions taking her Sunday Bible-class for her. It meant listening to the repetition by young women of whole

> epistles from the N.T. It was marvellous beyond everything to hear the correctness with which they did it – and their behaviour all the while was faultless. I always accompanied her to the Sewing-School and helped her there.

All the while practical tuition continued. 'I learnt to make butter and bread and pastry ... I learnt on my father's brown bread which I also shared at the table.'[88] Bessie in turn began to counsel Jane, before she too left Walthamstow Hall to return to Kuruman. 'And soon dear Janey, you will be coming to teach our Kuruman lasses and I think you will find much pleasure in the occupation, tho' at the same time much need of patience.'[89]

For missionary daughters, as for their mothers before them, mission activity was united in domestic concern, and even for the next generation of missionary women a sometimes uneasy balance had to be struck. Elizabeth Barker came to assist her father George after the death of her mother in 1836. 'Elizabeth returned from Cape Town to take charge of my house, she has resigned from a fine Infant school, left a circle of pious young people who were much attached to her, to share my seclusion.'[90] Like her mother before her, she too (and her younger sister Ann) had to juggle her new role as domestic exemplar with her more vocational roles. 'Elizabeth is housekeeper. She is a real Missionary. She has a number of children in the afternoon to teach needlework, twice a week a writing school for adults, and is teaching some of the youth to take notes of my sermons.'[91]

> Elizabeth instructs the three little girls [her sisters, Jane, Mary Ann and Harriet] at home ... As soon as they are up, the little ones go to their lessons, and the elder girls set the house in order, and get breakfast. At 9 o clock Elizabeth sits down with her little sisters, and Ann goes to the Infant school till 12 o clock, when we dine for convenience sake. After dinner the little ones attend to arithmetic. At 2 o clock school begins and Elizabeth has a class of little girls, from the Infant school, in addition to her sisters, until 4 o clock, when we take tea. On monday and wednesday evenings we have an adult school after tea. On Tuesday and Thursday evening preaching.[92]

Juvenile repatriation did little to disrupt this rhythm of generational activity, only delaying the involvement of adolescents until after their education. 'Our dear daughter at Walthamstow will have finished her term of education by the time this reaches England', wrote Charles Barff in 1850, 'and being the youngest we should like her to come out with the Directors permission, and take part in the Schools'.[93]

But this should by no means imply that missionary daughters were the only missionary children involved in active mission work. The

Moffat sons were also educated in the practicalities of mission life. 'In those days everyone had to be his own farmer, blacksmith, carpenter and builder. It was often my lot to take such a part as was possible in these activities for a youngster of my age', recalled John Moffat in his later life.[94] Charles Barff Jr was to be trained as a printer in 1830 in order that he could be of use to the mission, and numerous missionary sons (including sons of John Orsmond, Charles Barff and George Pritchard) were involved at various times with the SSM's sugar mill, and were thus connected with the secular side of mission work.[95] John Barff noted in his Candidate Papers (upon application to join the LMS in 1838) that he had 'taught in Sunday Schools both at Huahine, and London; and have assisted Mr [John] Williams in the translation of small religious publications'.[96] Wilberforce Buxton Philip 'was for more than a twelvemonth engaged in teaching the young in the School at Hankey (South Africa) both in the weekday school and in the Sabbath School'.[97]

As a source in this respect Candidate Papers are full of adolescent engagement, but can be somewhat problematic, given their direct purpose of convincing the LMS to undertake the education and training of future missionaries, and their bias towards missionary children who felt involved and engaged with the missionary enterprise. More commonly missionary parents were concerned about establishing secure secular careers for their sons. While missionary daughters had to wait for marriage opportunities, giving them time in which to work for the mission, their brothers had to use their own adolescence and early adulthood to establish themselves economically. This was a preoccupation for missionary parents who often used their personal contacts to secure their sons' entry into business. By 1842 George Barker's eldest son Edward was comfortably attached to his brother-in-law's apothecary, with the possibility of himself becoming part-owner of the business. 'Edward is with his brother Monro, who is doing a good business. Sarah [his older sister] writes me that Edward is very sturdy and attentive to business, and if all turns out well he has a prospect of a share in it.'[98]

While business was not always considered the most desirable career for missionary sons, it was more often than not the most practicable opportunity available to them. Charles Barff, talking of two of his sons 'who have gone astray' (Charles and Richard), decidedly placed the blame at their having 'enter[ed], in their little way, the commercial world, [where] they were brought into contact with evils and characters they were unable to withstand'.[99] George Barker described the problems to his sister when faced with the impending young adulthood of his second son John.

> I can place him in a printing office in Cape Town, but if he is willing I will put him into the school and relieve Elizabeth as it is too much for a female to manage big boys. Our Society do not do right, our children might be used in the schools, and would save the expense of sending men from England. Beside a European has to learn the language, and to know the people before he can be of any use. Whether John will consent to take the school remains to be known, he is 18 years old this month, and could earn at his business probably 30 or 40 shillings a week, and the missionary society would demur at giving him so much per month. Our school masters get about 60£ [*sic*] per annum, but they think missionaries['] children must work for nothing. They allow 15£ [*sic*] per year for our Infant school, a school with daily attendance of 80 children. We have no encouragements to make our children useful, we never had, and now the funds of the Society are low. It really requires a person to be a man of God, to be a missionary, for there are no worldly inducements.[100]

Missionary children well knew that the missionary vocation was not a lucrative one. 'I have good reason for believing, so far as human foresight avails, that my worldly circumstances will not be bettered by my becoming a missionary', wrote John Smith Moffat in his LMS application in 1853.[101] Recognising that the missionary life was a hard one, William Philip noted, 'I have had an opportunity of seeing some of the hardships to which Missionaries are exposed, and have I trust seriously considered them, and am willing to succumb to them.'[102] Perhaps unsurprisingly, John Barker did not pursue the hopes of his father in his young adulthood, instead joining a counting house and store, to 'give him an idea of mercantile business'.[103]

By the 1880s, controversy had also surfaced on the issue of paying missionary daughters for their co-opted service to mission. While 'the help of missionary daughters may have blunted the urgency of the need for single women who could provide full-time services and continuity',[104] in a context, from 1875, in which single female missionaries were systematically employed by the LMS, it was increasingly unsustainable for them to continue to utilise familial female labour in the former manner. In 1880 Annie Lea Duthie (daughter of James Duthie, India missionary 1856–1908) landed in India, after a Scottish education. She had applied to the Ladies Committee (founded in 1875) in order to return to the field as an agent of the Missionary Society, and had been told to contact them after she had been in India six months. Having done so, the LMS remained ambivalent about paying her as a missionary. 'As to the general question of the employment of Missionaries' Daughters', wrote her father in the face of continued LMS recalcitrance, 'I do not at all think that they should be employed except where there is work to be done ... But where, as here, there is work (*much* work in fact) and a readiness to engage in it, then it does seem to me that, while full Zenana Missionary's salary is not at all required, there should be given, at least, what will suffice for food and Clothes ... It is surely not too much for me to ask, on her behalf, this much.'[105] On a small mission salary, James Duthie could not afford to subsidise the continued involvement of his daughter in the mission, despite her utility. Numerous other missionaries weighed into the debate. James Emlyn argued in 1881 that, with more work in India than missionaries' wives could feasibly undertake, and the resources of the Society being unequal to the greater employment of lady missionaries proper, 'the decision to allow small salaries to qualified daughters of missionaries for work definitely undertaken by them while still living under their parents' roof, is not only natural, but thoroughly wise'.[106] William Lee also concurred. 'If the Ladies' Society is able to carry out this plan of employing the daughters of Missionaries when competent for special work to help their parents, it would certainly be productive of great benefit.'[107] The sticking point for the LMS was, as ever, monetary. Why pay for familial labour when it was so often proffered for free? While the labour of missionary children was systematically assumed, particularly where relative to missionary daughters, their informal work would remain unrecognised, fiscally or formally.

Conclusion

Missionary children were a constant source of anxiety and concern for their parents, and increasingly for the institution of which they were becoming recognised as a part. All of this worry and unease seemed often to be for good reason: missionary children around the world did have a propensity for misbehaviour and outright deviance. The LMS and its missionaries dealt with this by trying to mitigate against the negative effects of the missionary encounter – externally by separating children from the communities in which they were raised (first through the home; later through the school), and internally by inculcating a layer of western superiority into the very hearts of the next generation. Codes of superiority were at the heart of the missionary encounter, of course, but missionary parents in particular had to carefully juggle the universalism inherent in the missionary project, with the cultural prejudice that was also implicit within it.

This they did not always manage to do, but at the same time missionary children could be surprisingly resilient to the morality of their kin-folk – be it in the form of juvenile deviance, or more positively in ascribing a gentler social meaning to cultural interaction. Missionary children could also use their interstitial cultural identities to beneficent effect, creating a more understanding (if not totally hybridised) view of the missionary-indigene relationship. Thus John MacGregor Mills (son of William and Lillias Mills) wrote in 1861 that a missionary must 'deal faithfully with individuals in private as well as in public point out the errors of their systems, but that he do this in the Spirit of charity, without bitterness so that while conviction is carried to the minds of the people that Christianity is true, a spirit of opposition may not be provoked. I know not whether some in their zeal may be tempted to attack with violence the errors of idolatry, while others may lack the courage to point out firmly its folly.'[108]

John Mills used his bi-cultural upbringing to develop a more respectful theory of missionary practice than was always pursued by his forebears. At the same time, when he applied to the LMS to continue the vocation of his parents in 1861, he was fulfilling all of their hopes and dreams for his future (and spiritual) life. The fondest hope of all missionary parents was that their children should be missionaries. Second-generation missionaries such as John Mills fulfilled this promise, and were often only the beginning of large missionary dynasties that spanned both generations and geographical locations. It is to them that we shall now briefly turn.

Notes

1 Alexander Simpson to London, 18 May 1833, South Seas Incoming Letters (hereafter SSIL) 9/1/D.

2 This was also true of colonial children, though this was less worrying as racial hierarchies of power in no way undermined the colonial project. Elizabeth Buettner, *Empire Families: Britons and late imperial India* (Oxford: Oxford University Press, 2004); Ann Laura Stoler, *Race and the Education of Desire: Foucault's History of sexuality and the colonial order of things* (Durham, NC and London: Duke University Press, 1995), pp. 137–64; Ann Laura Stoler, *Carnal Knowledge and Imperial Power: race and the intimate in colonial rule* (Berkeley and London: University of California Press, 2002), pp. 112–39.

3 David C. Pollock and Ruth E. Van Reken, *Third Culture Kids: the experience of growing up among worlds* (Yarmouth, ME and London: Intercultural Press, 2001); Ruth Hill Useem and Richard D. Downie, 'Third-Culture Kids', *Today's Education* 65:3 (1976), 103–5; Ruth Hill Useem, *A Third Culture Kid Bibliography* (East Lansing, MI: [s.n.] 1999); Mary Langford, 'Global Nomads, Third Culture Kids and International Schools', in Mary Hayden and Jeff Thompson (eds), *International Education: principles and practice* (London: Kogan Page, 1998).

4 Elizabeth Price to Jane Moffat (hereafter Price to Moffat), 24 June 1866, in Una Long (ed.), *The Journals of Elizabeth Lees Price: written in Bechuanland, Southern Africa 1854–1883 with an Epilogue: 1889 and 1900* (London: Edward Arnold, 1956), p. 182.

5 Long, *Journals*, p. 47.

6 Neil Gunson, *Messengers of Grace: evangelical missionaries in the South Seas, 1799–1860* (Melbourne and Oxford: Oxford University Press, 1978), p. 159.

7 Ibid.

8 Neil Gunson, 'The Deviations of a Missionary Family: the Henrys of Tahiti', in James Wightman Davidson and Deryck Scarr (eds), *Pacific Islands Portraits* (Wellington, Auckland: A. H. & A. W. Reed, 1970), pp. 31–54. Quote on p. 33.

9 Diary of William Henry, Tahiti 1797, South Seas Journals (hereafter SSJ) 1.
10 See Chapter 5, p. 131.
11 John Smith Moffat, *The Lives of Robert and Mary Moffat* (London: T. Fisher Unwin, 1885), p. 88.
12 Robert Moffat to Alexander Moffat, 12 April 1823, in I. Shapera (ed.), *Apprenticeship at Kuruman: being the journals and letters of Robert and Mary Moffat, 1820–1828* (London: Chatto & Windus, 1951), p. 72.
13 Moffat, *Lives*, p. 88.
14 Price, 'Reminiscences', in Long, *Journals*, pp. 47–8.
15 Gunson, 'The Deviations of a Missionary Family', p. 35.
16 Ibid., pp. 31–54.
17 See Chapter 5, pp. 157–8.
18 John Orsmond to London, 1 January 1829, SSIL 7/1/A; Simpson to London, 18 November 1831, SSIL 8/3/B.
19 John Barff to London, 9 September 1845, SSIL 18A/4/B.
20 Orsmond to London, 1 January 1829, SSIL 7/1/A.
21 Simpson to London, 26 November 1844, SSIL 17/4/B.
22 Ibid., 16 August 1843, SSIL 16/3/B.
23 Orsmond to London, 1 January 1829, SSIL 7/1/A.
24 Simpson to London, 18 May 1833, SSIL 9/1/D.
25 Simpson to London, 18 November 1831 SSIL 8/3/B.
26 Ibid., 26 November 1844, SSIL 17/4/B.
27 Ibid.
28 Heath and Buzacott to Brethren, undated, SSIL 16/2/C.
29 Ibid.
30 Harriet Johnston to Brethren, undated, SSIL 16/2/C.
31 Eliza Darling to London, 20 June 1843, SSIL 16/2/C.
32 Ibid.
33 Mrs Louisa Thomson (nee Barff) to Brethren, undated, SSIL 16/2/C.
34 Charlotte Wilson to William Howe, 21 March 1843, SSIL 16/1/D.
35 Mary and Eliza Darling to Howe, 16 March 1843, SSIL 16/1/D.
36 Orsmond to London, 29 June 1843, SSIL 16/1/D.
37 Thomas Joseph to London, 24 June 1843, SSIL 16/2/C.
38 Ibid.
39 Orsmond to London, 29 June 1843, SSIL 16/2/D.
40 Ibid; William Howe to London, 15 July 1843, SSIL 16/2/D; David Darling to London, 25 July 1843, SSIL 16/3/A.
41 London to Thomas Joseph, undated, Western Outgoing Letters: South Seas (hereafter WOL:SS) 3, pp. 164–71.
42 Joseph to London, 24 June 1843, SSIL 16/2/C.
43 See Emily J. Manktelow, 'Rev Simpson's "Improper Liberties": moral scrutiny and missionary children in the South Seas Mission', *Journal of Imperial and Commonwealth History* 40:2 (2012), 159–81.
44 Joseph to London, 24 June 1843, SSIL 16/2/C.
45 Ibid.
46 Ibid.
47 Simpson to London, 16 August 1843, SSIL 16/3/B.
48 Joseph to London, 24 June 1843, SSIL 16/2/C.
49 Hayward's Answers to Queries, 1819, SSIL 3A/1/B.
50 Stoler, *Carnal Knowledge*, p. 129. See also Buettner, *Empire Families*, pp. 41–3, 85–7 and 99–101.
51 Anna Johnston, *Missionary Writing and Empire, 1800–1860* (Cambridge: Cambridge University Press, 2003), p. 135.
52 Richard Lovett, *The History of the London Missionary Society, 1795–1895* ([S.I.]: Frowde, 1899), vol. 1, p. 296.
53 Simpson to London, 18 May 1833, SSIL 9/1/D.
54 Ibid., 26 November 1844, SSIL 17/4/B.

55 Sarah Simpson to Howe, 23 July 1843, SSIL 16/3/A.
56 Joseph to London, 24 June 1843, SSIL 16/2/C.
57 London to Darling, 15 January 1845, WOL:SS 3, pp. 327–8.
58 Ibid.
59 Ann Laura Stoler, 'Tense and Tender Ties: The politics of comparison in North American and (post) colonial studies', *Journal of American History* 88:3 (2001), 829–65. Quote on p. 832.
60 Richard Price, *Making Empire: colonial encounters and the creation of imperial rule in nineteenth-century Africa* (Cambridge: Cambridge University Press, 2008), pp. 127–53.
61 Ibid., p. 127.
62 Though not explicit, there is some hint of this in Patricia Grimshaw, '"Christian Woman, Pious Wife, Faithful Mother, Devoted Missionary": conflicts and roles of American missionary women in nineteenth-century Hawaii', *Feminist Studies* 9:3 (1983), 489–521.
63 Simpson to London, 18 May 1833, SSIL 9/1/D.
64 Mary Moffat to her mother, 18 December 1818 in Moffat, *Lives*, p. 54.
65 Mary to John Moffat, 4 April 1860 in Moffat, *Lives*, pp. 348–9.
66 Moffat, *Lives*, p. 354.
67 Natasha Erlank, 'Jane and John Philip: partnership, usefulness and sexuality in the service of God', in John de Gruchy (ed.), *The London Missionary Society in Southern Africa: historical essays in celebration of the bi-centenary of the LMS in Southern Africa, 1799–1999* (Cape Town: David Philip, 1999), pp. 86–93. Quote on p. 91.
68 Livingstone to his children, 2 October 1853 in David Livingstone, *Family Letters, 1841–1856*, 2 vols. *Edited with an introduction by I. Schapera* (London: Chatto & Windus, 1959), vol. 2, p. 230.
69 Robert to Mary Moffat, April 1838 in Moffat, *Lives*, pp. 219–20.
70 David to Charles Livingstone, 16 May 1849, in Livingstone, *Family Letters*, vol. 2, p. 55.
71 Livingstone to his parents and sisters, 9 February 1851, in Livingstone, *Family Letters*, vol. 2, p. 122.
72 Price to Moffat, 22 August 1866, in Long, *Journals*, p. 216.
73 Hannah Crook Journal, 2 February 1820, National Library of New Zealand (hereafter NLNZ) Micro-MS-0726, p. 63.
74 Price to Moffat, 3 September 1866, in Long, *Journals*, p. 222.
75 Crook Journal, 12 December 1821, NLNZ Micro-MS-0726, p. 54.
76 See Adele Perry, 'From "the Hot-bed of Vice" to the "Good and Well-ordered Christian Home": First Nations Housing and Reform in Nineteenth-Century British Columbia', *Ethnohistory* 50:4 (2003), 587–610; Jean and John L. Comaroff, 'Home-Made Hegemony: modernity, domesticity, and colonialism in South Africa', in Karen Tranberg Hansen (ed.), *African Encounters with Domesticity* (New Brunswick: Rutgers University Press, 1992), pp. 37–74. See also Carol B. Stack and Linda M. Burton, 'Kinscripts', *Journal of Comparative Family Studies* 24/2 (1993), 157–70.
77 Darling to London, 2 April 1825, SSIL 5A/2/A.
78 Hephzibah Bicknell, 14; Ann Henry, 14; Ann Scott, 13; Mary Anna Bicknell, 13; and Martha Wilson, 12, to London, 13 March 1828, SSIL 6/5/C.
79 James Hayward's Answers to Queries, 1819, SSIL 3A/1/B.
80 Crook to London, 21 September 1827, SSIL 6/3/A.
81 Crook Journal, 13 April 1820, NLNZ Micro-MS-0726, p. 67. The Crook girls' fluency in Tahitian again speaks to the impossibility of entirely managing social contract, and the ultimate utility of bilingualism in the mission context.
82 Ibid., undated [probably Spring 1820], NLNZ Micro-MS-0726, p. 128.
83 William Crook to London, 4 December 1824, SSIL 4/5/B.
84 Mary was to become a missionary wife herself, in 1832.
85 Crook to London, 1 May 1829, SSIL 7/2/C.
86 Price, 'Reminiscences', in Long, *Journals*, pp. 45–64.

87 Ibid., pp. 59–60.
88 Ibid., p. 60.
89 Price to Moffat, 8 July 1857, in Long, *Journals*, p. 72.
90 George to Elizabeth Barker, 20 December 1837, National Library of South Africa (Cape Town) (hereafter NLSA(CT)) MSB 57 1 (14).
91 George Barker to his brother [unnamed], 4 April 1838, NLSA(CT) MSB 57 1 (14).
92 George to Elizabeth Barker, 5 May 1838, NLSA(CT) MSB 57 1 (14).
93 Charles Barff to London, 8 Feb 1850, SSIL 23/1/B.
94 Robert Unwin Moffat, *John Smith Moffat CMG Missionary: a memoir* (London: John Murray, 1921), p. 14.
95 Charles Barff to London, 30 September 1830, SSIL 7/6/B. See SSIL 12/4 for various letters relative to the sugar mill.
96 John Barff, Answers to Printed Querues (hereafter AtPQ) 2 May 1838, Candidate Papers (hereafter CP) 26/4/106.
97 Wilberforce Buxton Philip AtPQs 26 June 1842, NLSA(CT) MSB 57 1 (14).
99 Charles Barff to London, 9 September 1845, SSIL 18A/4/B.
100 George to Elizabeth Barker, 5 April 1842, NLSA(CT) MSB 57 1 (14).
101 John Smith Moffat, AtPQ, 26 April 1853, CP, 27/11/249.
102 William Philip, AtPQ, 20 July 1836, CP, 26/2/26.
103 George Barker to his sister [unnamed] 28 June 1842, NLSA(CT) MSB 57 1 (14).
104 Deborah Gaitskell, 'Rethinking Gender Roles: the field experience of women missionaries in South Africa', in Andrew Porter (ed.), *The Imperial Horizons of British Protestant Missions, 1880–1914* (Grand Rapids, MI: W.B. Eerdmans Publishers, 2003), pp. 131–57. Quote on p. 140.
105 James Duthie to Miss Bennett, 1 September 1881, CP 5/5.
106 James Emlyn's Remarks, 16 September 1881, CP 5/5.
107 Mr Lee's Remarks, 24 September 1881, CP 5/5.
108 John McGregor Mills, AtPQ, 15 January 1861, CP 27/16/375.

CHAPTER SEVEN

Epilogue: second-generation missionaries

From its very inception, the LMS's endeavour was embedded with mechanisms for its self-replication. For the Society it made fiscal and ideological sense for missionary children to be instruments of mission. From the idea that missionaries, by marrying into, and reproducing with, the local community, could create a generation of mixed race catechists, to the ideal of permanent establishment and an evangelical settler community, the LMS had attempted to implement ways in which missionary families would form the basis of a self-sustaining and self-replicating mission. Along such lines it was no coincidence that the regional schools, in inception or practice, were often linked with native seminaries.[1] Their ideal had always been that this would be an informal process of evangelical reproduction, requiring minimal financial investment from London. Even when these fiscally utopian visions and all the plans to keep missionaries' offspring in the regions of their birth had failed, the mission schools in London were still directed at 'the training of the [missionaries'] offspring for future useful service in the cause of Christ'.[2]

This short epilogue considers second-generation missionaries: their utility to the LMS; the encouragement they received from their parents; their unique stance on many missionary issues, including cultural sympathy, linguistic fluency and climactic suitability; and ultimately the informal apprenticeship they received at the hands of their missionary parents, the response of newer generations of missionaries to the vocational inheritance and replication involved in that apprenticeship (in other words, how second-generation missionaries perpetuated 'old-fashioned' theories and practices of mission), and finally how second-generation missionaries were often just the beginning of long-standing missionary dynasties who spanned the globe as well as the generations. There is much interesting work to be done here, particularly on the role of the missionary dynasty in shaping the way mission hagiography and mission history has been written over the last century and a half, and this chapter is (I hope) only the beginning of an interesting conversation. As the few examples in the Appendix so aptly show, missionary dynasties spanned the generations and the globe – and potentially shaped the networked dynamics of the missionary endeavour in the process.

Family connections

In the first century of LMS activity, fifty-seven missionary children became official LMS missionaries themselves, amounting to somewhere in the region of 5 per cent of missionaries dispatched. It is good to get an idea of numbers, but this is, it should be noted, a highly problematic one. Based on James Sibree's *Register of Missionaries*, it only takes into account those missionary children who formally joined the LMS, and who shared a surname with another missionary (so in other words, descended from the male missionary line). As such it is a number likely to be dwarfed by the number of missionary children (and particularly daughters) who married missionaries (likely to be a much more significant number); their offspring (who did not share surnames with official missionaries, such as their maternal grandparents); those who joined alternative missionary societies; nor those who pursued careers complementary to mission work, but not officially connected with it (as, for example, doctors, teachers and, indeed, colonial officials). In the families who appear in this book we can see numerous examples of such trends. In the Moffat family three of the girls married missionaries; in the Crook family at least the eldest, Mary, did so (marrying Johann Handt of the Church Missionary Society in 1832). Indeed, six of these forty-five male second-generation missionaries married the daughters of missionaries themselves. The missionary that Ann Moffat married, Jean Fredoux, worked for the Paris Missionary Society, and while one of their daughters became a LMS missionary, at least one other (and possibly two) joined an alternative society. Many of the children who have appeared within these pages became school teachers (including George Barker's eldest daughters) and pastors or ministers of various types. And of course, as previously mentioned, none of this includes those missionary children who stayed with their parents, as informal missionaries (and often particularly as teachers), such as the indomitable Jane Moffat (who ultimately inherited her mother's position as family matriarch).

The number of official second-generation missionaries, then, is probably insignificant compared to the number of informal second (and third) generation missionaries. Nonetheless, looking at their lives under the auspices of the LMS, their interactions with that institution and with their missionary vocation, can be both interesting and informative, highlighting many of the issues raised in this book. Second-generation missionaries were a success story for the LMS (and for their parents), but their relationship with the Society was a complex one. While missionary children had first-hand knowledge of the missionary enterprise it was the mission institution that retained all the power, and internecine squabbles (over education, placement and training) frequently broke out. Nonetheless, as prior to their formal connection with the enterprise, their utility was in many ways unparalleled: they were often fluent in the language, had at least some mediated access to the culture, and came with strong and useful networks of connection – among other missionaries, and sometimes among the local people. Ideologically and practically they could by no means be underestimated by the LMS, but their inclusion, like their very existence, resulted from complex negotiations between dedicated individuals on the one hand, and a pragmatic institution on the other.

Given the many advantages that being the child of a missionary could accrue when it came to becoming a missionary, second-generation missionaries were often surprisingly reticent about using their family connections to justify their application, however. On the contrary, they were careful to make clear their personal conversion experience, that their parents had not exercised undue influence on their applications and that a desire to return to their native lands, while certainly present (as explored below) was not definitive in their vocational feelings. James William Gordon, the first of the LMS's missionary children to become a missionary himself in 1834, made it clear in his application that 'my father [who had died four years previously] never expressed to me a wish that I might be a missionary.'[3] William Henry Hill, in his application of 1847 made clear that the 'thought of living, perhaps, [illegible] near my venerated Parents weighs not with me, for the office is too responsible a one to suffer such to influence my mind'.[4] To this end, he assured them, 'I make no choice of any Quarter of the globe, leaving it entirely in the hands of the Directors (should I be accepted) to send me where they think I may be most usefully employed.'[5] Wilberforce Buxton Philip took this distancing from his familial connections in the mission even further, excluding 'all references to Hankey and my brother' from his application.[6] It seems he was advised against this caution, however, as he went on to mention in his application form (know as Answers to Printed Questions in the LMS application process) both the religious education he had received from his parents, and the year he had spent working with his brother at Hankey mission station as a teacher.[7]

William Philip meanwhile, had taken this distancing even further in his application nearly twenty years previously, making very clear his father's hesitancy in referring his son to the Society. Indeed, it was not only the LMS that was cautious about the motivations of second-generation missionaries; surprisingly, so were some parents. At least three missionary parents within this cohort had serious reservations about their sons applying to the LMS to become missionaries. William Philip had applied to his father to become a missionary while living with him in Cape Town, 'but from the high standards of character which he always thought necessary to qualify for the Missionary work, and my deficiency in religious experience and general education, he disapproved of my leaving the profession to which I had then attached myself'.[8] His father, after some months, finally 'saw fit to accede to my wishes and proposed that I should offer myself to your Society', but only under the condition that William should 'obtain the education which would better prepare me for usefulness in my sphere of the Lord's vineyard'.[9]

Nor was John Philip the only missionary father to exercise such caution. In South Seas missionary George Turner's letter on behalf of his son George Alexander Turner, he noted that although from 'his earliest years, his mamma and I have prayed that God would raise him up to be a missionary', they had 'been careful however not unduly to press that work upon him, but rather to leave the decision as to his future course to his own unfettered judgment'.[10] He noted further that, 'I think I can speak with confidence as to the sincerity of his Christian character, and as his decision for Missionary work has come so entirely from himself I have good reason to conclude that it is of God.'[11] When Benjamin Rice wrote to the LMS on behalf of his son in 1863 he noted his first reaction to his son's vocational feelings:

> I did not at first encourage it, thinking it better that he should first engage in some secular employment feeling sure that if his wish to be a Missionary were from God, it would in due time fully manifest itself. Accordingly he commenced the study of Engineering, which he prosecuted for some time, apparently with energy, but, as he has since said, only as a temporary occupation, and because I wished it.[12]

It was only after 'consultation with my colleague, Mr Sewell' that Rice would even allow Henry to 'take some part in the labours of the Mission, in order that he might see a little more of the work in which he proposed to engage, and also that we might have still further opportunities of observing his qualifications'. It seems that Benjamin Rice did not only distrust his son's motivations for becoming a missionary, but his own motivations for supporting it. Having undoubtedly held the hope that his son would follow in his footsteps and carry on the vital work of the mission, it was only when his hopes were confirmed and shared by his colleague, and when he observed the success of his son's English and Bible classes, and even had this observation confirmed by his missionary son-in-law, that he allowed himself to support Henry's application.[13]

The LMS also needed to ascertain that missionary children were applying to be missionaries for the right reasons. Edwin Relfe Barrett (son of Jamaica missionary William Garland Barrett, 1834–48) noted in his letter to the Directors of May 1867, that in response to an earlier letter they had 'urged the necessity for care in making my choice, the responsibility of the work in which I should have to engage, and above all warning me lest I should endeavour to interpret the Will of Providence by my own desires' before he applied to become a missionary.[14] More generally, the LMS ascertained motivations through the following two questions in their Printed Questions:

> 7. What has been your occupation? Are you so employed at present as to be able to obtain a comfortable maintenance? Have you reasonable prospect of the same support in the future? Does the desire of improving your worldly circumstances enter into the motives of this application?[15]
>
> [...]
>
> 12. As there is too much reason to fear that some persons have become Missionaries under the influence of improper principles, you are desired seriously and sincerely to state what the MOTIVES by which you are actuated in offering yourself as a Missionary to the Heathen.[16]

The candidates themselves were not always so great at providing comforting answers to these questions. 'Have had no regular occupation. Do not apply for the sake of support', was John Barff's terse reply.[17] 'I have no future prospects of support', wrote John Smith Moffat in 1853; 'The desire of improving my worldly circumstances has no influence on my application to you.'[18] 'I have not been settled down to any occupation', wrote Wilberforce Buxton Philip in 1855, although in his case this was due to his continuance in his father's house and in education.[19]

Much more encouraging answers for the LMS were those which alluded to an actual occupation that had been relinquished in order to make the application. Edwin Relfe Barrett and George Alexander Turner had both had opportunities to successfully engage in business, while Thomas Durant Philip and John McGregor Mills both expressed a belief that they would be able to find positions in the home ministry if they needed to.[20] Even more encouragingly, William Henry Hill (son of India missionary Micaiah Hill) had turned down 'a lucrative situation offered me in India';[21] William Philip had worked both at sea and as a land surveyor in South Africa;[22] and Henry Rice had undertaken studies in engineering, at the insistence of his father.[23] They all hoped, in short, that these jobs would 'prove to the Society that the desire of improving my worldly circumstances does not enter into the motives of this application'.[24]

Of course, missionary children well knew that a career as a missionary was generally not a lucrative one. After all, their own parents had struggled to live on the allowances given by the Society, and had frequently requested increases in that allowance, and other forms of financial support from the Society, such as apprenticeships and education for their children. 'I have good reason for believing, so far as human foresight avails, that my worldly circumstances will not be bettered by my becoming a missionary', wrote John Smith Moffat in 1853.[25] Missionary children were also well aware that, not only was missionary life financially challenging, but that the life of a missionary was a hard one. 'I have had an opportunity of seeing some of the hardships to which Missionaries are exposed, and have I trust seriously considered them, and am willing to succumb to them', wrote William Philip.[26] He felt, however, that his constitution would be able to 'bear the ordinary fatigue of a Missionary life'.[27]

Indeed, second-generation missionaries had, in their health, a very good reason for feeling confident of their applications. They had, after all, been raised in missionary locations and thus, it was believed, were more able to tolerate and survive both the 'sultry clime' more generally, and the particular dangers of illness and disease. William Henry Hill's doctor was not the only one who went so far as to argue that the applicant's health would be *better* in the land of their birth.[28] Joseph Sturge cautioned that John Smith Moffat 'ought to return to Africa to save his life',[29] and William Philip used his health as a reason for his returning to Africa, rather than 'India [which] I have experienced has an enervating effect upon my system'.[30] His brother Wilberforce also argued that his health 'as a general rule ... [was] much better at the Cape than in England'.[31] Although this was a risky strategy in terms of proving the genuineness of one's missionary vocation, it could go some way in alleviating the LMS's fears over losing missionaries to an untimely death.

So far, so good then for the LMS. Among the ranks of the missionary children they had a small, but well-suited pool of future missionaries. They spoke the language, understood the local culture, and perhaps most importantly had a strong sense of the hardships they would have to face. The candidates themselves, meanwhile, seemed suitably humble, reticent about emphasising their family connections, fearing it might negate the personal nature of their conversion and desire to be missionaries. Not all second-generation missionary candidates were like this, however, and in those few who decided to use their family connections to get what they wanted, is evidenced the complex power dynamics between missionary children and the hierarchy of the LMS. It was at times knowledge v. power for second-generation missionary candidates, and it was not always clear who would win.

Knowledge v. power

William Turner, son of the South Seas missionary George Turner, first applied to the LMS to be a missionary in 1869. His application was deferred for a year, perhaps owing to his wish to be a medical missionary, but despite the Directors' wish that he wait until his father had returned from the South Seas before renewing his application, he applied again in 1870. Anxious to avoid delay in his appointment he informed the Board that, 'I am also willing to go to any field to which, when my course is finished, God may direct me'. 'I, of course', he continued, 'prefer Samoa or rather the South Seas, but am willing to leave the matter for the Directors to decide.'[32] The Directors apparently took him at his word and informed him in 1873 that he had been appointed to India.

Faced with the LMS's dismissal of his preference for the South Seas, the case of William Turner is instructive, highlighting the ways in which applicants could use their missionary childhood, and the knowledge it had provided them with, to their own advantage if they so wished, and perhaps most importantly, if the LMS refused to acquiesce to their desires and demands. For Turner, it seems, had not been quite genuine when he promised to go wherever the Directors saw fit to send him;

> I applied for the South Seas and I did so with reason, I was born there, and it was in connection with that Mission that I first had the desire, or call, to go out as a Missionary and it was to go to the South Sea Islands. I still desire it. All my sympathies are there, I have taken a deep interest in all the work there and do so still. I feel that it is there I can work best. I feel that while I am peculiarly qualified for the work there, so I lack the necessary qualifications for work in India or China ... It is to the South Seas that I feel I must go ... India I have always looked upon as perhaps the last place I would think of going to.

He confidently concluded his letter: 'sure you will see the propriety of my wishes. I ask you to reconsider your decision, and send me to that field for which I applied, for which I was received, for which I have been educated, for which I have laboured, in which I am interested, for which I long to spend all my energies.'[33]

Although the Directors wrote to him quoting his earlier agreement to go wherever they sent him, they decided in 1873 to appoint him to the South Seas, though to the New Guinea Mission rather than Samoa. 'Although I should have preferred the Samoan Mission I am willing to go to New Guinea', he grudgingly replied in November of that year.[34] In April, 1875 he 'suppose[d] that it is the time to tell you that I intend to get married before leaving to Miss Mary Colville. Please inform the Directors of this fact and formally percure [*sic*] their sanction.'[35] He and his new wife sailed for New Guinea in that year, Turner having essentially received all he had asked for from the Directors, including five years of education at their expense.

Turner's belligerent tone did not work for all second-generation missionary applicants who attempted it, however. John Smith Moffat applied to the LMS, with a raft of impressive references from Joseph Sturge, a Director, and John Jukes, a well-known and prominent Congregational minister, in 1853, and was accepted as a missionary student at Cheshunt College. In 1855 he wrote to the Directors in supplicant tone, requesting that he may be permitted to move to New College where he believed he could not only be afforded a more sound theological education, but where he could obtain certain practical sciences (Geology, Botany, Chemistry and Meteorology) which although 'not immediately connected with the higher duties of the Missionary ... would be of immense service as subsidiary means of action'.[36] He assured them that 'an increase of efficiency is likely to accrue' and in a moment of well-placed name-dropping informed them that 'the application is the result of general suggestions made by my honoured father'. His application was complied with and he commenced his studies at New College in October 1856, even though the move meant he would receive four years of education plus his time in preparatory school at Bedford, despite the general limit of education that the LMS were willing to fund being four years in total.[37]

Another controversy over his education soon ensued, however. In 1856 he applied to the Directors to be allowed an additional twelve months in England in order to pursue medical studies, at personal expense. His request was denied. In the summer of that year, however, having three months of vacation in front of him, he again went to the Mission House in order to apply to pursue medical studies during that time. The LMS's physician, Dr Risdon Bennett (whose daughter was later to head the female missionary board) informed him that it would be 'absurd' to attempt to fit in an entire medical knowledge in that time, but that he should 'pay attention to simple surgical cases'.[38] The experience was not a positive one. Being only 'tolerated' by the staff and students, he received 'very little practical knowledge – with a great deal of discouragement, and gave up before the end of the vacation'.

At the same time, the beginning of the academic session for 1856, his tutor applied on his behalf for him to be allowed to remain an extra year at New College as he was 'not in his last year's class'. Again, the request was denied: 'Now after the lengthened period which you have been preparing for the work, a period far exceeding that usually allotted to the studies of our Missionaries, we do not think it could be warrantable on our part to detain you in this country beyond the term of your present collegiate year.'[39] In an interesting inversion of Moffat's own use of his father's name, the LMS resorted to similar tactics, citing his brother-in-law David Livingstone's desire of opening a new mission in central Africa and the resultant need for more workers for the cause: 'This difficulty we felt strongly before your honoured relative, Dr Livingstone came to the country, but should it be resolved to commence a Mission in the region he has lately traversed, we shall require men even more urgently than now.' In some sense, the LMS had won at John's own game.

Thus John resigned himself to a swift removal to Africa at the close of his last session in June 1857. He was able in that summer, however, to undertake some more surgical training, which, although much more successful than his previous attempts, proved to him only that, 'it is a complete quagmire to a man who does not go into it more extensively than I could do under the circumstances'. Yet, in 1858, his departure seemingly interminably delayed, the LMS were themselves requesting that he undertake some more medical training, something he believed would only 'complete the chaos'.

> whence arise this deep conviction of the vale of medical knowledge – and thus spasmodic attempt to attain its advantages in the eleventh hour? If it *is* of so much importance why was it not more seriously thought of before? It is placing me in an unfair position to ask me to undertake obligations such as I shall incur, if I follow your suggestion. I decline because it would be a miserable sham on my part to accede, and because to quote your own words, *you did not think it could be warrantable on your part to detain me in this country beyond the term of my then current collegiate year – that* is, after June 1857. Hoping this free expression of my thoughts will meet with your approval, I am, Gentlemen, Your obedient servant, John Smith Moffat [original emphases].[40]

This forthright response did not meet the Directors' approval, and ultimately John Moffat was forced to go out to Africa under the direct and private pay of his brother-in-law David Livingstone in 1858, rather than as an employee of the LMS. He was not officially employed by the Society until 1864.

William Young Turner and John Smith Moffat took a determined tone with the Directors, based on what they presumed to be their superior knowledge of the mission and the mission world, though with mixed results. Not all second-generation missionary applicants were as forthright. Yet although some used a humble tone in their applications, many did indeed emphasise their prior knowledge and even experience of the mission in order to bolster their applications. Edwin Barrett argued that it was only natural, having been:

> Surrounded from my earliest years by reports and accounts of *other* missionary work, and observing in those around me the interest taken in such accounts, and, moreover, constantly having the opportunity of hearing lectures etc on such subjects by my own father, while agent for the London missionary Society ... that I should have early implanted in me, some knowledge of and corresponding interest in foreign missionary work.[41]

Joseph Hands noted that if a new missionary was to be sent out to India, James Gordon (son of missionary John Gordon) would be able to teach him 'Telagoo', 'which he is fully competent to impart'.[42] Language competency was also a recommendation for John McGregor Mills who argued that 'having known the Samoan language would, I think, enable me to acquire it more speedily than those who have never known it'. He also argued that his having spent time in the South Seas would enable his constitution to stand up to the climate, and further that 'the natives hearing that I am studying for the ministry have often expressed the hope that I might be sent out there'.[43] This was undoubtedly a great bonus for any missionary, to be wanted by the local people rather than being politely ignored or indeed actively despised.

Second-generation missionary applicants could also point out their particularly relevant experience in such work. While all applicants for the LMS had experience at teaching, usually at Sunday schools, and sometimes also preaching and tract distribution, only missionary children could point to their experience assisting their parents 'in the superintendence and inspection of the mission schools' as did James Gordon.[44] The younger Philip brothers could also point to their experience at William's station at Hankey. Wilberforce had worked as a weekday and Sunday school teacher there for a year and the 'knowledge I have gained and the tastes I have formed during a residence of three years upon the Missionary Institution' had, he believed, made him 'more suited to undertake the work of a Missionary'.[45]

These types of informal apprenticeships were undoubtedly useful for second-generation missionaries. They gave them the knowledge and experience required to pursue their careers once in the field for themselves, and prepared them for the trials and hardships they were likely to face – particularly on the spiritual frontier. The problem, however, was that through such apprenticeships, second-generation missionaries were socialised into an earlier form of missionary activity that did not always sit well with evolving mission strategies and objectives. This could make life particularly difficult for second-generation missionaries, who often felt torn between the practical education they had received at the hand of their parents, and the formal education and training they had received from the LMS.

John Smith Moffat's career was certainly one shaped by generational continuity in a time when the missionary profession and the missionary enterprise were shifting around him. As the missionary world became increasingly specialised, professionalised and institutionalised, he retained a strong faith in the precepts of practical evangelicalism, such as had befitted his father's generation (and location) on the spiritual frontier. In his education he had asked to be able to pursue those 'branches of study not immediately connected with the higher duties of the Missionary, but which would be of immense service … including Geology, Botany, Chemistry, and Meteorology'.[46] When seeking out medical training he wished to learn 'something of my Father's practice during the period which it then seemed profitable I should spend with him at the Kuruman station' and 'go in at the same end of the subject as he does', i.e. at a practical, rather than educational angle.[47] This preference for the practical was based not only on John's childhood in South Africa (which was of course disrupted by his return to England for his schooling), but on the informal apprenticeship he and his wife Emily (nee Unwin) received upon their arrival in South Africa (under the auspices of David Livingstone) in 1858. There, John particularly admired his father's practical knowledge: 'a wagon would come into collision with a stump hidden in the long grass … a breakage would occur, and a day would have to be spent in repairs. For these we had the valuable skill and experience of our leader, my father, who was equal to any difficulty of this kind'.[48]

Over the course of his career, John would thus embody this older style of missionary (and later, humanitarian consul in Bechuanaland), something which would ultimately involve him in conflicts with his colleagues. When the LMS proposed building a large, fixed missionary institution in South Africa, fittingly named the Moffat Institute, John would join with his father in condemning such a plan (despite its moniker) as ineffective in a region characterised by fluid physical boundaries, nomadic population movements, and an agricultural and pastoral economy that complicated any educational ideals the new social missionaries may have felt. The ensuing conflict between John and his colleagues at Kuruman became both heated and personal, and John preferred to move to Molepolole, there to temporarily replace his brother-in-law Roger Price (who was on furlough at the time). 'It was anti-Moffatism that led to my position in the Bechwana Mission's becoming intolerable', he wrote in 1914. 'I can quite make allowance for my brethren, who were fed up with the excessive prominence of the name and all connected with it.'[49]

Even in his later role as consul, John Moffat embodied the ideals of an earlier generation. Recent work by Esme Cleall has shown that the priorities of the South African mission shifted away from general humanitarianism as understood in the days of John Philip, Ordinance 50 (which secured some level of 'freedom and protection' for the indigenous peoples of southern Africa), and the anti-slavery movement, toward a more religion-focused and apolitical understanding of the missionary enterprise. Yet, John Smith Moffat would continue to understand the missionary movement in this humanitarian and politically functional way. As consul he would agitate against the indenture scandal of the late nineteenth century, in which nearly 2,000 so-called 'rebels' (including women and children) would be sentenced to five years' enforced labour for the colonial government. The way in which Moffat (with his wife and one Elizabeth Hepburn) 'framed their opposition to indenture bore many similarities to responses to violence in the Cape in the 1830s', argues Cleall.[50] Right in the centre of the controversy stood John Moffat, by now in his sixties, attempting to resolve the issue in favour of the Africans involved.

Second-generation missionaries generally tended to share an ideological and practical viewpoint inherited from an older missionary generation, and believed that all missionaries should have the facilities to turn their hand to any and all practical and spiritual objects. For them, practical evangelicalism was alive and well, and they urged the LMS to facilitate their education in practical and medical knowledge, citing their personal, and superior, knowledge of the mission and mission life to bolster their cases. William Charles Milne, son of the celebrated Robert Milne of China, wrote to the LMS that although he did not wish to 'underrate' classical studies, 'I do think that they should now give place to other subjects which may be, at least equally, if not more calculated to fit me for labour among the Heathen.'[51] He pinpointed three areas of education that were most important to him, the Chinese language, surgery and natural philosophy, and pointed to previous missionaries who had, in his experience, attended anatomical lectures at the University of London, and argued that 'very few have gone to a distant shore, without previously giving some degree of attention to one or other of the "*useful sciences*"'. In short, he asked that his studies could be 'modified as to have a *more direct* bearing on the Missionary work'.[52]

This type of practical evangelism did not always suit the LMS's evolving mission objectives, however, and second-generation missionaries often found themselves swimming against the tide of new mission strategies. Being part of a missionary family could certainly have its benefits, then, and some second-generation missionary candidates exemplified the superior knowledge of the enterprise they had through their juvenile and adolescent experience. Nonetheless, this did not always stand them in good stead, and just as in their youth, their relationship with the LMS was often fraught with tensions and difficulties which frequently threatened to boil over.

Conclusion

Despite this, however, for many missionary families, second-generation missionaries were just the start of much longer chains of mission service, and these dynasties became an important part of the missionary world – something as yet unexplored by mission historians. Such dynasties spanned the missionary enterprise well into the twentieth century, cross-pollinating and thereby creating vast networks based on missionary kinships around the world.[53] As the family trees in the Appendix show, these dynasties could have vast geographical and chronological reach. The Cousins family, whose reach would extend across the South Seas, Africa and China, spanned three generations and produced eleven official missionaries; the Dawson family in India spanned four generations, and produced six official missionaries; the Moffat dynasty stretched across three generations (in South Africa, India, Madagascar and China) and ultimately produced eleven LMS missionaries (and at least two missionaries with other societies); in India the Lewis family spanned four generations, with eight official missionaries; the Joyce-Rowlands dynasty spanned three generations (across the West Indies, the South Seas, China and India), with an extraordinary sixteen official missionaries; the Read-Brown dynasty spanned four generations (in South Africa, India, China and the South Seas) with fifteen official missionaries. Undoubtedly, there are many more, across the globe and across the numerous different evangelical missionary societies that operated in the nineteenth and twentieth-century. Nor do these examples of family dynasties include those promulgated through the female line. It seems likely that these missionary family dynasties would have had a huge impact on the missionary enterprise – in their particular regions and at times much more broadly (James Read and David Livingstone, both members of missionary dynasties, spring to mind as immediate examples of individuals who shaped mission history). Being part of a missionary dynasty could be highly beneficial. It provided a network of support in times of trouble or difficulty, a supply-line for materials, foodstuffs and emotional support, and often a way into a local community potentially hostile to new missionaries.

The .Moffats made extensive use of their dynasty. Mary Moffat, for example, was intimately involved in the well-being of her adult children and grandchildren, often restoring Mary Livingstone and her children back to health after long stretches in the interior. In 1847, the Livingstone's journeyed to Kuruman 'half withered away with fatigue and privation'. Mary Moffat 'laboured hard to fetch up their strength, and sent Mary back with her children like roses'.[54] At least ten of the Moffat grandchildren seem to have been born at Kuruman,[55] which also provided food, grain and tools to many of the outlying stations, more than a few of which were run by their own children: Chonuane and Kolobeng for the Livingstones; Motito for the Fredouxs; Linyati for the Moffat (Jr)s; Shoshong and Molepolole for the Prices. Robert, meanwhile, used his influence and experience to get missions started. When John started his mission in 1858 his father introduced him to all the major African leaders in the area. 'My father had, of course, immediately on our arrival, gone to salute the chief; but it was two days before he signalled his willingness that we, the younger men, should be introduced to him.'[56] Meanwhile, Mary Moffat also introduced the new Mrs Moffat to the chiefs and their wives. 'My father remained with us until the middle of 1860', wrote John, 'to see the mission fairly established on a workable footing.'[57] Much of Livingstone's early work too was made possible (or at least, easier) by his being married to the daughter of the famous RraMary, as Robert Moffat was locally known.

The missionary family may not have been self-sufficient then, but in many cases they were most certainly self-replicating. Being part of a mission dynasty could have its tensions: John Moffat's mission career certainly seems to have suffered from it. His wife's notice of the family hierarchies during their apprenticeship, meanwhile – 'We three juveniles (!) are pedestrians', she wrote of their journey from Cape Town in 1858 – suggest some of the strains that being part of a large, and close, family could undoubtedly cause. On the whole, however, the benefits seem to have largely outweighed the costs for those involved. As stated in the introduction, there is much work to be done here on the role of the family dynasty in mission history – and the very few mentioned here are really just the start. What they do show, as has this whole book, is that present-participling the missionary is a project well worth pursuing.

Notes

1 See LMS Board Minutes (hereafter BM), 15 January 1821, pp. 192–3; BM, 10 January 1825, p. 7; BM, 20 June 1825, p. 138; Ibid., pp. 138–41; Foster to London, 19 June 1826, South Africa Incoming Letters (hereafter SAIL) 10/1/C; *Annual Report* (1831), p. 76.
2 'Education of the Children of Missionaries', *Evangelical Magazine* (hereafter *EM*) (July 1837), p. 301.
3 James William Gordon, verbal examination, 23 July 1832, Candidate Papers (hereafter CP) 6/28.
4 William Henry Hill to London, 26 March 1847, CP 7/36.
5 Ibid.
6 Wilberforce Philip to unknown, 2 June 1855, CP 13/23.
7 Wilberforce Philip, Answers to Printed Question (hereafter AtPQ), 26 June 1855, CP 27/12/270.
8 William Philip to London, June 1836, CP 13/22.
9 Ibid.
10 George Turner to London, 2 August 1862, CP 16/51.
11 Ibid.
12 Benjamin Rice to London, 15 August 1863, CP 14/2.
13 Ibid. Rice's son-in-law was Mr Lake of the Nellore Free Church Mission.
14 Edwin Barrett to London, 23 May 1867, CP 1/33.
15 Original Printed Questions for Applicants.
16 Ibid.
17 John Barff, AtPQ, 2 May 1838, CP 26/4/106.
18 John Smith Moffat, AtPQ, 26 April 1853, CP 27/11/249.
19 Wilberforce Philip, AtPQ, 26 June 1855, CP 27/12/270.
20 Edwin Barrett to London, 23 May 1867, CP 1/33; George Turner (Sr) to London, 2 August 1862, CP 27/17/430; Thomas Durant Philip, AtPQ, 15 March 1843, CP 26/7/175; John McGregor Mills, AtPQ, 15 January 1861, CP 27/16/375.
21 William Henry Hill, AtPQ, 7 August 1843, CP 26/7/179.
22 William Philip, AtPQ, 20 July 1836, CP 26/2/26.
23 Benjamin Rice to London, 15 August 1863, CP 14/2.
24 John McGregor Mills, AtPQ, 15 January 1861, CP 27/16/375.
25 John Smith Moffat, AtPQ, 26 April 1853, CP 27/11/249.
26 William Philip, AtPQ, 20 July 1836, CP 26/2/26.
27 Ibid.
28 George Payne to London, 3 April 1847, CP 7/36.
29 Sturge to London, 1853 CP 12/1.
30 William Philip, AtPQ 20 July 1836, CP 26/2/26.
31 Wilberforce Philip, AtPQ 26 June 1855, CP 27/12/270.
32 Turner to London, 26 March 1870, CP 16/52.
33 Turner to London, 16 October 1873, CP 16/52.
34 Turner to London, 12 November 1873, CP 16/52.
35 Turner to London, 22 April 1875, CP 16/52.
36 John Smith Moffat to London, 7 June 1855, CP 12/1.
37 See Director's letter of 18 December 1856 quoted in Moffat to London, 2 February 1858, CP 12/1.
38 Moffat to London, 2 February 1858, CP 12/1.
39 Ibid.
40 Ibid.
41 Edwin Relfe Barrett to London, 23 May 1867, CP 1/33.
42 Joseph Hands to London, undated, CP 6/28.
43 John Mills to London, 7 March 1861, CP 11/34.
44 James Gordon's Examination by the Committee, 23 July 1832, CP 6/28.
45 Wilberforce Buxton Philip's AtPQ, 26 June 1855, CP 27/12/270.
46 John Smith Moffat to London, 7 June 1855, CP 12/1.

47 Moffat to London, 2 February 1858, CP 12/1.
48 Robert Unwin Moffat, *John Smith Moffat CMG Missionary: a memoir* (London: John Murray, 1921), p. 82.
49 Ibid., pp. 129–30.
50 Esme Cleall, 'Thinking with Missionaries: discourses of difference in India and southern Africa, *c.*1840–1895', PhD thesis (University College, London, 2009), p. 275.
51 William Milne to London, 9th June 1837, CP 11/41.
52 Ibid.
53 See Catherine Hall, 'Missionary Stories: gender and ethnicity in the 1830s and 1840s', in Catherine Hall, *White, Male and Middle Class: explorations in feminism and history* (Cambridge: Polity, 1992), pp. 205–55; p. 228.
54 Mary Moffat to her father, 17 March 1848, in John Smith Moffat, *The Lives of Robert and Mary Moffat* (London: T. Fisher Unwin, 1885), p. 265.
55 This according to the work done by family historians online and largely corroborated by surviving mission records.
56 Moffat, *Lives*, p. 85.
57 Ibid., p. 98.

CHAPTER EIGHT

Conclusion

Standing on the stage of the Barbican in July 2011, collecting my PhD certificate and cringing at the embarrassingly long and boring title of my then thesis, the gentleman shaking my hand and passing me the fake scroll used for the graduation pictures leaned in and whispered in my ear: 'My grandparents were LMS missionaries you know.'

This happens to me surprisingly regularly, though I wouldn't necessarily say often, and speaks, I think, to the fact that people are energised by their individual history of being part of a missionary family. In some ways it is easy to see why. While my family history consists of shepherds, smiths, wheelwrights and shopkeepers, some people's family history lies in the 'exotic' adventures of colonial actors whose actions can be tempered with a more placatory side of benevolence, philanthropy and a genuine desire to do good. Of course, scholarly reflections on the role of the missionary enterprise in the grassroots dynamics of the colonial and cultural encounter are rather different from this vision, but I can certainly see how having a missionary lurking in one's family history would be exciting.

The distance between public and academic understandings of empire – and mission – is large, and often seems a gap that's hard to bridge. Confronting people with the complexity and complicity of the past is not always a successful project – while soothing them with tales of past 'benevolence' and 'progress' seems to be the more emotionally and economically lucrative option. There is clearly more to do here, but certainly what we mustn't do is let our discomfort with this state of affairs stop us from engaging with the public (on the one hand), and from investigating fruitful avenues of analysis on the other. This is what has happened when it comes to missionary families – discomfort with the past and continuing calls for public heroisation has led us to ignore the role of the intimate, the personal and the emotional in the history of Christian mission. As this book has shown, this has had profound implications for our understanding of the missionary enterprise as a whole.

This book has had one overarching aim: to prove that the intimate and the personal should not be obscured by a focus on the public in history, and that mission history can be reshaped by attention to the role of the family therein. Taking the family as a legitimate unit of historical analysis in its own right sheds new light on sometimes well-worn historiographical debates. Assumptions about the ubiquity of the missionary wife have been dismantled through a close examination of early LMS policy and its utopian vision of racial intermarriage and cultural intermixing. Anchored by spiritual conformity, this was a mission ideal that was fundamental to the notion of a self-sufficient global evangelical community. 'Christianity, commerce and civilisation' as a mission slogan connecting secular culture to a conversionist enterprise from around the mid-nineteenth century, and the eventual encouragement of pre-embarkation marriage, both emanated from the breakdown of an earlier mission ideal. Our understandings of the professional identity of missionary wives, meanwhile, can be deepened and complicated by attention to their place within the missionary marriage. Within that paradigm it can be seen that missionary couples shared a conception of mission and marriage as rooted in mutuality of belief and vocational partnership. The fractures between these expectations and the realities of mission life were mediated, soothed and in its most successful manifestations resolved by the multi-layered understandings of missionary matrimony and spousal expectation held by individual missionaries. At the same time, that tense site of historiographical argument, missionary interactions with cultural and biological chauvinism, can equally be reframed through sensitivity to the role of parental anxiety in shaping missionary prejudice.

In shifting the focus of existing historiographical debates, meanwhile, this fresh approach to mission history has brought out aspects and actors in the missionary enterprise previously obscured by a focus on *public* history, and by the nature of the mission archive. There is definite scope for further development here. Our idea of the (male) missionary himself needs to be adjusted through an understanding of his familial identity and responsibilities, and the way in which these impacted on his ability to juggle multi-faceted personal identities fractured by the tensions between professional, spiritual and personal obligations. Historical understandings of the role, function and capabilities of the missionary wife need to be expanded to consider the importance of the regional, ethnographic and personal specificity of her spiritual agency and vocational desire. For missionaries' wives, so much depended on their material circumstances, the particulars of their mission station, and their current position within the life-cycle. Even more importantly, a focus on the missionary family demonstrates the role of missionary children as crucial determinants of and contributors to the character of the missionary enterprise. As bi-cultural beings caught in the interstitial space between two mutually exclusive cultures, missionary children negotiated a sense of belonging that deeply impacted the nature of mission, shaping racial and cultural interactions through their own active mission agency and the parental responses their presence elicited.

Missionary families were an integral component of the missionary enterprise, both as active agents on the global religious stage and as a force within the enterprise that shaped understandings and theories of mission itself. This book has argued for the importance of a historical understanding of the missionary enterprise informed by the complex context of the intimate, the personal *and* the professional. In so doing it has opened up numerous pathways to fruitful future research, and has posed a number of questions that still need to be answered. If the introduction of single female missionaries was a response to the practical and vocational difficulties of missionaries' wives, there is certainly scope to explore the dynamics of those relationships in the field from 1875. While lady missionaries felt that they had been employed by the LMS to fulfil a professional missionary role, firmly founded in their often extensive professional education and experience (as teachers, nurses and later doctors), missionary couples often understood the role of single female missionaries as one of assistance. The arrival of single female missionaries 'also created a certain amount of dismay among missionary wives'.

> Having worked alongside their husbands for decades to see their work ignored in missionary rhetoric, they now confronted unmarried women taking over some of their work as mission institutions expanded, and receiving the credit for what had been underway since the early nineteenth century.[1]

Tense arguments arose in many missionary stations between missionary couples clinging to an older form of missionary practice, which was being gently eroded by the introduction of professional missionary women. The LMS's rule that single female missionaries cohabit with missionary families, in order to protect evangelical respectability, only exacerbated these problems. Missionary wives felt unappreciated and replaced, but also superior and more experienced. Lady missionaries were unwilling to compromise their professional identity for the sake of mission harmony and an inferior position as an assistant. There is ample scope for future research to explore the arguments and difficulties that arose from this liminal period of change in the nature of female involvement in mission; and missionary families would once again have an important role to play in that research.

Along similar lines the generational role of missionary daughters remains a fruitful site for sustained historical analysis. Much close research is required to determine how many missionary daughters became the wives of missionaries, and thereby fulfilled their vocational desires, and the heartfelt wishes of their parents, through marriage. Regional analyses would probably be the most practical way of pursuing that research, and undoubtedly many interesting questions could thereby be answered, including whether or not missionary daughters also participated in the sense of generational continuity expressed by missionary sons (such as in requiring practical, over intellectual, knowledge in their training), and how missionary daughters were situated in the tense relationships between missionary wives and missionary women. As professional missionaries themselves from 1875, did their loyalties lie with the generation of their mothers, or with their own peers and colleagues? Did their experience shape the relationships their own parents had with single female missionaries? And more generally, how did women's individual passage between the two states (with so many early missionary women marrying missionaries in the field) affect the general mission atmosphere on the issue?

Throughout the many years it has taken to write this book, I have been intrigued by the conceptual similarities that existed between missionary children and indigenous converts. This has been most obvious in the fact that schools for missionary children were often attached to native seminaries (in South Africa and India), but also flows from the idea of interstitial space, and its capacity to both connect and demarcate social boundaries. That space is a conceptual and actual site of huge historical importance and interest and is certainly worthy of further study. Thinking about the ways in which missionary children and indigenous converts were similar opens doors to historical analyses of both these groups, often shadowy in the archive and obscure in mission history. The role of gossip networks and other informal structures of sanction could be a fruitful gateway into that discussion, illuminating not only the fabric of everyday life in mission stations, but giving a glimpse of how the powerless in those communities (women, children, converts) negotiated their own sense of themselves, and the structures of power and control they inhabited. While certain similarities certainly exist in the conceptual marginality of missionary children and indigenous converts, ultimately missionary children could be completely and unproblematically accepted by that community (particularly if they became missionaries themselves).

The question remains whether indigenous converts could ever inhabit the same level of acceptance as missionary children, and whether their conversions were ever considered above suspicion, and beyond the threat of backsliding, by missionaries whose unconscious cultural baggage included notions of cultural and racial superiority.

The history of missionary dynasties, the project with which this book began, and from which it has since diverted, also remains to be written. Their impact on the missionary enterprise cannot be underestimated, and various aspects of their history could provide thoughtful fodder for the historian. How far did they stultify changes and adaptations in mission theory through their generational continuity? How far, perhaps more beneficially, did their perpetuation of and socialisation into earlier mission norms (generally considered more optimistic and open, and less pessimistically racialist) shield the missionary enterprise from some of the less laudable intellectual trends in British domestic society (such as biological determinism and social Darwinism)? How far did being a member of a missionary dynasty secure one's acceptance in the enterprise, and how pressured was the childhood environment for members of those dynasties? These questions do not even begin to address the much broader potential of tracing family dynasties across related professions in medical, educational and religious practice.

Finally, this book has demonstrated the undeniable importance of the familial context to a complex and nuanced understanding of mission history. Its focus has been strictly with the LMS, however. There is undoubtedly potential to extend the scope of this research into the numerous alternative evangelical missionary societies that erupted at the turn of the eighteenth and nineteenth centuries. On certain points in particular, there is likely to be fascinating divergence, propelled by differences in socio-economic and educational make-up. The CMS, for example, employed ordained missionaries much more consistently, and from the very beginning of its enterprise. How did this impact on early ideas of cultural and racial intermixing such as have been uncovered for the LMS? With a strong tradition of female involvement in the Church of England, through the unofficial, but crucial work of the clergyman's wife, was the history of missionary women in the CMS dramatically different from that here explored of the LMS? Very recent work on the American Board of Commissioners for Foreign Missions by Char Miller suggests a strikingly similar chronology of family involvement, integration and disillusionment.[2] How far does this speak to transatlantic overlap and cooperation in both the theory and practice of evangelical mission?

By uncovering both occluded people and those elements of historical agency obscured by official bookkeeping, this project has promoted a more complex understanding of mission itself. It has explored the nature of female involvement in mission, the dynamics of missionary parenting, the bi-cultural, interstitial and semi-professional nature of missionary children, and the role of the missionary himself within a familial (as opposed to professional or spiritual) framework of understanding. Through an exploration of these partially obscured elements in the missionary enterprise, this book has examined the ways in which the seemingly intimate and personal (marriage, parenthood, family) utterly shaped and transformed the very nature of nineteenth-century mission itself.

Notes

1 Jeffrey Cox, *The British Missionary Enterprise since 1700* (London: Routledge, 2008), p. 190.

2 Char Miller, 'Domesticity Abroad: Work and Family in the Sandwich Islands Mission, 1820–1840', in Clifford Putney and Paul T. Burlin (eds), *The Role of the American Board in the World: Bicentennial Reflections on the Organisation's Missionary Work, 1810–2010* (Eugene, OR: WIPF & Stock, 2012), pp. 312–30.

APPENDIX

The following pages give the family trees of missionary dynasties, but only include those members who were offical missionaries (Figures 16–20):

1. Cousins Family Tree
2. Dawson Family Tree
3. Lewis Family Tree
4. Joyce-Rowlands Family Tree
5. Read-Brown Family Tree

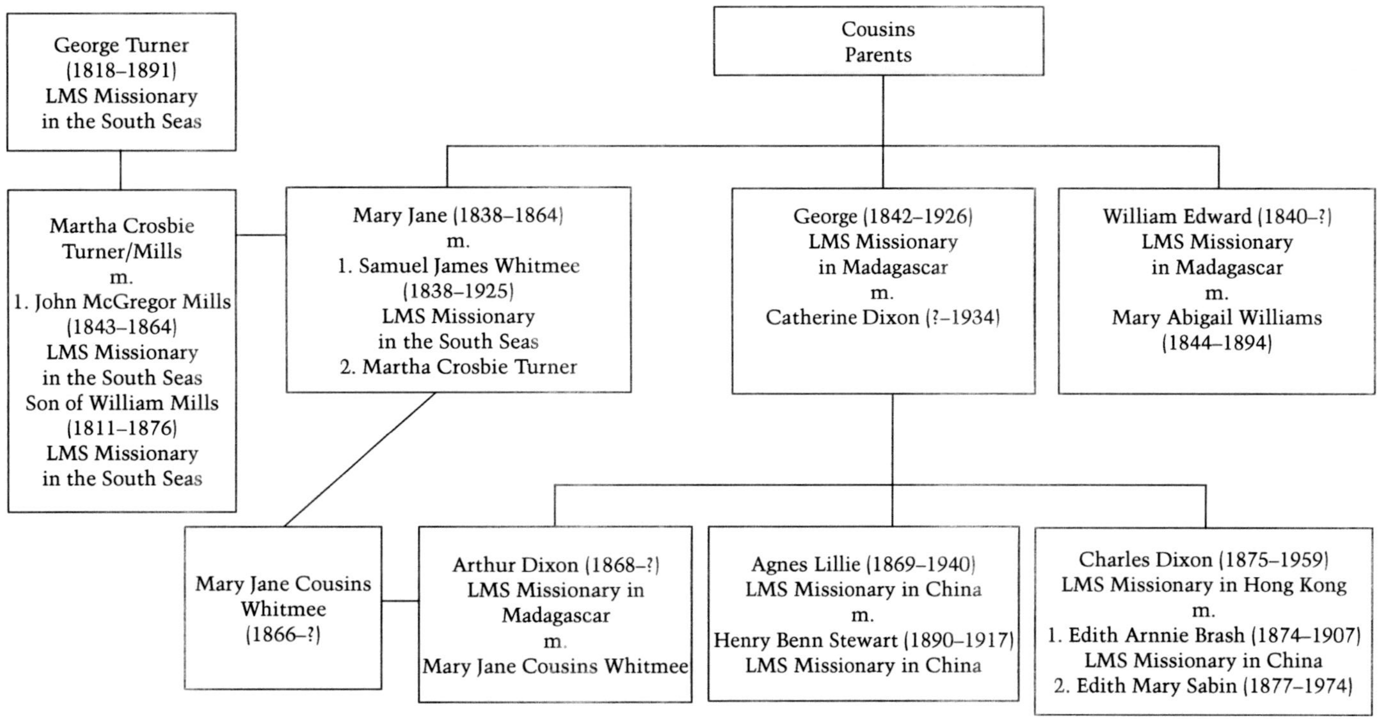

Figure 16 Cousins Family Tree (missionaries only).

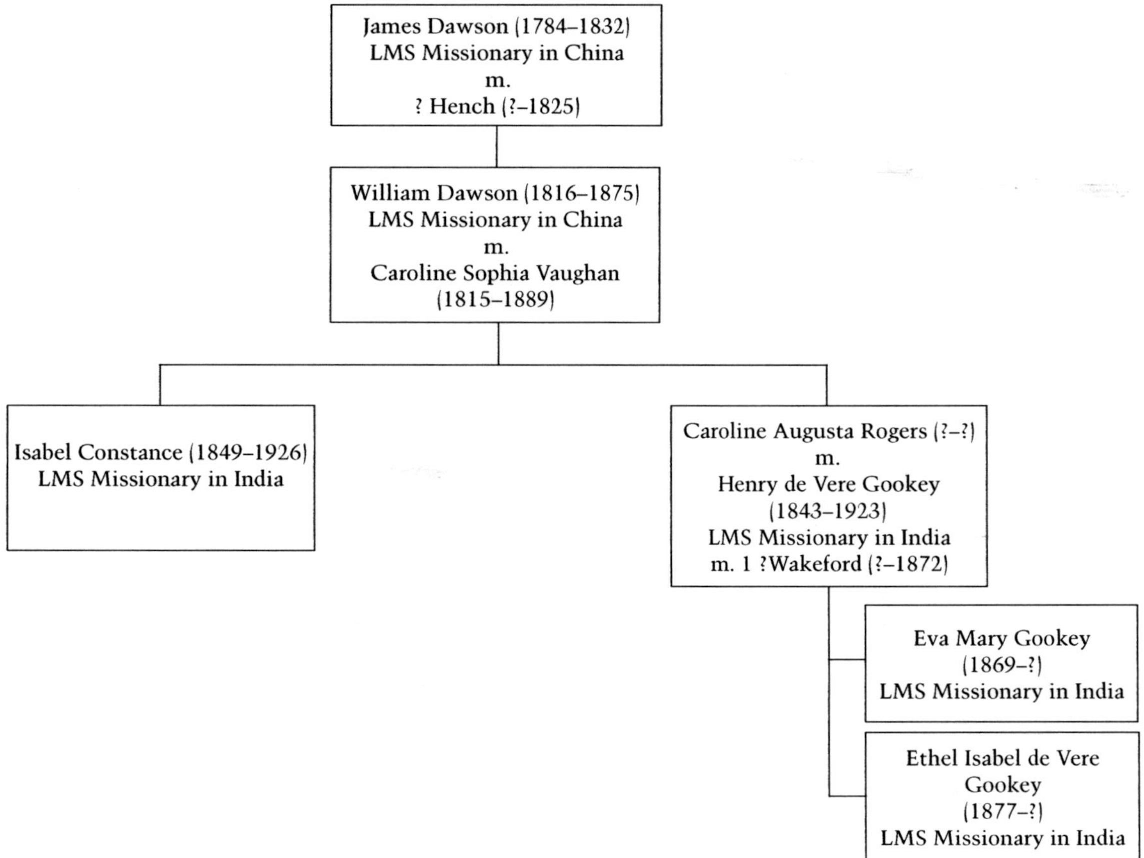

Figure 17 Dawson Family Tree (missionaries only).

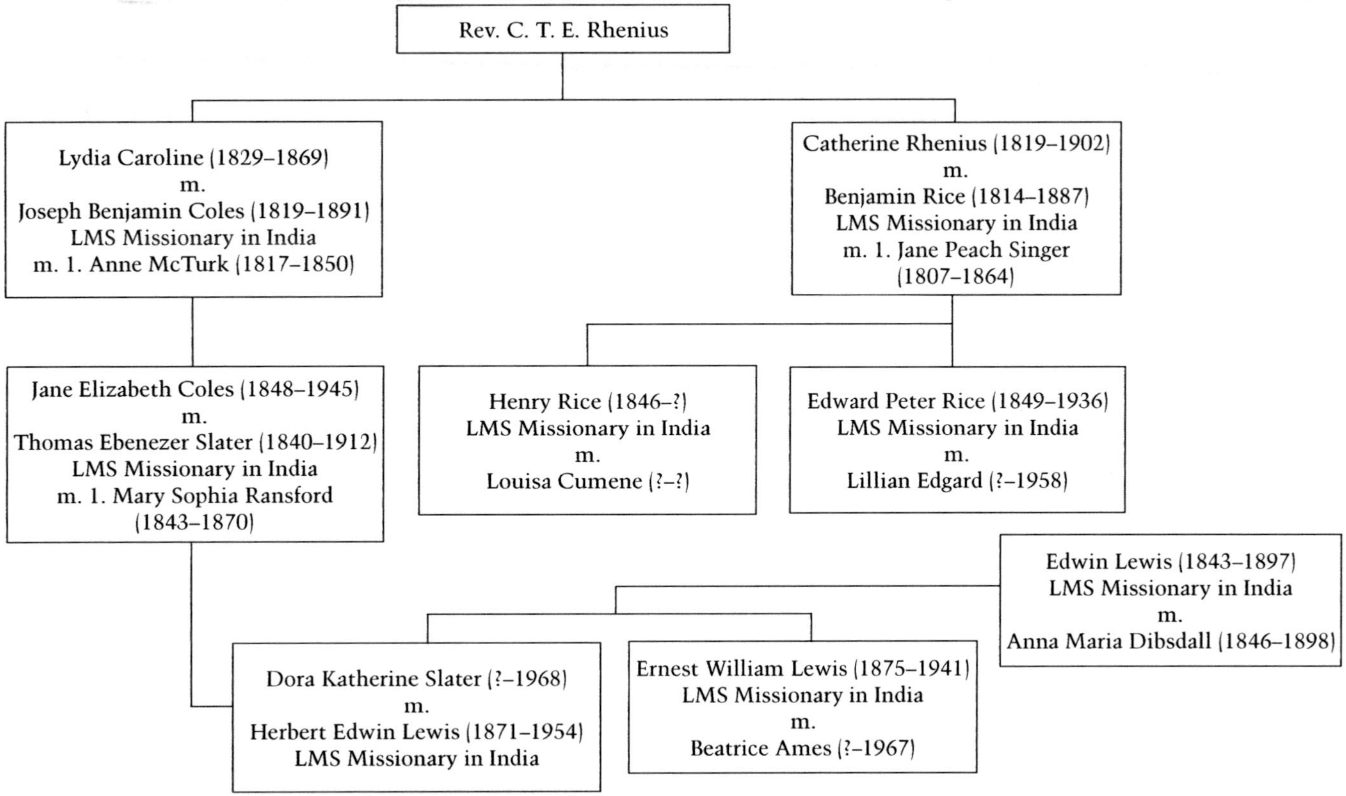

Figure 18 Lewis Family Tree (missionaries only).

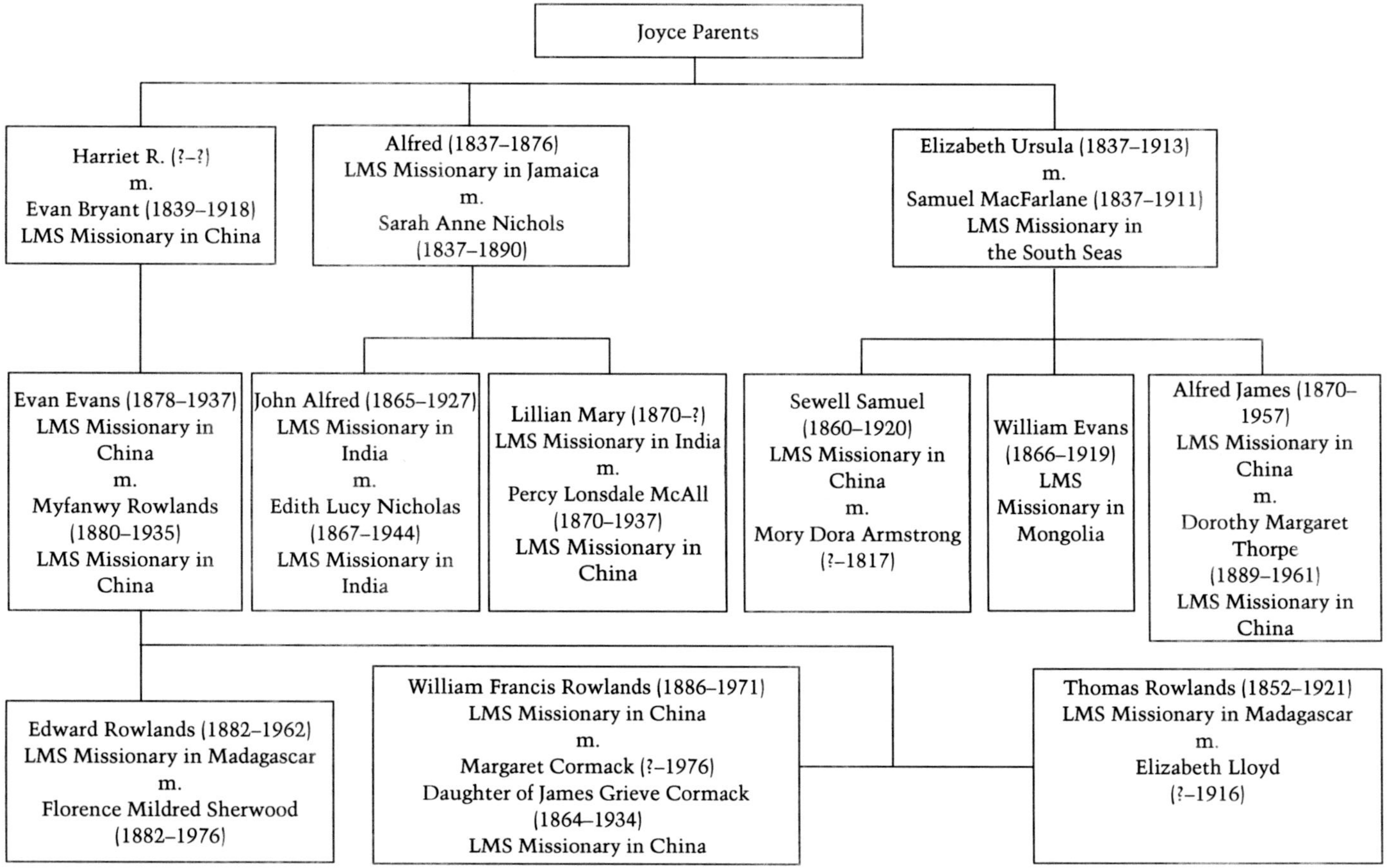

Figure 12 Joyce-Rowlands Family Tree (missionaries only).

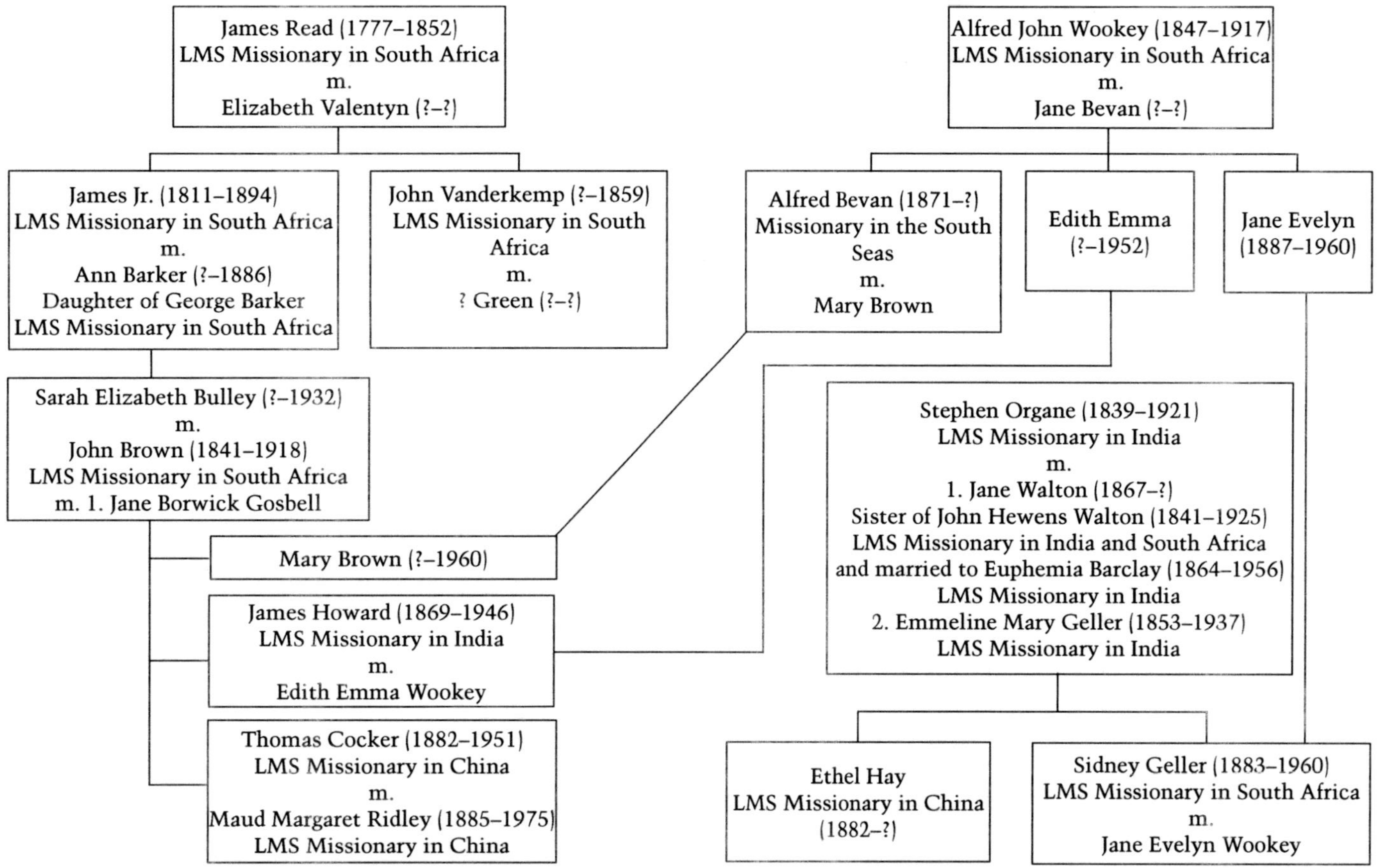

Figure 20 Read-Brown Family Tree (missionaries only).

BIBLIOGRAPHY

Archive material and manuscripts

Home

Archive of the Council of World Mission (formerly LMS), School of Oriental and African Studies, London.

Annual Reports, 1796–1875

Sermons Preached in London at the Formation of the Missionary Society, By Order of the Directors (T. Chapman, London, 1795–1815), vols 2–9.

Transactions of the Missionary Society (T. Williams, 1804–1818) vols. 1–4 (1795–1818)

Board Minutes, 1795–1875

Candidate Papers, 1795–1895, Boxes 1–28.

London Missionary Society Register of Missionary Children, 2 vols.

Miniature Portraits, Boxes 1–2.

Missionary Portraits, Boxes 1 and 4–6.

Papers of Deputation by Daniel Tyerman and George Bennet to the South Seas, Java, India, and Madagascar 1821–29. Home Odds. Box 10.

James Sibree, *A register of missionaries, deputations etc., from 1796–1923* (London Missionary Society 1923).

South Seas

Archive of the Council of World Mission (formerly LMS), School of Oriental and African Studies, London.

South Seas Incoming Letters, 1796–1875, Boxes 1(FBN 10)-34.

Western Outgoing Letters: South Seas and West Indies, 1822–1835, Boxes 1–4.

Western Outgoing Letters: South Seas, 1835–1875, Boxes 1–10.

South Seas Journal (SSJ), 1796–1816, Boxes 1–3.

Mary Williams Legacy Papers (uncatalogued)

National Archives at Kew, London, England

Convict List HO 11/2/5

The *Canada*'s Ship's Muster ADM 37/2738

Alexander Turnball Library, National Library of New Zealand, Wellington

Micro-MS-Coll-08–0129 [George Alexander Turner Papers]

Micro-MS-0726 [Hannah Crook Journal]

Micro-MS-Coll-08–0417 [Henry Nisbet Papers]

Micro-MS-Coll-08–0035 [John Williams and Robert Bourne Journal and Other Papers]

Micro-MS-0744 [Marsden Family Letters to Mrs Stokes, 1794–1824]

MS-Copy-Micro-0206 [Marsden Family Papers, 1802–1897]

Micro-MS-Coll-08–0095 [Samoan District Committee Minutes]
Micro-MS-0743 [Samuel Marsden Papers]
Micro-MS-0727 [Thomas Haweis Letters, 1791–1830]

Africa

Archive of the Council of World Mission (formerly LMS), School of Oriental and African Studies, London.
South Africa Incoming Letters, 1797–1875, Boxes 1–37.
Madagascar Incoming Letters, 1864–1895, Boxes 7–25.

National Archive of South Africa, Cape Archive Repository
Cape Town Manuscripts, MSB 858, LMS Miscellaneous
Cape Town Manuscripts, MSB 57: (George Barker Collection)
Cape Town Manuscripts, MSB 349: (Robert Moffat Collection)

Cory Library Rhodes University, Grahamstown South Africa
PR 343–345 [LMS missionary papers]
MS 5794–8398 [LMS missionary papers, including the letters and diaries of Elizabeth Price]

India

Archive of the Council of World Mission (formerly LMS), School of Oriental and African Studies, London.
North India, Bengal, Incoming Letters, 1824–1829, Box 2.
South India, Tamil, Incoming Letters, 1817–1830, Boxes 1–3.
South India, Canarese, Incoming Letters, 1817–1825, Box 1.
South India, Telegu, Incoming Letters, 1817–1835, Box 1.

Periodicals

Chronicle of the London Missionary Society
Evangelical Magazine
Missionary Magazine and Chronicle
Missionary Quarterly Sketches
Transactions

Books – pre-1900

Buckland, Rev. Augustus R., *Women in the Mission Field: Pioneers and Martyrs* (London, 1895).

Campbell, John, *Travels in South Africa, undertaken at the request of the London Missionary Society: being a narrative of a second journey in the interior of that country* (London, 1822).

Clough, Margaret M., *Extracts from the Journal and Correspondence of the late Mrs. M. M. Clough. With an introduction by Adam Clarke* (London, 1829).

Cook, James, *The voyages of Captain James Cook: illustrated with maps and numerous engravings on wood: with an appendix giving an account of the present condition of the South Seas Islands, etc.* (London, 1842).

Denison, Edward, Bishop of Salisbury, *Obedience to the Law of God and the End of Education: a sermon, preached at the opening of the school at Marlborough, for the sons of clergy and others, August 25, 1843* (London, 1843).

Drayson, Alfred Wilks, *Experiences of a Woolwich Professor during fifteen years at the Royal Military Academy* (London: Chapman and Hall, 1886).

Ellis, Sarah Stickney, *The Daughters of England: their position in society, characters and responsibilities* (London, 1845).

Ellis, William, *Memoir of Mrs. M. Ellis* (London, 1835).

Galt, John, *All the voyages round the world: from the first by Magellan in 1520 to Krusenstern in 1807/ now first collected by Capt. Samuel Prior [i.e. John Galt]* (London, 1820).

Fairchild, A. G., *Memoir of Mrs A. Lowrie of the Northern India Mission* (London, 1838).

Harvard, William Martin, *Memoirs of Mrs. Elizabeth Harvard, late of the Wesleyan Mission to Ceylon and India. With extracts from her diary and correspondence. By her husband* (London, 1825).

Judson, Ann Hasseltine, *An Account of the American Baptist Mission to the Burman Empire* (London, Joseph Butterworth and Son, 1823).

Knowles, James David, *Memoir of Mrs Ann H. Judson, late missionary to Burmah: including a history of the Baptist Mission in the Burman Empire* (Boston, MA: Gould, Kendall and Lincoln, 1835).

Lang, John Dunmore, *An historical and statistical account of New South Wales* (London: Cochrane and M'Crone, 1834).

Livingstone, David, *Missionary Travels and Researches in South Africa: including a sketch of sixteen years' residence in the interior of Africa, and a journey from the Cape of Good Hope to Loanda, on the west coast, thence across the continent, down the river Zambesi, to the eastern ocean* (London: John Murray, 1857).

London Missionary Society, *Is it nothing to you? A record of work among women (in connection with the London Missionary Society)* (London: London Missionary Society, 1899).

Lovett, Richard, *The History of the London Missionary Society, 1795–1895*, 2 vols. ([S.I.]: Frowde, 1899).

Moffat, John Smith, *The Lives of Robert and Mary Moffat* (London: T. Fisher Unwin, 1885).

Moffat, Robert, *Missionary Labours and Scenes in Southern Africa* (London: John Snow, 1842).

Moffat, Robert, *Scenes and Services in South Africa. The story of Robert Moffat's half-century of missionary labours* (London, 1876).

Newell, Harriet, *Memoirs of Mrs. Harriet Newell (Derived from her own writings)... To which is added a sermon on occasion of her death By Leonard Woods* (London: Booth and Co., 1815).

Philip, John, *Memoir of Mrs Matilda Smith late of Cape Town, Cape of Good Hope* (London: F. Westley, 1824).

Pitman, Emma Raymond, *Lady missionaries in foreign lands* (London: S. W. Partridge, 1889).

Shepheard, Henry, *A vindication of the Clergy Daughters' School and of the Rev. W. Carus Wilson from the remarks in the Life of Charlotte Bronte* (London: Robert Morphet, 1857).

Stuart (afterwards Wilson), Arabella M., *The lives of Mrs. A. H. Judson and Mrs S. B. Judson, with a biographical sketch of Mrs E. C. Judson, missionaries to Burmah* (London, 1852).

Thompson (afterwards Luke), Jemima, *Memoirs of British Female Missionaries: with a survey of the condition of women in heathen countries. And also a preliminary Essay on the importance of female agency in evangelizing Pagan Nations* (London, 1841).

Thompson, Ralph Wardlaw and Johnson, Arthur, *British Foreign Missions, 1837–1897* ([S.I.]: Blackie and Son Ltd, 1899).

Tyerman, Daniel and Bennett, George, *Journal of Voyages and Travels by the Rev Daniel Tyerman and George Bennet, Esq, deputed from the London Missionary Society to visit their various stations in the South Sea Islands, China, India etc. between the years 1821 and 1829 compiled from original documents by James Montgomery*, vol. I (London, 1831).

Veeson, George, *An Authentic Narrative of Four Year's Residence at Tongataboo* (London, 1810).

Walters, William, *Life and labours of Robert Moffat, D. D., missionary in South Africa* (Derby, 1882).

Winslow, Miron, *A Memoir of Mrs H. W. Winslow … combining a sketch of the Ceylon Mission … with an introductory essay by J. H. Evans* (London, 1838).

Books post-1900

Ajayi, A. F. Ade, *Christian Missions in Nigeria, 1841–1891. The making of a new elite* (London: Longmans, 1965).

Alderson, David, *Mansex Fine: religion, manliness and imperialism in nineteenth-century British culture* (Manchester: Manchester University Press, 1998).

Anderson, Benedict, *Imagined Communities: reflections on the origin and spread of nationalism* (London: Verso, 1983).

Anstey, Roger, *The Atlantic Slave Trade and British Abolition, 1760–1810* (London: Macmillan, 1975).

Armitage, David, *The Ideological Origins of the British Empire* (Cambridge: Cambridge University Press, 2000).

Ayandele, Emmanuel Avankanmi, *The Missionary Impact on Modern Nigeria, 1842–1914: a political and social analysis* (London: Longmans, 1966).

Bailey, Susan F., *Women and the British Empire: an annotated guide to sources* (New York and London: Garland, 1983).

Ballhatchet, Kenneth, *Race, Sex and Class under the Raj: Imperial attitudes and policies and their critics, 1793–1905* (London: Weidenfeld & Nicolson, 1980).

Ballantyne, Tony and Burton, Antoinette (eds), *Moving Subjects: gender, mobility, and intimacy in an age of global empire* (Urbana, IL: University of Illinois Press, 2009).

Bayly, C. A., *Imperial Meridian: the British Empire and the world, 1780–1830* (London: Longman, 1989).

Bayly, C. A., *The Birth of the Modern World, 1780–1914: global connections and comparisons* (Oxford: Blackwell, 2004).

Beaver, R. Pierce, *American Protestant Women in World Mission: history of the first feminist movement in north America* (Grand Rapids: William B. Eerdmans, 1980).

Bebbington, D. W., *Evangelicalism in Modern Britain: a history from the 1730s to the 1980s* (London: Unwin Hyman, 1989).

Bebbington, D. W., *The Nonconformist Conscience: chapel and politics, 1870–1914* (London: Unwin, 1982).

Bederman, Gail, *Manliness and Civilisation: a cultural history of gender and race in the United States, 1880–1917* (Chicago: University of Chicago Press, 1995).

Beidelman, Thomas O., *Colonial Evangelism: a socio-historical study of an East African mission at the grassroots* (Bloomington: Indiana University Press, 1982).

Berkeley, George Fitzhardinge, *Wellington College: the founders of the tradition* (Newport, Mon.: R. H. Johns, 1948).

Bertaux, Daniel and Thompson, Paul (eds), *Between Generations: family models, myths and memories* (Oxford: Oxford University Press, 1993).

Bickers, Robert and Seton, Rosemary (eds), *Missionary Encounters: sources and issues* (Richmond, Surrey: Curzon Press, 1996).

Blackburn, Robin, *The Overthrow of Colonial Slavery, 1776–1848* (London: Verso, 1988).

Blunt, Alison, *Travel, Gender and Imperialism: Mary Kingsley and West Africa* (New York and London: Guilford Press, 1994).

Bolt, Christine, *Victorian Attitudes to Race* (London: Routledge, 1971).

Bowie, Fiona, Kirkwood, Deborah and Ardener, Shirley (eds), *Women and Missions: past and present: anthropological and historical perspectives* (Providence, RI; Oxford: Berg, 1993).

Bowlby, John, *Attachment and Loss*, 3 vols (London: Hogarth Press, 1969–80).

Bradley, Ian C., *The Call to Seriousness: the Evangelical impact on the Victorians* (London: Jonathan Cape, 1976).

Bredekamp, Henry and Ross, Robert (eds), *Missions and Christianity in South African History* (Johannesburg: Witwatersrand University Press, 1995).

Brembeck, Cole Speicher, *Cultural Challenges to Education: the influence of cultural factors in school learning* (Lexington, MA and London: D. C. Heath, 1973).

Bridenthal, Renate, Koonz, Claudia and Stuard, Susan (eds), *Becoming Visible: women in European history* (Boston, MA: Houghton Mifflin, 1987).

Broughton, Trev Lynn and Rogers, Helen (eds), *Gender and Fatherhood in the Nineteenth Century* (Basingstoke: Palgrave Macmillan, 2007).

Brouwer, Ruth Compton, *New Women for God: Canadian Presbyterian women and India missions, 1876–1914* (Toronto; Buffalo: University of Toronto Press, 1990).

Brown, Judith and Louis, Roger (eds), *Oxford History of the British Empire*, vol. 4 *Twentieth Century* (Oxford: Oxford University Press, 1999).

Brown, Kathleen M., *Good Wives, Nasty Wenches, and Anxious Patriarchs: gender, race, and power in colonial Virginia* (Chapel Hill; London: Published for the Institute of Early American History and Culture, Williamsburg, Virginia by the University of North Carolina Press, 1996).

Brumberg, Joan Jacobs, *Mission for Life: the story of the family of Adoniram Judson, the dramatic events of the first American foreign mission, and the course of evangelical religion in the nineteenth century* (New York: Free Press, 1980).

Buettner, Elizabeth, *Empire Families: Britons and late imperial India* (Oxford: Oxford University Press, 2004).

Burman, Sandra (ed.), *Fit Work for Women* (London: Croom Helm, 1979).

Burn, William Laurence, *The Age of Equipoise: a study of the mid-Victorian generation* (London: Allen & Unwin, 1964).

Burton, Antoinette, *Burdens of History: British feminists, Indian women and imperial culture, 1865–1915* (Chapel Hill and London: University of North Carolina, 1994).

Burton, Antoinette, *At the Heart of Empire: Indians and the colonial encounter in late-Victorian Britain* (Berkeley; London: University of California Press, 1998).

Burton, Antoinette (ed.), *After the Imperial Turn: thinking with and through the nation* (Durham and London: Duke University Press, 2003).

Bush, Barbara, *Slave Women in Caribbean Society 1650–1838* (London: Currey, 1990).

Caine, Barbara, *Bombay to Bloomsbury: a biography of the Strachey family* (Oxford; New York: Oxford University Press, 2005).

Cairns, H. Alan C., *Prelude to Imperialism: British reactions to Central African society, 1840–1890* (London: Routledge & Kegan Paul, 1965).

Callan, Hilary and Ardener, Shirley (eds), *The Incorporated Wife* (London: Croom Helm, 1984).

Cannadine, David, *Ornamentalism: how the British saw their empire* (London: Allen Lane, 2002).

Capp, Bernard, *When Gossips Meet: women, family and neighbourhood in early modern England* (Oxford: Oxford University Press, 2003).

Carey, Hilary M. (ed.), *Empires of Religion* (Basingstoke: Palgrave Macmillan, 2008).

Chaudhuri, Nupur and Strobel, Margaret (eds), *Western Women and Imperialism: complicity and resistance* (Bloomington: Indiana University Press, 1992).

Cluassen, Dane S., *The Promise Keepers: essays on masculinity and Christianity* (Jefferson, NC: McFarland Publishers, 1999).

Comaroff, John and Jean, *Of Revelation and Revolution. Vol. 1, Christianity, colonialism, and consciousness in South Africa* (Chicago: University of Chicago Press, 1991).

Comaroff, Jean and John, *Of Revelation and Revolution. Vol. 2, The dialectics of modernity on a South African frontier* (Chicago, London: Chicago University Press, 1997).

Cooper, Frederick and Stoler, Ann Laura (eds), *Tensions of Empire: colonial cultures in a bourgeois world* (Berkeley, CA and London: University of California Press, 1997).

da Costa, Emilia Viotti, *Crowns of Glory, Tears of Blood: the Demerara Slave Rebellion of 1823* (Oxford: Oxford University Press, 1994).

Cox, Jeffrey, *Imperial Fault Lines: Christianity and colonial power in India, 1818–1940* (Stanford, California: Stanford University Press, 2002).

Cox, Jeffrey, *The British Missionary Enterprise since 1700* (London: Routledge, 2008).

Craton, Michael, *Testing the Chains: resistance to slavery in the British West Indies* (Ithaca, NY and London: Cornell University Press, 1982).

Crossick, Geoffrey (ed.), *The Lower Middle Class in Britain, 1870–1914* (London: Croom Helm, 1977).

Curtin, Philip, *Image of Africa British Ideas and Action, 1780–1850* (London: Macmillan and Co. Ltd, 1965).

Davidoff, Leonore and Hall, Catherine, *Family Fortunes: men and women of the English middle class, 1780–1850* (London: Hutchinson, 1987).

Davidoff, Leonore, *Worlds Between: historical perspectives on race and class* (Cambridge: Polity, 1995).

Davidoff, Leonore, Doolittle, Megan, Fink, Janet, and Holden, Katherine, *The Family Story: blood, contract and intimacy, 1830–1960* (London and New York: Longman, 1999).

Davidson, James Wightman and Scarr, Deryck (eds), *Pacific Islands Portraits* (Wellington, Auckland: A. H. & A. W. Reed, 1970).

Davis, David Brion, *Slavery and Human Progress* (New York and Oxford: Oxford University Press, 1984).

Dening, Greg, *Islands and Beaches: Discourse on a silent land Marquesas, 1774–1880* (Honolulu: Hawai'i University Press, 1980).

Dening, Greg, *Performances* (Chicago: Chicago University Press, 1996).

Dickson, Mora, *Beloved Partner: Mary Moffat of Kuruman* (London: Victor Gollancz Ltd, 1974).

Earle, Rebecca (ed.), *Epistolary Selves: letters and letter-writers, 1600–1945* (Aldershot, Brookfield, Singapore and Sydney: Ashgate, 1999).

Edmond, Rod, *Representing the South Pacific: colonial discourse from Cook to Gauguin* (Cambridge: Cambridge University Press, 1997).

Edmond, Rod and Smith, Vanessa (eds), *Islands in History and Representation* (London: Routledge, 2003).

Elbourne, Elizabeth, *Blood Ground: Colonialism, missions, and the contest for Christianity in the Cape Colony and Britain, 1799–1853* (Montreal and London: McGill-Queen's University Press, 2002).

Elphick, Richard and Davenport, Rodney (eds), *Christianity in South Africa: a political, social and cultural history* (Oxford: James Currey, 1997).

Elshtain, Jean Bethke, *Public Man, Private Woman: women in social and political thought* (Princeton, NJ: Princeton University Press, 1981).

Enklaar, Ido H., *Life and work of Dr. J. Th. van der Kemp, 1747–1811: missionary pioneer and protagonist of racial equality in South Africa* (Balkema, Southern African Biographical and Historical Studies, 28: 1988)

Etherington, Norman, *The Great Treks: the transformation of South Africa, 1815–1854* (Harlow: Longman, 2001).

Etherington, Norman (ed.), *Missions and Empire* (Oxford: Oxford University Press, 2005).

Ferguson, Niall, *Empire: how Britain made the modern world* (London: Penguin, 2004).

Flemming, Leslie A., *Women's Work for Women: missionaries and social change in Asia* (Westview Press, 1989).

Fletcher, Anthony and Hussey, Stephen (eds), *Childhood in Question: children, parents and the state* (Manchester: Manchester University Press, 1999).

Foucault, Michel, *The History of Sexuality. Volume 1, An Introduction*, trans. Robert Hurley (London: Allen Lane, 1979).

Foyster, Elizabeth A., *Manhood in Early Modern England: honour, sex, and marriage, women and men in history* (London: Longman, 1999).

Ghosh, Durba, *Sex and the Family in Colonial India: the making of empire* (Cambridge: Cambridge University Press, 2006).

Gill, Sean, *Women and the Church of England from the eighteenth century to the present* (London: SPCK, 1994).

Gillis, John R., *A world of their Own Making: myth, ritual, and the quest for family values* (New York: Basic Books, 1996).

Godber, Joyce and Hutchins, Isabel, *A Century of Challenge: Bedford High School, 1882–1982* (Bedford: Bedford High School, 1982).

Goodall, Norman, *A History of the London Missionary Society 1895–1945* (London: Oxford University Press, 1954).

Gowing, Laura, *Domestic Dangers: women, words, and sex in early modern London* (Oxford: Oxford University Press, 1998).

Gowing, Laura, *Common Bodies: women, touch and power in seventeenth-century England* (New Haven & London: Yale University Press, 2003).

Grimshaw, Patricia, *Paths of Duty: American missionary wives in nineteenth-century Hawaii* (Honolulu: University of Hawai'i Press, 1989).

Groves, C. P., *The Planting of Christianity in Africa. Vol. 2, 1840–1878* (London: Lutterworth Press, 1954).

de Gruchy, John W. (ed.), *The London Missionary Society in Southern Africa: historical essays in celebration of the bicentenary of the LMS in Southern Africa, 1799–1999* (Cape Town: David Philip, 1999).

Guha, Ranajit and Spivak, Gayatri Chakravorty (eds), *Selected Subaltern Studies* (New York and Oxford: Oxford University Press, 1998).

Gunson, Neil, *Messengers of Grace: evangelical missionaries in the South Seas, 1799–1860* (Melbourne, Oxford: Oxford University Press, 1978).

Hall, Catherine, *White, Male and Middle Class: explorations in feminism and history* (Cambridge: Polity, 1992).

Hall, Catherine, *Civilising Subjects: metropole and colony in the English imagination, 1830–1867* (Oxford: Polity, 2002).

Hall, Catherine and Rose, Sonya (eds), *At Home with the Empire: metropolitan culture and the imperial world* (Cambridge: Cambridge University Press, 2006).

Harlow, Vincent T., *The Founding of the Second British Empire, 1763–1793*,

2 vols. (London: Longmans, 1952–64).
Hastings, Adrian, *The Church in Africa: 1450–1950* (Oxford: Clarendon Press, 1994).
Hastings, Adrian, *The Construction of Nationhood: ethnicity, religion and nationalism* (Cambridge: Cambridge University Press, 1997).
Healey, Edna, *Wives of Fame: Mary Livingstone, Jenny Marx, Emma Darwin* (London: Sidgwick & Jackson, 1986).
Hetherington, Penelope, *Settlers, Servants and Slaves: Aboriginal and European children in nineteenth-century Australia* (Nedlands, WA: University of Western Australia Press, 2002).
Hill, Patricia Ruth, *The World their Household: the American woman's foreign mission movement and cultural transformation, 1870–1920* (Ann Arbor: University of Michigan Press, 1985).
Hilton, Boyd, *Age of Atonement: the influence of evangelicalism in social and economic thought, 1795–1865* (Oxford: Clarendon Press, 1988).
Hiney, Tom, *On the Missionary Trail: the classic Georgian adventure of two Englishman, sent on a journey around the world, 1821–1829* (London: Vintage, 2001).
Hobsbawm, Eric and Ranger, Terence (eds), *The Invention of Tradition* (Cambridge: Cambridge University Press, 1983).
Hopkins, A. G. (ed.), *Globalisation in World History* (London: Pimlico, 2002).
Horne, C. Sylvester, *The story of the LMS* (London: London Missionary Society, 1908).
Huber, Mary Taylor and Lutkehaus, Nancy C. (eds), *Gendered Missions: women and men in missionary discourse and practice* (Ann Arbor: University of Michigan Press, 1999).
Hunt, Lynn (ed.), *The New Cultural History* (Berkeley: University of California Press, 1989).
Hunter, Jane, *The Gospel of Gentility: American women missionaries in turn of the century China* (New Haven and London: Yale University Press, 1984).
Hyam, Ronald, *Empire and Sexuality: the British experience* (Manchester: Manchester University Press, 1990).
Isichei, Elizabeth Allo, *A History of Christianity in Africa: from antiquity to the present* (London: SPCK, 1995).
Jakobsson, Stiv, *Am I not a man and a brother? British mission and the abolition of the slave trade and slavery in West Africa and the West Indies, 1786–1838* (Lund: Gleerup, 1972).
Jeal, Tim, *Livingstone* (New Haven and London: Yale Nota Bene, 2001 [first published London: Futura Publications, 1979]).
Johnston, Anna, *Missionary Writing and Empire, 1800–1860* (Cambridge: Cambridge University Press, 2003).
Jolly, Margaret and Macintyre, Martha (eds), *Family and Gender in the Pacific: domestic contradictions and the colonial impact* (Cambridge: Cambridge University Press, 1999).
Knapman, Claudia, *White Women in Fiji 1835–1930: the ruin of Empire* (London: Allen & Unwin, 1986).
Kreider, Alan and Shaw, Jane (eds), *Culture and the Nonconformist Tradition*

(Cardiff: University of Wales Press, 1999).

Laidlaw, Zoe, *Colonial Connections, 1815–45: patronage, the information revolution and colonial government* (Manchester: Manchester University Press, 2005).

Lamb, Jonathan, Smith, Vanessa, and Thomas, Nicholas (eds), *Exploration and Exchange: a South Seas anthology, 1680–1900* (Chicago, London: Chicago University Press, 2000).

Lambert, David and Lester, Alan (eds), *Colonial Lives across the British Empire: imperial careering in the long nineteenth century* (Cambridge: Cambridge University Press, 2006).

Langmore, Diane, *Missionary Lives: Papua, 1874–1914* (Honolulu: University of Hawai'i Press, 1989).

Latourette, Kenneth S., *A History of the Expansion of Christianity*, 7 vols (London: Eyre & Spottiswoode, 1937–45).

Lester, Alan, *Imperial Networks: creating identities in nineteenth-century South Africa and Britain* (London: Routledge, 2001).

Levine, Philippa, *Prostitution, Race, and Politics: policing venereal disease in the British Empire* (New York; London: Routledge, 2003).

Levine, Philippa (ed.), *Gender and Empire* (Oxford: Oxford University Press, 2004).

Lewis, Gail (ed.), *Forming Nation, Framing Welfare* (London: Routledge, 1998).

Lewis, Jane (ed.), *Labour and Love: women's experience of home and family, 1850–1940* (Oxford: Blackwell, 1986).

Livingstone, David, *Family Letters, 1841–1856*, 2 vols. *Edited with an introduction by I. Schapera* (London: Chatto & Windus, 1959).

Livingstone, David, *Livingstone's Private Journals, 1851–1853. Edited with an introduction by I. Schapera* (London: Chatto & Windus, 1960).

Livingstone, William Pringle, *Mary Slessor of Calabar: pioneer missionary* (London: Hodder & Stoughton, 1916).

Long, Una (ed.), *The Journals of Elizabeth Lees Price: written in Bechuanaland, Southern Africa 1854–1883 with an Epilogue: 1889 and 1900* (London: Edward Arnold, 1956).

Lorimer, Douglas A., *Colour, Class and the Victorians: English attitudes to the Negro in the mid-nineteenth century* (Leicester: Leicester University Press, 1978).

McClintock, Anne, *Imperial Leather: race, gender and sexuality in the colonial conquest* (New York and London: Routledge, 1995).

McClintock, Anne, Mufti, Aamir and Shohat, Ella (eds), *Dangerous Liaisons: gender, nations, and postcolonial perspectives* (Minneapolis, London: University of Minnesota Press, 1997).

McClintock, Anne, *Double Crossings: madness, sexuality and imperialism: the 2000 Garnett Sedgewick memorial lecture* (Vancouver: Ronsdale Press, 2001).

MacKenzie, John, *Propaganda and Empire: the manipulation of British public opinion, 1880–1960* (Manchester: Manchester University Press, 1984).

MacKenzie, John (ed.), *Imperialism and Popular Culture* (Manchester: Manchester University Press, 1986).

Macmillan, W. M., *Bantu, Boer and Briton: the making of the South African native problem* (London: Faber and Gwyer, 1929).

Malik, Kenan, *The Meaning of Race: race, history and culture in western society* (Basingstoke: Macmillan, 1996).

Mangan, J. A. and Walvin, James (eds), *Manliness and Morality: middle-class masculinity in Britain and America, 1800–1940* (Manchester: Manchester University Press, 1987).

Mangan, J. A. (ed.), *Benefits Bestowed: education and British imperialism* (Manchester: Manchester University Press, 1988).

Marshall, P. J. (ed.), *Cambridge Illustrated History of the British Empire* (Cambridge: Cambridge University Press, 1996).

Marshall, P. J., *Oxford History of the British Empire*, vol. 2, *the eighteenth century* (Oxford: Oxford University Press, 1998).

Martin, Roger, *Evangelicals United: ecumenical stirrings in pre-Victorian Britain, 1795–1830* (Metuchen, NJ and London: Scarecrow, 1983).

Matsuda, Matt, *Empires of Love: histories of France and the Pacific* (Oxford: Oxford University Press, 2005).

May, Andrew and Grimshaw, Patricia (eds), *Missionaries, Indigenous Peoples and Cultural Exchange* (Brighton: Sussex Academic Press, 2010).

Mead, Margaret, *Coming of Age in Samoa: a study of adolescence and sex in primitive societies* ([S.I.]: Penguin, 1928).

Medick, Hans and Sabean, David Warren (eds), *Interest and Emotion: essays on the study of family and kinship* (Cambridge: Cambridge University Press, 1977).

Messenger, Charles, *Unbroken Service: the history of Lloyd's Patriotic Fund 1803–2003* (London: The Fund, 2003).

Midgley, Clare (ed.), *Gender and Imperialism* (Manchester: Manchester University Press, 1998).

Midgley, Clare, *Feminism and Empire: women activists in imperial Britain, 1790–1865* (London: Routledge, 2007).

Mintz, Steven, *A Prison of Expectations: the family in Victorian culture* (New York, London: New York University Press, 1983).

Moffat, Robert, *The Matabele Journals of Robert Moffat, 1829–1860* 2 vols. Edited by Wallis, J. P. R. (London: Chatto & Windus, 1945).

Moffat, Robert, *Apprenticeship at Kuruman. Being the journals and letters of Robert and Mary Moffat 1820–1828*, ed. by I. Schapera (London: Chatto & Windus, 1951).

Moffat, Robert Unwin, *John Smith Moffat CMG Missionary: A Memoir* (London: John Murray, 1921).

Morris, Rosalind C. (ed.), *Can the Subaltern Speak?: reflections on the history of an idea* (New York and Chichester: Columbia University Press, 2010).

Mountford, Roxanne, *The Gendered Pulpit: preaching in American Protestant spaces* (Carbondale, IL: Southern Illinois University Press, 2003).

Murdoch, Lydia, *Imagined Orphans: poor families, child welfare, and contested citizenship in London* (New Brunswick, NJ and London: Rutgers University Press, 2006).

Neill, Stephen, *A History of Christian Missions* ([S.I.]: Penguin, 1964).

Newell, Jennifer, *Trading Nature: Tahitians, Europeans and ecological exchange* (Honolulu: University of Hawai'i Press, 2010).

Newsome, David, *A History of Wellington College, 1859–1959* (London: John Murray, 1959).

Newsome, David, *Godliness and Good Learning: four studies on a Victorian ideal* (London: Cassell, 1961).

Newton, Judith L., Ryan, Mary P. and Walkowitz, Judith R. (eds), *Sex and Class in Women's History* (London: Routledge, 1983).

Nock, O. S., *A History of the London Missionary Society* 2 vols. (London: Allen & Unwin, 1982).

Noll, Mark, *The Rise of Evangelicalism: the age of Edwards, Whitefield and the Wesleys* (Nottingham: IVP, 2004).

Obeyesekere, Gananath, *The Apotheosis of Captain Cook: European myth-making in the Pacific* (Princeton, NJ: Princeton University Press and Honolulu, Hawaii: Bishop Museum Press, 1992).

O'Brien, Patty, *The Pacific Muse: exotic femininity and the colonial Pacific* (Seattle, Washington and London: University of Washington Press, 2006).

O'Connor, Daniel (ed.), *Three Centuries of Mission: the United Society for the Propagation of the Gospel 1701–2000* (New York, London: Continuum, 2000).

Oddie, Geoffrey, *Social Protest in India: British Protestant missionaries and social reforms* (New Delhi: Manohar, 1979).

Oliver, Roland, *The Missionary Factor in East Africa* (London: Longmans Green and Co., 1951).

Osborne, Honor, *A History of the Royal School for Daughters of Officers of the Army, 1864–1965* (London: Hodder & Stoughton, 1966).

Parsons, Janet Wagner, *The Livingstones at Kolobeng 1847–1852* (Gaborone, Botswana: Botswana Society, 1997).

Pascoe, Charles Frederick, *Two Hundred Years of the SPG: An historical account of the Society for the Propagation of the Gospel in Foreign Parts, 1701–1900*, 2 vols (London: SPG, 1901).

Pateman, Carole, *The Sexual Contract* (Cambridge: Polity, 1988).

Pateman, Carole, *The Disorder of Women: democracy, feminism and political theory* (Cambridge: Polity, 1989).

Peacocke, Douglas, *William Pascoe Crook, 1775–1846* (Perth: Peacocke Press, 1995).

Perry, Adele, *On the Edge of Empire: gender, race, and the making of British Columbia, 1849–1871* (Toronto and London: University of Toronto Press, 2001).

Philips, Adam and Taylor, Barbara, *On Kindness* (London: Hamish Hamilton, 2009).

Piggin, Stuart, *Making Evangelical Missionaries, 1789–1958: the social background, motives and training of British protestant missionaries to India* ([S.l.]: Sutton Courtney Press, 1984).

Pike, Elsie, *The Story of Walthamstow Hall. A century of girls' education. Material collected by E. Pike and Constance E. Curryer* (London: Carey Press, 1938).

Pitman, Emma Raymond, *Ann H. Judson: missionary heroine of Burma* (London: Pickering and Inglis, 1935).

Pollock, David C. and Reken, Ruth E. Van, *Third Culture Kids: the experience of growing up among worlds* (Yarmouth, ME and London: Intercultural Press, 2001).

Porter, Andrew (ed.), *Atlas of British Overseas Expansion* (London: Routledge, 1991).

Porter, Andrew (ed.), *Oxford History of the British Empire*, vol. 3 *the nineteenth century* (Oxford: Oxford University Press, 1999).

Porter, Andrew (ed.), *The Imperial Horizons of British Protestant Missions, 1880–1914* (Grand Rapids, MI: W.B. Eerdmans Pub., 2003).

Porter, Andrew, *Religion Versus Empire? British protestant missionaries and overseas expansion, 1700–1914* (Manchester: Manchester University Press, 2004).

Porter, Bernard, *The Lion's Share: a short history of British imperialism 1850–1970* (London: Longman, 1975).

Porter, Bernard, *The Absent-minded Imperialists: empire, society and culture in Britain* (Oxford: Oxford University Press, 2004).

Price, Richard, *Making Empire: colonial encounters and the creation of imperial rule in nineteenth-century Africa* (Cambridge: Cambridge University Press, 2008).

Pratt, Mary Louise, *Imperial Eyes: travel writing and transculturation* (London: Routledge, 1992).

Prochaska, F. K., *Women and Philanthropy in Nineteenth-century England* (Oxford: Clarendon Press, 1980).

Procida, Mary, *Married to Empire: gender, politics and imperialism in India, 1883–1947* (Manchester: Manchester University Press, 2002).

Putney, Clifford, and Burlin, Paul T. (eds), *The Role of the American Board in the World: Bicentennial Reflections on the Organisation's Missionary Work, 1810–2010* (Eugene, OR: WIPF & Stock, 2012).

Robert, Dana L., *American Women in Mission: a social history of their thought and practice* (Macon, GA: Mercer University Press, 1996).

Robert, Dana L. (ed.), *Gospel Bearers, gender barriers: missionary women in the twentieth century* (New York: Orbis, 2002).

Roper, Michael and Tosh, John (eds), *Manful Assertions: Masculinities in Britain since 1800* (London and New York: Routledge, 1991).

Ross, Andrew C., *John Philip (1775–1851): missions, race and politics in South Africa* (Aberdeen: Aberdeen University Press, 1986).

Ross, Andrew C., *David Livingstone: mission and empire* (London: Hambledon & London, 2002).

de Rougement, Herbert, *A History of the Lloyd's Patriotic Fund from its foundation in 1803* (London: Leadenhall Press, 1914).

Ruether, Rosemary Radford, *Christianity and the Making of the Modern Family* (London: SCM Press, 2001).

Rutherdale, Myra, *Women and the White Man's God: gender and race in the Canadian mission field* (Vancouver: University of British Columbia Press, 2002).

Said, Edward, *Orientalism: western conceptions of the Orient* (London: Routledge & Kegan Paul, 1978).

Said, Edward, *Culture and Imperialism* (London: Knopf, 1993).

Sales, Jane, *Mission Stations and the Coloured Communities of the Eastern Cape 1800–1852* (Cape Town and Rotterdam: Balkema, 1974).

Scarr, Deryck, *A History of the Pacific Islands: passages through tropical time* (Richmond: Curzon, 2001).

Scott, James C., *Weapons of the Weak: everyday forms of peasant resistance* (New Haven & London: Yale University Press, 1985).

Scott, Joan Wallach, *Gender and the Politics of History* (New York: Columbia University Press, 1988).

Scully, Pamela, *Liberating the Family? Gender, professionalism, and the Victorian idea of Christian mission* (Woodbridge: Boydell Press, 2003).

Seaver, George, *David Livingstone: his life and letters* (London: Lutterworth Press, 1957).

Sellers, Ian, *Nineteenth-century Nonconformity* (London: Edward Arnold, 1977).

Semple, Rhonda A., *Missionary Women: gender, professionalism and the late Victorian idea of Christian mission* (Woodbridge: Boydell, 2003).

Singh, Maina Chawla, *Gender, Religion, and 'Heathen Lands': American missionary women in South Asia, 1860s–1940s* (New York: Garland Publishers, 2000).

Sinha, Mrinalini, *Colonial Masculinity: the 'manly Englishman' and the 'effeminate Bengali' in the late nineteenth century* (Manchester: Manchester University Press, 1995).

Sivasundaram, Sujit, *Nature and the Godly Empire: science and evangelical mission in the Pacific, 1795–1850* (Cambridge: Cambridge University Press, 2005).

Schoeman, Karel (ed.), *The British Presence in the Transorange, 1845–1854* (Cape Town: Human and Rousseau, 1992).

Schoeman, Karel, *A Thorn Bush that Grows in the Path: the missionary career of Ann Hamilton, 1815–1823* (Cape Town: South African Library, 1995).

Smart, Carol (ed.), *Regulating Womanhood: historical essays on marriage, motherhood and sexuality* (London: Routledge, 1992).

Smith, Vanessa, *Literary Culture and the Pacific: nineteenth-century textual encounters* (Cambridge: Cambridge University Press, 1998).

Smyth, John George, Right Hon. Sir, Bart, *Sandhurst. The history of the Royal Military College, Sandhurst, and the Royal Military Academy Sandhurst, 1741–1961* (London: Weidenfeld & Nicolson, 1961).

Spivak, Gayatri Chakravorty, *A Critique of Postcolonial Reason: towards a history of the vanishing present* (Cambridge, MA; London: Harvard University Press, 1999).

Stanley, Brian, *The Bible and the Flag: Protestant missions and British imperialism in the nineteenth and twentieth centuries* (Leicester: Apollos, 1990).

Stanley, Brian, *A History of the Baptist Missionary Society 1792–1992* (Edinburgh: T. & T. Clark, 1992).

Stanley, Brian (ed.), *Christian Mission and the Enlightenment* (Grand Rapids, MI: W B Eerdmans Pub., 2001).

Stock, Eugene, *The History of the Church Missionary Society: its environment, its men and its work*, 4 vols (London: Church Missionary Society, 1899–1916).

Stocking, George W., Jr, *Victorian anthropology* (New York: Free Press, 1987).

Stoler, Ann Laura, *Race and the Education of Desire: Foucault's History of sexuality and the colonial order of things* (Durham, NC and London: Duke University Press, 1995).

Stoler, Ann Laura, *Carnal Knowledge and Imperial Power: race and the intimate in colonial rule* (Berkeley and London: University of California Press, 2002).

Stoler, Ann Laura, *Haunted by Empire: geographies of intimacy in North American history* (Durham, NC and London: Duke University Press, 2006).

Stoler, Ann Laura, *Along the Archival Grain: epistemic anxieties and colonial common sense* (Princeton, NJ: Princeton University Press, 2009).

Stone, Lawrence, *The Family, Sex and Marriage in England, 1500–1800* (London: Weidenfeld & Nicolson, 1977).

Strobel, Margaret, *European Women and the Second British Empire* (Bloomington: Indiana University Press, 1991).

Talboys, Rollo St Clare, *A Victorian School. Being the history of Wellington College* (Oxford: Blackwell, 1943).

Tebbutt, Melanie, *Women's Talk? A social history of 'gossip' in working-class neighbourhoods, 1880–1960* (Aldershot: Scolar Press, 1995).

Thompson, Andrew, *The Empire Strikes Back? The impact of imperialism on Britain from the mid-nineteenth century* (Harlow: Pearson, 2005).

Thompson, F. M. L., *The Rise of Respectable Society: a social history of Victorian Britain, 1830–1900* (London: Fontana, 1988).

Thompson, Henry Paget, *Into all Lands: the history of the Society for the Propagation of the Gospel in Foreign Parts, 1701–1950* (London: SPCK, 1951).

Thorne, Susan, *Congregational Missions and the Making of an Imperial Culture in Nineteenth-century England* (Stanford, CA: Stanford University Press and Cambridge: Cambridge University Press, 1999).

Tolley, Christopher, *Domestic Biography: the legacy of evangelicalism in four nineteenth-century families* (Oxford: Clarendon Press, 1997)

Tosh, John, *A Man's Place: masculinity and the middle-class home in Victorian England* (New Haven, CT and London: Yale University Press, 1999).

Tosh, John, *The Pursuit of History: aims, methods and new directions in the study of modern history*, 3rd edn (Harlow: Longman, 2000).

Tosh, John, *Manliness and Masculinities in Nineteenth-century Britain: essays on gender, family and empire* (Harlow: Pearson Longman, 2005).

Twells, Alison, *The Civilising Mission and the English middle classes, 1792–1850: the 'heathen' at home and overseas* (Basingstoke: Palgrave Macmillan, 2009).

Turner, Mary, *Slaves and Missionaries: the disintegration of Jamaican slave society, 1787–1834* (Urbana, IL: University of Illinois Press, 1982)

Useem, John and Ruth Hill, *The Western-Educated Man in India: a study of his social roles and influence* (New York: Dryden Press, 1955).

Useem, Ruth Hill, *A Third Culture Kid Bibliography* (East Lansing, MI: [s.n.] 1999).

Vance, Norman, *Sinews of the Spirit: the ideal of Christian manliness in Victorian literature and religious thought* (Cambridge: Cambridge University Press, 1985).

Van Kirk, Sylvia, *Many Tender Ties: women in fur-trade society in Western Canada, 1670–1870* (Winnipeg: Watson and Dwyer Publications, 1980).

Vicinus, Martha (ed.), *A Widening Sphere: changing roles of Victorian women* (Bloomington and London: Indiana University Press, 1997).

Walls, Andrew F., *The Missionary Movement in Christian History: studies in the transmission of faith* (Edinburgh: T. & T. Clark, 1996).

Ward, Keith and Stanley, Brian (eds), *The Church Mission Society and world Christianity,1799–1999* (Grand Rapids, MI and Cambridge: Eerdmans Pub., 2000).

Ware, Vron, *Beyond the Pale: white women, racism and history* (London, New York: Verso, 1992).

Weeks, Jeffrey, *Sex, Politics and Society: the regulation of sexuality since 1800*, 2nd edn (London: Longman, 1989).

West, Shearer (ed.), *The Victorians and Race* (Aldershot: Scolar Press, 1996).

Westaway, Katherine Mary, *A History of Bedford High School* (Bedford: F. R. Hockliffe, 1932).

Williams, M., *Notes on the Clergy Daughters' School, Casterton* (Beverley: Minister Press, 1935).

Wilson, Kathleen (ed.), *A New Imperial History: culture, identity, and modernity in Britain and the Empire, 1660–1840* (Cambridge: Cambridge University Press, 2004).

Winks, Robin (ed.), *Oxford History of the British Empire*, vol. 5, *Historiography* (Oxford: Oxford University Press, 1999).

Witting, Clifford, *The Glory of Sons. A history of Eltham College school for the sons of missionaries* (London: Board of Governors, Eltham College, 1952).

Wohl, Anthony (ed.), *The Victorian Family: structure and stresses* (London: Croom Helm, 1978).

Woollacott, Angela, *Gender and Empire* (London: Palgrave, 2006).

Yates, Timothy, *Christian Mission in the Twentieth Century* (Cambridge: Cambridge University Press, 1994).

Young, G. M., *Portrait of an Age* (Oxford: Oxford University Press, 1953).

Chapters in edited collections

Ballantyne, Tony and Burton, Antoinette, 'Introduction: The Politics of Intimacy in an Age of Empire', in Tony Ballantyne and Antoinette Burton (eds), *Moving Subjects: gender, mobility, and intimacy in an age of global empire* (Urbana, IL: University of Illinois Press, 2009), pp. 1–28.

Bammer, Angelika, 'Mother Tongues and Other Strangers: Writing "Family" across Cultural Divides', in Angelika Bammer (ed.), *Displacements: cultural identities in question* (Bloomington and Indianapolis: Indiana University Press, 1994), pp. 90–109.

Barker, John, 'Where the Missionary Frontier Ran Ahead of Empire', in Norman Etherington (ed.), *Missions and Empire* (Oxford: Oxford University Press, 2005), pp. 86–106.

Beidelman, Thomas O., 'Altruism and Domesticity: Images of Missionary Women among the Church Missionary Society in Nineteenth-century East Africa', in Mary Taylor Huber and Nancy C. Lutkehaus (eds), *Gendered Missions: women and men in missionary discourse and practice* (Ann Arbor: University of Michigan Press, 1999), pp. 113–43.

Buettner, Elizabeth, 'Parent-child Separations and Colonial Careers: the Talbot family correspondence in the 1880s and 1890s', in Anthony Fletcher and Stephen Hussey (eds), *Childhood in Question: children, parents and the state* (Manchester: Manchester University Press, 1999), pp. 115–32.

Comaroff, John, 'Images of Empire, Contests of Conscience: Models of Colonial Domination in South Africa', in Frederick Cooper and Ann Laura Stoler (eds), *Tensions of Empire: colonial cultures in a bourgeois world* (Berkeley, California, London: University of California Press, 1997), pp. 163–97.

Comaroff, Jean and John L., 'Home-Made Hegemony: Modernity, Domesticity, and Colonialism in South Africa', in Karen Tranberg Hansen (ed.), *African Encounters with Domesticity* (New Brunswick: Rutgers University Press, 1992), pp. 37–74.

Cox, Jeffrey, 'The Missionary Movement', in D. G. Paz (ed.), *Nineteenth-century English Religious Traditions: retrospect and prospect* (Westport, Conn.; London: Greenwood, 1995), pp. 197–220.

Cunningham, Valentine, '"God and Nature Intended You for a Missionary's Wife': Mary Hill, Jane Eyre and Other Missionary Women in the 1840s', in Fiona Bowie, Deborah Kirkwood and Shirley Ardener, *Women and Missions: past and present: anthropological and historical perceptions* (Providence RI and Oxford: Berg, 1993), pp. 85–105.

Cutherbertson, Greg, 'Preaching Imperialism: Wesleyan Methodism and the War', in David Omissi and Andrew Thompson (eds), *The Impact of the South African War* (Basingstoke: Palgrave, 2002), pp. 157–72.

Davidoff, Leonore, 'Class and Gender in Victorian England', in Judith L. Newton et al. (eds), *Sex and Class in Women's History* (London: Routledge, 1983).

Davidoff, Leonore, 'The family in Britain' in F. M. L. Thompson, *The Cambridge Social History of Britain, 1750–1950*, vol. 2, *People and their Environment* (Cambridge: Cambridge University Press, 1990), pp. 71–130.

Davidoff, Leonore and Hall, Catherine, 'The Architecture of Public and Private Life: English middle class society, in a provincial town 1780–1850', in Derek Fraser and Anthony Sutcliffe (eds), *The Pursuit of Urban History* (London: Edward Arnold, 1983).

Dening, Greg, 'Towards an Anthropology of Performance in Encounters in Place', in Donald H. Rubenstein (ed.), *Pacific History: papers from the 8th Pacific History Association Conference* (Mangilao, Guam, 1992).

Elbourne, Elizabeth, 'Mothers Milk: gender power and anxiety on a South African mission station, 1839–40', in Andrew May and Patricia Grimshaw (eds), *Missionaries, Indigenous Peoples and Cultural Exchange* (Brighton: Sussex Academic Press, 2010).

Elbourne, Elizabeth and Ross, Robert, 'Combating Spiritual and Social Bondage: Early Missions in the Cape Colony', in Richard Elphick and Rodney Davenport (eds), *Christianity in South Africa: a political, social and cultural history* (Oxford: James Currey, 1997), pp. 31–50.

Erlank, Natasha, 'Jane and John Philip: partnership, usefulness and sexuality in the service of God', in John de Gruchy (ed.), *The London Missionary Society in Southern Africa: historical essays in celebration of the bi-centenary of the LMS in Southern Africa, 1799–1999* (Cape Town: David Philip, 1999), pp. 86–93.

Etherington, Norman, 'Gender Issues in South-East African Missions, 1835–85', in Henry Bredekamp and Robert Ross (eds), *Missions and Christianity in Southern African History* (Johannesburg: Witwatersrand University Press, 1995).

Etherington, Norman, 'Missions and Empire', in Robin W. Winks (ed.), *Oxford History of the British Empire*, vol. 5, *Historiography* (Oxford: Oxford University Press, 1999), pp. 303–14.

Gaitskell, Deborah, '"Wailing for Purity": prayer unions, African mothers and adolescent daughters, 1912–1940', in Shula Marks and Richard Rathbone (eds), *Industrialisation and Social change in South Africa: African class formation, culture, and consciousness, 1870–1930* (Harlow: Longman, 1982), pp. 338–57.

Gaitskell, Deborah, 'Race, Gender and Imperialism: A Century of Black Girls' Education in South Africa', in J. A. Mangan (ed.), *Benefits Bestowed: education and British imperialism* (Manchester: Manchester University Press, 1988), pp. 150–73.

Gaitskell, Deborah, 'Devout Domesticity? A century of African women's Christianity in South Africa', in Cherryl Walker (ed.), *Women and Gender in Southern Africa to 1945* (Cape Town: David Philip, 1990), pp. 251–72.

Gaitskell, Deborah, 'Rethinking Gender Roles: the Field Experience of Women Missionaries in South Africa', in Andrew Porter (ed.), *The Imperial Horizons of British Protestant Missions, 1880–1914* (Grand Rapids, MI: W.B. Eerdmans Pub., 2003), pp. 131–57.

Grimshaw, Patricia, 'Faith, Missionary Life, and the Family', in Philippa Levine (ed.), *Gender and Empire* (Oxford: Oxford University Press, 2004), pp. 260–280.

Grimshaw, Patricia and Sherlock, Peter, 'Women and Cultural Exchanges', in Norman Etherington (ed.), *Missions and Empire* (Oxford: Oxford University Press, 2005), pp. 173–93.

de Groot, Joanna, 'Metropolitan Desires and Colonial Connections: reflections on consumption and empire', in Catherine Hall and Sonya Rose (eds), *At Home with the Empire: metropolitan culture and the imperial world* (Cambridge: Cambridge University Press, 2006), pp. 166–90.

Gunson, Neil, 'The Deviations of a Missionary Family: the Henrys of Tahiti', in James Wightman Davidson and Deryck Scarr (eds), *Pacific Islands Portraits* (Wellington, Auckland: A. H. & A. W. Reed, 1970), pp. 31–54.

Haggis, Jane, '"Good wives and mothers" or "dedicated workers"? Contradictions of domesticity in the "mission of sisterhood", Travancore, South

India', in Kalpana Ram and Margaret Jolly (eds), *Maternities and Modernities: Colonial and postcolonial experience in Asia and the Pacific* (Cambridge: Cambridge University Press, 1998), pp. 81–113.

Haggis, Jane, 'White Women and Colonialism: towards a non-recuperative history', in Clare Midgley (ed.), *Gender and Imperialism* (Manchester: Manchester University Press, 1998), pp. 45–75.

Hall, Catherine, 'The early formation of Victorian domestic ideology', in Sandra Burman (ed.), *Fit Work for Women* (London: Croom Helm, 1979).

Hall, Catherine, 'Private Persons versus Public Someones: class, gender and politics in England, 1780–1850', in Carolyn Steedman, Cathy Urwin and Valerie Walkerdine (eds), *Language, Gender and Childhood* (London: Routledge & Kegan Paul, 1985), pp. 10–33.

Hall, Catherine, 'Missionary Stories: gender and ethnicity in the 1830s and 1840s', in Catherine Hall, *White, Male and Middle Class: explorations in feminism and history* (Cambridge: Polity, 1992), pp. 205–55.

Hall, Catherine, 'A Family for Nation and Empire', in Gail Lewis (ed.), *Forming nation, framing welfare* (London and New York: Routledge, 1998), pp. 9–48.

Hall, Stuart, 'The Multi-Cultural Question', in Barnor Hesse (ed.), *Un/settled Multiculturalisms: diasporas, entanglements, "transruptions"* (London and New York: Zed Books; New York: St Martin's Press, 2000), pp. 29–41.

Heuman, Gad, 'The British West Indies', in Andrew Porter (ed.), *Oxford History of the British Empire*, vol. III (Oxford: Oxford University Press, 1999), pp. 470–94.

Hilton, Boyd, 'Manliness, Masculinity and the Mid-Victorian Temperament', in Lawrence Goldman (ed.), *The Blind Victorian: Henry Fawcett and British Liberalism* (Cambridge: Cambridge University Press, 1989), pp. 60–70

Huber, Mary Taylor and Lutkehaus, Nancy C., 'Introduction: Gendered Missions at Home and Abroad', in Mary Taylor Huber and Nancy C. Lutkehaus (eds), *Gendered Missions: women and men in missionary discourse and practice* (Ann Arbor: University of Michigan Press, 1999), pp. 1–38.

Johnston, Anna, 'A Blister on the Imperial Antipodes: Lancelot Edward Threkheld in Polynesia and Australia', in David Lambert and Alan Lester (eds), *Colonial Lives across the British Empire: imperial careering in the long nineteenth century* (Cambridge: Cambridge University Press, 2006), pp. 58–87.

Kirkwood, Deborah, 'Protestant Missionary Women: Wives and Spinsters', in Fiona Bowie, Deborah Kirkwood and Shirley Ardener (eds), *Women and Missions: past and present: anthropological and historical perspectives* (Province, RI and Oxford: Berg, 1993), pp. 23–42.

Lake, Marilyn, 'Australian frontier feminism and the marauding white man', in Clare Midgley (ed.), *Gender and Imperialism* (Manchester: Manchester University Press, 1998), pp. 123–36.

Langford, Mary, 'Global Nomads, Third Culture Kids and International Schools', in Mary Hayden and Jeff Thompson (eds), *International Education: principles and practice* (London: Kogan Page, 1998).

Langmore, Diane, 'the Object Lesson of a Civilised, Christian Home', in Margaret Jolly and Martha Macintyre (eds), *Family and Gender in the*

Pacific: domestic contradictions and the colonial impact (Cambridge: Cambridge University Press, 1999).

Lester, Alan, 'Humanitarians and White Settlers in the Nineteenth Century', in Norman Etherington (ed.), *Missions and Empire* (Oxford: Oxford University Press, 2005), pp. 64–85.

Lester, Alan and Lambert, David, 'Missionary Politics and the Captive Audience: William Shrewsbury in the Caribbean and the Cape Colony', in David Lambert and Alan Lester (eds), *Colonial Lives across the British Empire: imperial careering in the long nineteenth century* (Cambridge: Cambridge University Press, 2006), pp. 88–112.

Macdonald, Charlotte, 'Intimacy of the Envelope: Fiction, Commerce, and Empire in the Correspondence of Friends Mary Taylor and Charlotte Bronte, *c.* 1845–55' in Tony Ballantyne,and Antoinette Burton (eds), *Moving Subjects: gender, mobility, and intimacy in an age of global empire* (Urbana, IL: University of Illinois Press, 2009), pp. 89–109.

Mackenzie, John, 'David Livingstone: the construction of the myth', in Graham Walker and Tom Gallagher (eds), *Sermons and Battle Hymns* (Edinburgh: Edinburgh University Press, 1990).

McLeod, Hugh, 'White Collar Values and the Role of Religion', in Geoffrey Crossick, (ed.), *The Lower Middle Class in Britain, 1870–1914* (London: Croom Helm, 1977), pp. 61–88.

Midgley, Clare, 'Bringing the Empire Home: women activists in imperial Britain, 1790s-1930s', in Catherine Hall and Sonya Rose (eds), *At Home with the Empire: Metropolitan Culture and the Imperial World* (Cambridge: Cambridge University Press, 2006), pp. 230–50.

Miller, Char, 'Domesticity Abroad: Work and Family in the Sandwich Islands Mission, 1820–1840', in Clifford Putney and Paul T. Burlin (eds), *The Role of the American Board in the World: Bicentennial Reflections on the Organisation's Missionary Work, 1810–2010* (Eugene, OR: WIPF & Stock, 2012), pp. 312–30.

Orwell, George, 'Shooting an Elephant', in George Orwell, *Shooting an Elephant and other Essays* (London: Secker & Warburg, 1950).

Perry, Adele, 'Islands of Intimacy: Community, Kinship, and Domesticity, Salt Spring Island, 1866', in Tony Ballantyne, and Antoinette Burton, (eds), *Moving Subjects: gender, mobility, and intimacy in an age of global empire* (Urbana, IL: University of Illinois Press, 2009), pp. 296–314.

Porter, Andrew, 'Trusteeship, Anti-Slavery, and Humanitarianism', in Andrew Porter (ed.), *Oxford History of the British Empire*, vol. III (Oxford: Oxford University Press, 1999), pp. 198–222.

Porter, Andrew, 'Religion, Missionary Enthusiasm, and Empire', in Andrew Porter (ed.), *Oxford History of the British Empire* vol III (Oxford: Oxford University Press, 1999), pp. 222–46.

Predelli, Line Nyhagen and Miller, Jon, 'Piety and Patriarchy: Contested Gender Regimes in Nineteenth-century Evangelical Missions', in Mary Taylor Huber and Nancy C. Lutkehaus (eds), *Gendered Missions: women and men in missionary discourse and practice* (Ann Arbor: University of Michigan Press, 1999), pp. 67–112.

Rapp, Rayna, Ross, Ellen and Bridenthal, Renate, 'Examining Family History', in Judith L. Newton, Mary P. Ryan and Judith R. Walkowitz (eds), *Sex and Class in Women's History* (London, Boston, Melbourne and Henley: Routledge & Kegan Paul, 1983).

Roberts, David, 'The Paterfamilias of the Victorian Governing Classes' in Anthony Wohl (ed.), *The Victorian Family: Structure and Stresses* (Croom Helm, London, 1978), pp. 59–81.

Ross, Andrew C., 'Christian Missions and Mid-Nineteenth-Century Change in Attitudes to Race: The African Experience' in Andrew Porter (ed.) *The Imperial Horizons of British Protestant Missions, 1880–1914* (Grand Rapids, MI: W.B. Eerdmans Pub., 2003), pp. 85–105.

Rotundo, Anthony E., 'Patriarchs and Participants: A Historical Perspective on Fatherhood', in Michael Kaufman (ed.), *Beyond Patriarchy: Essays on Pleasure, Power, and Change* (Toronto and New York: Oxford University Press, 1987), pp. 64–80.

Ryan, Mary P., 'The Power of Women's Networks', in Judith L. Newton, Mary P. Ryan, and Judith R. Walkowitz (eds), *Sex and Class in Women's History* (London, Boston, Melbourne and Henley: Routledge & Kegan Paul, 1983).

Scott, Joan W., 'Gender: A Useful Category of Analysis', in Joan W. Scott, *Gender and the Politics of History* (New York: Columbia University Press, 1988).

Seton, Rosemary, '"Open Doors for Female Labourers": Women Candidates of the London Missionary Society, 1875–1914', in Robert Bickers and Seton, Rosemary (eds), *Missionary Encounters: sources and issues* (Richmond, Surrey: Curzon Press, 1996), pp. 50–69.

Spivak, Gayatri Chakravorty, 'Can the Subaltern Speak?', in Cary Nelson and Lawrence Gossberg, *Marxism and the interpretation of culture* (Basingstoke: Macmillan Education, 1988), pp. 271–315.

Stoler, Ann Laura, 'Carnal Knowledge and Imperial Power: Gender, Race and Morality in Colonial Asia', in Micaela di Leonardo, *Gender at the Crossroads of Knowledge: feminist anthropology in the postmodern era* (Berkeley: University of California Press, 1991), pp. 51–101.

Stoler, Ann Laura, 'Cultivating bourgeois bodies and racial selves', in Catherine Hall (ed.), *Cultures of Empire: colonisers in Britain and the Empire in the Nineteenth and twentieth centuries* (Manchester: Manchester University Press, 2000), pp. 87–119.

Thompson, Paul, 'Family Myth, Models, and Denials in the Shaping of Individual Life Paths' in Daniel Bertaux and Paul Thompson (eds), *Between Generations: family models, myths and memories* (Oxford: Oxford University Press, 1993), pp. 13–38.

Thorne, Susan, 'Missionary-Imperial Feminism', in Mary Taylor Huber and Nancy C. Lutkehaus (eds), *Gendered Missions: women and men in missionary discourse and practice* (Ann Arbor: University of Michigan Press, 1999), pp. 39–66.

Tosh, John, 'Domesticity and manliness in the Victorian middle class: the family of Edward White Benson', in Michael Roper and John Tosh (eds), *Manful Assertions: masculinities in Britain since 1800* (London: Routledge, 1991), pp. 44–73.

Twells, Alison, '"Let Us Begin at Home": Class, Ethnicity, and Christian Motherhood in the Writing of Hannah Kilham, 1774–1832', in Eileen Yeo (ed.), *Radical Femininity: women's self-representation in the public sphere* (Manchester: Manchester University Press, 1998), pp. 25–51.

Twells, Alison, 'Missionary "Fathers" and Wayward "Sons" in the South Pacific, 1797–1825', in Trev Lynn Broughton and Helen Rogers (eds) *Gender and Fatherhood in the Nineteenth Century* (Basingstoke: Palgrave Macmillan, 2007).

Vibert, Elizabeth, 'Writing "Home": Sibling Intimacy and Mobility in a Scottish Colonial Memoir', in Tony Ballantyne and Antoinette Burton (eds), *Moving Subjects: gender, mobility, and intimacy in an age of global empire* (Urbana, IL: University of Illinois Press, 2009), pp. 67–88.

Walker, Pamela J., '"I Live Not Yet For Christ Liveth in Me": Men and masculinity in the Salvation Army, 1865–90', in Michael Roper and John Tosh (eds), *Manful Assertions: masculinities in Britain since 1800* (London: Routledge, 1991), pp. 92–112.

Williams, C. Peter, '"The Missing Link": The Recruitment of Women Missionaries in some English Evangelical Missionary Societies in the Nineteenth Century', in Fiona Bowie, Deborah Kirkwood and Shirley Ardener (eds), *Women and Missions: past and present: anthropological and historical perspectives* (Province, RI and Oxford: Berg, 1993), pp. 43–69.

Articles

Abarbanel, Janice, 'Moving with Emotional Resilience between and Within Cultures', *Intercultural Education* 20: Supplement Nos. 51–2 (2009), 5133–41.

Anderson, Nancy Fix, 'Cousin Marriage in Victorian England', *Journal of Family History* 11 (1986), 285–301.

Baker, D. W. A., 'John Dunmore Lang', *Australian Dictionary of National Biography*.

Ballantyne, Tony, 'Race and the Webs of Empire: Aryanism from India to the Pacific', *Journal of Colonialism and Colonial History* 2:3 (2001).

Ballantyne, Tony, 'Introduction: Debating Empire', *Journal of Colonialism and Colonial History* 13:1 (2002).

Ballantyne, Tony, 'Religion, Difference, and the Limits of British Imperial History', *Victorian Studies* 47:3 (2005), 427–55.

Barnhart, William C., 'Evangelicalism, Masculinity, and the Making of Imperial Missionaries in Late Georgian Britain, 1795–1820', *The Historian* 67:4 (2005), 712–32.

Beidelman, Thomas O., 'Social Theory and the Study of Christian Missions in Africa', *Africa* 44 (1974), 235–49.

Beidelman, Thomas O., 'Contradictions between the Sacred and the Secular Life: The Church Missionary Society in Ukaguru, Tanzania, East Africa, 1875–1914', *Comparative Studies in Society and History* 23 (1981), 73–95.

Berger, Mark, 'Imperialism and Sexual Exploitation: a response to Ronald Hyam's "empire and sexual opportunity"', *Journal of Imperial and Commonwealth History* 17:1 (1988), 83–9.

Binfield, Clyde, 'Congregationalism's Baptist Grandmothers and Methodist Great Aunts: The Place of Family in a Felt Religion', *Journal of the United Reformed Church History Society* 2:1 (1978), 2–9.

Blake, Lynn A., 'Pastoral Power, Governmentality and Cultures of Order in Nineteenth-Century British Columbia', *Transactions of the Institute of British Geographers* 24:1 (1999), 79–93.

Boyd, Mary, 'Samuel Williams', *New Zealand Dictionary of National Biography*.

Breen, T. H., '"Baubles of Britain": The American and Consumer Revolutions of the Eighteenth Century', *Past and Present* 119 (1988), 73–104.

Buettner, Elizabeth, 'Problematic Spaces, Problematic Races: defining "Europeans" in late colonial India', *Women's History Review* 9:2 (2000), 277–98.

Burstyn, Joan N., 'Women's Education in England during the nineteenth century: A review of the literature, 1970–1976', *History of Education* 6:1 (1977), 11–19.

Calder, Alex, 'The Temptations of William Pascoe Crook: an experience of cultural difference in the Marquesas, 1796–98', *Journal of Pacific History* 31 (1996), 144–61.

Capp, Bernard, 'The Double Standard Revisited: plebeian women and male sexual reputation in early modern England', *Past and Present* 162 (1999), 70–100.

Carey, Hillary M., 'Companions in the Wilderness? Missionary Wives in Colonial Australia, 1788–1900', *Journal of Religious History* XIX (1995), 227–48.

Chilton, L., 'A New Class of Women for the Colonies: *The Imperial Colonist* and the construction of Empire', *Journal of Imperial and Commonwealth History* 31 (2003), 36–56.

Cleall, Esme, 'Missionaries, Masculinities and War: The London Missionary Society in Southern Africa, *c.*1860–1899', *South African Historical Journal* 61:2 (2009), 232–53.

Comaroff, Jean, 'Missionaries and Mechanical Clocks: an essay on religion and history in South Africa', *The Journal of Religion* 71:1 (1991), 1–17.

Cooper, Frederick and Stoler, Ann Laura, 'Introduction Tensions of Empire: colonial control and visions of rule', *American Ethnologist* 16:4 (1989), 609–21.

Crozier, Dorothy, 'Kinship and Occupational Succession', *The Sociological Review* New Series 13 (1965), 15–43.

Dachs, Anthony J., 'Missionary Imperialism – the case of Bechuanaland', *The Journal of African History* 13:4 (1972), 647–58.

Darwin, John, 'Imperialism and the Victorians: the dynamics of territorial expansion', *English Historical Review* 112 (1997), 614–42.

Davidoff, Leonore, 'Kinship as a Categorical Concept: a case study of nineteenth-century English siblings', *Journal of Social History* 39:2 (2005), 411–28.

Davin, Anna, 'Imperialism and Motherhood', *History Workshop Journal* 5:1 (1978), 9–66.

Doolittle, Megan, 'Close Relations? bringing together gender and family in English history', *Gender and History* 11:3 (1999), 542–54.

Douglas, Bronwen, 'Encounters with the Enemy? Academic Readings of Missionary Narratives on Melanesians', *Comparative Studies in Society and History* 43:1 (2001), 37–64.

Dube, Saurabh, 'Conversion to Translation: colonial registers of a vernacular Christianity', *South Atlantic Quarterly* 101 (2002), 807–37.

Elbourne, Elizabeth, 'Review Article: concerning missionaries: the case of Van der Kemp', *Journal of Southern African Studies* 17:1 (1991), 153–64.

Endfield, Natasha and Nash, David, 'Missionaries and Morals: climatic discourses in nineteenth-century Central Southern Africa', *Annals of the Association of American Geographies* 92:4 (2002), 727–42.

Erlank, Natasha, 'Missionary views on sexuality in Xhosaland in the nineteenth century', *Le Fait Missionnaire* special issue 'Sex and Mission', 11 (2001), 9–43.

Erlank, Natasha, 'Sexual Misconduct and Church Power on Scottish Mission Stations in Xhosland, South Africa, in the 1840s', *Gender and History* 15:1 (2003), 69–84.

Fox-Genovese, Elizabeth, 'Placing Women's History in History', *New Left Review* 133 (1982), 5–29.

Francis, Martin, 'The Domestication of the Male? Recent research on nineteenth- and twentieth-century British masculinity', *The Historical Journal* 45:3 (2002), 637–52.

Gaitskell, Deborah, 'Housewives, Maids or Mothers: some contradictions of domesticity for Christian women in Johannesburg, 1903–39', *The Journal of African History* 24:2 (1983), 241–56.

Gaitskell, Deborah, 'Female Faith and the Politics of the Personal: Five Mission Encounters in Twentieth-Century South Africa', *Feminist Review* 65:1 (2000), 68–91.

Gibson, Mary Ellis, 'Henry Martyn and England's Christian Empire: Rereading *Jane Eyre* through Missionary Biography', *Victorian Literature and Culture* (1999), 419–42.

Gillis, John, 'Making Time for Family: the invention of family time(s) and the reinvention of family history', *Journal of Family History* 21:1 (1996), 4–21.

Goodman, Joyce, 'Languages of Female Colonial Authority: the educational network of the Ladies Committee of the British and Foreign School Society, 1813–1837', *Compare: a Journal of Comparative Education* 30:1 (2000), 7–19.

Gowing, Laura, 'Gender and the Language of Insult in Early Modern London', *History Workshop Journal* 35 (1993), 1–21.

Gowing, Laura, 'Secret Births and Infanticide in Seventeenth-century England', *Past and Present* 156 (1997), 87–115.

Grimshaw, Patricia, '"Christian Woman, Pious Wife, Faithful Mother, Devoted Missionary": conflicts and roles of American missionary women in nineteenth-century Hawaii', *Feminist Studies* 9:3 (1983), 489–521.

Gunson, Neil, 'Christian Encounters with the Other', *Journal of Pacific History* 39:2 (2004), 259–66.

Gutierrez, Ramon A., 'What's Love Got to Do with It?', *Journal of American History* 88:3 (2001), 866–9.

Haggis, Jane, 'Ironies of Emancipation: Changing Configurations of "Women's Work" in the "Mission of Sisterhood" to Indian Women', *Feminist Review* 65:1 (2000), 108–26.

Hall, Catherine, 'White Visions, Black Lives: the free villages of Jamaica', *History Workshop Journal* 36:1 (1993), 100–32.

Humphrey, David C., 'Colonial Colleges and English Dissenting Academies: A Study in Transatlantic Culture', *History of Education Quarterly* 12:2 (1972), 184–97.

Hyam, Ronald, 'Empire and Sexual Opportunity', *Journal of Imperial and Commonwealth History* 14:2 (1986), 34–90.

Jolly, Margaret, '"To Save the Girls for Brighter and Better Lives": Presbyterian missions and women in the south of Vanuatu, 1848–1870', *Journal of Pacific History* 26:1 (1991), 27–48.

Kosambi, Meera and Haggis, Jane, 'Reconstructing Femininities: colonial intersections of gender, race, religion and class', *Feminist Review* 65:1 (2000), 1–4.

Koss, Stephen, 'Wesleyanism and Empire', *Historical Journal* 18:1 (1975), 105–18.

Krenis, Lee, 'Authority and Rebellion in Victorian Autobiography', *Journal of British Studies* 18 (1978), 107–30.

Lauer, L. E., 'Dorothea Foulger', *Oxford Dictionary of National Biography*.

Leavy, Barbara Fass, 'Fathering and the *British Mother's Magazine*, 1845–1864', *Victorian Periodicals Newsletter* 13 (1980), 10–17.

Lee, Janet, 'Between Subordination and She-Tiger: social constructions of white femininity in the lives of single, Protestant missionaries in China, 1905–1930s', *Women's Studies International Forum* 19 (1996), 621–32.

Di Leonardo, Micaela, 'The Female World of Cards and Holidays: women, families, and the work of kinship', *Signs: Journal of Women in Culture and Society* 12/3 (1987), 40–53.

Lester, Alan, 'British Settler Discourse and the Circuits of Empire', *History Workshop Journal* 54 (2002), 24–48.

Lester, Alan, 'Imperial Circuits and Networks: geographies of the British Empire', *History Compass* 4:1 (2006), 124–41.

Manktelow, Emily J., 'Rev. Simpson's "improper liberties": moral scrutiny and missionary children in the South Seas Mission', *Journal of Imperial and Commonwealth History* 40:2 (2012), 159–81.

Martin, Mary Clare, 'Women and Philanthropy in Walthamstow and Leyton, 1740–1870', *London Journal*, 19/2 (1995), 119–50.

Maude, H. E., 'Beachcombers and Castaways', *Journal of the Polynesian Society* LXXIII (1964), 254–93.

Midgley, Clare, 'Can Women be Missionaries? Envisioning female agency in the early nineteenth-century British Empire', *Journal of British Studies* 45 (2006), 335–58.

Milne-Smith, Amy, 'Club Talk: gossip, masculinity and oral communities in late nineteenth-century London', *Gender and History* 21 (2009), 86–106.

Moss, Barbara A., '"And the Bones Come Together": women's religious expectations in Southern Africa, *c.*1900–1945', *Journal of Religious History* 23 (1999), 108–127.

Newman, L., 'Critical Theory and the History of Women: what's at stake in deconstructing women's history?', *Journal of Women's History* 2:3 (1991), 58–68.

Newsome, David, 'Father and Sons: review of Ford K. Brown's *Fathers of the Victorians*', *Historical Journal* 6 (1963), 295–310.

Pedersen, Joyce Senders, 'The Reform of Women's Secondary and Higher Education: Institutional Change and Social Values in Mid and Late Victorian England', *History of Education Quarterly* 19:1 (1979), 61–91.

Pedersen, P., 'Anxious Lives and Letters: family separation, communication networks and structures of everyday life', *Culture and History* 8 (1990), 7–19.

Peel, J. D. Y., 'For Who Hath Despised the Day of Small Things? Missionary Narratives and Historical Anthropology', *Comparatives Studies of Society in History* 37:3 (1995), 581–607.

Perry, Adele, '"Fair Ones of a Purer Caste": white women and colonialism in nineteenth-century British Columbia', *Feminist Studies* 23:3 (1997), 501–24.

Perry, Adele, 'The State of Empire: reproducing colonialism in British Columbia, 1849–1871', *Journal of Colonialism and Colonial History* 2:2 (2001).

Perry, Adele, 'From "The Hot-bed of Vice" to the "good and well-ordered Christian Home": First Nations Housing and Reform in Nineteenth-Century British Columbia', *Ethnohistory* 50:4 (2003), 587–610.

Philips, Richard, 'Histories of Sexuality and Imperialism: what's the use?', *History Workshop Journal* 63 (2007), 136–53.

Pomeranz, Kenneth, 'Social History and World History: from daily life to patterns of change', *Journal of World History* 18:1 (2007), 69–98.

Poovey, Mary, 'Feminism and Deconstruction', *Feminist Studies* 14:1 (1988), 51–65.

Porter, Andrew, 'Cambridge, Keswick, and late Nineteenth-Century Attitudes to Africa', *Journal of Imperial and Commonwealth History* 5 (1976), 5–34.

Porter, Andrew, 'Evangelical Enthusiasm, Missionary Motivation and West Africa in the Late Nineteenth Century: the Career of G. W. Brooke', *Journal of Imperial and Commonwealth History* 6 (1977), 23–43.

Porter, Andrew, 'Commerce and Christianity: the rise and fall of a nineteenth-century missionary slogan', *The Historical Journal* 28:3 (1985), 597–621.

Porter, Andrew, 'Religion and Empire: British expansion in the long nineteenth century, 1780–1914', *Journal of Imperial and Commonwealth History* 20:3 (1992), 370–90.

Porter, Andrew, '"Cultural imperialism" and Protestant missionary enterprise, 1780–1914', *Journal of Imperial and Commonwealth History* 25:3 (1997), 367–91.

Porter, Andrew, 'Evangelical Visions and Colonial Realities', *Journal of Imperial and Commonwealth History* 38:1 (2010), 145–55.

Potter, Simon, 'Empire, Cultures and Identities in Nineteenth and Twentieth-Century Britain', *History Compass* 5:1 (2007), 51–71.

Predelli, Line Nyhagen, 'Sexual Control and the Remaking of Gender: the attempt of nineteenth-century Protestant Norwegian women to export western domesticity to Madagascar', *Journal of Women's History* 12:2 (2000), 81–103.

Predelli, Line Nyhagen, 'Marriage in Norwegian Missionary Practice and Discourse in Norway and Madagascar, 1880–1910', *Journal of Religion in Africa* 31:1 (2001), 4–48.

Reay, Barry 'Kinship and the Neighbourhood in Nineteenth-Century Rural England: The Myth of the Autonomous Nuclear Family', *Journal of Family History* 21:1 (1996), 87–104.

Robert, Dana L., 'Evangelist or Homemaker? Mission strategies of early nineteenth-century missionary wives in Burma and Hawaii', *International Bulletin of Missionary Research* 17:1 (1993), 4–12.

Rooke, Patricia T., '"Ordinary Events of Nature and Providence": reconstructing female missionary experience in the British West Indies, 1800–45', *Journal of Religious History* 19 (1995), 204–26.

Ross, Robert, 'Missions, Respectability and Civil Rights: the Cape Colony, 1828–1854', *Journal of Southern African Studies* 25:3 (1999), 333–45.

Rountree, Kathryn, 'Re-making the Maori Female Body: Marianne Williams's mission in the Bay of Islands', *Journal of Pacific History* 35:1 (2000), 49–66.

Rowbotham, Judith, '"Soldiers of Christ"? Images of female missionaries in late nineteenth-century Britain: issues of heroism and martyrdom', *Gender and History* 12:1 (2000), 82–106.

Ruether, Kirsten, 'Heated Debates over Crinolines: European clothing on nineteenth-century Lutheran mission stations in the Transvaal', *Journal of Southern African Studies* 28:2 (2002), 359–78.

Sagner, Andreas, '"The Abandoned Mother": aging, old age and missionaries in early and mid-nineteenth-century South-East Africa', *The Journal of African History* 42:2 (2001), 173–98.

Scott, Ann L., 'Physical Purity Feminism and State Medicine in Late Nineteenth-Century England', *Women's History Review* 8:4 (1999).

Scully, Pamela, 'Rape, Race, and Colonial Culture: the sexual politics of identity in the nineteenth-century', *The American Historical Review* 100 (1995), 335–59.

Semple, Rhonda, 'Missionary Manhood: professionalism, belief, and masculinity in the nineteenth-century British imperial field', *Journal of Imperial and Commonwealth History* 36:3 (2008), 397–415.

Smyth, Charles, 'The Evangelical Movement in Perspective', *The Historical Journal* 7 (1943), 160–74.

Stack, Carol B., and Burton, Linda M., 'Kinscripts', *Journal of Comparative Family Studies* 24/2 (1993), 157–70.

Stanley, Brian, '"Commerce and Christianity": providence theory, the missionary movement, and the imperialism of free trade', *The Historical Journal* 26:1 (1989), 71–94.

Stanley, Brian, 'The Church of the Three Selves: a perspective from the World Missionary Conference, Edinburgh, 1910', *Journal of Imperial and Commonwealth History* 36:3 (2008), 435–51.

Stanley, Brian, 'From the "Poor Heathen" to the "Glory and Honour of all Nations": Vocabularies of Race and Custom in Protestant Missions, 1844–1928', *Yale Divinity School Library Occasional Publication* 21 (2009), 1–14.

Stearns, Peter N., 'Social History and World History: prospects for collaboration', *Journal of World History* 18:1 (2007), 43–52.

Stoler, Ann Laura, 'Making Empire Respectable: The Politics of Race and Sexual Morality in Twentieth-Century Colonial Cultures', *American Ethnologist* 16:4 (1989), 634–60.

Stoler, Ann Laura, 'Rethinking Colonial Categories: European communities and the boundaries of rule', *Comparative Studies in Society and History* 31:1 (1989), 134–61.

Stoler, Ann Laura, 'Matters of Intimacy as Matters of State: a response', *Journal of American History* 88:3 (2001), 893–7.

Stoler, Ann Laura, 'Tense and Tender Ties: the politics of comparison in North American and (Post) Colonial Studies', *Journal of American History* 88:3 (2001), 829–65.

Stoler, Ann Laura and Strassler, Karen, 'Castings for the Colonial: memory work in 'New Order' Java', *Comparative Studies in Society and History* 42:1 (2000), 4–48.

Summers, Carol, 'Mission Boys, Civilised Men, and Marriage: educated African men in the missions of Southern Rhodesia, 1920–1945', *The Journal of Religious History* 23:1 (1999), 75–91.

Tennant, Margaret, 'Pakeha Deaconesses and the New Zealand Methodist Mission to Maori: 1893–1940', *Journal of Religious History* 23 (1999), 309–26.

Twells, Alison, '"So Distant and Wild a Scene": language, domesticity and difference in Hannah Kilham's writing from West Africa, 1822–1832', *Women's History Review* 4:3 (1995), 301–18.

Twells, Alison, '"Happy English Children": class, ethnicity, and the making of missionary women in the early nineteenth century', *Women's Studies International Forum* 21:3 (1998), 235–45.

Twells, Alison, 'Missionary Domesticity, Global Reform and "Woman's Sphere" in Early Nineteenth-Century England', *Gender and History* 18:2 (2006), 266–84.

Useem, Ruth Hill and Downie, Richard D., 'Third-Culture Kids', *Today's Education* 65:3 (1976), 103–5.

Van Kirk, Sylvia, 'From "Marrying-In" to "Marrying-Out": changing patterns of aboriginal/non-aboriginal marriage in colonial Canada', *Frontiers* 23:3 (2002), 1–11.

Vickery, Amanda, 'From Golden Age to Separate Spheres? A Review of the Categories and Chronology of English Women's History', *Historical Journal* 36:2 (1993), 383–414.

Wallace, Lee, 'A House is not a Home: gender, space and Marquesan encounter, 1833–34', *The Journal of Pacific History* 40:3 (2005), 265–88.

Wiesner-Hanks, Merry, 'World History and the History of Women, Gender, and Sexuality', *Journal of World History* 18:1 (2007), 53–67.

Welch, Edwin, 'Thomas Haweis', *Oxford Dictionary of National Biography.*

Wells, Julia C., 'The Scandal of Rev James Read and the Taming of the London Missionary Society by 1820', *South African Historical Journal* 42 (2000), 136–60.

Wells, Julia C., 'Curing the "Public Evils": the contested terrain of male missionary sexuality in early nineteenth-century LMS missions at the Cape of Good Hope', *Le Fait Missionnaire* special issue 'Sex and Mission' 11 (2001), 45–72.

Wells, Julia C., 'The Suppression of Mixed Marriages among LMS Missionaries in South Africa before 1820', *South African Historical Journal* 44 (2001), 1–20.

Welter, Barbara, 'She Hath Done What She Could: Protestant Women's Missionary Careers in Nineteenth-Century America', *American Quarterly* 30:5 (1978), 624–38.

Willis, Justin, 'The Nature of a Mission Community: the universities' mission to Central Africa in Bonde', *Past and Present* 140 (1993), 127–54.

Unpublished sources

Cleall, Esme, 'Thinking with Missionaries: discourses of difference in India and southern Africa, *c.*1840–1895', PhD thesis (University College London, 2009).

Daily, Christopher, 'From Gosport to Canton: a new approach to Robert Morrison and the beginnings of Protestant missions in China', PhD thesis (University of London, 2010).

Manktelow, Emily, 'Female Missionaries in Madagascar: the London Missionary Society and Conceptions of Gender, 1865–1895', MA dissertation (University of London, 2006).

Martin, Mary Clare (Hewlitt), 'Children and religion in Walthamstow and Leyton, 1740–1870', PhD thesis (University of London, 1997).

Maughan, Stephen, 'Regions Beyond and the National Church: Domestic Support for the Foreign Missions of the Church of England in the High Imperial Age, 1870–1914', PhD thesis (University of London, 1995).

Murray, Kirsteen, 'Scandals and Failure in the South Seas, Representations of the First London Missionary Society Mission', Paper presented to Yale-Edinburgh Conference 'Representations and Misrepresentations of the Missionary Movement', Edinburgh, 6–8 July 2000.

Perry, Adele, 'Ties of Kin and Bonds of Empire: Gender, Family, and Colonialism in the Connolly-Douglas Family', keynote paper 'Gendering Imperialism: home, colony and the construction of gender identities' conference, University of Edinburgh, 8 November 2008.

Potter, Sarah Caroline, 'The social origins and recruitment of English Protestant missionaries in the nineteenth century', PhD thesis (London: University of London, 1974).

Stuart, Doug, '"Of Savages and Heroes": Discourses of Race, Nation and Gender in the Evangelical Missions to Southern Africa in the Nineteenth Century', PhD thesis, Institute of Commonwealth Studies (University of London, 1997).

Urban-Mead, Wendy, 'The "Civilising" Mission of Elizabeth Lees Price: Domesticity, Christianity, and Imperialism in Southern Africa, 1854–1883', MA thesis (University of Albany, 1995).

Vickery, Amanda, 'The Din of Visiting Day: Publicising the Private Sphere', Keynote Paper at the University of Northampton Visiting Rites: accessing the English home, *c.*1550–1850 symposium, 10 September 2009.

INDEX

CPSIA information can be obtained
at www.ICGtesting.com
Printed in the USA
FFOW02n1240121115
18449FF